P9-DBX-872

CONTENTS

THE BASICS

You may have seen wizardry with water buckets before, but now it's time for the magic power of the paintbrush. After he's sucked into Wasteland by the ominous Shadow Blot monster, you guide Mickey Mouse and his special Paint and Thinner abilities on an epic journey from chains in Dark Beauty Castle to the heights of Mickeyjunk Mountain. Do you have what it takes to save a world?

Before you dissolve in a Thinner bath or get flattened by a Slobber, read through the following chapter and learn basic strategies in *Disney Epic Mickey*, along with a few advanced tips for the experts-in-training. Before you know it, you'll be wielding Mickey's paintbrush like a magical Picasso.

Your Screen

You have a lot to absorb the first time you start playing *Disney Epic Mickey*. Luckily, the interface is very streamlined, and clicking around will soon become second nature. Here's a breakdown of the user interface to help you get started:

1. **Health Status:** The top left corner shows Mickey's health status. If he's smiling and you have five red health pips, you're in great shape. As you lose health pips, Mickey becomes less happy. Reach zero and you have to restart in your area. You can add more health pips later in game.
2. **Guardian Bar:** The more Paint or Thinner you use, the faster these guardian bars fill up. When you fill up one bar segment, you receive a corresponding guardian (tint for Paint and turp for Thinner). Fill a second bar and you get two guardians, followed by a third guardian if you fill the last bar.
3. **Sketches:** The top right corner keeps track of your three sketch types: TV, Anvil, and Watch. You can cycle through them or deploy them from here, and the current number available is displayed below the sketch.
4. **Thinner Capacity:** The bottom left corner indicates how much Thinner you have to use. Once you dip into a lower segment, you can't refill it without a power-up. However, the lowest segment will always refill over time so you have some Thinner available.
5. **Mickey:** Guide Mickey around in Wasteland. When you want to use the paintbrush, guide the reticle to a target on the screen and fire away.
6. **Paint Capacity:** The bottom right corner indicates how much Paint you have to use. Once you dip into a lower segment, you can't refill it without a power-up. However, the lowest segment will always refill over time so you have some Paint available.

Your Moves

Walk

Usually, you'll want to run everywhere, but there are times when walking comes in handy. If you're crossing along a dangerous, narrow path, slow down and take each step carefully. Against a Spladoosh, it's best to walk gently and leave it sleeping, unless you want to cause a big goo explosion.

Run

Your standard mode of traveling, running gets you from point A to point B most efficiently, unless you have dangerous obstacles to avoid. In most fights, you want to keep on the move, so running around and dodging is the best option.

Jump

A small hop jumps you over short obstacles and lifts you up to short platforms. A single jump limits your hang time, which can be useful in certain circumstances, such as jumping over a pit trap without hitting a low spiked ceiling.

Double-Jump

Most of the time you jump, you'll want to perform the double-jump. The double-jump gives you the most hang time, and when combined with a running start, allows you to cross the greatest distances. A double-jump is also useful in combat to avoid enemy attacks, and, while you're in the air, you can plan where to touch down and set up your next combat maneuver.

Spin Move

This is your most useful action. Perform a spin move to smash open resources and gain power-ups. Swat enemies aside. Activate gears and levers. Extend a jump with a spin move on the end. Experiment often and you'll be rewarded with new maneuvers.

Resources

Resources are all over Wasteland in everyday objects: barrels, statues, boxes, bottles, and even more fanciful objects like suits of armor and decorative banners. These objects shimmer to signify that the resource can be shattered with your spin move. You may even spot translucent resources that can be painted to spill their contents.

Generally, resources will give you power-ups in the following order: health (pink Mickey ears to fill up health pips if you're low), Paint or Thinner (to fill up your containers if you're low), and finally, if your primary needs are all met, e-tickets.

Paint

Blue Paint fills in translucent objects and befriends Blotling enemies if you douse them with enough of it. Paint slows down Beetleworx enemies. You can spray a burst of Paint up close, or deliver a continuous stream for as long as your capacity holds out. If you use Paint to defeat a boss, you permanently gain an extra segment in your Paint capacity.

Thinner

Green Thinner erases toon objects and dissolves Blotling enemies if you douse them with enough of it. Against Beetleworx enemies, Thinner removes their armor and leaves them vulnerable to your spin move. You can spray a burst of Thinner up close, or deliver a continuous stream for as long as your capacity holds out. If you use Thinner to defeat a boss, you permanently gain an extra segment in your Thinner capacity.

While jumping, you can spray Paint or Thinner straight down underneath you.

Combat

As much as you may yearn for the peace and comfort of your bed back home, it's inevitable that you'll run into enemies in Wasteland and have to defend yourself. These various attacks will get you through enemy encounters:

Painting

Paint befriends Blotlings, so against Seers, Spatters, Sweepers, Spladooshes, and Slobbers use your blue mixture to create allies. Once you transform an enemy to an ally with Paint, they fight for you against other hostile enemies. Just don't douse allies with Thinner or they become hostile again. Against Beetleworx enemies, Paint gums up their machinery and slows them down. Practice streaming Paint at long range to get a feel for how far it travels, and wash enemies from far away to avoid close combat (where most of your damage occurs).

Thinning

Thinner erases Blotlings, so against Seers, Spatters, Sweepers, Spladooshes, and Slobbers use your green mixture to eliminate them. Against Beetleworx enemies, Thinner erodes their outer shell so you can attack their vulnerable insides. Practice streaming Thinner at long range to get a feel for how far it travels, and wash enemies from far away to avoid close combat.

Spin Move

You can use the spin move offensively and defensively. Swat enemies around with the spin move and knock them back. When you're near Thinner pools or cliff edges, it's generally more efficiently to swat foes into the Thinner or over the edge to remove the threat. When enemies get too close, or try to swarm you like Bunny Children, a spin move repels the aggressors and gives you valuable space to reposition yourself.

Jumping

Avoid enemy attacks with frequent double-jumps. While you're in the air, you can quickly glance at open space and steer toward it on the landing. You can also jump on the head of many enemies to temporarily stun them.

Sketches

You can drop your sketches anywhere to affect enemies or alter the environment to your advantage. Experiment with your sketches and see what kind of tricks you can pull off. At various points in the game, allies and resources give you more sketches.

TV

This sketch produces a TV that sits on the ground and affects any character within a small radius, until the TV fades away. Blotlings and NPCs watch the TV and ignore you. Beetleworx attack the TV and get shocked. The TV can also power up platforms that activate larger machines (such as in Tomorrow City), or a TV can be dropped to serve as a platform to increase your jumping distance.

Anvil

When you use this sketch, an anvil appears some distance over the target and immediately falls to the ground, damaging anything underneath it. Don't forget to use the anvil to activate pressure plates and serve as a platform to increase your jumping distance.

Watch

This sketch causes everything in the world to slow down, except for you and your abilities, for a certain time. A large pocket watch appears in the air above the targeting cursor. The hands on the watch start at 12 and move clockwise. Once the hands reach 12 again, time returns to normal. It's great for battling large group of foes, slowing environmental hazards, and beating timing-based puzzles.

Guardians

The guardians represent the primal forces of Wasteland: Paint and Thinner. Guardians born of Thinner are known as "turps." They wield the power of Thinner on your behalf. Thin your environment to draw turps to you. Copious use of Paint summons "tints," the guardians representing the power of Paint in Wasteland. In either case, the more you use Paint or Thinner, the more guardians you attract.

All guardians serve as guides and protectors. On command they fly forth and show the way to the next destination or goal. They can also influence your opponents, but in very different ways: Turps will melt opposing Blotlings, while tints will make them friendly. Shake the Nunchuck to send a single guardian on the attack; shake the Nunchuck and the Remote together to send all your guardians on the attack. When guardians are used in this way they are dispelled, but new ones can always be summoned according to how you use your Paint or Thinner in the world around you.

Inert

The original fabric of Wasteland is all made of "toon." You can see toon that has been "thinned out," which you can restore. However, there is a third form of matter called "inert." Things from the "real world" that enter Wasteland are almost always made of inert, a substance that is usually muted in color and resistant to any effects from Paint and Thinner. It is not invulnerable, however, and you can shatter many weaker inert objects using your spin move.

The highest concentration of inert objects can be found at Mickeyjunk Mountain. In fact, the mountain is mostly composed of the stuff. Old and lost items representing Mickey Mouse end up here. Toys, lunch boxes, comics, and even more exotic items have entered Wasteland from the real world, and Mickey can see a library of relics spanning more than 80 years, all bearing his likeness.

Gremlins and Pals

Gremlins and pals like Animatronic Goofy, Daisy, and Donald are among your best allies in the game. Thirty gremlins are trapped in Wasteland, each caged and hidden in remote locations. Some gremlins might be behind a toon wall, or atop a high ledge, or even inside a rotating painting. Save as many as you can, because they always offer you a pin or other resource as a reward, and if you save all 30 gremlins, you receive a special pin for your efforts. The pal quests to restore your animatronic friends require you to find each pal's missing parts to reassemble him or her. Not only do you gain a pin for your faithfulness, but you change the game's ending with each pal that you restore.

Junction Points

Junction Points are quests or events that influence your game's future and can be decisions such as whether you decide to defeat a boss with Paint or Thinner, the animatronic pal quests, whether you choose to help an NPC with a task or not, and other game-changing moments. Pay close attention to Junction Points so that you can guide the game toward a conclusion that will be the most satisfying for your play style.

Questing

Go out and explore the many worlds in Wasteland. There are tons of challenges, but even more moments of exhilaration as you inspire the citizens around you and save the day from the Shadow Blot's minions.

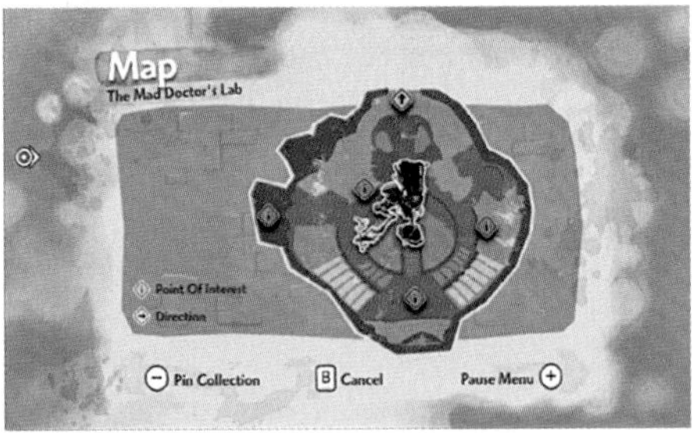

As you travel around, consult your map frequently. Each new level holds a unique map; study that map to figure out your positioning and the optimal paths through the zone. For detailed maps and step-by-step progressions through each level, see the walkthrough chapters later in this guide.

Travel between worlds in Wasteland via screen projectors. Quests frequently involve solving puzzles or aiding NPCs to open the door to an exit projector. Most projectors send you to a 2D transition level before you reach your final 3D destination.

Speak with as many NPCs as you can. Many will be allies, supplying you with helpful pieces of advice, or giving out quests. As you adventure in Wasteland, you discover the main storyline: Mickey must track down Oswald for answers so that he can eventually escape Wasteland and return home. Along the journey, you encounter many characters, some of whose quests can alter future events and the game's ending, and some whose side quests simply entertain and bolster your treasure hoard.

Pins, Extra Content, and Film Reels

Every 3D level has hidden pins and extra content, whether it be in a red chest out in the open or a floating concept art sketch behind a toon wall. Each 2D level has a film reel that may require some serious jumping skills to capture. Turn the film reels in to the Usher at Mean Street's Cinema for special rewards, ranging from e-tickets to power sparks to cartoons that you can watch on the entry menu. Collect as many pins and extra content as you can for bragging rights.

E-tickets and Power Sparks

Think of e-tickets and power sparks as "currency." Use e-tickets to buy various objects in the shops, and services from certain NPCs. You collect e-tickets from resources and as rewards on certain quests. Gremlins will ask for power sparks to start up many of the projector screens in Wasteland. You can find some power sparks in the world, usually in secluded locations or in shops, though most of your power sparks will be earned by completing optional quests.

Shops

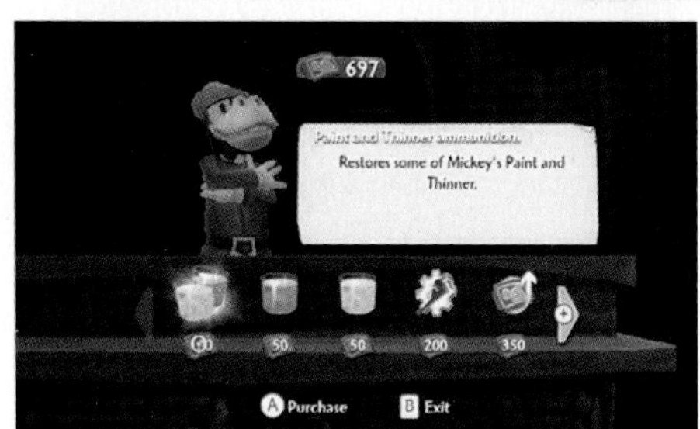

Each major town has a shop, such as Mean Street's Emporium. Visit shops to spend e-tickets on power-ups, pins, extra content, power sparks, and permanent upgrades. If you leave an area and then return later in the game, always check the local shop; a shop's inventory can change as the game progresses, and you will find some very interesting items if you're paying close attention.

Enemies

Wasteland enemies come in two major types: Blotling and Beetleworx. Blotlings come from the Shadow Blot and are fluid creatures. Beetleworx come from the Mad Doctor's handiwork and are robotic. Paint and Thinner affect Blotlings and Beetleworx differently.

Blotlings

Paint can befriend a Blotling, while Thinner makes it disappear. The following Blotlings are listed in the order that you encounter them in the game:

SEER

The weakest of the Blotlings, Seers are generally scouts that spot your presence and alert fellow Blotlings. On the attack, Seers roll up into a ball and try to bowl you over. Spray them at range, and when they roll toward you, jump up in the air or dodge to the side and avoid them.

SPATTER

Spatters are the most common Blotling. They usually congregate in groups, and rush forward when they catch sight of you. They cause damage with a head butt, so keep your distance and hose them down with Paint or Thinner if you want to walk away clean.

SWEEPER

The dangerous Sweeper has two primary attacks: a ranged bucket of Thinner and its namesake body sweep that can knock you around. Prioritize Sweepers because they can attack you both at range and up close, and the Sweeper's Thinner frequently removes toon objects, which can cause further hazards in combat.

SPLADOOSH

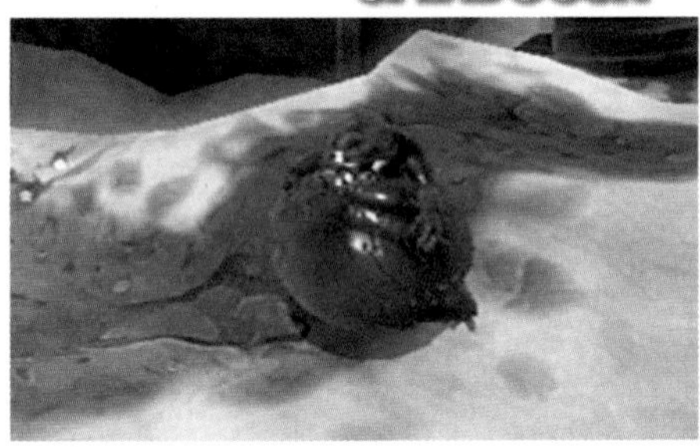

The Spladoosh is the easiest Blotling to deal with, as long as you treat them with a healthy dose of respect. A Spladoosh begins in a sleeping state, and only awakes if you make noise or motion next to it. If you walk carefully past it, or stay far away, the Spladoosh won't react. If you do get close, let the Spladoosh expand and then race out of its blast radius to eliminate it without taking damage yourself. Anvils also blow them up.

SLOBBER

The hardest Blotling is the Slobber with its massive claws, suction breath, and Thinner spit. The claws rake you for damage, the suction breath pulls you in closer, and its Thinner spit can hit you at range, much like the Sweeper's Thinner buckets. However, when the Slobber uses its suction breath, its mouth opens wide, and you can spray Paint or Thinner in the mouth to damage it.

Hard Enemies

Seers, Spatters, Sweepers, and Slobbers have hard versions. Later in the game, you can face tougher versions of these Blotlings, and you should be aware of the differences.

- **Seer:** Increased toughness and faster rolling speed in ball form
- **Spatter:** Increased toughness and damage to player
- **Sweeper:** Increased toughness and faster and more accurate ranged attack
- **Slobber:** Increased toughness

Beetleworx

Paint only slows a Beetleworx down, while Thinner strips its armor and exposes the inner workings to your spin move. The following Beetleworx are listed in the order that you encounter them in the game:

HOPPER

The weakest of the Beetleworx, the birdlike Hoppers bounce around and peck at you. They have good mobility, so maintain better position first and foremost while defending. Coat the outer shell with Thinner to expose its vulnerable insides and spin move to defeat it.

SPINNER

Spinners have a wide arc of cutting buzz saws, so it's best to give them wide berth. When you have to get in close, double-jump to the flank and try to position yourself at its rear. As with the Hopper, spill Thinner on the Spinner's armor to expose a weakness. When the Spinner flips over, avoid any sharp protrusions and spin move to short-circuit it.

TANKER

The toughest of the Beetleworx to defend against, the Tanker attacks with a potent punch and both a Paint and Thinner cannon. Its cannon can have unforeseen consequences on the environment, because it vanishes toon objects it hits with Thinner and restores objects it strikes with Paint. Take these enemies out first on the battlefield with the standard Thinner and spin move combination.

BASHER

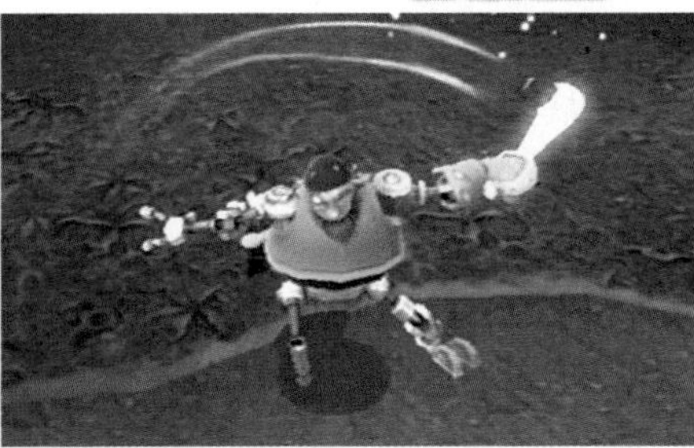

Avoid the long reach of the Basher, which is more likely to cut you to pieces if you aren't careful. Bashers move about quickly, so you won't have as much time to position yourself against other enemies. Rely on Thinner at range to strip its armor down, then dodge or double-jump to avoid its attack and counterstrike.

Bunny Children

Neither Blotling or Beetleworx, the Bunny Children are annoying creatures unto themselves. They move around in packs, but don't damage you directly. Rather, they swarm around you, which slows you down. If enough of them gather, they pick you up and carry you toward the nearest hazard (usually a Thinner pool). Swat them away with a spin move. A well-positioned TV draws their attention and gives you time to escape.

Auto-Save

Remember that *Disney Epic Mickey* auto-saves at certain key moments during the level. If you quit or have to restart, double check your quest status to make sure you have everything you had before the restart. You don't want to accidentally move on without completing something you thought you completed earlier. The good news is that no matter the circumstances, you always remain on your current level, so you can always finish the task.

ENTERING WASTELAND

Dragged into Wasteland by the mysterious Shadow Blot creature, Mickey enters a world filled with forgotten cartoons and dangerous creations that were formed due to his earlier mistake in the magical workshop. Playing as Mickey, you must guide him from sinister worlds like Dark Beauty Castle to twisted worlds like Mickeyjunk Mountain and finally to a confrontation with the Shadow Blot itself.

Wasteland and Its Worlds

The main worlds in *Disney Epic Mickey*, such as Gremlin Village and Tomorrow City, are primarily filled with 3D levels, where you can talk to NPCs, complete quests, and rely on Mickey's Paint and Thinner abilities to navigate the many surprises and obstacles.

When you jump through a projector screen to reach another world, you first arrive in a 2D transition level. These 2D levels are side-scrolling adventures (either horizontally or vertically) and rely on Mickey's jumping and acrobatic skills (plus some puzzling out) to scoop up lots of e-tickets and gain each level's film reel on the way to the exit screen into another 3D level.

For a list of all worlds and levels, see the "World Progression" sidebar at the end of the chapter.

Critical Path and Side Quests

As you adventure in Wasteland, you'll slowly discover the main storyline: Mickey must track down Oswald for answers so that he can eventually escape Wasteland and return home. Along the journey, you will encounter many characters, some of whose quests can alter future events and the game's ending, and some whose side quests simply entertain and bolster your treasure hoard.

Junction Points

Each time you meet a quest or event that influences your game future, we'll call these out in the walkthrough chapters as "Junction Points." Junction Points can be decisions such as whether you defeat a boss with Paint or Thinner, whether you help an NPC with a task or not, and other game-changing moments. Pay close attention to Junction Points so that you can guide the game toward a conclusion that will be the most satisfying for your play style.

Maximizing Your Resources

You can use your spin move on many objects around Wasteland to uncover power-ups. Everything from barrels, plants, banners, statues, and more can be a resource, so smack things on a regular basis to see what you find. You may even spot translucent resources that can be painted to spill their contents. Generally, resources will give you power-ups in the following order: health (pink Mickey ears to fill up health pips if you're low), Paint or Thinner (to fill up your containers if you're low), and finally, if your primary needs are all met, e-tickets.

Collecting Extras

Besides completing quests to eventually bring Mickey home, you should also collect as many pins, film reels, concept art, and cartoons as you can find. Not only are they fun to look at, but some have effects on the game. By saving the 30 gremlins in the game, for example, you earn a special pin, but you also uncover a lot more of the hidden places in *Disney Epic Mickey*. Once you reach Mean Street, you gain a direct benefit by turning in film reels to Usher at the Cinema, so pick up as many as you can.

Playthroughs

Disney Epic Mickey is so, um, epic that you can't complete everything in a single playthrough. It will probably take you three playthroughs to gain all the pins, film reels, concept art pieces, and cartoons. Play through the game once using primarily Paint, then play through using primarily Thinner and you'll experience a whole different set of events, including a different ending. After you complete your first playthrough, make notes on the important Junction Points and, in your second playthrough, make sure you do the opposite the second time around. For example, if in the first playthrough, you chose to retrieve Small Pete's ship log and gained a free pass through the Colosseum (and a trip into the treasure room!), skip the ship log in your second playthrough and you'll fight dozens of enemies in the Colosseum arena. After two playthroughs you should have nearly every reward, and your third playthrough should pick up the few missing stragglers.

How to Use the Walkthroughs

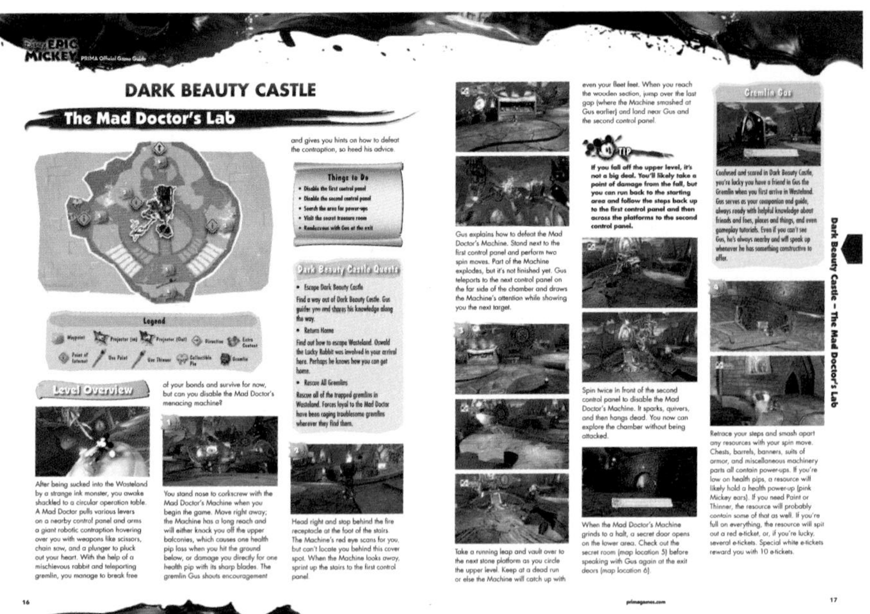

Each 3D level comes with a map labeling important points of interest, where to use Paint and Thinner, hidden pins and extra content, projector screen locations, and more. The map also numbers the most logical route through the level; follow the numbers and read the corresponding text and screens for strategies on how to overcome each obstacle. A "Things to Do" scroll at the beginning of each walkthrough quickly outlines your main tasks on the level. We also begin each section with a list of available quests in that area. Because many quests can be performed in any order you choose, we always list them alphabetically. Sidebars draw your attention to key elements of the level, such as Junction Points, enemies, bosses, gremlins, pins, extra content, and optional quests. If you read an entire walkthrough section, you should have no trouble finding everything in the level, from the fastest path to the exit projector screen to the craziest hidden item.

For 2D levels, it's much easier. The 2D levels look like film reel–themed pages and show you the step-by-step progression through the level. Each screenshot captures an important action on the level, and the caption below explains what to do. Follow the screenshots and captions to collect every e-ticket and the important film reel on your way toward the projector screen exit.

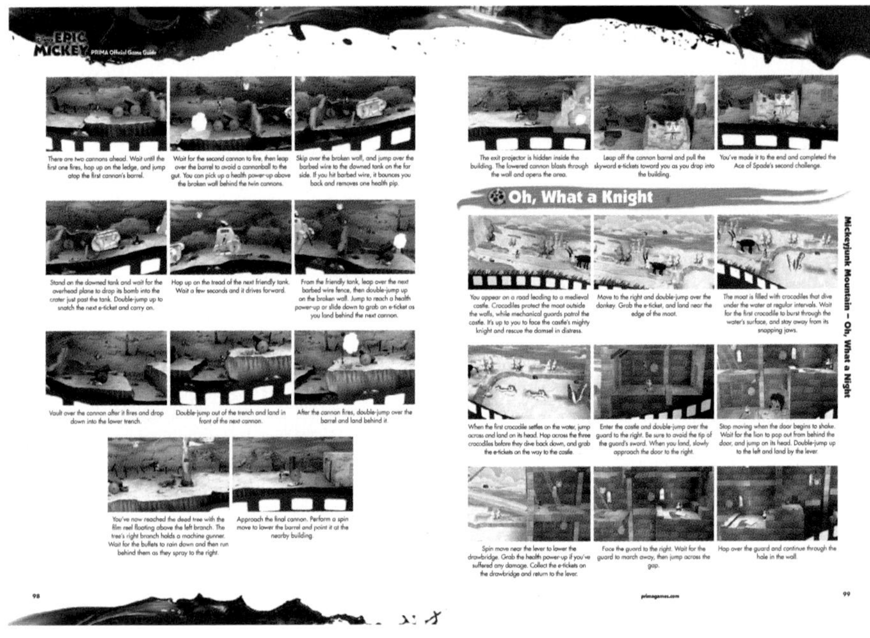

World Progression

Once you get the projector screens working in Wasteland, jumping back and forth between worlds is a snap. With so many quests and so many talkative NPCs, the whirlwind of activity may quickly have you seeing those little birdies spinning around your head. To help set you on the best path through Wasteland, here's a list of the levels in the order you'll most likely encounter them:

Dark Beauty Castle

- The Mad Doctor's Lab
- Utilidor III
- Castle Entrance
- Mickey and the Beanstalk (2D level)

Gremlin Village

- Slalom
- Ticket Booth
- Jungle Boat Ride
- Asian Boat Ride
- Steamboat Willie 1 (2D level)
- World of Gremlins
- Clock Cleaners 1 (2D level)
- World of Gremlins (outside of tower)
- Steamboat Willie 2 (2D level)
- Clock Cleaners 2 (2D level)
- European Boat Ride
- Steamboat Willie 3 (2D level)
- The Clock Tower

Mean Street and OsTown

- Mean Street
- Thru the Mirror (2D level)
- OsTown
- Mickey's Steamroller (2D level)

Mickeyjunk Mountain

- The Heaps
- Alpine Climbers 1 (2D level)
- The Piles
- Alpine Climbers 2 (2D level)
- Mt. Osmore: Slopes
- Mt. Osmore: Caverns
- Trolley Trouble (2D level)
- Great Guns (2D level)
- Oh, What a Knight (2D level)
- OsTown
- Mean Street
- Plutopia 1 (2D level)

Tomorrow City

- Notilus
- Mickey's Mechanical Man 1 (2D level)
- Tomorrow City Lagoon
- Great Big Tomorrow
- Plutopia 2 (2D level)
- Tomorrow City Square
- Mickey's Mechanical Man 2 (2D level)
- Space Voyage
- Petetronic
- Mean Street
- Jungle Rhythm 1 (2D level)

Pirates of the Wasteland

- Ventureland
- Castaway 1 (2D level)
- Tortooga
- Jungle Rhythm 2 (2D level)
- Jungle
- The Whalers (2D level)
- Tortooga
- Castaway 2 (2D level)
- Pirate Voyage
- Shanghaied (2D level)
- Skull Island
- The Jolly Roger
- Ventureland
- Mean Street
- Lonesome Ghosts 1 (2D level)

Lonesome Manor

- Bog Easy
- Lonesome Ghosts 2 (2D level)
- Manor House
- Mad Doctor 1 (2D level)
- Foyer
- Haunted House 1 (2D level)
- Stretching Room
- Mad Doctor 2 (2D level)
- Library
- Haunted House 2 (2D level)
- Ballroom
- Haunted House 3 (2D level)
- Mad Doctor's Attic

Beating the Blot

- Bog Easy
- Mean Street
- OsTown
- Mt. Osmore Caverns
- Ye Olden Days (2D level)
- The Shadow Blot
- OsTown
- Mean Street
- Ventureland
- Bog Easy
- Tomorrow City
- Space Voyage
- The Mad Doctor's Lab
- Sleeping Beauty (2D level)
- Throne Room
- Fantasia 1 or Fantasia 2 (2D levels)
- Fireworks Control Tower
- Utilidor IV
- Sorrow Tower
- Fantasia 3 (2D level)
- Grief Tower
- Fantasia 4 (2D level)
- Loss Tower
- Utilidor VII
- Inside the Blot

DARK BEAUTY CASTLE

The Mad Doctor's Lab

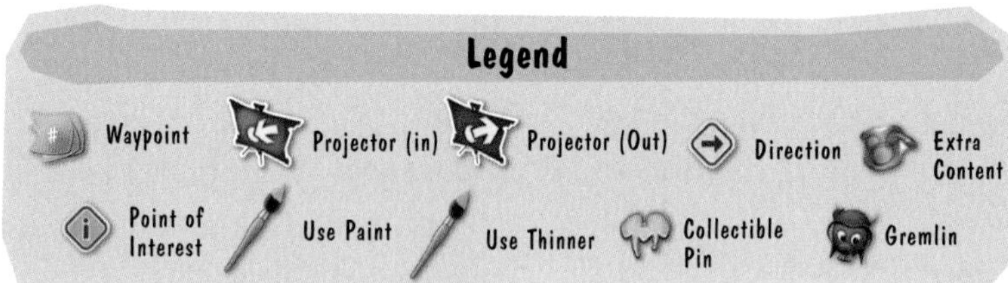

Level Overview

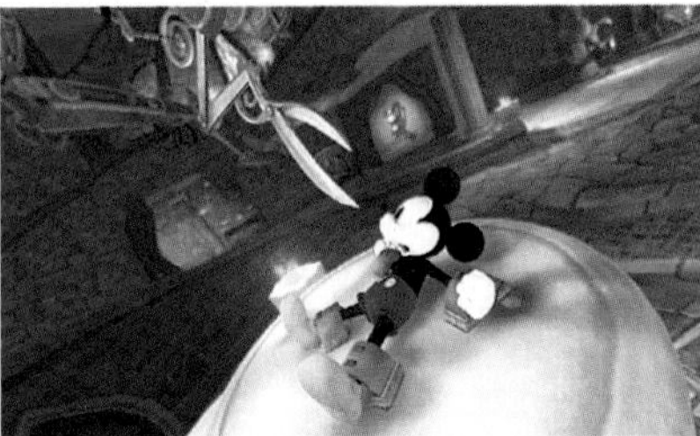

After being sucked into the Wasteland by a strange ink monster, you awake shackled to a circular operation table. A Mad Doctor pulls various levers on a nearby control panel and arms a giant robotic contraption hovering over you with weapons like scissors, chain saw, and a plunger to pluck out your heart. With the help of a mischievous rabbit and teleporting gremlin, you manage to break free of your bonds and survive for now, but can you disable the Mad Doctor's menacing machine?

You stand nose to corkscrew with the Mad Doctor's Machine when you begin the game. Move right away; the Machine has a long reach and will either knock you off the upper balconies, which causes one health pip loss when you hit the ground below, or damage you directly for one health pip with its sharp blades. The gremlin Gus shouts encouragement and gives you hints on how to defeat the contraption, so heed his advice.

Things to Do

- Disable the first control panel
- Disable the second control panel
- Search the area for power-ups
- Visit the secret treasure room
- Rendezvous with Gus at the exit

Dark Beauty Castle Quests

- Escape Dark Beauty Castle

Find a way out of Dark Beauty Castle. Gus guides you and shares his knowledge along the way.

- Return Home

Find out how to escape Wasteland. Oswald the Lucky Rabbit was involved in your arrival here. Perhaps he knows how you can get home.

- Rescue All Gremlins

Rescue all of the trapped gremlins in Wasteland. Forces loyal to the Mad Doctor have been caging troublesome gremlins wherever they find them.

Head right and stop behind the fire receptacle at the foot of the stairs. The Machine's red eye scans for you, but can't locate you behind this cover spot. When the Machine looks away, sprint up the stairs to the first control panel.

Gus explains how to defeat the Mad Doctor's Machine. Stand next to the first control panel and perform two spin moves. Part of the Machine explodes, but it's not finished yet. Gus teleports to the next control panel on the far side of the chamber and draws the Machine's attention while showing you the next target.

Take a running leap and vault over to the next stone platform as you circle the upper level. Keep at a dead run or else the Machine will catch up with even your fleet feet. When you reach the wooden section, jump over the last gap (where the Machine smashed at Gus earlier) and land near Gus and the second control panel.

If you fall off the upper level, it's not a big deal. You'll likely take a point of damage from the fall, but you can run back to the starting area and follow the steps back up to the first control panel and then across the platforms to the second control panel.

Spin twice in front of the second control panel to disable the Mad Doctor's Machine. It sparks, quivers, and then hangs dead. You now can explore the chamber without being attacked.

When the Mad Doctor's Machine grinds to a halt, a secret door opens on the lower area. Check out the secret room (map location 5) before speaking with Gus again at the exit doors (map location 6).

Gremlin Gus

Confused and scared in Dark Beauty Castle, you're lucky you have a friend in Gus the Gremlin when you first arrive in Wasteland. Gus serves as your companion and guide, always ready with helpful knowledge about friends and foes, places and things, and even gameplay tutorials. Even if you can't see Gus, he's always nearby and will speak up whenever he has something constructive to offer.

Retrace your steps and smash apart any resources with your spin move. Chests, barrels, banners, suits of armor, and miscellaneous machinery parts all contain power-ups. If you're low on health pips, a resource will likely hold a health power-up (pink Mickey ears). If you need Paint or Thinner, the resource will probably contain some of that as well. If you're full on everything, the resource will spit out a red e-ticket, or, if you're lucky, several e-tickets. Special white e-tickets reward you with 10 e-tickets.

Use spin moves on all the machinery on the Mad Doctor's stage and fill up on power-ups and e-tickets.

Continue around the chamber looking for any resources that will give you more e-tickets, which you'll save up to spend on valuable items later. On the lower level, watch that you don't step in the Thinner stream that clogs up a quarter of the area.

Enter the secret room unlocked from the Mad Doctor's Machine's demise. Pick up more e-tickets from the suits of armor and chest on the right side.

The red chest in the back corner holds a Bronze Pin, your first of 105 pins if you want to collect them all. Most pins are unique and commemorate specific events or places.

On your way out of the secret room, grab the Extra Content doodle from between the two large statues. This unlocks "The Mad Doctor's Lab II" content.

Scour the chamber one last time for anything you missed. When you're happy that you've exhausted all resources, return to the Gus and the exit doors. He trains you to properly use Paint and Thinner.

Bronze Pin and Mad Doctor's Lab II Extra Content

After you defeat the Mad Doctor's Machine, search the secret treasure room for your first Bronze Pin and your first extra content (Mad Doctor's Lab II). You have 19 more Bronze Pins to go, and 49 pieces of extra content, if you want to collect them all.

Utilidor III

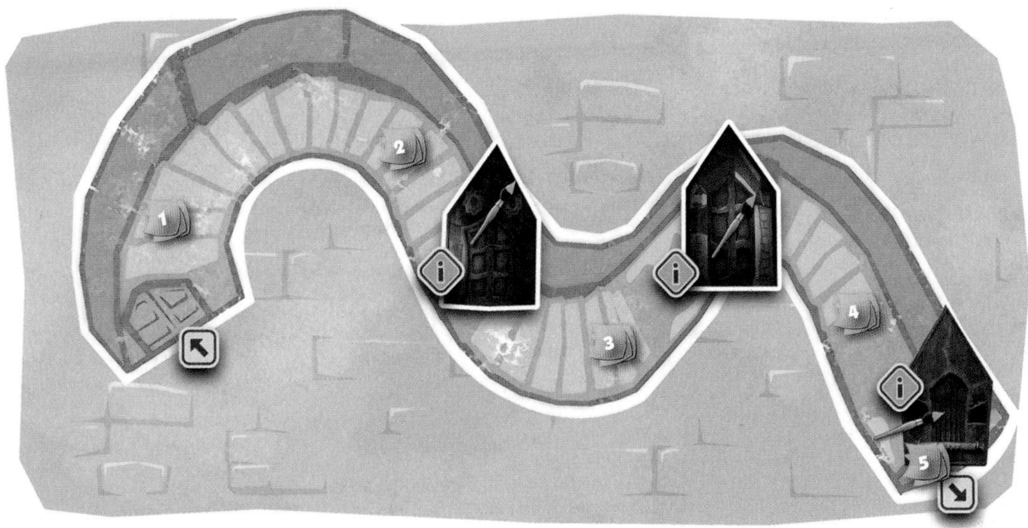

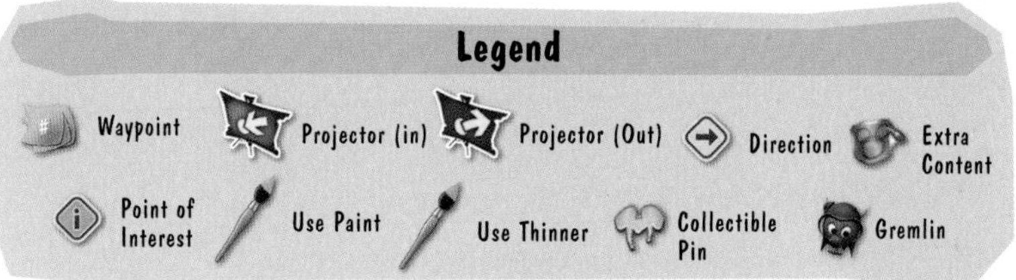

Level Overview

Outside the first chamber, Gus teaches you the basic ins and outs of working with Paint and Thinner. You learn to paint in gears, remove Paint to collapse floors and doors, and navigate Wasteland with a flick of your brush. After the tutorial, you should be ready to face the foes in the next area.

Gus explains how to work with Paint and Thinner in the corridor outside the Mad Doctor's chamber. Practice spurting and spraying your blue and green mixtures on the wall targets and the three obstacles that block your path. Don't worry about using too much Paint or Thinner; the suits of armor and barrels scattered down the corridor provide plenty of extra resources.

Things to Do

- Learn how to use Paint
- Learn how to use Thinner
- Bypass the three obstacles

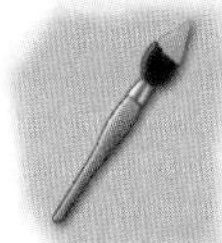

Paint the middle gear above the closed door to open the lock.

At the first door, you learn to use Paint. In Wasteland, painting is a powerful tool; it can create objects, start up machinery, befriend enemies, and more. Look above the door and you'll see a translucent gear slightly below and between the two visible gears. Use Paint to fill in the translucent gear and the door will open.

Remove the painted door frame to drop the second door.

At the second door, Gus gives you a lesson on Thinner. Use Thinner to erase certain painted objects, reveal secret areas, stop machinery, vanish enemies, and more. The frame holding the second door in place is made with cartoon Paint. Use Thinner to remove that Paint and the door falls, bridging the pool of Thinner blocking your way. Hop over the door and into the final area.

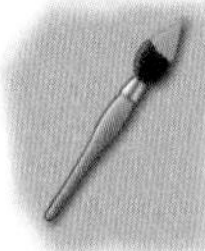

Erase the floor in front of the third obstacle and it collapses out of sight.

Your path appears to be a dead end. Fortunately, you control a magical brush that can produce quite a few tricks. Here we'll use both Thinner and Paint. First, thin out the floor so that

the rock and wall behind it collapse into the magically vanished spot. Next, restore the floor again with Paint and the corridor is back to normal, minus the dead-end wall.

March over the newly fashioned floor and into the final area. With the knowledge of Paint and Thinner, you can now face off against some of Wasteland's enemies.

Castle Entrance

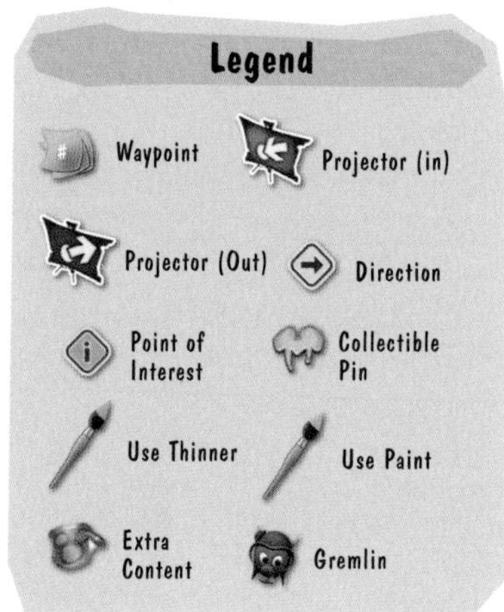

Level Overview

You run into your first Blotlings in the Castle Entrance. A pair of Seers tries to roll you flat as a cartoon pancake while you dance around the courtyard. Deal with the Seers while you befriend Gremlin Calvin and figure out a way to open the large portcullis that seals the Dark Beauty Castle exit.

1

When you enter the Castle Entrance, you spot the Dark Beauty Castle exit on the far side; unfortunately, the way out is barricaded by a huge portcullis. You must free Gremlin Calvin and spin two gears on the upper balconies to open the portcullis.

Things to Do

- Beat the two Seers
- Free Gremlin Calvin
- Gain the Gold Pin
- Learn about blue guardians (tints)
- Spin the first portcullis gear
- Learn about green guardians (turps)
- Spin the second portcullis gear
- Search the area for power-ups
- Retrieve the Dark Beauty Castle Pin
- Retrieve the Dark Beauty Castle I extra content
- Complete the "Escape Dark Beauty Castle" quest by exiting through the projector screen

Paint or Thinner? Enemies can be defeated by either mixture. With enough Paint, you can turn an enemy into an ally who will fight other enemies for you. Thinner, on the other hand, erases the enemy completely. It's really a matter of your play-style preference, and, remember, the more Paint or Thinner you use, the quicker the matching guardian bar will fill up.

First, though, you have to deal with a new enemy: the Seer. As soon as you set foot in the main courtyard, a Seer spots you and calls forth a partner from a large pipe to your right. See the "Enemy: Seer" sidebar for more details on your first Blotling foe. Use Paint to befriend the Seers, Thinner to erase them, or a combination of both to use one Seer to eliminate the other.

2

After you defeat the Seers, approach the columned structure in front of the portcullis and hop on the short, bejeweled platform alongside it.

Stepping on this platform activates the machinery holding Gremlin Calvin's cage. Spin three times to lower the cage to the ground.

Enemy: Seer

A Seer looks like a giant eyeball with two legs that fold in when the Seer lowers to the ground and rolls. It tries to damage you by rolling over you. Once a Seer begins a roll, it heads in a straight line, which you can dodge easily or jump over if you're not caught by surprise. Alone, a Seer isn't that dangerous; however, a Seer's true strength lies in its ability to spot you at a distance and alert reinforcements to your presence.

Gremlin Calvin

Calvin is trapped in his cage high up inside a mechanized claw. Jump on the pink glowing platform and spin three times to drop the claw to the ground. Perform a spin move to shatter the cage and release Calvin. Don't go for the chest inside the columned structure or you won't be able to release Calvin.

Avoid the chest on the pressure plate inside the columned structure. If you go for the reward, you won't be able to rescue Gremlin Calvin.

Head over to Calvin's cage and spin to shatter it to pieces. Calvin rewards you with a Gold Pin, and you can now seek out the two gears on the balconies above you to open the exit gate.

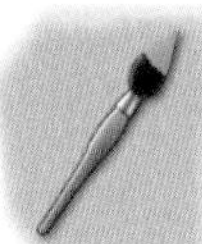

Remove the collapsed stone on the balcony turn to reach the upper level.

If you're facing the portcullis, head to the ramp on your left. At the first turn, several chunks of collapsed stone block the path. Pull out your brush and spray green Thinner to clear the way. Search the chest and barrels behind the stone for more power-ups.

On the next ramp Gus explains guardians to you. You summon guardians by using Paint or Thinner in the world around you. One blue guardian (tint) appears if you fill one of the bars beneath your health pips. Use more Paint to fill two bars, and two blue guardians circle around you. Fill all three bars for three guardians. The guardians stay until you activate them or until you use enough of the opposite mixture to reduce the guardian bars.

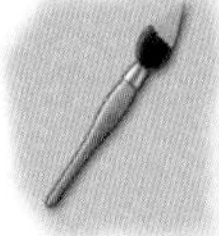

Fill in the upper balcony holes to safely traverse to the first portcullis gear.

In this section, the balcony has large holes that are challenging to cross. If you paint as you move along, it's much easier to cross without a damaging fall to the floor below.

Continue painting a safe path until you reach the first portcullis gear.

A spin move activates the first portcullis gear. Now seek out the second gear to completely open the gate.

Dark Beauty Castle Pin

You can retrieve the Dark Beauty Castle Pin in the Castle Entrance area at any time. Look for the lit door on the left wall as you first enter the courtyard. Wash down the door with Thinner and open the chest hidden behind the door for the pin.

6

Take a running leap off the balcony near the first gear and double-jump down to the next balcony. Raid the resources nearby to fill up on health pips, Paint, Thinner, and e-tickets.

7

Continue along the balcony and Gus tells you about green guardians (turps). After you learn about those

guardian spirits, solidify the balcony with more Paint and continue.

Near the end of the long straightaway, jump over the small gap and land near the blocked stone. This stone cannot be removed with Thinner, but you can use Thinner on the floor beneath it to make the stone fall away.

Instead, hop up on the balcony railing and carefully inch to the rock outcropping. Double-jump over the rock and land on the far side of the balcony.

At the corner, you face another rock obstruction that can't be removed with Thinner. Again, use Thinner on the floor beneath the rocks or hop up on the railing and jump to the other side. Don't jump too far or you'll fall through the unpainted floor.

8

Fill in the floor with Paint and cross to the second portcullis gear. Spin once to activate the gear and raise the exit gate.

9

With the portcullis out of the way, you now have a clear path to your first projector screen. Gus explains that projector screens operate like portals to other worlds. Jump through one and you exit the current location and enter a new one, which can be either a 2D level or a 3D level. The Castle

Entrance projector screen sends you to "Mickey and the Beanstalk," your first 2D level.

Extra Content: Dark Beauty Castle I

If you're facing the portcullis, the Dark Beauty Castle I extra content is hidden under the left ramp. Walk to the foot of the ramp and coat the area in Thinner to find the special item floating underneath the ramp.

Mickey and the Beanstalk

You have escaped Dark Beauty Castle, but now you start the epic "Return Home" quest and climb to the top of a giant beanstalk.

Run forward and jump to snatch the first e-ticket. Vault up on both branches of the dead tree to gain the next two e-tickets.

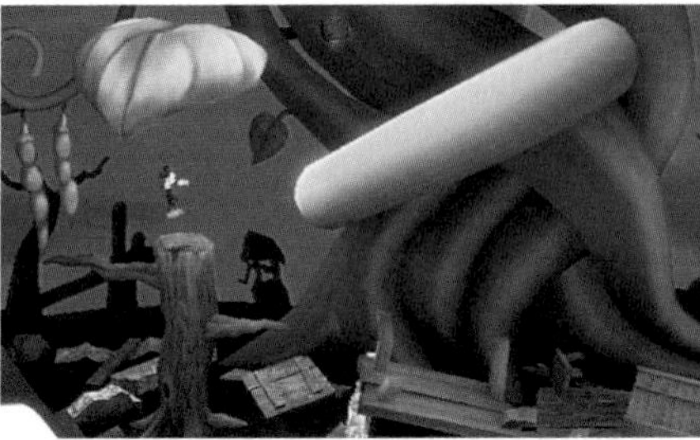
Leap over to the beanstalk and hop up the diagonal stem to gain the string of e-tickets.

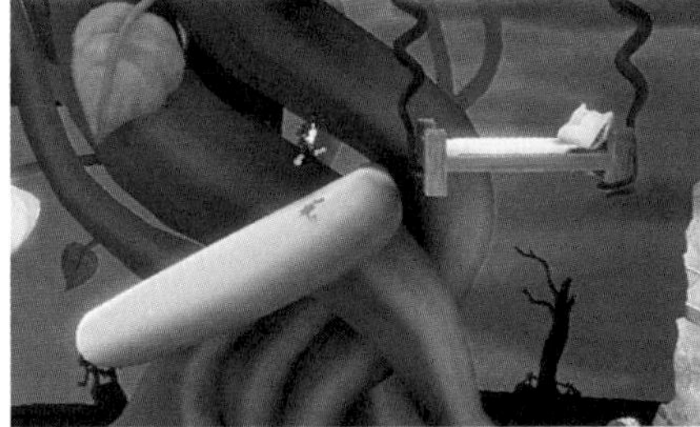
Wait for the first bed to lower and jump onboard.

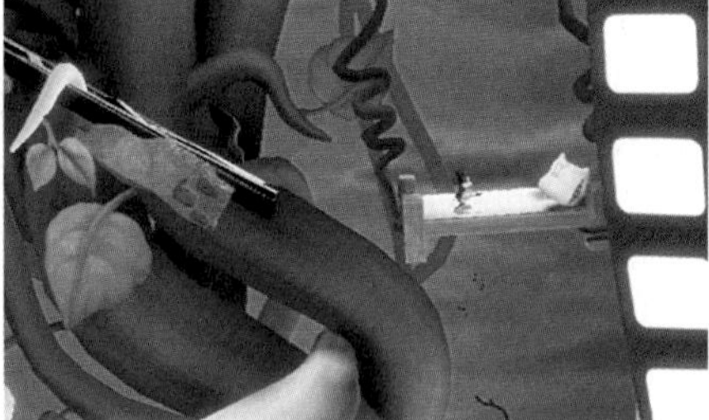
As the bed springs up, collect the hanging e-ticket above and then flip over to the beanstalk again.

Race up the next beanstalk stem and hop up on the far leaf.

Double-jump to reach the e-ticket above you.

Run and double-jump to reach the roof spread out on the next set of stems.

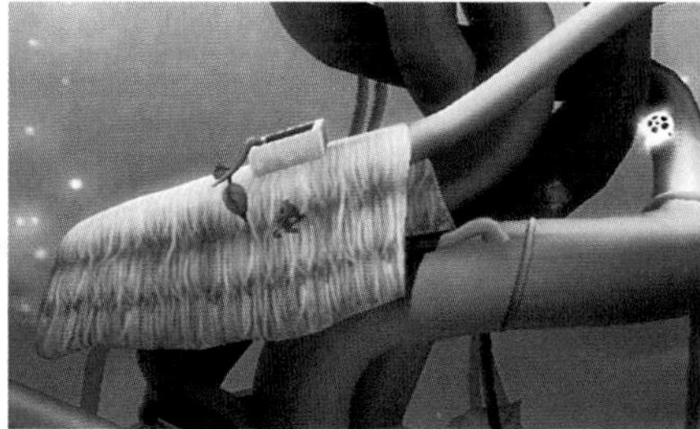

Drop down through the roof's chimney hole.

Walk out on the stem ledge and collect your first film reel. Naturally, it's "Mickey and the Beanstalk." All future 2D levels contain a self-titled film reel. Collect them all to help you later in the game.

Return to the chimney and jump back up. Collect another e-ticket as you climb higher.

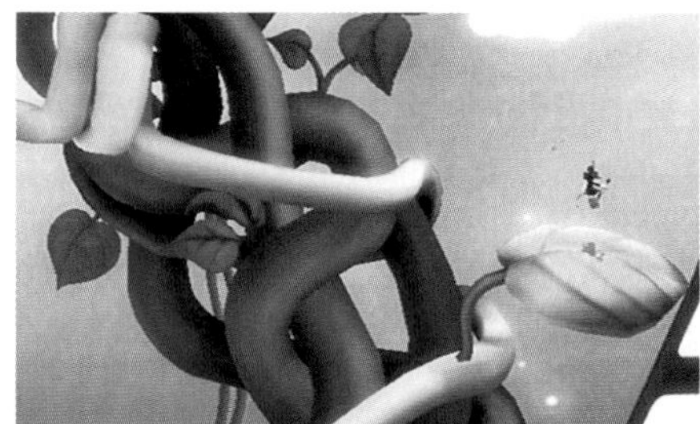

Double-jump up on the next leaf and gather e-tickets as you spring back to the left to land on the main stem cluster.

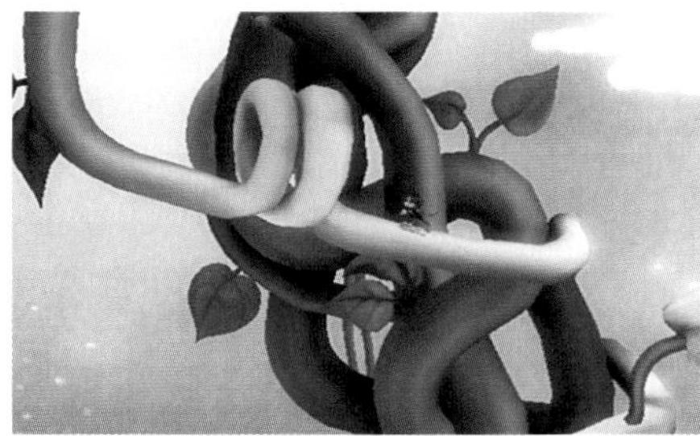

Run and double-jump on top of the twin coil in the middle of your current stem.

Wait for the second bed to swing toward you and jump onto the mattress.

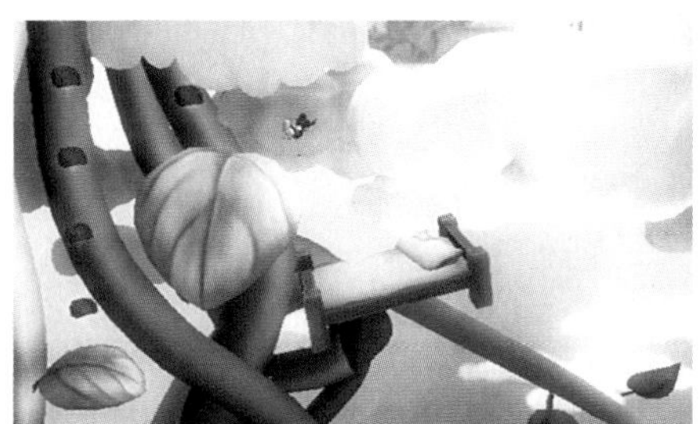

As the bed swings close to the highest leaf, double-jump to reach safety.

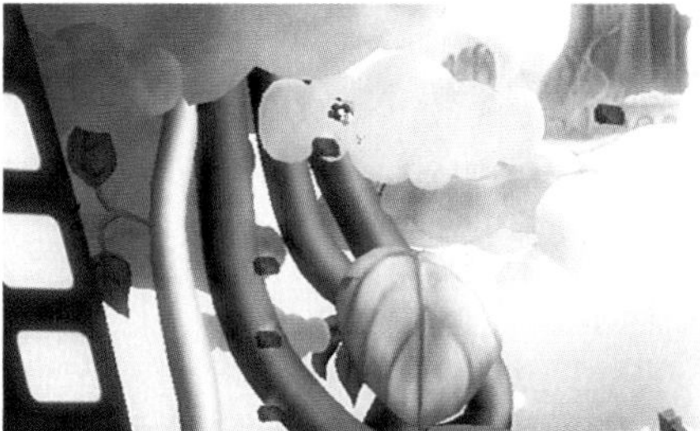

If you want more e-tickets, jump off the leaf's left side and suck up a string of e-tickets on your way down.

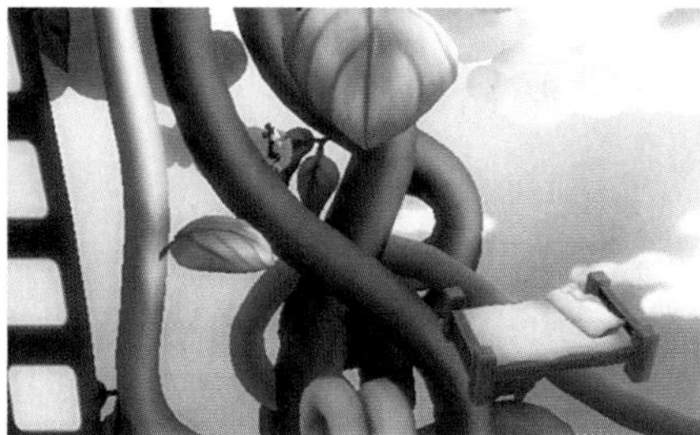

Land on the small leaf below and wait for the bed again to circle back up to the top.

Return to the highest leaf and execute a well-timed double-jump to reach the clouds. Hit your second jump while at the height of your first jump to land on clouds and not on stems below.

If you have a healthy dose of e-tickets in pocket and your film reel, jump through the projector screen to enter Gremlin Village.

GREMLIN VILLAGE

Slalom

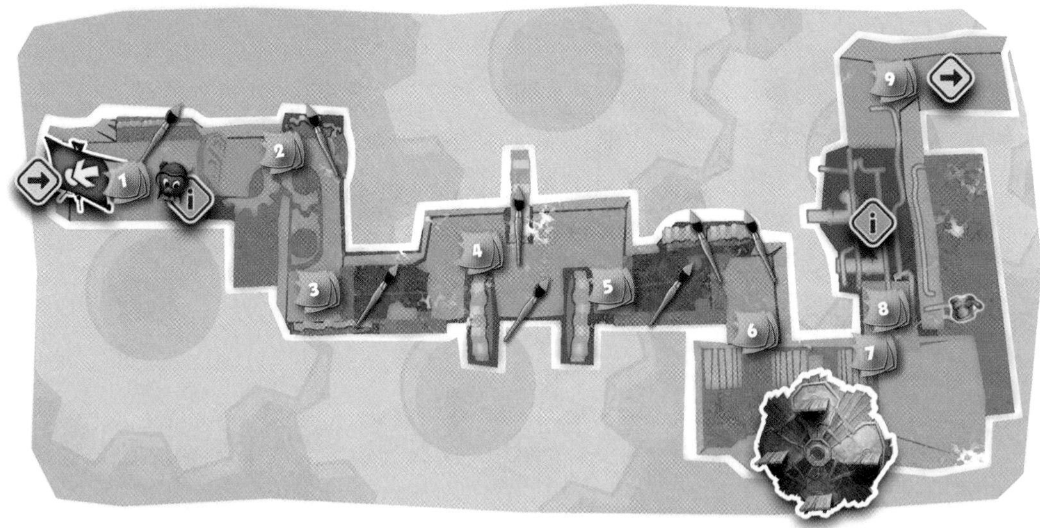

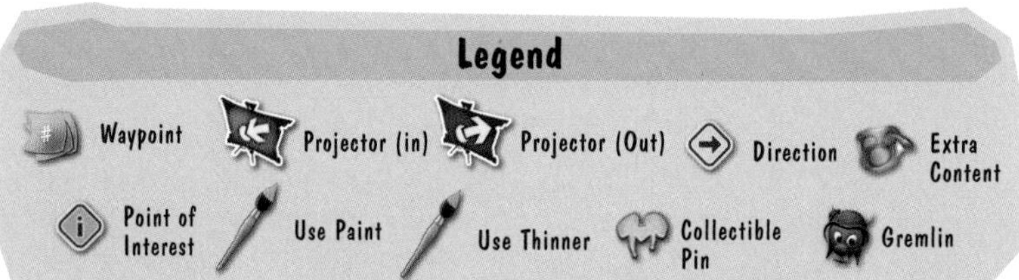

Level Overview

The first level in Gremlin Village is a maze of gears, valves, and steam vents. You meet Gremlin Tiestow and offer to assist him on repairing the various steam valves to pass through to the far side. A careful examination will get you through the passages safely, until a trap springs on you at the end and you must battle your second Blotling enemies, the Spatters.

1

You don't have to rescue the next gremlin you meet; Gremlin Tiestow is already free and looking for some help repairing the machinery in the next set of corridors.

Paint the two gears near Gremlin Tiestow to unlock the first door.

Pull out your paintbrush and aim it at the two gears on the wall left of the locked door. Painting in the gears activates the door, which unlocks and gives you access to the rest of the level. Or, you can knock down the door; spray the gears with Thinner or use the Spin Attack to take out the gear in the middle. With the door out of your way, you can pass through to the rest of the level—but Gremlin Tiestow won't be happy with you.

Things to Do

- Meet up with Gremlin Tiestow
- Repair the door
- Patch the steam pipes
- Paint multiple floor sections to pass safely
- Defeat the Spatters
- Search the area for power-ups
- Exit to the Ticket Booth area

Gremlin Village Quests

- Ambush Down Below

Either defeat the Spatters with Thinner or turn them friendly with Paint.

- Clock Tower

Defeat or befriend the Clock Tower. Use Thinner to defeat the Clock Tower or Paint to make it an ally.

- Find Small Pete's Ship's Log

Recover the ship's log from Small Pete's crashed boat.

- Get Inside the Colosseum

To reach the Colosseum, either topple the Parisian Tower or take the cloud path.

- The Leaning Tower

Cause the Leaning Tower to fall over and form a bridge or fix the whirlpool problem.

- Navigate the Asia Boat Ride

Find the path to the door leading out of the Asia Boat Ride. Talk to the trapped gremlins, repair the machines, and explore to find hidden clues to navigate the Asia Boat Ride.

- Open the Gate

The exit from World of Gremlins is controlled in the village tower. Reach the top of the village tower, and then operate the pump at the top.

Gremlin Village Quests (cont'd)

- Patch Steam Pipes

Paint in all of the leaking steam pipes in the tunnels. Patch leaking steam pipes by painting in the area around the leak, from a safe distance.

- Raise the Fire Bridge

Use the machinery to escape. The machinery in the back corner of the Asia Boat Ride controls something called the fire bridge.

- Reach the Clock Tower

Proceed through the European Boat Ride to reach the Clock Tower.

- Save Gus's House

Stop the Thinner from continuously spraying on Gus's house by repairing some of the damage in World of Gremlins.

- Ticket Booth

Gremlin Tim needs help! Blotlings have trapped Gremlin Tim in the ticket booth. Remove the threat and stop new Blotlings from entering the area.

- Tiestow's Door

Gremlin Tiestow wants to get the door open. Repair the door by painting the gears. Or take the direct approach and use your spin move to break it.

- Tiestow's Treasure

Gremlin Tiestow asked you to paint in all of the pipes as you go through the tunnels. Patch leaking steam pipes by painting in the area around the leak, from a safe distance.

Assuming you cooperate with Gremlin Tiestow, he offers to help you later on and disappears. Gus points out the blasts of steam that block your way ahead and gives you the "Patch Steam Pipes" quest to fix them. When

you see translucent sections of pipe spewing out hot steam, paint the section and seal up the pipe to get credit for a fix. If you fix them all, you complete the quest and earn the Tunnels extra content at the end of the level. The first steam pipe lies in the top corner of the first turn beyond the front doors.

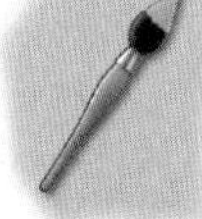

Paint all four steam pipes to complete the "Patch Steam Pipes" quest.

Extra Content: Tunnels

You can weave through the Slalom area by dodging steam vents, and, in some instances, using Thinner to foul up the works. However, if you do this, you miss out on the Tunnels extra content. To receive the extra content, you must seal every steam pipe. Proceed slowly and use Paint on any translucent pipes near where you see steam. If you reach the end and have closed all steam pipes, Gremlin Tiestow will raise the gate in the alcove that holds the Tunnels extra content. Retrieve it after you defeat the Spatters.

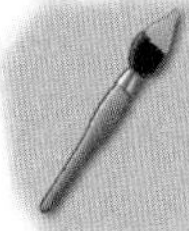

Coat the floor in Paint for any of the larger gaps on the level. You need additional flooring to make the jumps.

Continue down the corridor and slow up when you reach the next turn. The floor here is gone, and you'll fall through if you advance. Spray a nice coat of Paint down on the floor to seal things up and continue.

In the Gears Room, move near the second gear and stand back from the steam. Shoot a long stream of Paint across the room and seal up the second steam pipe to continue. It's also possible to continue by using Thinner on the second gear, but if you leave the steam pipe active you can't finish the "Patch Steam Pipes" quest.

Fill in the next section of floor with Paint. After you spill out some Paint, you can cross easily, but don't forget

about the steam pipe halfway across on the left side.

Paint in the next two steam pipes. Once you do that, you complete the "Patch Steam Pipes" quest when you see Gremlin Tiestow in the final corridor, and Tiestow will unlock the outer door for you, plus reward you with the Tunnels extra content.

A huge crank turns in the next room. You can jump on the wooden platform jutting out of the crank and follow the machine as it rotates counterclockwise, or squirt Paint on a second platform if you miss the first one. You can also drop to ground level, stock up on some of the power-ups in barrels and chests, and then jump on the wooden platform as it reaches its low point.

Ride the wooden platform around the crank. Don't slip off or you'll drop into the Thinner pool below and slowly dissolve.

Wait for the platform to approach the ledge on the far side of the chamber. Take a running leap off the platform and double-jump to safety on the ledge.

As soon as you enter the final corridor, the door seals behind you. It's a trap, and a Spatter immediately drops out of the nearby pipe and attacks. A few seconds later, a second

Spatter forms in the middle of the corridor and joins the attack.

Enemy: Spatter

These small purple Blotlings can liquefy and drop out of pipes or fit through grilles. In its solid form, a Spatter rushes in close to you and tries to strike you with a head butt. If successful, you lose one health pip and get knocked back several feet. A spin move will brush the Spatter back, and a little bit of Paint or Thinner either teams it up with you or wipes it clean.

Dodge around long enough to put some space between you and your Spatter target and let the Blotling have it with a healthy dose of Paint or Thinner. If a Spatter gets too close, perform a spin move to knock it back.

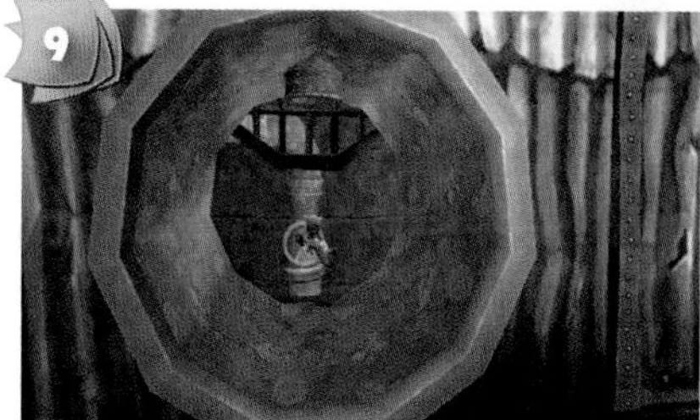

Once the Spatters are puddles, Gremlin Tiestow unlocks the exit door for you, and, if you completed the "Patch Steam Pipes" quest, opens the gate in the first side pipe to reach the Tunnel extra content. Exit through the door and into the Ticket Booth area.

Ticket Booth

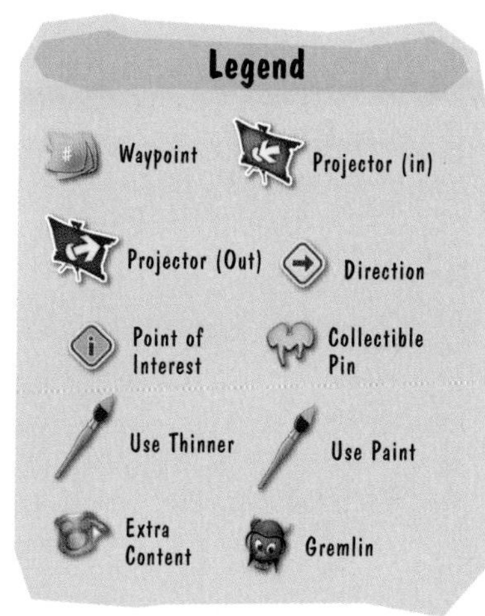

Level Overview

In a broken theme park, you must rescue Gremlin Tim, who's stuck in a ticket booth surrounded by Blotling enemies. After you spring Tim, he asks you to fix the theme park rides, which requires savvy paintbrush skills and acrobatic prowess.

1

Blotlings will spot you a few steps into the Ticket Booth area, so prepare for a battle. You must defeat the three Spatters and a Seer to reach Gremlin Tim in the booth.

Things to Do

- Free Gremlin Tim from the Blotlings
- Find Tim's wrench
- Fix the Tea Cup Ride
- Search the area for power-ups
- Exit to the Jungle Boat Ride

2

Combat the Blotlings with your favorite fighting technique. You can paint one or two to battle on your side, or break out the Thinner to liquidate them all. You have plenty of room to move around in front of Gremlin Tim, so avoid the tumbling Seer while using your paintbrush on the Spatters. If any enemies get close, use a spin move to knock them back.

Once all enemies are defeated, approach Gremlin Tim in the booth. He thanks you for helping him escape, but he can't help you with the rides until you find his missing wrench. He remembers using it last near the Tea Cup Ride.

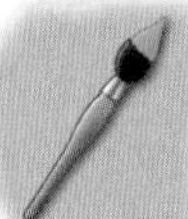

Erase the red-striped tea cup to uncover the missing wrench.

3

Head over to the Tea Cup Ride and look for a red-striped cup. Spray Thinner on the cup until it dissolves completely.

If you've picked the correct cup, you'll see the wrench floating inside the now translucent cup. Grab the wrench and return it to Gremlin Tim.

4

Gremlin Tim is back over by the Elephant Ride. When you return his wrench to him, Tim activates the Elephant Ride, which now rises high enough that you can use it to reach the striped tent.

Gremlin Tim

Gremlin Tim is trapped inside the ticket booth, surrounded by Spatters and a Seer. Even after you defeat the Blotlings and free Gremlin Tim, he realizes that he's forgotten his wrench somewhere and can't help you until you find it for him.

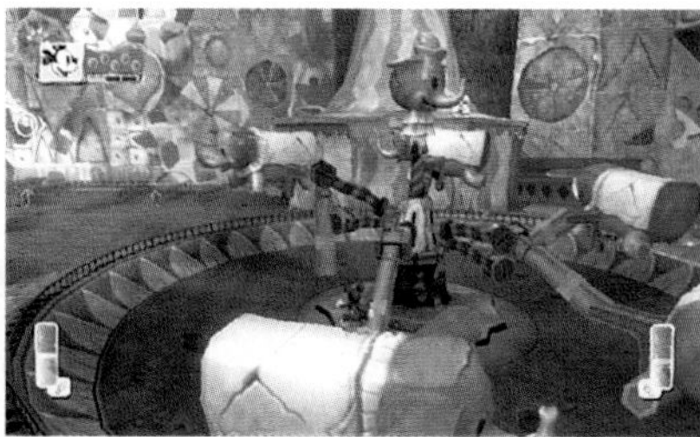

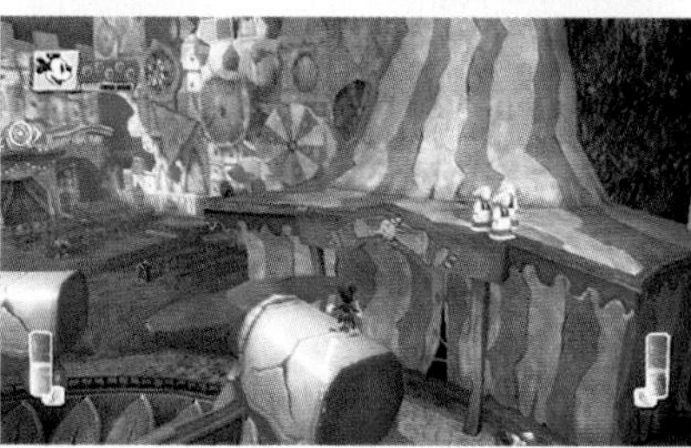

Double-jump up on the lowest elephant and jump from back to back. On the fourth elephant, turn toward the striped tent and make the long leap over to the roof.

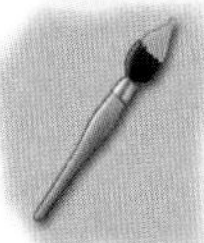

Paint in the bridge to cross the Thinner river and reach the maintenance area.

5

Follow the striped tent roof until you reach the half-finished wooden bridge. Paint the bridge in so you can walk across the Thinner river and enter the maintenance area.

6

Inside the maintenance area, three gears turn above a Thinner pool below. If you spray Thinner on the

gear, it will stop; spray Paint on that same gear, and it will rotate again.

Use your Thinner and Paint to stop the gears so that they form three flat platforms. Double-jump carefully from one platform to the next.

Walk to the edge of the last platform and double-jump across the final stretch to land on the machinery in the corner. Walk out on the machinery pipes and double-jump out through the building opening and onto the half-formed bridge.

Extra Content: Spatter Springs Up

Thinner has spread into the maintenance area, and several boats float in the goo beneath the gears you need to cross to reach the pump. Hovering above one of these boats is the Spatter Springs Up extra content. Instead of making the final jump to the outside ledge by the pump room, drop to the stone near the Thinner and hop safely over to the boat to get the extra content.

7

Traverse the bridge and enter the pump room through the hole in the wall to your right.

Fill the pump with either Paint or Thinner to start the Tea Cup Ride machinery running again.

If you fill a pump with Paint, machinery will run smoothly again. If you fill a pump with Thinner, expect the machinery to operate erratically.

Patch the two pipes near the pump to finally activate the Tea Cup Ride. You can drop near the pipes for a shortcut back out to the Tea Cup Ride and Gremlin Tim.

Bronze Pin

If you go the extra mile and fix the Tea Cup Ride for Gremlin Tim, he opens the secret treasure room that holds a Bronze Pin. Look for the open doors below the pump room and in front of the Tea Cup Ride.

To reward you for helping him, Gremlin Tim opens the treasure room below the pump room. Collect your pin and hop a ride on one of the jungle boats cruising down the Thinner river.

Jungle Boat Ride

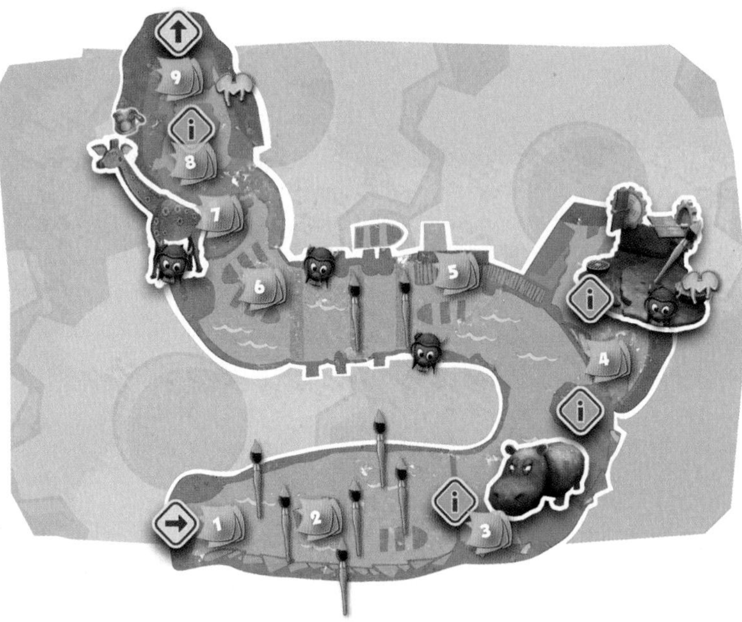

Level Overview

The long Jungle Boat Ride weaves you through a boat bottleneck, a battle with a Sweeper, ups and downs on moving cylinders, a heavily guarded set of bridges, whirlpools, multiple caged gremlins, and a race to release steam valves before time expires. There are certainly lots of challenges along the way, but more than a few rewards too.

The river bumps you along until you bounce into a room full of boats in a bottleneck before a jammed door. You can either paint the three hippos that spray Thinner in the room, or thin out three pipes on the side walls to open the door.

Things to Do

- Open the jammed river door
- Beat the Sweeper
- Free Gremlin Tringo
- Free Gremlin Habel
- Free Gremlin Hyperion
- Free Gremlin Pinza
- Defeat the four Sweepers
- Exit to the Asian Boat Ride

Four Gremlins

The Blotlings have caged four gremlins inside the Jungle Boat Ride. Release Gremlin Tringo in the room past the first Sweeper. Gremlins Habel and Hyperion are in the alcoves by the river bridges. Finally, Gremlin Pinza has been locked up underneath the giraffe statue near the end of the ride.

The boats make a path to the jammed door. Jump from boat to boat to get closer. Look to your left as you jump to the first boat. The first pipe springs up out of the Thinner near the yellow flower. Use Thinner to put a hole in the white section of piping.

CAUTION

Overturned boats will sink when you land on them. When you jump to an overturned boat, plan to jump off as soon as possible to avoid the encroaching Thinner.

Jump over to the boat adjacent to the first hippo. The broken hippo sprays Thinner in your path. Rather than risk damage, paint in the hippo.

Continue following the boat path. At the tip of the boat in front of the second hippo, spray blue Paint and reform two out of the three hippos you need to open the door.

Turn left and jump onto the nearby overturned boat. Run quickly along the boat's underside and leap off to the rocky shore before the Thinner touches you. Thin the pipe on the wall in front of you if you plan on opening the door with Thinner.

Jump back out onto the boats and paint the third hippo for the easiest

way to release the door. You can also jump across more boats to the far shore and thin out the third pipe if you like. Once you've interacted with the third hippo or third pipe, the door opens and boats begin pouring out.

Enemy: Sweeper

As the name implies, a Sweeper likes to sweep you off an edge and into Thinner any chance it can get. If you keep your distance, a Sweeper will throw buckets of Thinner at you, so be cautious that Sweeper Thinner doesn't strike you directly or remove Paint at your feet and drop you into something more dangerous. If you're quick on your feet, you can dodge Sweeper Thinner while gushing back Thinner of your own, or you can get in close and use a spin move to stun the Sweeper and push it over a ledge or into deadly Thinner.

Use the shore again as a stepping stone to reach the final set of boats near the open door. Hop from boat to boat to exit the area.

Jump on the last two boats before springing off onto the side by the frog and hippo statues.

There's an e-ticket to collect if you repaired the pipes. Hop up on the hippo platform and collect the white e-ticket inside the hippo's mouth for 10 extra e-tickets. Circle around the front of the hippo, careful not to fall in the Thinner, and drop on the lower platform beyond.

On the next yellow platform you face off against a new Blotling enemy, the Sweeper. You can turn a Sweeper into your ally with Paint, or you can either douse it with a lot of Thinner, or jump in close and use your spin move to knock it off the platform and into the

Thinner river. Just don't let the Sweeper hit you with too many buckets of Thinner; it's good at pegging you with Thinner if you don't move often.

With the Sweeper vanquished, you can thin out the wall next to the yellow platform and enter the cylinder area.

Bronze Pin

In the cylinder room, paint all gears and lower the tallest cylinder. Retrace your steps and avoid the Thinner pool to return to the first platform. Jump over to the lowered cylinder and retrieve the Bronze Pin from the chest.

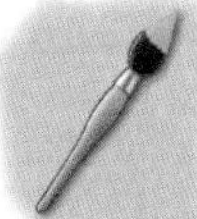

Paint in the gears in the room past the Sweeper to operate the cylinders.

Gremlin Tringo stands locked in a cage just inside the cylinder room. Spin move to shatter the cage and release him. He pledges to help you out later on (against the four Sweepers at the end of the level).

Paint in the bridge to cross the cylinder room.

Get the first gear working with some Paint, then double-jump over the Thinner pool and paint in the dormant gear on the room's far side.

Once all gears are in motion, the tall cylinder drops and new cylinders spring up on the wall near the entrance. You can pick up a Bronze Pin on the chest atop the tall cylinder.

Time your jump for when the first cylinder sinks to its lowest position. Clear the Thinner and stay to the left near the wall so that you don't overshoot into the whirlpool.

Wait for the first cylinder to rise and the second to lower. Jump to the second cylinder, then take a running leap off the cylinder and double-jump

to the upper platform. Smash open the chest for some power-ups.

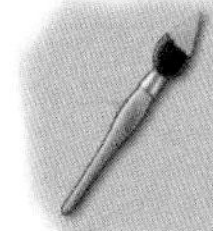

Disintegrate the river bridges to drop the Blotling guards into the Thinner below and avoid close combat.

Use Thinner on the orange wall and open a path back to the Thinner river. Follow the wooden ledge to the three bridges ahead.

Look left to see the second gremlin, Habel, in the alcove across the river.

To reach Habel, you first have to deal with the Spatter on the first bridge. When the Spatter patrols in the center of the bridge, coat the center with Thinner. The Spatter will drop into the Thinner below. Repaint the bridge so it's safe to walk on.

Double-jump over to the ledge in front of Habel. Spin move to smash the cage and release the gremlin. He'll aid you later against the four Sweepers near the end of the level.

Attack the second bridge enemy in the same fashion: Thin out the center, let the enemy drop, then repaint the center so it's not a liability to you.

Run along the bridge until you enter paintbrush range of Gremlin Hyperion's ledge. Paint the tip of the ledge so that it's safer to reach. Jump over to the first ledge, then to the second ledge in front of Gremlin Hyperion. Like his brethren, Hyperion vows to aid you at the first opportunity.

On the third bridge, either jump down onto one of the floating boats, or jump down to the shore and then hop over onto one of the boats.

Ride the boat as it bounces off the hippo head and circles the whirlpool. Don't panic. As the boat speeds up and it looks like you're going to be sucked down the whirlpool, you have a chance to jump off to your right and land safely on the stone ledge.

Turn around and double-jump back to the platform beneath the giraffe statue.

Free Gremlin Pinza from his cage and gain his assistance in the next area against the four Sweepers.

Extra Content: Pirate Gate

Atop the giraffe statue where Gremlin Pinza stands caged, the Pirate Gate extra content floats out of sight. Climb the yellow trees to get in range of a double-jump to the reach the giraffe head.

7

On the stone shelf next to the whirlpool, you can either bypass an optional Sweeper or battle it to pick up some extra power-ups on its ledge. After you deal with the Sweeper (or ignore it), jump down on the tall cylinder in the star area.

8

When you land on the cylinder, it sinks into the Thinner. Jump off before you touch the Thinner and land on the stones to either side.

Four Sweepers on retractable platforms guard the star room. Four corresponding valves around the room retract the platforms. Each gremlin that you saved releases one of the valves and retracts a platform, sending a Sweeper into the Thinner. If you saved all four gremlins, your friends will eliminate all of the Sweepers for you. If you left any gremlin behind, then you'll have to manually turn the valves yourself.

After you've removed the Sweeper threat, spray the yellow wall with Thinner. It reveals a hidden passage on the right wall. Creep up on the first

smasher and wait for it to retract. Run across the gap and stop between the smashers. Wait again and run across after the second smasher retracts.

Double-jump up on the elevator and ride it to the top. Jump off it at an angle and land on the corner of the retractable platform closest to the exit door. Don't forget to grab the Silver Pin the alcove at the end of the retractable platform.

Jump down to the stone platform in front of the exit door. Twist the valve to open the door and exit into the final chamber.

To escape the Jungle Boat Ride, you must turn three steam valves in 10 seconds. To start your timer, step on the jeweled disk on the floor.

Run to the left wall and use a spin move on the valve. Double-jump up to the first platform and spin the second valve. Double-jump again to the next platform and spin the third valve before the 10 seconds are up.

When you release all three steam valves, the door opens and Small Pete storms out to bark at you. He asks you to find his ship's log to prove he hasn't done the gremlins wrong. Keep this quest in the back of your mind because it'll play a big part in the World of Gremlins level.

Asian Boat Ride

Level Overview

You'll need your wits about you to puzzle through the Asian Boat Ride. Two of the three gremlins on the level call for help out in the open, but one is hidden, along with the flying carpets he can loan to you. You'll also have to survive a difficult fan blade challenge, and figure out what exactly is a "fire bridge."

There are two ways to get through this level. If you want more combat, take the left path through the Magic Carpet Ride. If you want more exploration, take the right path. We cover both so you can collect everything in this area.

You're safe on the platform you first enter in the Asian Boat Ride. In front of you lies a half-finished bridge. Paint the bridge to cross safely, or double-jump to the other side and over the Thinner pool.

Keep the bridge unfinished. Lure the Spatters back to the bridge and jump over to the entrance side. They might just follow you and drop through the hole to their demise.

Things to Do

- Free Gremlin Braun
- Find Gremlin Sam and the magic carpets
- Free Gremlin Herman
- Overcome the fan blade challenge
- Activate the fire bridge
- Unlock the exit door
- Search for power-ups on the level
- Exit to Steamboat Willie: Part 1

Two Spatters guard the pagoda courtyard. Take them out with your favorite combat maneuvers. With the surrounding Thinner pool, you can easily swat them over the edge if you don't feel like using up Paint or Thinner.

Use your spin move on the gear alongside the pagoda. Two blocks slide out of the base, giving you a platform to jump up the building.

Wind around the second story until you reach machinery on the back end and hop up those as steps.

Smash Gremlin Braun's cage at the top of the pagoda and release him. As a thank you, Braun activates the boats in the area, which you can use to better navigate from island to island.

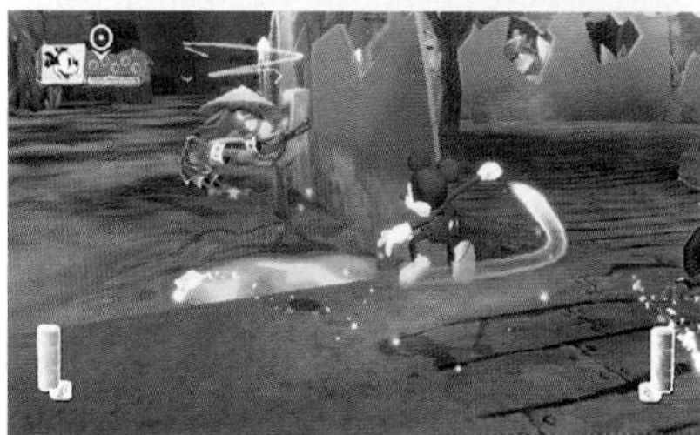

Jump on the circling boat between the pagoda and the Magic Carpet Ride and reach the second island in two leaps. As soon as you arrive, several more Spatters attack. Knock them off into the Thinner or let them have it with your paintbrush.

Three Gremlins

You have three gremlins to rescue in the Asian Boat Ride. Gremlin Braun pounds on his cage atop the pagoda. Gremlin Sam is hidden inside the central shaft of the Magic Carpet Ride; release him by spinning the gear on the side of the shaft and then smashing his cage. The last gremlin, Herman, is an easy one: He's atop the circular island with the rotating purple statues.

Look for the central shaft on the ride and spin the gear on the far side. A wooden panel drops to the floor and reveals Gremlin Sam inside. Free him by shattering the cage. Sam starts up the ride, which you can use if you can activate the magic carpets.

Jump up the gears to reach the second floor's broken wooden floor. A Sweeper guards the area. You're in tight quarters up here, so rather than take any chances, repeatedly swat the Sweeper with a spin move and knock it over the edge and into the Thinner pool.

Move out to the edge facing the pagoda. The magic carpets float translucent and inactive a few feet off the edge. Paint the magic carpets to activate them. They circle out to the exit platform and back to the Magic Carpet Ride. If you don't want to go for any of the pins on this level, you can use the magic carpets as a shortcut to reach the exit.

If you want to skip through the level quickly, jump on a magic carpet to bypass the other areas and directly access the exit platform.

Assuming you want to pick up the level's two pins, double back to the pagoda island and jump off onto one of the boats heading out to the circular island that holds Gremlin Herman. Jump onto the purple statue island and shatter each statue for an e-ticket as you head to the top to free Gremlin Herman.

If you accept Gremlin Herman's offer to turn off the whirlpool for 100 e-tickets, you won't get the Bronze Pin in the area.

When you release Herman, he offers to shut off the whirlpools for 100 e-tickets. It's a good bargain if you want to proceed quickly through the level; however, if you accept, you will miss out on the pin.

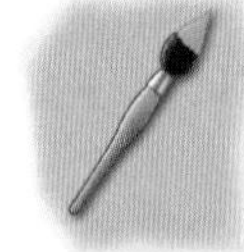

In the maintenance corridor, remove all the fan blades that you can before attempting to turn the valves.

If you want to get things working properly yourself, exit the circular island via the multicolored bridge that you can easily fill in with a little Paint. Cross to the wooden platform on the other side.

Run along the wooden platform and leap through the red wall to a second wooden platform in the corner. Turn left and jump up to a small platform jutting out of the wall. If you want some security, spray Paint on the platform to extend it.

Double-jump up to the next platform. Double-jump again to reach the roof of the maintenance corridor. The path straight across the roof is blocked by a wall (which raises and grants access to the Bronze Pin after you turn all the valves in the maintenance corridor). Instead, drop into the hole and land inside the maintenance corridor.

To deactivate the whirlpools, you must turn all four valves in the maintenance corridor. You only have 10 seconds to turn each valve, so deal with the spinning fan blades first.

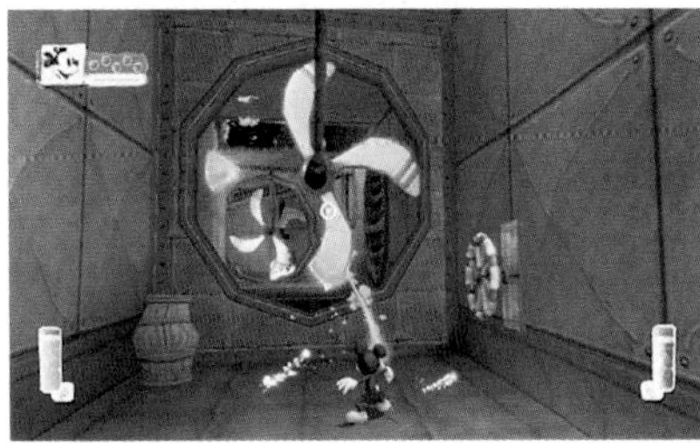

Thin out as many of the blades as you can. On the first fan, you can thin out all four blades; the second fan, three; the third fan, two; and only a single blade on the exit fan.

Once you've reduced the number of blades, return to the first room and use your spin move on the valve. Race to the next valve within 10 seconds, then the third, and fourth. With the blades reduced, it should be easy enough to trigger all four valves, but if you have trouble, restart at the first valve after the time expires and try again.

Bronze Pin

After you turn the valves in the maintenance corridor protected by spinning fans, circle back around to the start again and climb back up to the roof where you originally entered the maintenance corridor. The valves have removed the wall that had been blocking access to the other side of the roof. Instead of dropping into the corridor, jump over the opening and head across the roof to pick up the Bronze Pin at the far edge.

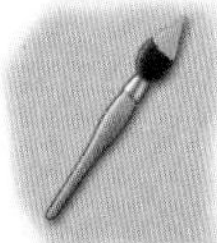

Activate the fire bridge by painting in all the gears on the nearby wall.

With the whirlpools gone, the boats travel around the Thinner pool. Jump on a boat and ride it to the next area with the giant gears. Paint in each of the gears on the wall, and a secret passage opens on the wall to your right.

Double-jump up into the secret passage area. Open the chest for the Gold Pin, and turn around to face back out at the gears. Take a running jump and land on the closest gear platform as it rotates flat, then jump again to land on the fire bridge activation pad a little higher up on the wall after the painted gear.

Gold Pin

To reach the platform that activates the fire bridge, you'll probably use the Gold Pin platform as a jumping point, so collecting this pin should be a piece of cake. Activating the fire bridge gears opens the door to the hidden Gold Pin, which you simply grab before leaping over to the fire bridge activation pad.

7

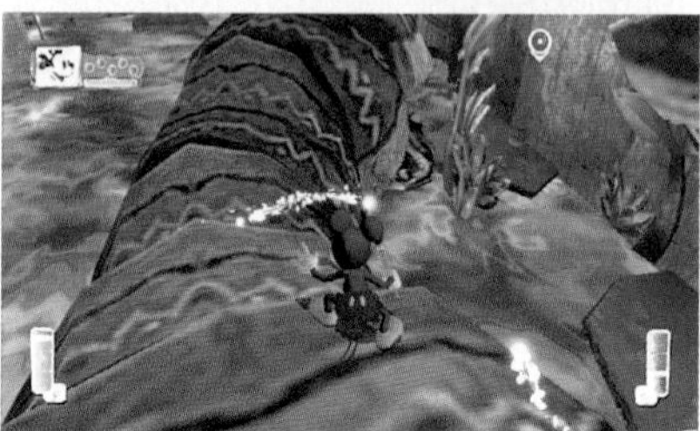

The "fire bridge" turns out to be a long red dragon that connects the gear platform with the exit platform. Hop up on the overturned boat and double-jump onto the back of the red dragon.

The dragon wiggles around and it's easy to fall off into the Thinner unless you stay to the middle and walk slowly. Patiently cross along its back until you can double-jump safely over to the exit platform.

Extra Content: World of Gremlins II

Look for the World of Gremlins II extra content behind the veil under the sun on the wall near the exit door. You can hop on a cloud to get in close enough to jump over to the blue platform in front of the veil. Thin a section of the veil and pick up another valuable piece of extra content.

8

Now you just have to open the exit door to reach the screen projector behind it. An orange canopy bobs up and down to your right. Double-jump off the exit platform and atop the orange canopy.

Ride the orange canopy up to its apex and then double-jump across to the floating cloud.

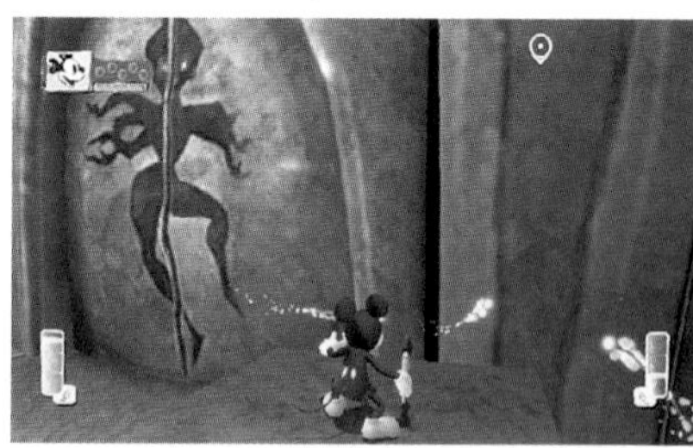

Turn toward the exit door. There's one stable platform directly above the door, and two activation platforms (dark gray) flanking the door. Leap off the cloud and land on the closest activation platform.

Repeat the process and land back up on the cloud. Jump over to the stable platform above the door and then hop onto the second activation platform. The exit door opens and you can enter another 2D adventure, Steamboat Willie: Part 1.

Steamboat Willie: Part 1

You appear on the bustling docks of a classic cartoon. Chickens spring from their crates, heavy cargo swings from cranes, and a steamboat's stacks erupt at the slightest touch.

Jump to grab the e-ticket to the right, and hop on the first chicken crate to spring high into the air.

Land on the stack of boxes, and continue to the right to collect another e-ticket from the floating barrels.

Jump onto the steamboat. There is a chicken crate on a group of boxes, and a cow hangs from the crane to the right.

Jump onto the boxes, and hop onto the chicken crate. Spring up to grab the e-ticket above you. Continue to bounce on the chicken crate until the cow is lowered toward the deck of the steamboat, then jump across to the right.

Land on the cow, and notice the two paths marked by e-tickets. You can ride the cow to the upper path to collect the film reel, or drop to the lower path to head straight to the exit projector.

To take the lower path, drop to the boxes on the cow's right side. Continue to the right to collect the e-tickets inside the steamboat.

Continue to the right, and drop to the steamboat's deck.

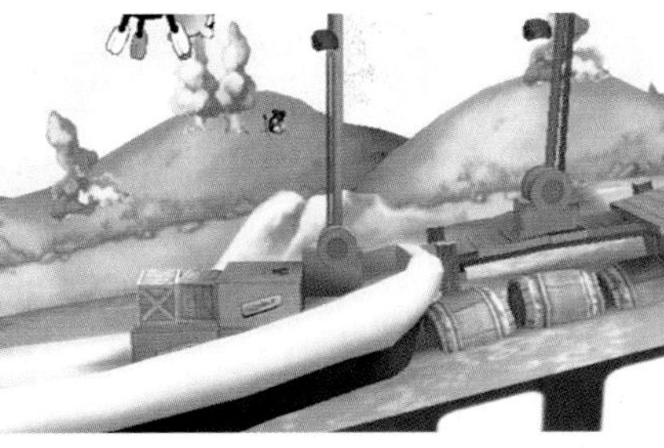

Jump onto the boxes near the end of the steamboat, and double-jump to grab the e-ticket above you. Grab the health power-up if you've taken any damage, and continue across the floating barrels.

Continue to the right to reach the exit projector. The film reel is on the tall platform just past the projector. You can complete the level right away, or you can head back to the steamboat to follow the upper path.

To take the upper path (before or after taking the lower path), jump onto the cow on the left side of the steamboat.

Ride to the top of the crane, and jump to the right before the cow drops back down. Grab the e-ticket and land near the whistles on the steamboat's cabin.

Drop down to grab the e-ticket in the steamboat's first stack, and spring into the air with a burst of steam.

Move to the second stack to spring up and double-jump from the top of the steam to collect the e-tickets above you. Wait for the cow on the right to swing within range, and hop across to it before it moves away.

Ride the cow over to the right, and jump up to collect any e-tickets above you. When the cow pauses, double-jump onto the box hanging from the next crane.

When you land, stand on the box to force it down toward the deck. As the first box lowers, the box on the other side of the crane is pulled higher into the air.

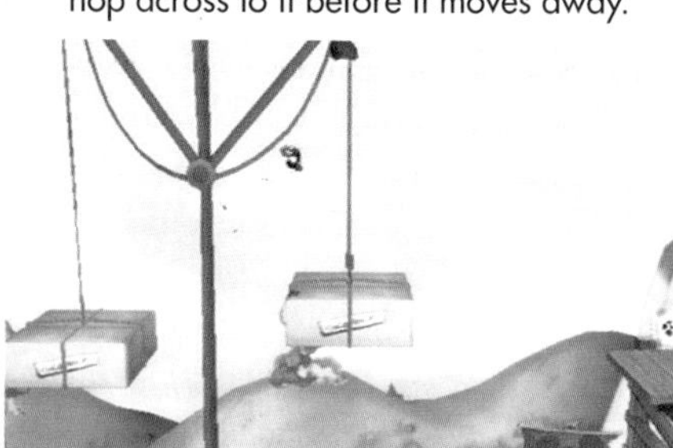

Jump over to the next box. When you land, double-jump straight into the air to grab the e-tickets above you.

Double-jump from the box's right side to collect the film reel above the exit projector.

After you collect the film reel, drop to the exit projector. If you followed the upper path from the start, you can continue to the left to grab the e-tickets along the lower path. When you're ready, activate the exit projector to complete the level.

World of Gremlins

See map on the following page

Level Overview

You've made it to Gus's home, except it's been attacked. Gus asks you to help repair the village, including the main steam pipes, the theme park rides, the windmill, the village tower, and even Gus's house, which has been doused in Thinner. The most important section of the village might be Small Pete's boat, which holds the ship log that can exonerate him.

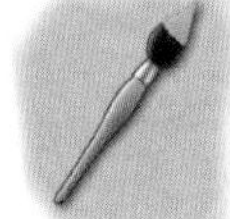

Paint all broken steam pipes to repair the first part of the gremlin village.

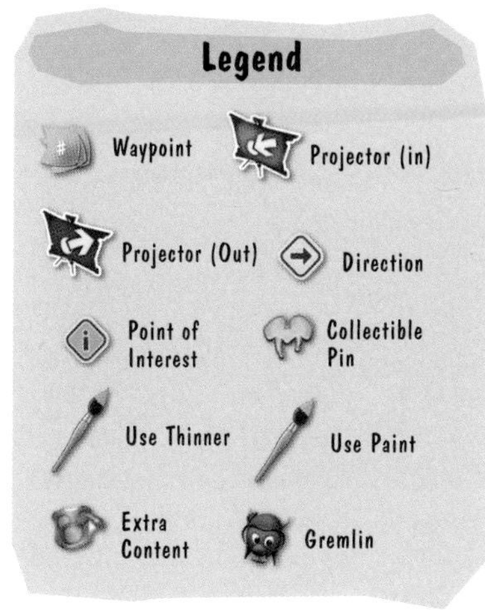

To start repairs, enter the circle of steam pipes near the entrance. Completing this area activates other areas around the village.

Run around the perimeter and paint four hissing steam pipes.

With the steam pipes filled in, head to the center and spin the valve. This finishes the repair, and activates the rides around the village. It also shuts off the Thinner washing out Gus's house.

Things to Do

- Repair the village steam pipes
- Paint Gus's House
- Retrieve Small Pete's ship log (or not)
- Free Gremlin Ditto inside the windmill
- Search for power-ups on the level
- Exit to Clock Cleaners: Part 1

Extra Content: World of Gremlins I

After you restore the village pipe system, the smashers in the side alcove next to the entrance spring to life. Jump down into the hole to the right of the entrance and watch the pattern for a few seconds. Get as close as you can to the first smasher, and run as soon as it rises. Either stop in front of the second smasher (if you can judge your space correctly between the two), or time it so you can dash down the corridor while both smashers are raised. Collect the extra content and exit carefully in the same fashion.

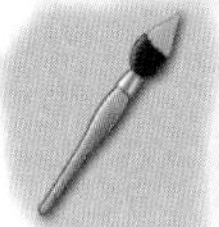

Return Gus's house to him by painting the building after you've shut off the Thinner spray drenching it.

Jump up to Gus's house and paint it like brand new. You can also enter the house and discover a Bronze Pin as a reward.

Bronze Pin

After you save Gremlin Gus's house, you can enter it. Once inside, open the red chest for another Bronze Pin as a reward for helping out your friend.

If you plan on retrieving Small Pete's ship log, jump across the giant gears and hilly terrain to get near the Airplane Ride.

Jump on one of the airplanes and adjust your position to stay on it as the ride spins in a fast circle. When you spin close to Small Pete's ship, double-jump off the airplane and land on the ship's deck.

Junction Point: Small Pete

At the end of the Jungle Boat Ride, Small Pete asks you to find his ship log and prove his innocence to the gremlins. Small Pete's ship smashed into the gremlin village by accident (see map location 4), and you can choose to either retrieve the log and show it to Gremlin Bennet to befriend Small Pete or leave him as an outcast and annoy him. If you retrieve the ship log and prove Small Pete's innocence, he will not attack you in the European Boat Ride Colosseum and will instead reward you with a pin and extra content (plus you gain another pin in Mean Street later). If you choose to skip the ship log quest, Small Pete will attack you in the Colosseum and won't open the treasure room. As with many important characters, Small Pete will have a bigger role in the ending if you complete his quest.

Walk to the back of the ship and spin the wheel. This opens the locked door at the front of the ship.

Use Thinner on the compartment at the back of the ship to recover a hidden chest.

Open the red chest at the front of the ship to recover Small Pete's ship log. To complete the quest, you must give the log to Gremlin Bennet back in the village center.

Gremlin Pin

You could also give the ship log to Gremlin Shaky, who is near the Clock Tower. Trade the log for the Gremlin Pin if you like, but Pete will not be happy if you do.

CAUTION

If you lose all your health at any point during the level and restart, check your quest log to see where you last auto-saved. You don't want to miss anything crucial. For example, if you restart after turning in the ship log to Gremlin Bennet but before you exit the World of Gremlins, you might have to give the ship log to Gremlin Bennet again.

5

Return to the village center and see Gremlin Bennet. Turn Small Pete's ship log into him, and Bennet makes sure that all the gremlins know that it wasn't Small Pete's fault that his ship crashed into their village. You've befriended Small Pete, which affects later game events in your favor.

6

Next, seek out the windmill. Jump up to the central area above the Thinner pool and time a leap safely onto one of the magic carpets.

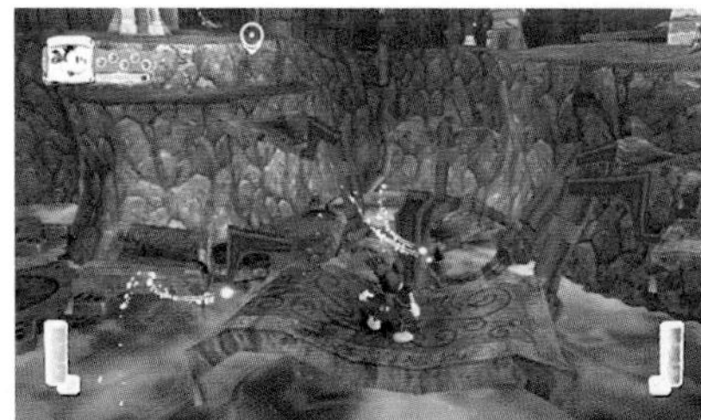

Follow the Magic Carpet Ride around until you can safely jump off on the grass beneath the village tower. Anytime you want to reach the far side of the gremlin village, it's easiest to take the Magic Carpet Ride and jump off at the village tower.

7

Head left and stick to the village perimeter to reach the windmill. First, double-jump up on the multicolored house, then double-jump across to the first wooden platform against the exit wall.

Take a running start and double-jump to the next platform overlooking the exit landing. Jump down to the exit landing and then back up on the second multicolored house.

Double-jump up to the platform above the multicolored house, then drop to the next platform beneath it. Back up against the wall and get as much of a running start as you can. Leap off the platform and double-jump to reach the windmill landing on the far side.

8

Look for the broken wall in front of the windmill. Hop on the section closest to the exit landing and wait for the windmill's outer platform to rotate near you. It doesn't matter which one you jump on; just don't leap out too far and fall off the windmill landing entirely.

Ride the windmill platform high overhead. You can jump off the platform to land on the right side or the left side of the windmill. The right side holds the entrance to Gremlin Ditto's prison and the secret screen projector (see the "Gremlin Ditto" sidebar for details). The left side holds a yellow e-ticket worth 100 e-tickets, so it's well worth timing a successful double-jump to reach that platform.

Gremlin Ditto

A Spatter has trapped Gremlin Ditto in the windmill. After restoring the village pipes and painting Gus's house, head off to the windmill in search of Ditto. Ride the windmill platform to the top and jump off to the small platform on the right side. Eliminate the Spatter guard and smash Gremlin Ditto out of his cage. He rewards you by activating a secret screen projector that takes you midway through the European Boat Ride. You must pass through Clock Cleaners: Part 2 to enter the European Boat Ride.

When you're ready to enter the village tower, return to the tower landing either by retracing your steps to the windmill or starting all over at the Magic Carpet Ride. Entering the screen projector at the tower base sends you into the Clock Cleaners: Part 1 2D level and then out atop the village tower.

Clock Cleaners: Part 1

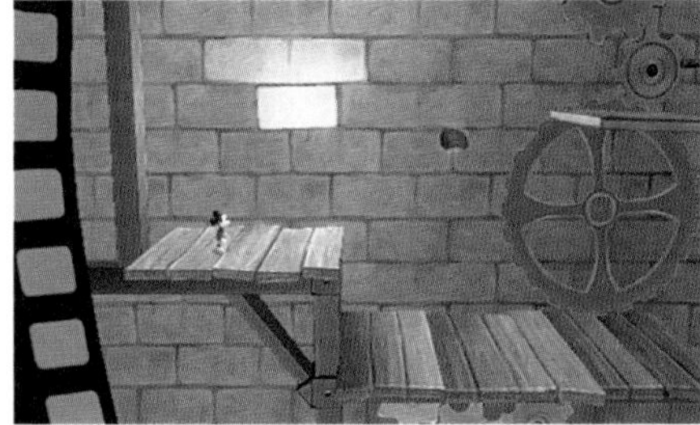

You arrive among the inner workings of a giant clock. Spinning gears, swinging pendulums, and flipping platforms all move in time with the clock.

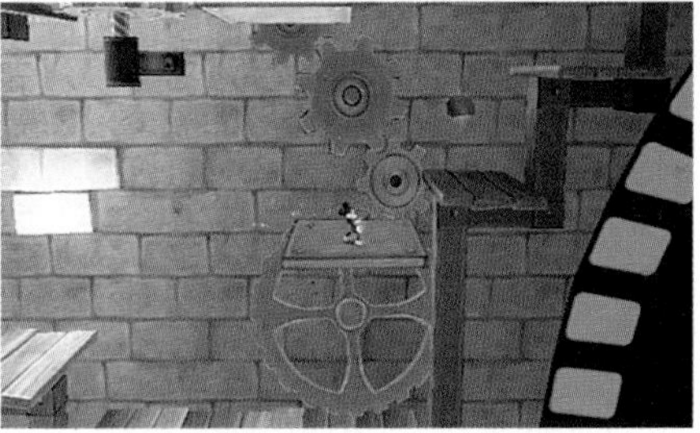

Wait for the metal platform to move into range as the large gear rotates. Jump up to grab the e-ticket, then land on the platform. Wait for the gear to bring the metal platform back up, and ride up to the wooden platforms to the right.

Jump onto the first wooden platform and collect the e-ticket. When you land, double-jump up to the next wooden platform, and face back to the left.

The metal platform to the left flips over at regular intervals, so time your jump to avoid a fall. When the platform begins to flip over, jump across to grab the e-ticket and land on the metal platform as it pauses between flips.

When the gear to the left spins down to the bottom of the dowel screw, jump across and land on the gear. If the metal platform begins another flip before the gear is in place, double-jump across to the wooden platform and grab the e-ticket to the left.

When you're ready, ride the gear to the top of the dowel screw. To the right, you can see a metal platform attached to a series of gears. Wait for the platform to flip over, and hop onto it before the gear spins back down the dowel screw.

Notice the film reel on the wooden platform below the nesting bird. The film reel is blocked by a metal door and a second metal door blocks the path in front of you.

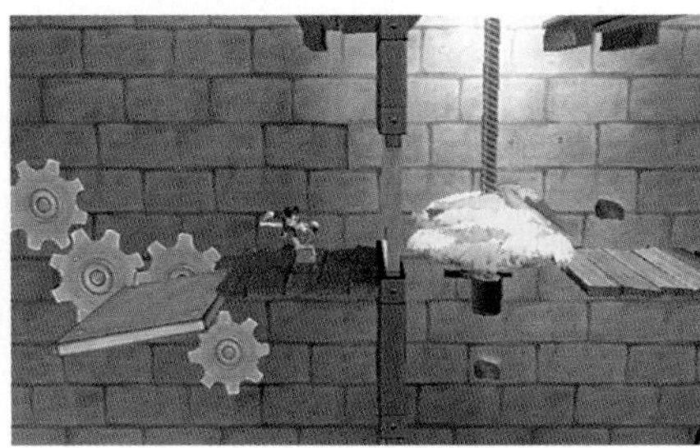

Jump over to the lever before the metal platform begins another flip. Use your spin move on the lever to activate the gear under the nesting bird.

The gear springs to the top of the dowel screw, launching the bird right out of the clock in the process. Wait for both metal doors to retract into the wooden barrier.

Drop to collect the film reel before the gear spins back down the dowel screw, or hop down to the wooden platforms below the lever.

Be careful around the metal platform to the left of the film reel; make sure you're not standing on it when it flips down. Collect the film reel, and grab the two e-tickets nearby.

Move across the metal platform to the left, and jump onto the gear spinning around the dowel screw.

Ride back up to the top of the dowel screw. Wait for the metal platform to flip over, then jump across to return to the lever.

When the gear reaches the bottom of the next dowel screw, jump onto it. Grab the e-ticket to the right, and wait for the gear to spin up to the platforms above you.

Collect the e-tickets from the wooden platforms, and jump across to the door on the left.

An automaton is moving along the track that runs through the two doors. Wait for the automaton to move out of the way, or double-jump over it as it slides along the track.

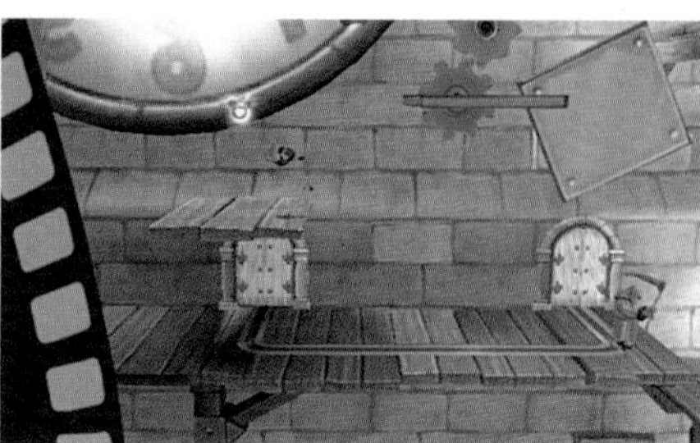

Jump onto the platform above the door to the left. Grab the health power-up if you're running a little low, and face the metal platforms to the right.

Wait for the first platform to flip over, then jump across and grab the e-ticket. Run across the second metal platform before it flips down, or jump across the gap to reach the wooden platforms to the right.

When the metal platform rotates to the bottom of the large gear, double-jump onto it and grab the e-ticket above you.

Ride up along the gear, and jump over to the metal platform attached to the pendulum. Begin your jump as the pendulum approaches to make sure you land before the pendulum swings away.

Ride on the platform as the pendulum swings back to the left. Jump up to collect the e-tickets above you, or drop to grab the e-ticket below the exit projector.

Once you've collected the film reel and any desired e-tickets, return to the swinging pendulum. Ride across the pendulum as it swings to the left. Jump over to the exit projector to continue to the top of the village tower.

World of Gremlins (Village Tower)

To fix the village tower, walk around the ledge to the front of the clock face. Fill the pump with Paint (or Thinner, if you want some crazy results) and you've accomplished your task.

If you continue along the ledge, it looks like a dead-end, but it's not. A platform on the side takes you directly down to the ground.

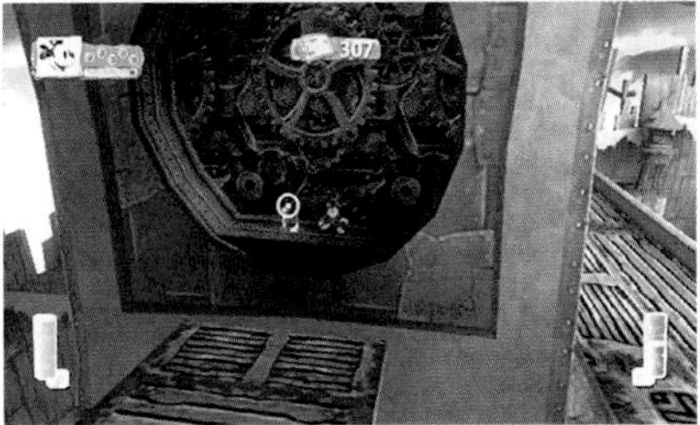

When you jump on the exit platform, immediately jump again to the small ledge with the yellow e-ticket. The platform drops quickly; if you don't get off immediately, you'll miss your chance at the yellow e-ticket—it's not possible to come back for this one later.

From the tower's platform, you can take the same path that you took to the windmill to reach the now opened exit door (see map location 7). When you reach the exit landing halfway toward the windmill, enter the alcove and use the screen projector to access your next 2D level, Steamboat Willie: Part 2.

NOTE

Steamboat Willie: Part 2 can be accessed through the normal exit projector in the World of Gremlins. If you freed Gremlin Ditto in the windmill, he activates the secret screen projector. This projector takes you into Clock Cleaners: Part 2, and then to the projector midway through the European Boat Ride level.

Steamboat Willie: Part 2

Return to the steamboat to find yourself in a new port. Crates and cranes are still the business of the day, but a helpful goat is hanging around the docks.

Before you move onto the docks, head left and grab the e-tickets inside the steamboat.

Return to the deck, and jump onto the pile of boxes near the edge of the steamboat. Hop onto the chicken crate to spring into the air. Grab the e-ticket to the left, then use the chicken crate to launch yourself onto the boxes.

Jump across to the box hanging on the crane's left side. You can jump to the next box to take the upper path, or drop to the dock to take the lower path. The upper and lower paths both lead to the goat standing on the docks, and both paths offer e-tickets.

To take the lower path, drop to the dock and continue to the right. Collect the e-ticket near the base of the crane, and jump across the floating barrels to collect a few more.

Continue to the next group of floating barrels. Jump up to grab the health power-up if you need to recover from any damage.

Grab the e-tickets above the floating barrels, and jump up to the chicken crate ahead of you.

Hop onto the chicken crate to spring up to the goat.

To take the upper path, jump across to the pile of boxes just past the crane.

Double-jump to the top of the boxes, and drop on the chicken crate to spring into the air. Grab the e-ticket above you, and bounce onto the cow as it swings into range.

Ride the cow over to the right, and double-jump to grab the e-tickets. When you land, you've reached the goat standing on the docks.

Approach the goat, and jump onto its back. When you land, the goat bleats out a few musical notes.

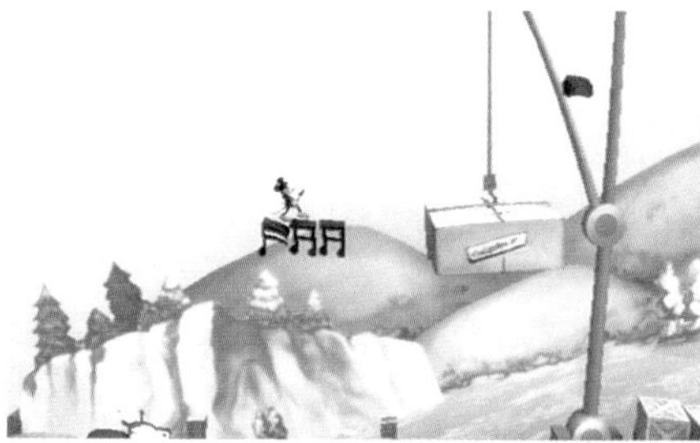

Hop onto the musical notes, and ride up to the box hanging from the next crane. The notes disappear quickly, so jump across to the box when you're within range.

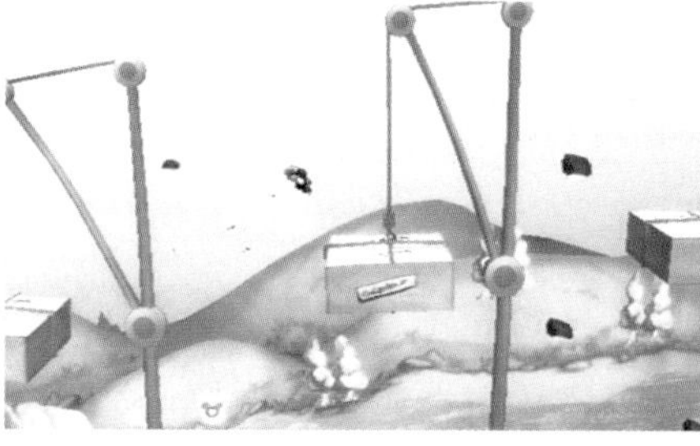

Move to the box's right edge, and watch for movement from the next crane. When the next box starts to swing toward you, double-jump to the right. Grab the e-tickets ahead of you, and land on the box as it comes to a stop.

Ride on the box as it swings back to the right. The film reel is just above the next box.

When the swinging box stops, jump across to the next crane and grab the film reel.

Drop from the box's right side to reach the exit projector, or drop from the left side to collect a few more e-tickets. If you need it, grab the health power-up across the floating barrels.

When you're satisfied with your haul of e-tickets, activate the exit projector at the end of the docks to complete the level.

Clock Cleaners: Part 2

You return to the spinning gears of the giant clock. This time, however, there are several holes along the wooden platforms; take extra care to avoid costly falls.

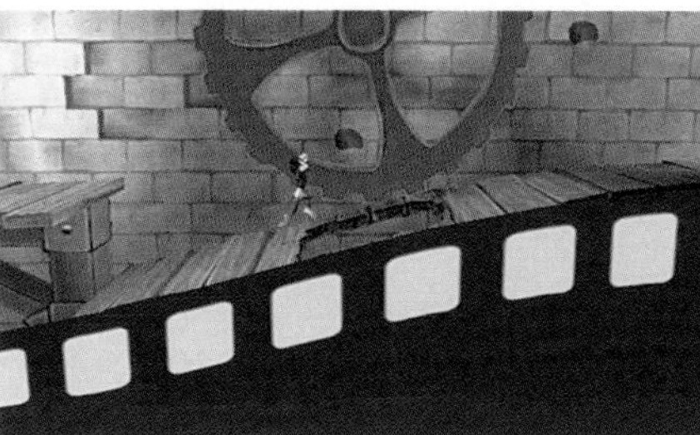

At the start of the level, you can take the upper path directly to the film reel, or the lower path to collect some extra e-tickets.

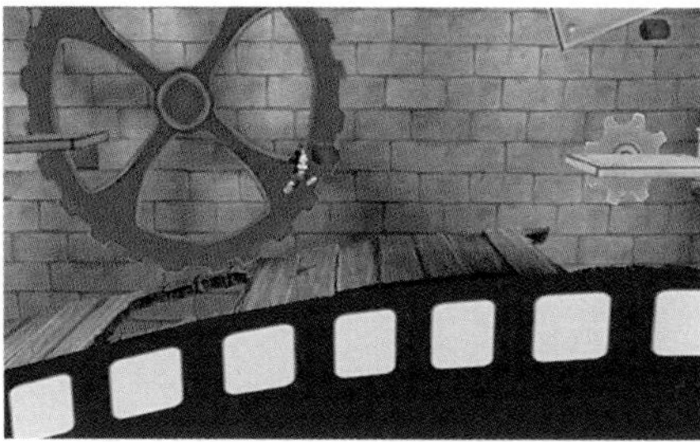

To get the most out of your time in the clock, drop to the wooden platform to the right. Jump over the hole below the large gear, and collect the e-tickets on the way to the metal platform.

Hop onto the metal platform just after it flips over, then hop across to the doors on the right. Double-jump to avoid the automaton running along the track.

Collect the two e-tickets between the doors and continue to the right. Grab the health power-up if you've taken any damage.

Drop to the wooden platforms past the second door. Run under the large platform sliding across the gears above you. Jump over the hole to the right to grab two more e-tickets, then jump back up to the two doors on the left.

Continue to the left, and avoid the automaton as it slides along the track. Wait for the metal platform to flip over, and jump across to head back to the start of the level.

After you return to your starting point, wait for the large gear to rotate the metal platform into range. Double-jump to land on the metal platform, and ride up to the wooden platform near the top of the gear.

Jump up to grab the e-ticket above the gear, and hop across to the wooden platform. Wait for the metal platform to flip into place, and continue to the right. Double-jump to grab the e-ticket above you, and move to the next wooden platform.

Three metal platforms are attached to the gear above the two doors. The platform at the center of the gear flips over at regular intervals.

Jump onto the first platform, and use your weight to rotate the large gear. As the first platform drops, the third platform moves upward.

Wait for the platform at the center of the gear to flip over, and jump across to collect the e-tickets near the top of the gear. Without your weight, the platforms slowly return to their starting positions. Grab the health power-up near the top of the gear, if needed.

Move quickly to reach the third platform before it drops too low. Double-jump to reach the wooden platform next to the gear. When you land, jump up to grab the e-ticket above you.

Wait for the metal platform to flip into place, or double-jump across the gap to collect the film reel to the right.

Stand on the metal platform and wait for it to flip back down. Drop to grab the e-ticket, and land on the sliding platform as it pauses below you.

If you fall from the sliding platform, simply jump up to the platforms on the left, and double-jump onto the sliding platform when it comes within range.

Ride the sliding platform as it moves to the right. Jump up to grab another e-ticket, and hop across to the wooden platforms.

Grab the health power-up above the wooden platform if you need to recover from any damage. When the gear reaches the bottom of the dowel screw, jump on and wait for it to head back up.

Jump onto the metal platform near the top of the dowel screw. Continue to the left before the metal platform flips over and drops you back to the platforms below.

Jump up along the wooden platforms to grab the e-ticket at the top.

Double-jump across the gap to reach the door to the right. When you land, continue to the bell at the end of the platform.

Double-jump to reach the exit projector above the bell. If you wait for the automaton to ring the bell, you can collect two more e-tickets. When you're ready, activate the exit projector to complete the level and take your shortcut into the European Boat Ride.

European Boat Ride

Level Overview

Whether you helped Small Pete with his ship log or not has a major impact on how this level plays out. You still have to cross the various obstacles in the European Boat Ride. However, if you supported Pete, you won't have to fight in the Colosseum. If you skipped Small Pete's quest, you'll have several rounds of enemies to battle in the Colosseum arena.

You start in a long tunnel leading to the Leaning Tower island. Blotlings attack once you exit the tunnel, so prepare yourself before stepping out into the light.

Things to Do

- Defeat the Blotlings in front of the Leaning Tower
- Turn the valve on the Leaning Tower
- Use the cloud path to reach the Colosseum (optional)
- Use the Parisian Tower to reach the Colosseum (optional)
- Search for power-ups on the level
- Speak with Small Pete in the Colosseum
- Battle the Colosseum enemies (if you didn't befriend Small Pete)
- Exit to Steamboat Willie: Part 3

The Blotlings converge on you. Dodge the rolling Seers and charging Spatters as you angle toward the small pillars.

Jump up on the shortest of the pillars and attack the Blotlings from your secure location. The enemies can't reach you up here, so it's only a matter of time before your paintbrush does them in.

Wait until you've disabled all enemies before continuing. It's easy to fall off the pillars, and you don't want to land in the midst of angry enemies.

Jump across the line of pillars, and then double-jump up to the Leaning Tower's first tier. Spin the valve to stop the whirlpool and activate the boats.

Drop off the Leaning Tower and hop on one of the crossing boats. Double-jump off the boat and land at the corner of the Parisian Tower area, where you can hide from the nearby Blotlings while you get your bearings.

Use your spin move to whack the Blotlings off the landing and into the Thinner pool. Thin out the orange spots on the landing to open the platform up to the Thinner beneath, and you can easily drop enemies into the dissolving goop.

Two paths lead to the Colosseum at the end of the level: the cloud path and the Parisian Tower path. The Parisian Tower is shorter, but the cloud path offers more rewards. Start out on the cloud path by stopping the giant gears on the back wall.

Once you have the gear platforms level enough to traverse, climb across them to the first cloud.

Ride the first cloud to the upper tier of the Parisian Tower. When the second clouds softly bumps into the first cloud, hop over to the second cloud.

Ride the second cloud until it hovers near the third cloud. Double-jump across to the third cloud. The third cloud passes close enough to the far side to make the leap across; just be careful you don't bounce off the cut-out tulips that line the ledge. You can also jump over to the fourth cloud and then make an easier jump to the far side.

You land near a screen projector. This projector connects with the windmill in the World of Gremlins and can be a shortcut for you if you freed Gremlin Ditto.

Watch out for a Sweeper that patrols the area. You can try to swat it back several times to launch it off the edge near the Silver Pin chest, but it's a long distance. It's more efficient to drown the Sweeper in Thinner.

To reach the upper entrance to the Colosseum, use your Paint and Thinner to flatten out the big gears on the back wall. When you have the first gear where you want it, jump off the platform near the screen projector and begin your long journey across the gears.

Slowly work on each gear until you have it flat and can jump safely to it.

Silver Pin

If you take the long road to the Colosseum, this pin is along your path after you beat the Sweeper near the secret projector screen from the World of Gremlins. Pick up the Silver Pin before you cross the gears to the Colosseum's upper entrance.

If you fall off the first few, you'll land on the platform below; after that, you drop into the Thinner pool and it's a difficult path back.

The last gear is on a slant. You can either try to straighten it out, or you can jump onto it and then immediately double-jump to the Colosseum before you stumble off it and into the Thinner.

7

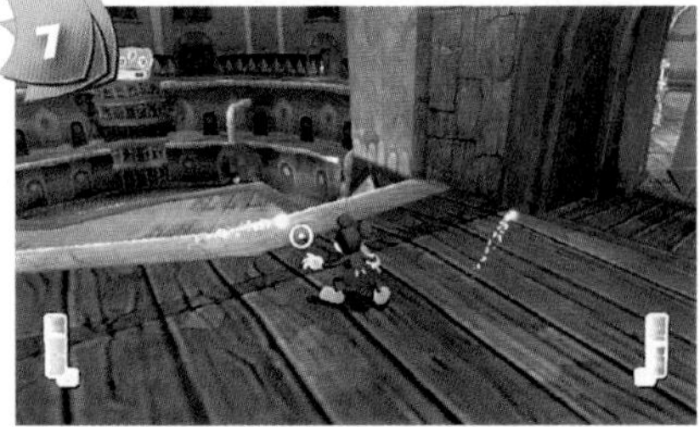

Jump up to the next tier and you're in the Colosseum. Step forward to speak with Small Pete. If you helped him out with his missing ship log, he'll open the exit and the treasure room off to your right.

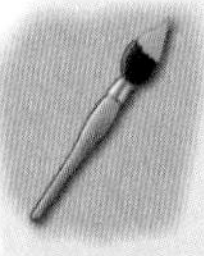

To drop the Parisian Tower, thin out its upper support structure at the corner facing the Colosseum. Jump down the fallen tower as a shortcut to the Colosseum.

8

To access the Colosseum's lower entrance (and get there quicker), jump on the first cloud as if you're taking the longer cloud path, but double-jump off onto the Parisian Tower's upper tier. Walk over to the corner and look for cartoon support on the opposite corner.

Thin out that cartoon support and the whole tower topples over. Run down the tower to reach the Colosseum's lower entrance.

9

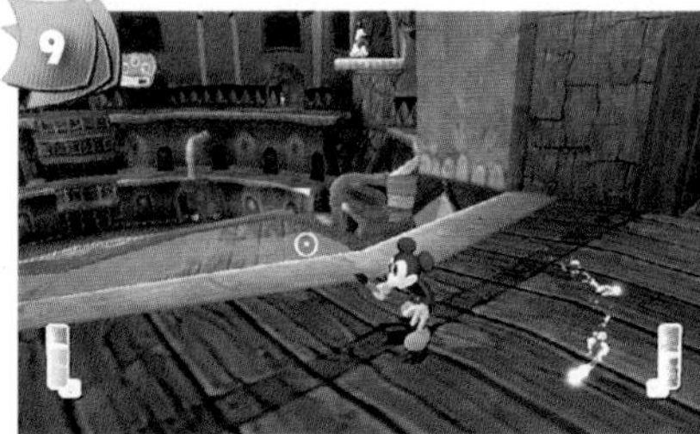

Depending on what you did with Small Pete's ship log quest, you either have an easy or difficult time in the Colosseum arena.

If you completed the ship log quest, Small Pete opens the exit door for you without a fight.

Small Pete also rewards you by opening the treasure room near the upper entrance. Visit the treasure room for lots of e-tickets, a Bronze Pin, and the Inky Mickey extra content.

Bronze Pin and Inky Mickey Extra Content

The treasure room in the Colosseum holds both of these items. If you completed Small Pete's ship log quest, he opens the treasure room by the upper entrance so you can retrieve the items. If you skipped Small Pete's ship log quest, he won't open it for you.

If you didn't complete Small Pete's ship log quest, he sends wave after wave of Blotlings after you to teach you a lesson.

The Blotlings drop out of pipes all around you. The arena floor is actually thinnable, so dissolve it as enemies converge and you can liquefy a bunch of them in one nasty maneuver.

Continue battling the Blotlings as you race around the Colosseum perimeter. You don't have a lot of time to stand still, so it's probably best to spin move enemies away from you and try to angle them into the central Thinner pool that you've uncovered.

Once you eliminate all the Blotling enemies, you can finally escape the arena. If your health drops low, seek out the resources in the side alcoves around the perimeter.

Whether you defeat all the enemies and cause Small Pete to retreat, or you get the free pass from a friendly Small Pete, proceed to the exit portal and take the screen projector to Steamboat Willie: Part 3.

Steamboat Willie: Part 3

You arrive at yet another port, with still more cranes and cargo. This time you get a peek inside the steamboat, so watch out for the stray coals tumbling from the steamboat's furnace.

Hop onto the chicken crate and spring into the air. Grab the e-ticket above you, and double-jump to land on the box to the right.

Ride the box to the top of the crane, and jump across to the wooden platform.

Collect the e-tickets above the platform, and continue to the right. Drop down and collect the e-ticket under the platform, then jump up to the crane on the right.

Wait for the cow to approach, and jump onto the chicken crate to spring into the air.

To collect the film reel, land on the cow to take the upper path. Ride across to the right, and double-jump to reach the box ahead of you.

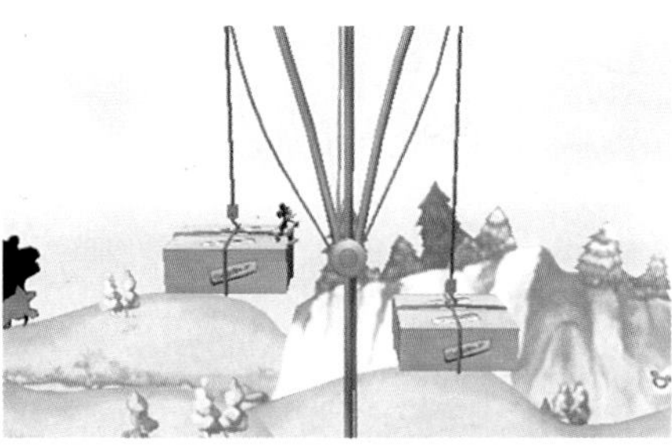
Stand on the first box, and use your weight to pull the second box up a bit.

When you land, move quickly and double-jump to the right. Collect the film reel next to the steamboat's stacks.

From this area, you can see the projector to the right, but the steamboat's stacks are too tall to jump over.

Move to the platform's left edge, and drop to the boxes below. Jump up to grab the health power-up if you've suffered damage from any falls.

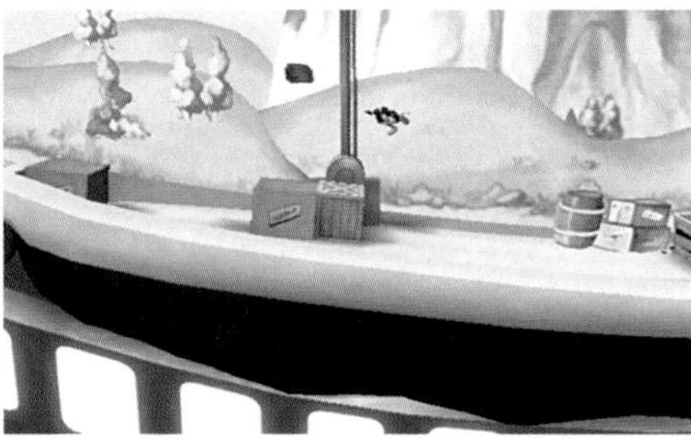
To collect some extra e-tickets, move back to the left. Jump over the boxes to collect the e-ticket near the crane.

Continue to the left, and jump onto the floating barrels to grab another e-ticket.

Hop back onto the steamboat, and follow the deck to the right. Jump onto the chicken crate to spring into the air, and land on the boxes to the right.

To grab the e-ticket near the top of the room, stand on the coal pile and double-jump onto the wooden platform.

Drop to the floor, and approach the stairs. Whenever the screen shakes, a piece of coal is thrown from the furnace. Wait for the coal to tumble down the stairs, and position yourself so that it bounces right over you.

When you get near the top of the stairs, take a moment to wait for another piece of coal to pop out of the furnace. Dodge the coal as it bounces down the stairs, and jump onto the furnace when the coast is clear.

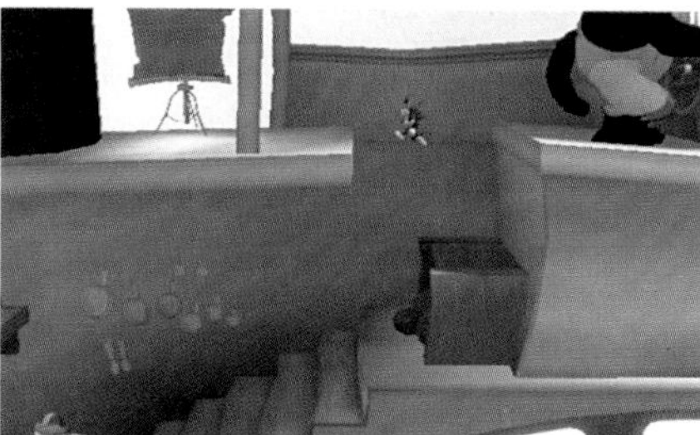

When you land, face to the left, and double-jump up to the platform.

Move to the steamboat's stacks, and activate the exit projector to complete the level and head to your boss encounter against the Clock Tower.

The Clock Tower

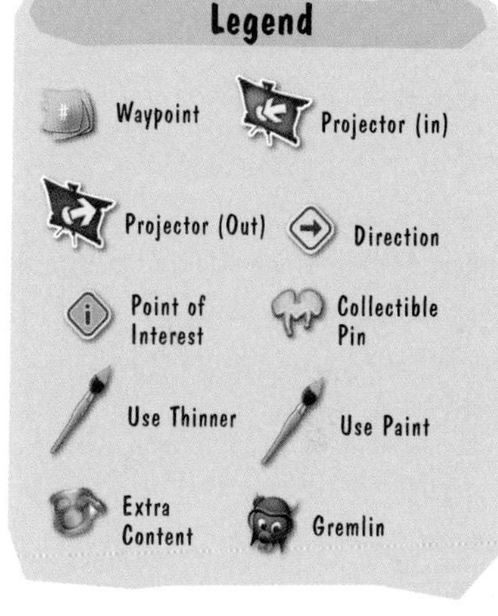

Level Overview

The Clock Tower boss stands in your way at the end of the Gremlin Village world. Its mechanical fists are imposing, and when those same fists smash the street under your feet, you feel the shockwaves. If you're quick on your toes and quick with your paintbrush, you can defeat the final foe before you move on to Mean Street.

You begin the fight in the center of the street, between the Clock Tower's menacing, mechanical fists. Don't stand there for too long.

But don't run under one of the fists as it slams down, either. Watch the position of the fists and don't run underneath one unless you're sure it's not ready to strike.

If you're running low on health, use your spin move on any of the statues on the near edge of the street and grab a health power-up. Snatch the Paint/Thinner power-ups when they appear on the street too.

Things to Do

- Defeat the Clock Tower's left arm
- Defeat the Clock Tower's right arm
- Cross safely across the Thinner pool
- Increase your Paint or Thinner capacity
- Exit to Mean Street

Junction Point: The Clock Tower

Whether you battle the Clock Tower with Paint or Thinner affects your reward after the battle. If you wield Thinner against the Clock Tower, when you defeat the machine you'll gain one permanent extra Thinner slot; wield Paint, and you gain a permanent Paint slot. Your decision also affects the game's ending.

Fight each arm by itself so you don't get caught dodging two different massive attacks. Head to the left first and focus on the right arm. Always dodge the fist first, and only use Paint/Thinner on the fist when you're to the side and not directly under it. If you're using Paint, keep it up until the arm turns completely blue and stops working.

Pour on the Paint/Thinner until you weaken the fist enough that it shatters on the street when it next attacks.

With the fist out of the picture, concentrate on the forearm section. Continue your pattern of dodging first to avoid damage, then spray the forearm to weaken it.

Stay near the left wall and hit the Clock Tower's right forearm with enough Paint/Thinner to finish it off.

Now you only have to worry about attacks from one direction. Switch over to the right side and douse the left fist with Paint/Thinner.

With more room to maneuver now, it should be easier to dodge the Clock Tower attacks and hit the left fist with your attacks. Wait for the fist to break apart, then concentrate on the forearm.

You might go through all your health power-ups, but eventually the Clock Tower's right arm will weaken and it'll concede.

In defeat, the Clock Tower drops down into the Thinner and forms a path to reach the exit projector.

Your choice of using Paint or Thinner is an important one. If you chose Paint, your Paint capacity increases by one at the end of the fight. If you chose Thinner, your Thinner capacity increases by one.

To escape the arena, you must cross the Thinner pool and reach the exit projector at the base of the defeated Clock Tower.

Double-jump off the street and onto the right arm. Run carefully along the metal shaft and double-jump again onto the second arm section.

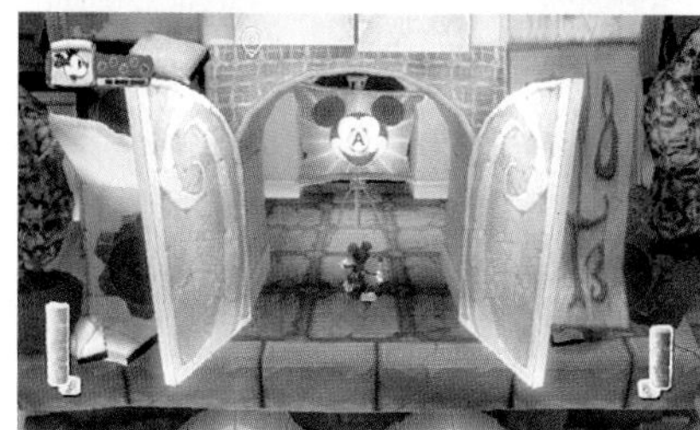

Finally, double-jump onto the Clock Tower face and up into the tower base. The exit projector takes you to Mean Street, the next major destination on your adventure to find Oswald and answers.

Stop the Music Pin

If you defeat the Clock Tower solely with Paint, you gain the Stop the Music Pin as a reward. Defeat the Clock Tower with Thinner, and you earn the Unwind the Clock Pin. To get both of these pins, you'll have to play through the game twice, alternating your paintbrush mixtures to take down the Clock Tower.

MEAN STREET AND OSTOWN

Mean Street

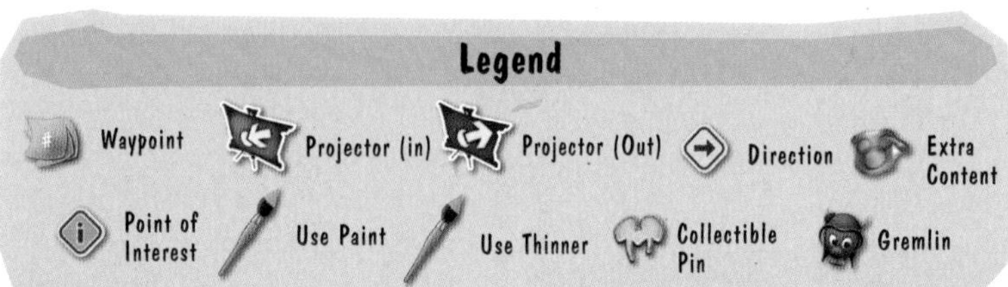

Things to Do

- Speak with Big Bad Pete
- Finish Gilda's race and get the first gear
- Retrieve Horace's book and get the second gear
- Deliver the gears to Gremlin Markus
- Gain a power spark
- Deliver the power spark to Gremlin Markus so he can fix the projector to OsTown
- Search the area for power-ups
- Complete any optional quests
- Exit to OsTown

Level Overview

You enter a bustling community with toons going about their daily business, and you notice new variations of the same characters (sketches left on the drawing table or new identities from different cartoons). Speak to everyone you can, and visit all the points of interest, including the City Hall, Museum, Cinema, Emporium, Ice Cream Shop, and Detective Agency.

When you first arrive, Gremlin Markus greets you at the projector. He gives you the lowdown on Mean Street and explains that the projectors have broken. He can fix them up, but you'll have to track down two gears and a power spark before he can work his magic.

Mean Street Quests (Visit 1)

- Collect Film Reels

The Usher rewards you for collecting film reels from the cartoons around Wasteland.

- Find Casey's Key

Casey dropped his storeroom key somewhere near the Ice Cream Parlor. Recover it.

- Gilda's Lost Axe

Gilda lost her climbing axe on Mickeyjunk Mountain. If you find it for her, she'll reward you.

- Museum Power Spark

Find something to trade for the power spark in the Museum. Ask the Usher at the Cinema about getting an item to trade for the power spark.

- OsTown Projector Screen

Gremlin Markus needs you to collect the gears from Pete and Horace to get the projector screen to OsTown working again.

- Recover Horace's Book

Horace needs his book back. Horace will give you a machine gear if you recover his book from Casey, the Emporium owner.

After Gremlin Markus leaves, walk down into the upper courtyard and speak with Big Bad Pete. If you helped his cousin, Small Pete, Big Bad Pete hands you some e-tickets and the Small Pete Pin as a reward. If you didn't aid Small Pete on his ship log's quest, Big Bad Pete gives you nothing but a jaw full of how you'd better not mess with him. Despite the rumor that Big Bad Pete had one of the gears, he doesn't; Pete gave it to Gilda when he lost a race to her.

Extra Content: Mean Street

This piece of concept art sits atop the train station behind the entrance projector. Paint in the lower roof, double-jump up to the new roof, and then double-jump up to the higher roof and nab the extra content.

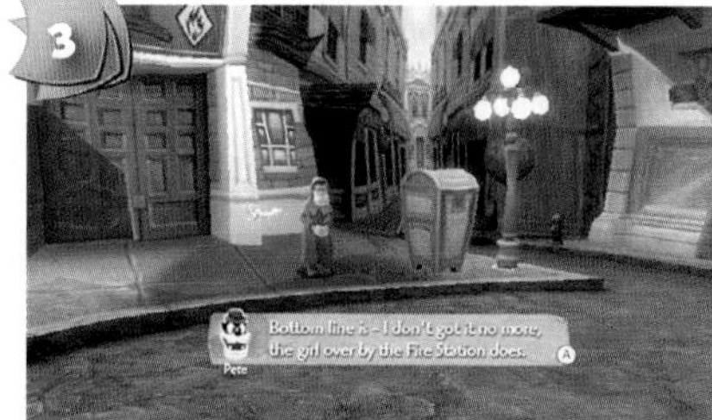

Head down to the fire station (right next to the City Hall) to find Gilda. She offers to hand over the gear if you can beat her race time. You have one minute to follow the white guardian around Mean Street and cross the finish line.

Optional Quest: Gilda's Lost Axe

Gilda is certainly the adventurous type. She's just returned from a trip to Mickeyjunk Mountain; unfortunately, she lost her favorite axe in a dangerous section of the mountain. Accept the quest before you begin the foot race, and you can complete it later when you brave Mickeyjunk Mountain yourself.

You begin in front of Gilda and race across the courtyard toward the museum.

The guardian then circles around and heads back up the ramp toward the entrance projector.

Silver Pin

Circle around the back of the train station building to find a small alley that holds the Silver Pin right out in the open. You won't have trouble finding it if you take a stroll.

When you chase the guardian up the ramp, it dances along the ledge and then darts over to the City Hall roof.

Double-jump over to the City Hall roof and follow the guardian to the other side.

Leap off the City Hall roof and land at the courtyard near where you started.

The guardian rushes down the center of Mean Street. Follow it. At the end of the block it ducks to the left at the corner.

Follow the guardian as it weaves back to the other side of the street in front of the Cinema. Once you reach the Cinema, the guardian zips to the lower courtyard in front of the four projector screens. Touch the finish line flag in under a minute and you win.

Return to Gilda and she gives you the first gear. Now you need the second one from Horace.

Cross the street to the Detective Agency (the one with the magnifying glass sign). Enter and speak to Horace. He says he'll gladly trade you the second gear if you return the book he lent to Casey.

Bronze Pin

This pin is hidden inside a rooftop wall of the New Sounds for a New Century building, which is adjacent to the Detective Agency. Vault up to the roof and spray Thinner back toward the Detective Agency. This reveals a secret room with two e-tickets and the Bronze Pin.

Casey is in the Emporium (the shop with the gift sign). He tells you that he finished reading Horace's book and lent it to Paulie, so off you go to the Ice Cream Shop.

Enter the Ice Cream Shop (the one with the ice cream cone sign), and speak with Paulie. He isn't quite done with the book yet, but he's a nice guy and hands it over to you anyway.

Return to Horace in the Detective Agency and hand him the missing book. Horace rewards you with the second gear.

Travel farther down the street and speak with Gremlin Markus in front of the machinery opposite the Cinema. He's happy to put those two gears to good use; however, he needs a power spark to get the OsTown projector working.

ICE CREAM STORE INVENTORY			
Item	**Price**	**Available**	**Notes**
Health Pip Upgrade 1	250	Visit 3	Can only buy once
Health Refill	50	Visit 1	None
Ice Cream Quest Item	100	Visit 1 and Visit 3	None

The first way to gain a power spark is to run back up to the Museum and speak with Laralee. Her prime exhibit is a power spark, and she'll only trade it for something equally valuable.

Gold Pin

Look for the Gold Pin high up on the Museum rooftop. Use the overhanging canopies to bounce from the street up to the roof and grab this coveted collectible.

Fortunately, it's easy to find something valuable for Laralee. Return to the Cinema and speak with the Usher. If you have a film reel, he trades you Hook's Cutlass and rewards you with the Swashbuckler Pin. If you don't have a film reel, he'll still give you the Cutlass, but it will cost you 30 e-tickets.

Return to Laralee in the Museum. She loves Hook's Cutlass and swaps it for the power spark.

Double back to Gremlin Markus and give him the power spark. He pounds on the machinery and eventually fixes the exit projector to OsTown.

Power Sparks

There are plenty of opportunities to gain power sparks In Mean Street (and later in OsTown as well). Several citizens have optional quests that reward you with a power spark, or you can buy power sparks from the Emporium after you return from Mickeyjunk Mountain. To get your first power spark and aid Gremlin Markus, complete either Laralee's optional quest in the Museum or Casey's optional quest in the Emporium.

Cinema Rewards

You'll love the Usher soon enough, because he rewards you more than any other toon in Mean Street. When you first visit him, he hands you the Swashbuckler Pin on your Museum quest for Laralee. If you have another film reel, the Usher rewards you with a Bronze Pin. Keep handing in film reels and you'll earn your first cartoon, "Oh, What a Knight," and more!

THE USHER'S FILM REEL REWARDS

Turned In	Reward
2	E-tickets
4	Bronze Pin
6	"Oh, What a Knight" cartoon
8	Power Spark
10	Wallet upgrade
12	Silver Pin
14	"Mad Doctor" cartoon
16	TV capacity upgrade
18	Gold Pin
22	Watch capacity upgrade
26	Anvil capacity upgrade
28	Health upgrade
30	Concept art (Mickey Grabbed)
32	Max wallet capacity upgrade (9,999) and 1,000 e-tickets
36	All 3 sketch types +50 capacity, Cartoon Buff Pin

EMPORIUM STORE INVENTORY

Item	Price	Available	Notes
Blot Scare	200	Visit 2 and on	Can only buy once
Bog Easy Bell Piece	300	After player returns from Lonesome Manor and the ghosts have gone back	Can only buy once
Dual Ammo Refill	100	Visit 1	None
Gear and Wrench Pin	200	Visit 1	Can only buy once
Goofy Part 1	1,000	After player returns from Tomorrow City	Only available if the player did not find this part
Goofy Part 2	1,000	After player returns from Tomorrow City	Only available if the player did not find this part
Goofy Part 3	1,000	After player returns from Tomorrow City	Only available if the player did not find this part
Goofy Part 4	1,000	After player returns from Tomorrow City	Only available if the player did not find this part
Mickey Faces I	200	Visit 1	Can only buy once
Mickey Faces II	200	Visit 2 and on	Can only buy once
Mickey Faces III	200	Visit 3 and on	Can only buy once
Mickey Faces IV	200	Visit 4 and on	Can only buy once
Moonliner Rocket Pin	200	After player returns from Tomorrow City	Can only buy once
Paint Refill	50	Visit 1	None
Power Spark 1	50	Visit 2 and on	Can only buy once
Power Spark 2	100	Visit 2 and on	Can only buy once
Power Spark 3	150	Visit 2 and on	Can only buy once
Power Spark 4	200	Visit 2 and on	Can only buy once
Thinner Falls	200	Visit 2 and on	Can only buy once
Thinner Refill	50	Visit 1	None
Train Station Pin	200	Visit 5—After the player comes back from Lonesome Manor	Can only buy once
TV Sketch Capacity Increase	500	After player returns from Tomorrow City	Can only buy once
TV Sketch	100	After player returns from Tomorrow City	None
Wallet Increase 1	350	Visit 1	Can only buy once

10

Before you leave for OsTown, finish up anything else you'd like to accomplish in Mean Street. Visit Casey again in the Emporium and accept the "Find Casey's Key" optional quest. This quest gives you a power spark, which you may need to fix the OsTown projector, and completing the quest opens the Emporium for business.

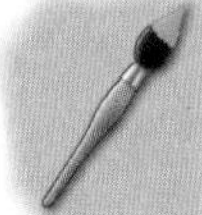

Spray the manhole cover in the alley next to the Ice Cream Shop to discover Casey's lost key.

To find Casey's lost key, head back to the Ice Cream Shop, but don't go in. The key is in the alley, underneath the manhole cover. Coat the manhole cover with Thinner, jump in, and grab the key. Return to Casey for the power spark reward.

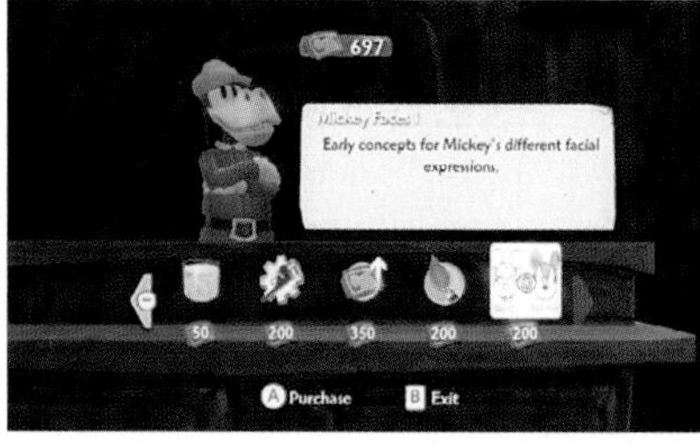

Once you complete the "Find Casey's Key" quest, you can shop in the Emporium. Spend e-tickets to buy Paint and Thinner refills, the Gremlin Village Pin (costs 200 e-tickets), the Large Wallet to carry many more e-tickets (costs 350 e-tickets), the Welcome to Wasteland Pin (costs 200 e-tickets), and the Mickey Faces I extra content (costs 200 e-tickets).

Check back at the Emporium each time you visit Mean Street. Casey's merchandise will change, and you can find some great items for your collection.

Thru the Mirror

Explore Mickey's home to find a wonderland of household objects. Playing cards, sewing needles, and spinning globes can be huge obstacles to a tiny adventurer.

Move to the right, and jump onto the mantle. Approach the mirror to cross into a new world of familiar objects.

When you pass through the mirror, you shrink to a fraction of your normal size. Land on the mantle, and continue to the right.

Grab the e-ticket from the end table, and approach the globe. Double-jump up to the e-tickets near the top of the globe, and hop across to the deck of playing cards.

Stand near the health power-up, and wait for fresh cards to float down from the upper path. The King of Hearts is patrolling the area to the right; avoid the lower path for the moment, and jump onto the playing cards as they approach.

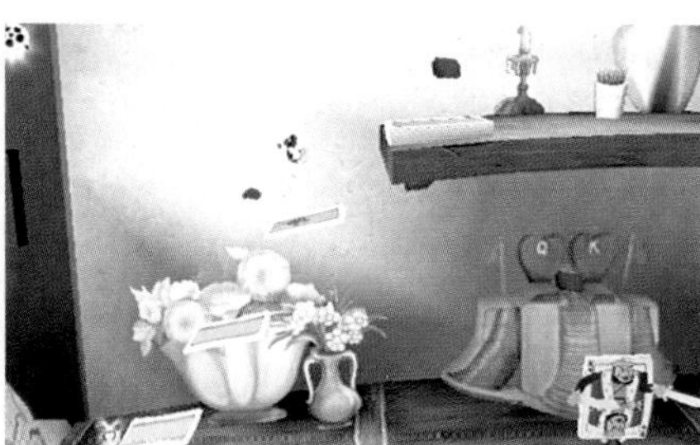

Jump up along the cards to reach the deck above you. The film reel is to the left of the upper path. Double-jump from the floating cards to collect the film reel. If you're not in position to make this jump, hop over to the shelf and wait for a new line of playing cards to appear.

When you land, return to the deck of cards on the lower path. Grab the health power-up if you took damage from the fall.

Jump back up along the falling cards to return to the upper path.

Hop onto the bowl of thread, and double-jump to grab the e-ticket. Be sure to avoid the sewing needle as you land. Grab the health power-up if you need it, or jump down from the right side of the bowl.

Stand on the deck of cards at the end of the shelf. Hop onto the playing cards as they float over to the right. Grab the e-ticket in front of the clock, then jump across to the next shelf.

When you land, grab the e-ticket to the right, and continue to the end of the shelf.

Drop down to the top hat below you. From this point, you can continue to the right or follow the lower path to the left for some extra e-tickets.

To collect more e-tickets, jump over to the piece of wood, and push it down to the ground.

Run up along the wood, and double-jump to grab the e-ticket above you.

Jump up along the books to find the Queen of Hearts dancing near the edge of the desk.

Hop onto the queen to gain some extra height, then double-jump up to the e-tickets above you. Try to stay clear of the king's blades, and grab the health power-up if he lands a successful attack. Before you move on, use your spin move with the queen for two extra e-tickets.

Jump back over to the piece of wood, and leap across to the top hat.

Continue to the right, and wait for the shuffling cards to approach. Jump over the cards, and grab the e-tickets above the dresser.

Jump across the walnuts to reach the mantle, and approach the mirror to the right.

Pass through the mirror to return to normal size, and activate the exit projector to complete the level and travel to OsTown.

OsTown

Level Overview

A broken bridge in harmonious OsTown needs fixing before you can climb Mickeyjunk Mountain. But where's OsTown's resident gremlin, and what's that strange noise coming from the Old Gag Factory? The colorful characters around town will help you find your way, and don't forget to pick up the special pal quest from Animatronic Goofy.

You stroll into the scenic OsTown on the trail of Oswald, and after speaking with the citizens, it's clear that you have to follow Oswald to Mickeyjunk Mountain. Unfortunately, the bridge to that exit projector is broken and the resident gremlin, Prescott, is nowhere to be found.

Things to Do

- Speak with Clarabelle
- Talk to Moody and paint his house
- Free Gremlin Prescott from the safe
- Speak with your house Telephone
- Side with Telephone or Gremlin Prescott to repair the bridge
- Search the area for power-ups
- Complete any optional quests
- Exit to the Mickey's Steamroller level

As you approach the buildings, Clarabelle stops you near her front lawn. She's heard weird noises coming from the Old Gag Factory and directs you to Moody for answers.

Optional Quest: Ice Cream Cake

Instead of pies, Clarabelle is thinking of making a special ice cream cake for Horace from Mean Street. If you accept this optional quest, return to Mean Street and visit the Ice Cream Parlor. For 100 e-tickets, you can buy an ice cream cone and bring it back to Clarabelle so she has the secret ingredient for her new treat. After your visit to Mickeyjunk Mountain, Clarabelle will have the ice cream cake ready and you can deliver it to Horace, which sets up a quest chain to earn both the Mean Street Romance Pin and the Happy Birthday Pin. If you fail to bring Clarabelle ice cream, she will still make a pie for Horace and you can earn the Pie Pin instead.

Moody has been hearing strange noises from the safe dangling out in front of the Old Gag Factory. He offers to give you the combination to the safe if you give his house a paint job.

Cross town to the stick-frame house on the end, between Mickey's yellow house on the left and the Thinner pool on the right. Walk around the house and coat it in Paint, from the doorstep to the rooftop. When you've completed the job, return to Moody and he gives you the safe combination.

Use the hopping mailbox behind Moody to jump up to the Old Gag Factory rooftop. Approach the safe to free Gremlin Prescott who is trapped inside. Thin the safe support to let Prescott out.

Gremlin Prescott offers to fix the bridge, but first he wants you to deal with the rogue Telephone who locked him in the safe. He sends you to your yellow house across the street.

Optional Quest: Thin the Gag Factory

Abner strolls around near the Gag Factory, and you can actually gain two power sparks from this quest if you're paying attention. Abner doesn't want strangers to think the Gag Factory is still in business, so he wants you to thin out the building as much as you can. Wash the walls in thick Thinner coats, then climb to the roof and do the same. Once you completely erase the tallest tower, you'll discover a power spark hidden at the base. Collect it before gaining a second power spark when you complete the quest.

Run over to your house and talk to Telephone inside. Apparently, Telephone claims that Gremlin Prescott was going to dismantle him, so he locked the gremlin inside the safe out of self-preservation.

If you help Telephone with his "OsTown Phone Network" optional quest, he'll get out of town, leave Prescott in peace, and give you a Bronze Pin. You must find three circuit breaker boxes hidden around town and paint them to switch them on. The first breaker box is up on the Old Gag Factory rooftop, directly behind where you freed Prescott in the safe. The second breaker box is on the small strip of land past the Old Gag Factory and directly below Donald's tugboat and the Thinner pool. Thin out the pink wall and look for the breaker box inside a hidden alcove. The third breaker box is underneath Clarabelle's garden.

You can also side with Prescott and let him in your house. It's the quick way of fixing the bridge; however, Prescott will dismantle Telephone and you won't earn the Bronze Pin that Telephone has for you.

Extra Content: Ortensia's House

Walk down the thin alley between the orange and pink houses and face the back wall behind the houses. Spray Thinner around the area to open a secret alcove with Ortensia's House extra content and two e-tickets.

Before you depart for Mickeyjunk Mountain, check around town to make sure you've covered all the quests you wanted to pick up and collected all the power-ups and e-tickets you can hold. Remember to check on the rooftops too; you'll find some interesting things up there, including a power spark atop Mickey's house! Definitely speak with Animatronic Goofy to pick up the "Find Goofy's Parts" pal quest, which affects the game's ending.

Junction Point: Animatronic Goofy

Before you head off to Mickeyjunk Mountain, speak with Animatronic Goofy and pick up his "Find Goofy's Parts" quest. The parts are located far from OsTown, in Tomorrow City, but you need the quest to recover them. If you do restore Animatronic Goofy, he becomes your pal, gives you a special pin, and plays a more friendly role in the game's ending.

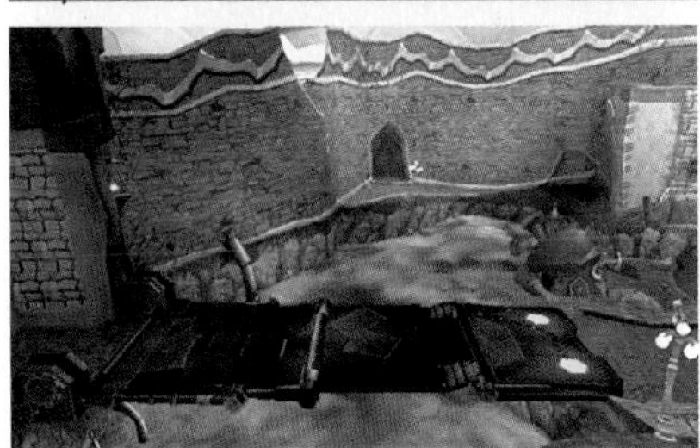

When you're ready to exit OsTown, speak with Gremlin Prescott at the edge of the Thinner pool. He puts the finishing touches on the bridge mechanism, and the whole thing lowers for you to cross to the exit projector.

Mickey's Steamroller

You enter a sleepy little town full of stone buildings and softly glowing streetlights. This quiet town is in for a rude awakening, however, with a little help from an unattended steamroller.

Move to the left, and jump onto the building to collect two e-tickets.

Turn around, and drop back to the ground. Hop onto the shed, and double-jump up to the window to collect more e-tickets.

Jump up to grab the e-ticket past the window, then drop straight down to the small roof below you.

Collect the e-tickets in front of the next house, and continue to the end of the buildings.

Run to the right to find two youngsters standing on a steamroller. What could go wrong?

Jump onto the steamroller, and continue up to the planks running along the wooden beams.

When you land, run along the planks to the right. Grab the e-ticket, and keep moving to stay ahead of the runaway steamroller.

Collect the film reel to the right, and continue to the end of the planks.

When you reach the end of the planks, jump across to the building in front of you. Stand on the low roof and wait for the steamroller to approach.

Just before the steamroller crashes into the building, double-jump to avoid getting caught in the wreckage. Land on the steamroller, and drop to the ground as it continues up the hill.

To grab some extra e-tickets, move back to the left. Jump over the exposed nails along the row of planks, and collect any e-tickets and health power-ups you might need.

When you reach the end of the planks, turn around and move back to the right. Remember to avoid the nails on your way back to the damaged buildings.

Run through the holes left by the steamroller, and move to the top of the hill.

Jump up along the row of bathtubs. From this point you can reach the exit screen on the building to the right, or collect the e-tickets on the buildings to the left.

If you wish, stand on the second tub and double-jump to the left. Grab the e-tickets above the buildings, and drop down to collect the health power-up if you need a little boost.

Double-jump from the top of the bathtubs to reach the last e-ticket.

When you're ready, jump up along the bathtubs to reach the exit projector to the right. Activate the projector to complete the level and travel to Mickeyjunk Mountain.

MICKEYJUNK MOUNTAIN

The Heaps

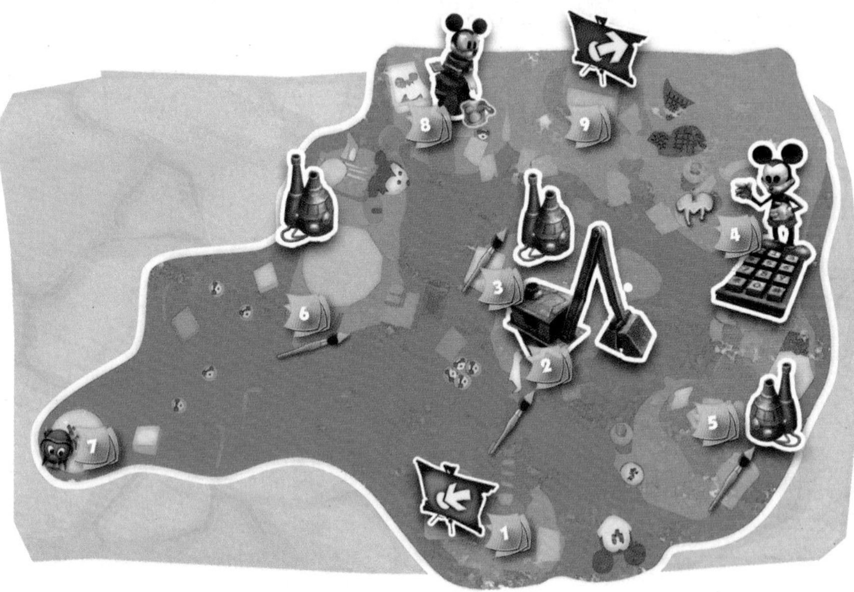

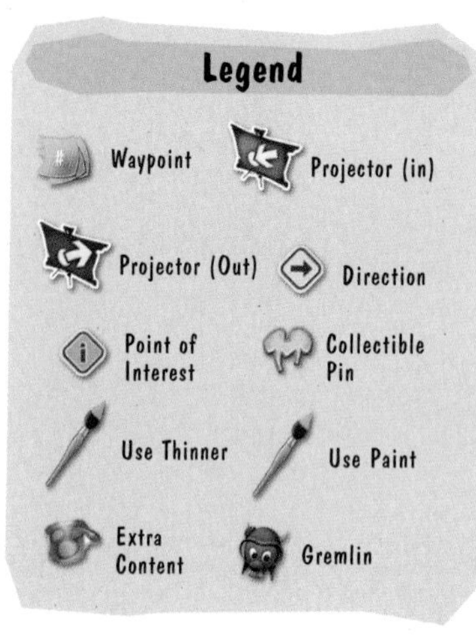

Level Overview

Oswald's sanctuary lies at the top of Mickeyjunk Mountain, and it will be a long, dangerous climb to the top, especially in your miniaturized form. The Heaps spread out at the bottom of the mountain, a junkyard of forgotten Mickey-related merchandise. Your task is to get the crane working and open the lunch box lid to expose the exit area. Of course, the new Bunny Children and the old Spatters won't want you do anything productive, unless you can entertain them in some way.

Look around the junkyard and plan your paths carefully. Unlike normal terrain, the footing in the Heaps can be treacherous. If you slip off a pile of garbage or stand too long on a bobbing block, you'll fall in the surrounding Thinner sea.

Things to Do

- Speak with Decker at the crane
- Battle through Bunny Children and Spatters to paint the three TVs
- Activate the crane and open the exit area
- Free Gremlin Kip
- Search the area for power-ups and collectibles
- Exit to the Piles

Mickeyjunk Mountain Quests

- Ascend the Mountain

Proceed to the top of Mickeyjunk Mountain. Oswald is somewhere atop this mountain that's crawling with Beetleworx, Blotlings, and other hazards.

- Knock Knock

Subdue the Blotlings so Jack Trade can repair the door, or repair it yourself by restoring TVs in the area.

- Power the Crane

Paint in the TVs to power the crane. Decker has informed you that the crane runs on TV power. The nearby TVs require Paint to be recharged.

- Three Challenges

Complete three challenges, based on Oswald's adventures, to gain audience with Oswald.

To make crossing the junkyard terrain easier, spray Paint in areas that close gaps over the Thinner, such as the guitar neck near the crane island.

Jump down on the base of the guitar below you. Paint the neck and walk carefully out over the Thinner and onto the island with the crane.

2

Speak with Decker, the playing card operating the crane. He's happy to help you pull down the lunch box lid and open the exit to the Piles; however, the crane needs powering up. Either Paint in the three TVs around the area for power, or free Gremlin Kip out to sea on the scattered debris and he'll start up the crane.

As soon as you leave Decker, Bunny Children arrive. These small bunnies only slow you down at first, but the more that gather, the worse for you. If enough swarm you, they pick you up and run you over to the Thinner sea. To avoid getting tossed into the Thinner, spin move when the bunnies arrive and knock them out of your way.

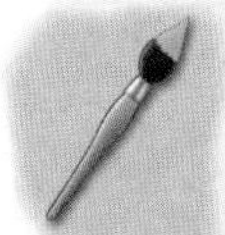

The first TV rests behind the crane.

3

Paint in the first TV behind the crane. If you have Bunny Children on your tail, the TV will absorb their attention and they won't bother you anymore. The TV even placates nearby Spatters.

4

Search for the second TV on the right side of the Heaps. While you're traveling over there, you'll pass one of the Thinner falls with an old telephone to the right. If you jump on the buttons and punch out the secret code (349), the falls dries up, revealing a hidden cave behind it. Paint in the platform below the hidden cave, then jump up and retrieve the Silver Pin.

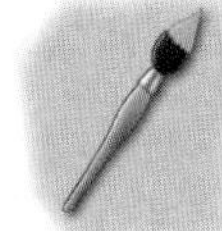

The second TV stands on the right side, past the old telephone.

Enemy: Bunny Children

These small blue bunnies might look cute bouncing around and acting like rambunctious toddlers, but they can get out of hand quickly. One or two tugging at your legs will only slow you down; once a large group clusters around you, the Bunny Children will hoist you up in the air and carry you to the nearest Thinner spot to toss you in. Fortunately, a single spin move can bat all of them away, and if you knock them into Thinner, Bunny Children dissolve just like other enemies. The most effective method of corralling them is to set up a TV to entertain their young minds.

Two Spatters guard the second TV on the Mickey Mouse Club island. Swat the Spatters into the nearby Thinner sea, or spray Paint on the second TV to occupy their attention. With the second TV painted, you only have one more to go.

The third TV hides behind the "Fantasia" poster.

Return to the starting area and hop over the floating debris to reach the left side of the Heaps.

Climb to the top of the stacked junk and look down. Two Spatters guard the third TV area. Surprise them from above and spin move them off the platform and into the Thinner. You can try to battle with Paint or Thinner; however, the fight is in close quarters and it may prove difficult to douse them before they smack you.

Look for the third TV behind the blue "Fantasia" poster. Follow the power cables on the ground to locate the TV.

As soon as you spray Paint on the third TV, Decker operates the crane and pulls open the lunch box lid that hides the exit screen.

From the third TV area, scan out to sea. You'll spot some merchandise floating in the Thinner, and way out in the distance, you should see Gremlin Kip trapped out on a drum. Begin double-jumping from toy to toy.

You may want to use a Watch sketch to free Gremlin Kip. It gives you more time to hop across the toys out in the Thinner sea before the goo creeps in.

The toys sink into the Thinner as soon as you land, so immediately jump off a toy after landing. The buttons sink faster than the blocks, so use your time on the block to adjust direction. When you reach the drum, smash Gremlin Kip's cage. If you haven't found all three TVs yet, Kip will start the crank for you. Don't forget to open the chest on the drum; it contains valuable power-ups, including health power-ups if you've taken damage on the journey out.

Before you depart the Heaps, you may want to visit the Mickey gumball machine next to the second Thinner falls.

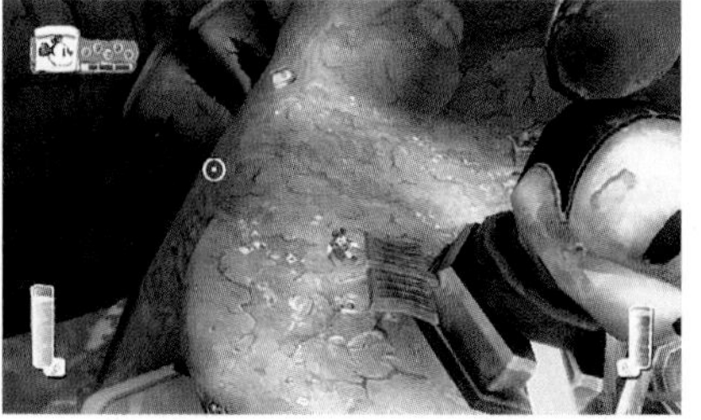

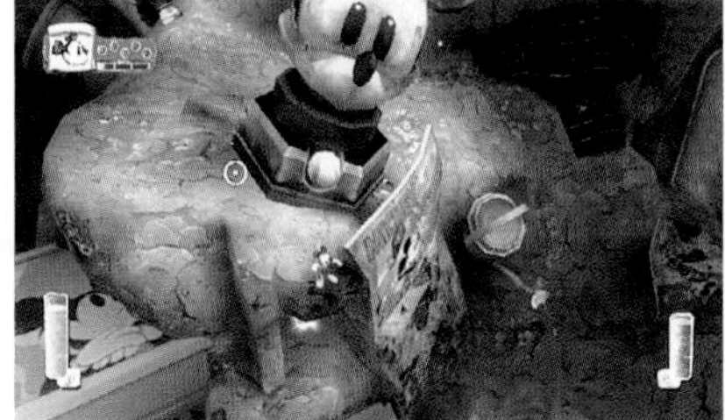

Climb up to the top plateau with the gumball machine and spin the lever on the side. This shuts off the Thinner falls. Inch out to the edge and shoot Paint straight down to fill in the platform beneath the hidden cave. Jump down on the new platform, then jump back into the cave and recover the Bunny Children extra content. Do all this quickly because the Thinner falls will start back up soon.

Bounce up the debris to reach the lunch box lid. The exit screen hides in the lunch box. When you're ready, jump into the screen and head toward the Piles, after you run through the "Alpine Climbers: Part 1" 2D level.

Alpine Climbers: Part I

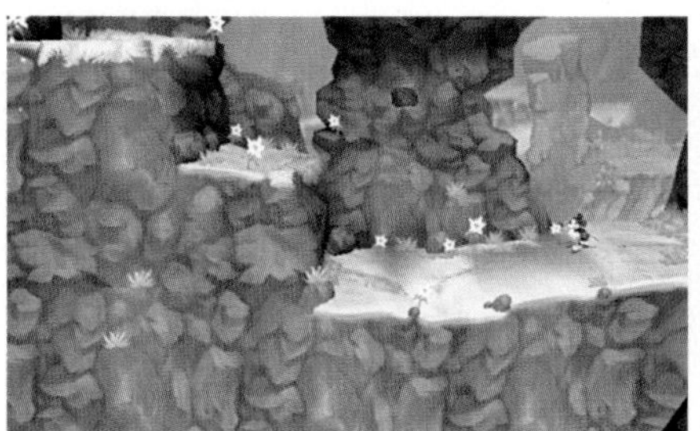

You appear high in the Alps, and you need to climb even higher. Watch out for falling rocks, flimsy branches, and hostile wildlife as you scale these massive mountains.

Run to the left, and double-jump up to the ledge. Move quickly to avoid falling rocks during tremors.

Jump to grab the e-tickets along the first two ledges, then double-jump to the right.

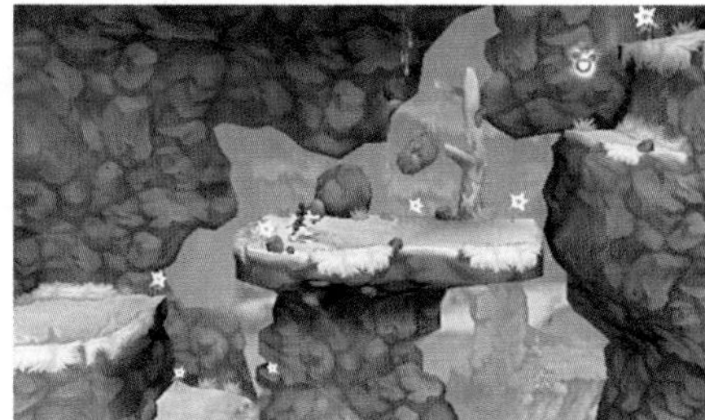

When you land, stand near the ledge's left side. Wait for the next tremor to shake another group of rocks loose, and stay clear to avoid damage. When it's safe to move on, jump up to grab the e-ticket and continue to the right.

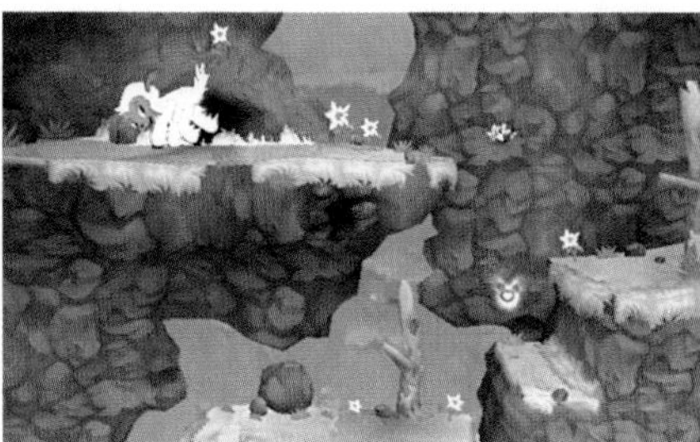

Jump up to the next set of ledges, and grab the health power-up if you need it. Double-jump over to the baby mountain goat running across the ledge to the left.

Hop onto the baby mountain goat, and jump up to collect the e-tickets above you. Double-jump onto the branch sticking out from the ledge and continue to the right.

Wait for the hatching egg to float within range, and hop onto it.

Ride up to the next ledge. Jump to grab the e-ticket above you, then hop to the ledge. Continue to the next hatching egg.

Jump onto the egg, and wait for it to fly back up. When the egg pauses below the health power-up, collect the e-tickets above you and double-jump to the nearby branch.

Move all the way to the ledge, and wait for the next egg to fly within range. Jump up and ride the egg to the e-ticket above you.

After you grab the e-ticket, jump over to the baby goat on the ledge. Hop onto the goat, and double-jump up to the nest in the next branch.

When you land on the nest, the branch begins to sag. Hop over to the ledge on the right, and let the branch return to its starting position. Run across the branch and leap up to grab the two e-tickets. Use the baby mountain goat to return to the nest and continue up the mountain.

A large bird is tied to the next branch. When the bird flies down, the branch moves into range. Jump up and run across the branch.

When the bird flies back up, run to the right and jump up to the ledge. Collect the e-ticket, and grab the health power-up if you've suffered any damage.

Run back across the branch, and jump along the ledges to the left. Hop onto the bird, and ride up to the top of its path. Hop over to the right, and watch out for the angry mountain goat when you land.

Wait for the mountain goat to finish its charge, then run over and hop on its back. Grab the e-tickets in the area, and double-jump from the goat to reach the branches of the dead tree.

Jump over to the branch sticking out of the mountain, and wait for the hatching egg to fly over from the right. Jump across to the egg and collect the e-tickets above you.

Ride over to the right, and jump to the next hatching egg. Face the ledges to the right. The film reel is on the upper ledge and the exit screen is on the ledge below.

Ride the hatching egg to the upper ledge to collect the film reel. Hop back to the egg, and ride down toward the lower ledge.

Hop down to the exit screen, and use a spin move to break your fall. If you've collected all of the desired e-tickets, activate the exit screen to complete the level.

The Piles

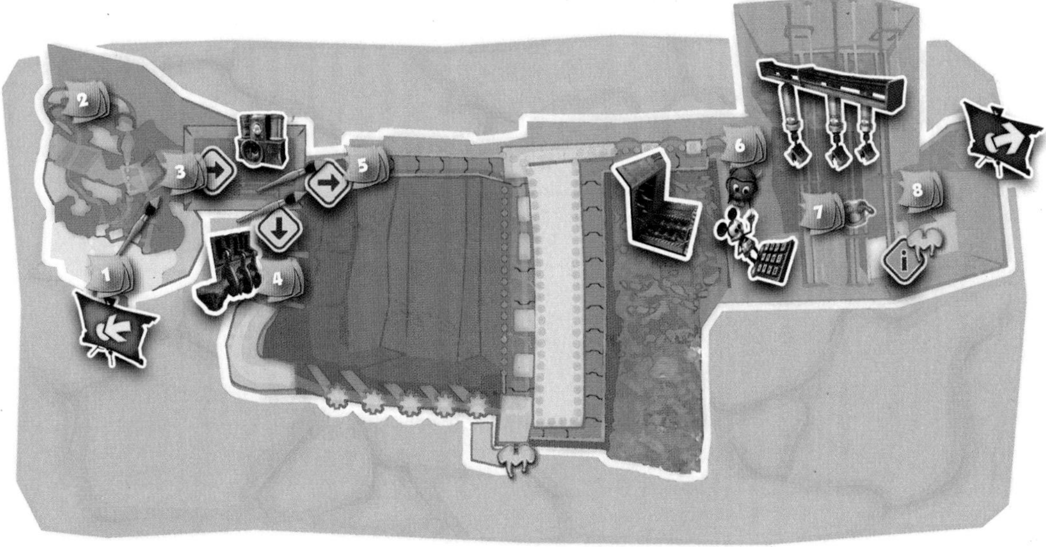

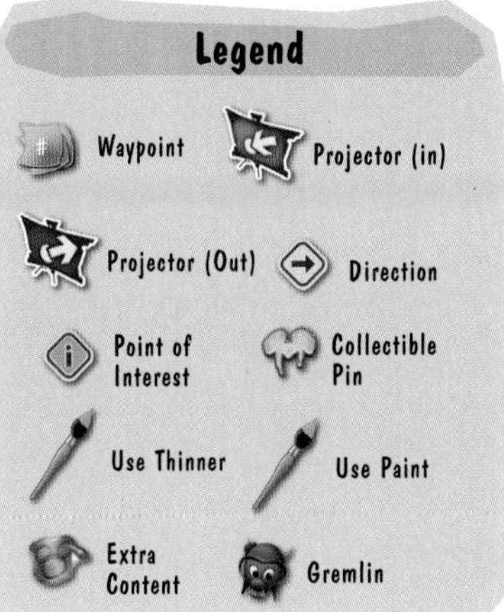

Level Overview

The path gets more difficult, because you now have new enemies to battle, a dangerous climb on the outside of the mountain to survive, and even more dangerous route inside the factory once you reach the next summit. This is the most dangerous part of the mountain. It's not exactly downhill after the Piles—you still have one more level to climb to the top—but fewer machines try to crunch your bones.

At the start of the Piles, you confront your first Beetleworx creature. Where the Blotlings were created with liquid, Beetleworx are more machine. To defeat a Beetleworx such as the Hopper, you must first dissolve its armor with Thinner, exposing its weak spots, and then use your spin move to damage the creature.

Enemy: Hopper

The robotic, bird-like Hoppers will peck your health away if given a chance. Unlike Blotlings, which you can befriend with Paint, Beetleworx creatures such as the Hopper only slow down when you gum up their machinery with Paint. Thinner, however, dissolves the Hopper's armor and exposes its inner parts. Use a spin move while the parts are exposed to deliver the disabling stroke.

After you defeat the first Hopper, two more join the fray. Repeat your Thinner and spin move attacks on the new Hopper pair, or swat them off the mountainside to save on your paintbrush mixtures.

Things to Do

- Defeat the Hoppers
- Climb farther up the mountainside
- Avoid the Spladoosh creatures
- Fill the pump with either Paint or Thinner
- Navigate the dangerous path through the factory
- Free Gremlin Ronald
- Cross the Thinner pool via the claws
- Search the area for power-ups and collectibles
- Exit to Mt. Osmore Slopes

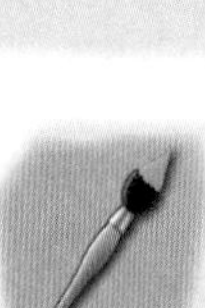

Paint in the guitar on your climb up the mountain to traverse the more difficult stretches on the cliff face, and slow the Mickey Thinner sprayers with a squirt of Paint.

Enter the tunnel from which the Hoppers emerged and climb up the mountain.

Paint in the guitar neck and travel across the long gap. When you reach the guitar base, turn right and double-jump up to the first carton sticking out of the mountainside.

Continue up the cartons until you reach the top one. Spray Paint directly above you to fill in the second guitar. Jump straight up, grab onto the guitar neck, and pull yourself up.

Fire Paint at the Mickey head to stop the green toxic gas from spraying out. Cross the guitar and jump onto the steel mesh grate. You're about to enter the factory.

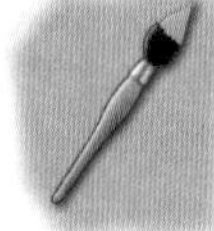

Fill the pump with Paint to take the easier, lower path through the conveyor belt.

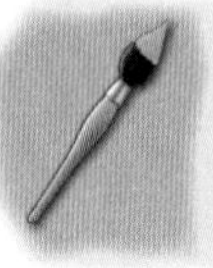

Fill the pump with Thinner to take the harder, upper path through the gears and pistons.

The large pump room holds multiple Spladoosh Blotlings. These sleeping giants won't stir (and explode!) if you tread quietly. Walk slowly across the room to the front of the pump. If you fill the pump with Thinner, it opens the door to your right and gives you access to the upper path through the factory. If you fill the pump with Paint, it opens the door straight ahead and gives you access to the lower path through the factory.

Enemy: Spladoosh

The good news: a Spladoosh doesn't move. The immense blobs stay in one position and sleep most of the time. If you walk quietly by the sleeping giants, they'll stay asleep. The bad news: If you wake them up, they expand and eventually explode with the force of a goo bomb. You don't want to get caught in that mess, so don't rush into hectic combat around them.

The Thinner path is more dangerous, but offers more potential rewards. If you decide on the Thinner path, walk slowly past the remaining Spladoosh Blotlings and exit through the open doorway to your right.

NOTE

If you take the upper (Thinner) path and fall off inside the factory, you may survive and land on the lower (Paint) path. Follow the tips on the lower path (map location 5) to still reach Gremlin Ronald.

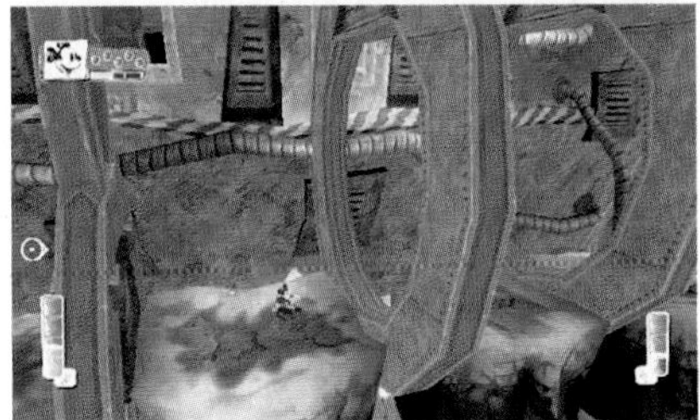

Exit outside and stand on the ledge in front of the first mechanized claw. The giant claw raises and lowers; stand in front of it for several seconds to understand the pattern. Double-jump through when the claw rises and land on the next ledge. Repeat for the second and third claws.

Walk past the Spladoosh out on the snowy corner ledge. You have no other threat around, so there's no reason to stir him up unless you want to see a goo explosion.

Four giant pistons churn up and down in the next section. Double-jump onto the first piston as it drops to its lowest point. Ride it up until it's flush with the next piston at their highest point and jump across. Continue in the same fashion until you land on the last piston.

Ride the last piston down to its low point and jump off to pick up the Silver Pin out on the snow ledge. If you don't want the Silver Pin, jump off at the high point and land on the steel grate.

Wait at the edge of the steel grate and watch the giant spinning wheels. Each wheel has a section missing, and it's possible to double-jump through this open section to bypass the wheel. Get a running start and time your jump to pass through the wheel and land on the next grate. Unfortunately, this next grate holds a Spladoosh in the corner. Back up slowly when you land and prepare for the next jump.

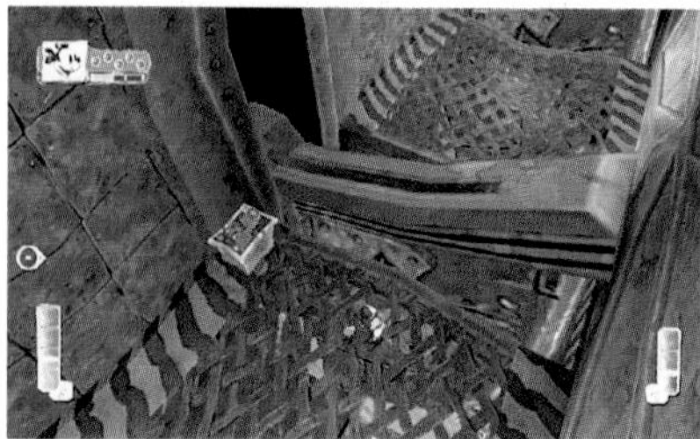

Time your run and jump to pass through the wheel. You'll wake up the Spladoosh, but you'll be long gone before it has a chance to explode. Jump through one more wheel and you're past this section.

The final section holds a series of grinders that chew up and compact garbage chunks falling out of the slots in the wall.

There's also a Spladoosh sitting on the platform beyond the first grinder. You can't get away from this Spladoosh, so you have to time your jump to clear the first two grinders one after the other. Wait for the grinders to gobble up the garbage chunks, and as soon as you can clear the garbage, run and double-jump over the first grinder. Continue running and double-jump over the second grinder.

Take a deep breath and wait for the next garbage square to grind down. Run and double-jump over the grinder to reach the final area with Gremlin Ronald.

The Paint path is the easier of the two factory paths. If you decide on the Paint path, walk slowly past the remaining Spladoosh Blotlings and exit through the open doorway straight ahead.

When you reach the doorway, run toward the opening and double-jump over the gap and onto the moving conveyor belt. If you stand on the conveyor belt, it will carry you toward the rollers, which is sometimes the direction you want to go and sometimes the opposite direction. Jumping up in the air stops you from moving, and you can hop if you need to move against the conveyor belt direction. Corner platforms can also help you get your bearings while you pause and refuel with any resources stuck in the corner.

Continue along the conveyor belt and avoid the garbage chunks that shuffle down the middle of the belt. In the second passage, toxic gas shoots out of nozzles on the sides. Run along the conveyor belt until you get near a nozzle and wait for the gas to spray out. As soon as the gas pauses, double-jump forward to give yourself some momentum and clear the danger area. Patiently wait in front of each nozzle and jump when it's clear to avoid toxic gas damage.

As you navigate the passages, watch for new nozzles. They may be closer or farther down the wall, and can catch you in a poison blast if you rush through.

In the final passage, watch for garbage chunks dropping out of the right wall. Stay to the left and avoid the garbage chunks as you exit the conveyor belt area.

If you enter the final chamber from the upper (Thinner) path, drop over the edge and land on the next floor next to Gremlin Ronald. If you enter the final chamber from the lower (Paint) path, you'll have to double-jump up to him. Use your spin move to free Gremlin Ronald, and he fixes the machinery so that the three cranes line up and form a makeshift bridge across the Thinner pool.

Instead of freeing Ronald, you have the option to go straight to the old phone and enter one of the codes from the Address Book in Heaps. This will align the machinery and let you cross the Thinner pool.

Gremlin Ronald

Gremlin Ronald waits imprisoned on the middle platform near the old phone in the final factory chamber. Releasing him gets you another gremlin closer to the Gremlin Guardian Pin, and he directly rewards you by setting up the claws so that you can jump safely across the Thinner pool.

On the lower level next to the old phone, several Spatters and a Spladoosh guard the area. You're safe on the higher platforms, but as soon as you step on the lower platform, they attack. Swat the Spatters over the side and into the Thinner pool for some quick eliminations, then run up and tag the Spladoosh. Run back past the middle platform wall and you'll be safe from the Spladoosh's explosion.

Extra Content: Mickeyjunk Mountain

Bobbing atop the floating block in the corner of the Thinner pool, the Mickeyjunk Mountain extra content is one of the more dangerous ones to try to collect. You can easily drop down on the concept sketch from atop the third claw; unfortunately, the block begins to sink as soon as you land on it. It's recommended that you only attempt it with full health.

7

After Gremlin Ronald lines up the claws, walk over to the old phone and turn toward the Thinner pool. Double-jump out and up onto the first claw. Continue along to the second and third claws. Look down and in the corner of the Thinner pool to spot the Mickeyjunk Mountain extra content hovering above the green "B" block.

Gold Pin

After you cross the claws and reach the far side of the Thinner pool, look for the Gold Pin on the top platform. Follow the platform around the corner and the Gold Pin chest rests in a small alcove.

8

Spatters and Hoppers guard the large courtyard in front of the exit tunnel. You have a lot of room to maneuver here;

pick your favorite strategy for eliminating the enemies, though if you lure them close to the Thinner pool and swat them into the goop, you'll stay wide of the Spladoosh in front of the tunnel.

You can run by the Spladoosh and should clear the blast radius before the explosion hits the front of the tunnel. If you want to finish off the Spladoosh first, release an Anvil sketch over its head and stand back. Anvils are an excellent tactic for removing a Spladoosh threat. The exit screen waits for you in the back of the tunnel.

Alpine Climbers: Part 2

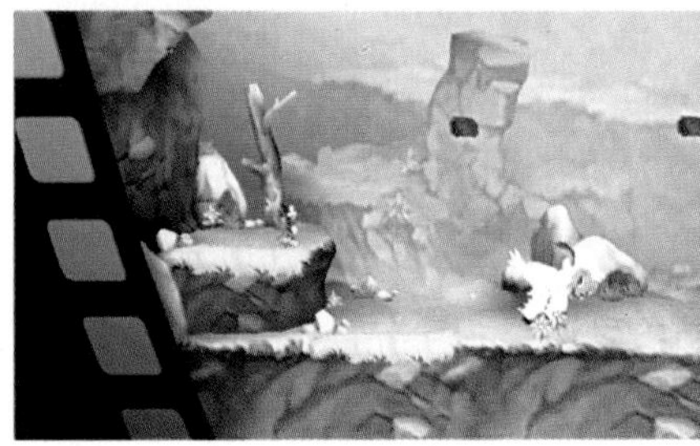

You return to the steep drops and falling rocks of the mountains. The wildlife offers some help during your climb, but a misguided rescue dog isn't quite up to the task.

Hop up and collect the e-tickets to the right, and land on the baby mountain goat. Double-jump to reach the next ledge.

Wait for the hatching egg to fly within range, and jump on to take a ride.

When the egg reaches the top of its path, jump over to the right and grab another e-ticket.

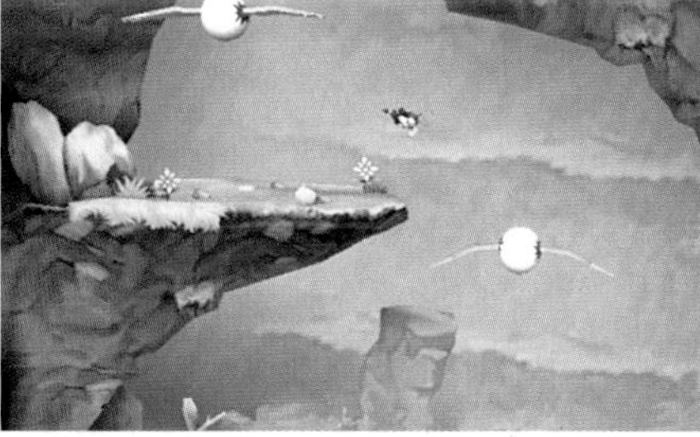
Leap back to the egg, and hop across to the next ledge.

Hop onto the next egg when it flies into range, and wait for it to head back up.

Ride the egg up to the top of its path. Grab the e-ticket above you, then jump across to the right. Try to land on the end of the ledge to avoid the kegs rolling down the mountain.

Wait for the keg to crash down on the ledge. Jump over the wreckage and continue to the right.

Follow the e-tickets up to the rescue dog. Each time the dog pops out of its house, it rolls a new keg down the mountain.

Hop over any rolling kegs and jump onto the doghouse. Continue up along the ledges to the right.

If you've taken any damage, grab the health power-up near the dead tree. Face back to the left, and jump up to the next ledge.

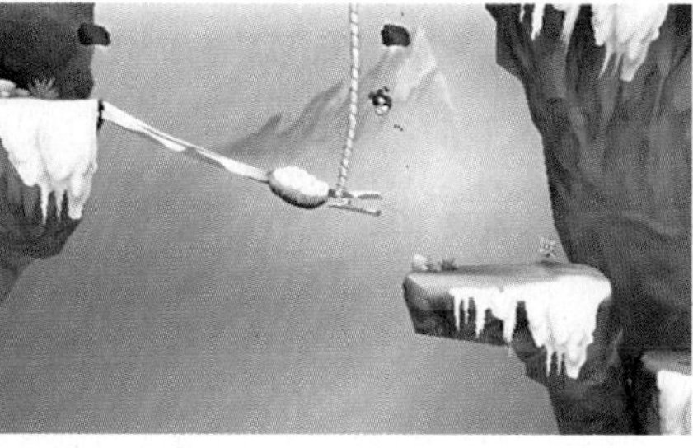
Wait for the large bird to fly down, and jump across to the nest.

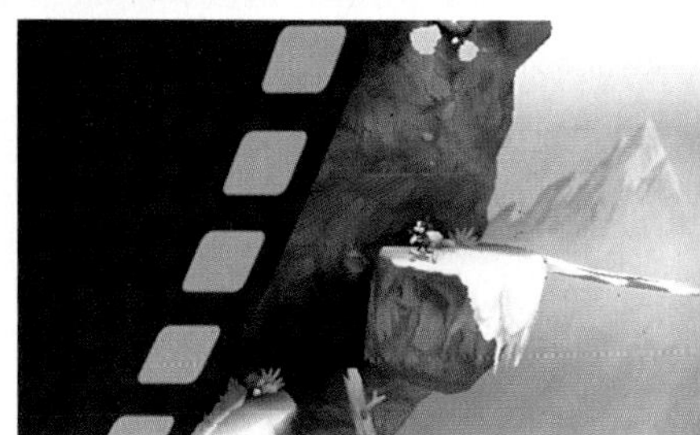
Run across the branch to reach the ledge. Run all the way to the ledge's left side to avoid the falling rocks. Drop through the e-ticket to reach the ledge below you.

Move back to the right, and hop down to collect two more e-tickets. When you land, grab the film reel from the ledge below you.

Hop back down to the rescue dog, and avoid the rolling kegs. Jump back up the ledges and return to the bird's nest.

When the large bird flies down, hop onto the branch and run to the left.

Wait for the bird to fly back up, then run to the right and jump to the next ledge.

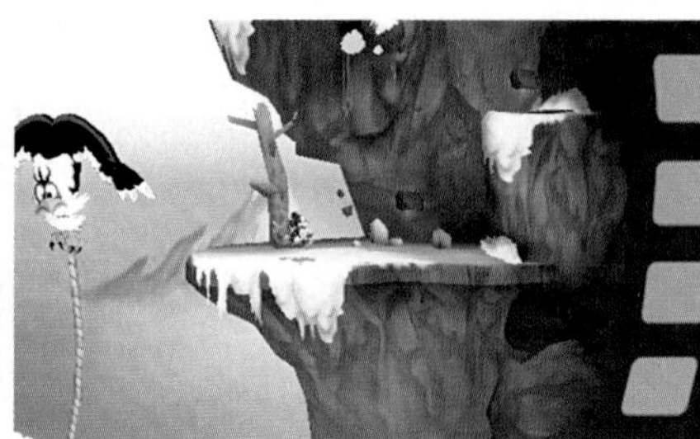
When you land, continue to the right and jump onto the small ledge in front of you. Move quickly to avoid the falling rocks.

Jump to the next ledge, and run back to the left. Hop onto the large bird, then double-jump to the ledge in front of you.

Jump up to the health power-up near the dead tree. The exit screen is on the ledge to the right.

Double-jump to the right, and grab the last e-ticket. When you're ready, activate the exit screen to complete the level.

Mt. Osmore Slopes

Level Overview

Massive closed doors seal off Oswald's headquarters. You can open it after a big battle, or use your brain to figure out a way to power up the mechanism. Side tasks can prove valuable here: you can pick up Gilda's lost axe and discover a secret treasure room with a basketball hoop!

Speak with Jack Trade at the entrance screen. The playing card tells you that the passage to Oswald is closed, unless you can open the big gate doors. One method involves defeating all of the enemies swarming around the place; the other method involves a difficult puzzle to power the machines operating the gate.

Things to Do

- Battle through the enemies in the front courtyard
- Defeat all enemies or use Paint on the two TVs to open the main gate
- Enter the secret room and claim your rewards
- Find Gilda's axe
- Search the area for power-ups and collectibles
- Climb the spiraling ramp in Oswald's room
- Exit to Mt. Osmore Caverns

Whether you decide to fight it out with the Slopes' enemies or not, you have to pass through the main courtyard many times and will encounter multiple Spatters and Spladoosh Blotlings when you do. Spin move to knock the enemies away, and use Paint or Thinner to gradually reduce the threat.

The puzzles on the courtyard ground can be thinned to reveal pools underneath. If you plan to defeat the enemies, thin out the puzzles with Spatters over them to quickly eliminate some, and then spin move others into them.

You can play tag with each Spladoosh when you want to eliminate it. Run up to the Spladoosh, touch it quickly, then run in a safe direction. If you practice stopping just out of range, you'll explode the Spladoosh before it shrinks back down and falls asleep again. The Spladoosh blast will also stun any Spatters caught in the blast.

A translucent clock hangs on the back wall. Paint that clock and time slows down in the courtyard. Eventually, you can use a Watch sketch for the same effect, which greatly aids your combat prowess.

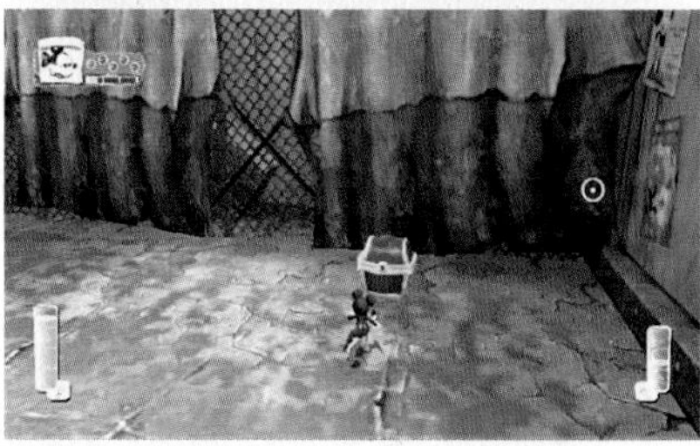

If you dash through the yellow Mickey Mouse Birthday Show poster in the back corner you discover a secret treasure room. Inside, a red chest contains another Gold Pin.

Play the basketball game to capture the *Disney Epic Mickey* extra content. Jump into the steam and let it carry you up toward the hoop. Grab the rim and pull yourself up to win the *Disney Epic Mickey* concept art.

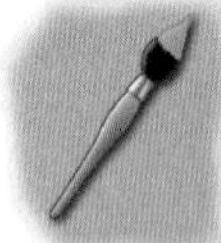

Erase the giant hand to start the platforms that lead to Gilda's lost axe.

4

Exit the secret treasure room and approach the far wall in the courtyard. You'll see a giant hand high up in the right corner. Spray Thinner on this hand to release an anvil. The anvil lands on a pressure plate and activates the moving platforms to your left.

Jump on the first platform when it nears the ground and ride it up. Wait for the second platform to slide close to the first platform and double-jump across to it. Wait for the third platform to slide up and out of the way, then double-jump across to the rooftop in the corner by the Thinner falls.

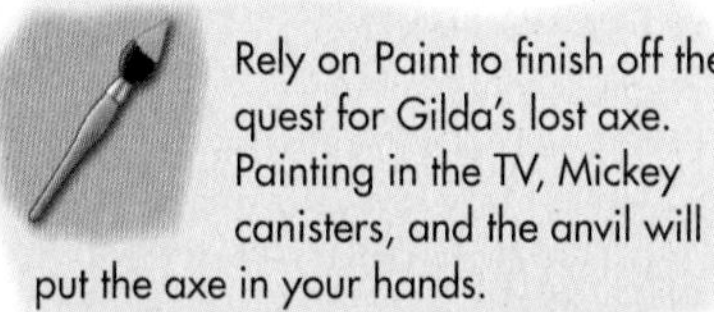

Rely on Paint to finish off the quest for Gilda's lost axe. Painting in the TV, Mickey canisters, and the anvil will put the axe in your hands.

Coat the TV in the junk pile to your right with Paint. This lowers the Thinner falls and reveals a path of debris. Double-jump across this new path to the concrete beyond.

Paint the Mickey canisters to stop the poison gas. Double-jump over to the block and then again to the higher ledge.

Paint in the hanging, translucent anvil ahead of you. The weight of the newly formed anvil lowers the pulley's cable and lifts the wall to your left.

Enter the shack and recover Gilda's lost axe. You can either return the axe to Gilda for a reward, or use the axe in the secret chamber beneath Mt. Osmore Caverns.

If you want to activate the machines to open the main gate, jump up on the anvil on the right side of the courtyard and jump again to reach the snowy ledge. You're safe from enemies up on this ledge. Paint the Mickey canister to stop the toxic gas, jump up on the crate, then double-jump up to the next snowy ledge.

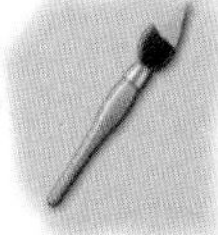

Use Paint to bypass the Mickey canister and activate the first TV near the Tic Tac Toe board.

The machine that operates the gate is on your left. You can see the first TV you need to activate in the small compartment above the ledge you're on. Shoot Paint through the broken fencing and activate the first TV.

Paint in the missing Tic Tac Toe blocks so that it's easier to cross the next section. Wait until the blocks are flat to jump onto them. When they're angled, it's easy to slip through the cracks and go splat. Double-jump from one flat block to the next to gain the other side.

A Sweeper guards the area. Spin move repeatedly to keep the Sweeper off balance and move it slowly toward the ledge. Swat the Sweeper over the side to get rid of it without firing a Paint or Thinner gush.

Jump on the wooden platform inside the machine and over the small Thinner pool. Paint the hanging translucent anvil. The anvil's weight pulls the wooden platform up. Double-jump to your left and onto the platform before the anvil hits the Thinner and the elevator drops again.

Climb the rotating gear platforms. Time your jumps to land on a platform just after it has flipped. If you need some help, slow down time by painting in the clock above the gears.

Double-jump off the last rotating gear platform and onto the ledge in front of the smashers. Watch the pattern and jump (not double-jump!) across the spike pit and onto the second platform when the smasher is fully raised. The second smasher pushes upward, but it's the same principle: wait until the smasher is fully lowered before crossing with a single jump. One more safe jump gets you across without a nick.

Walk on the elevator at the end and shoot Paint straight up to deactivate the Mickey canister. Before the toxic gas

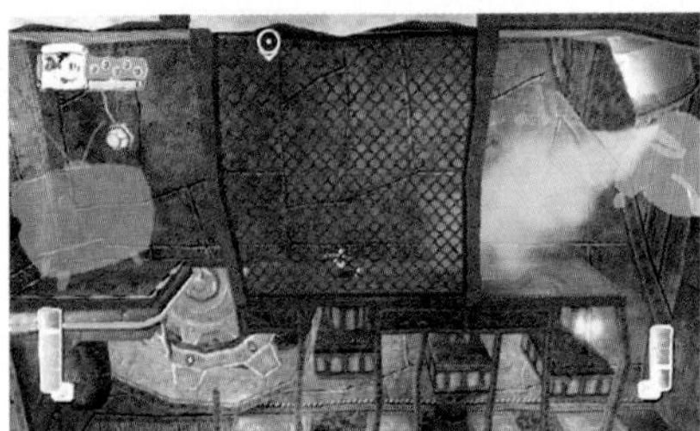

turns back on, double-jump to the higher platform and rush to the left out of range.

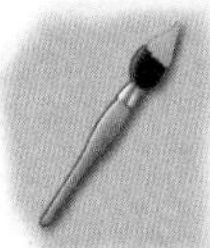

Paint in the second TV at the top of the machine to open the main gate.

With a coat of Paint, the second TV activates and the main gates open. You've successfully entered Oswald's domain with minimal casualties.

Enter the long passage and stop in Oswald's room. Gus explains Oswald's history to you, and you finally understand that Oswald was the first cartoon to be forgotten and that he built this place in remembrance of lost toons like himself.

After hearing Oswald's tale, ascend the spiraling stairs. Fill in any big holes with Paint to provide a safer surface. At the top, enter the room into Mt. Osmore Caverns.

Mt. Osmore Caverns

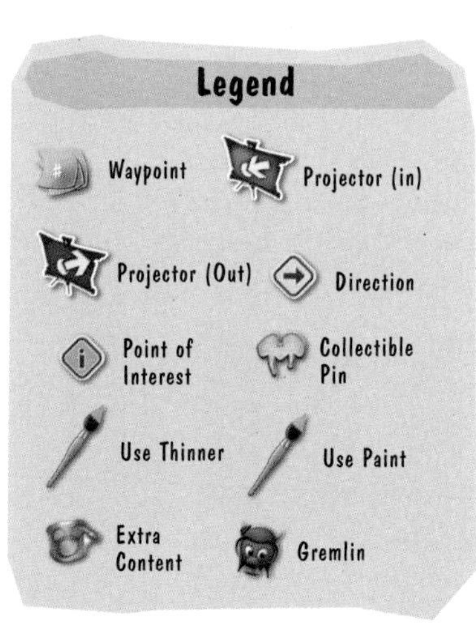

Level Overview

You've finally made it to Oswald's throne room and can almost speak with the toon in charge. First, however, you must pass the Ace of Spades and his three challenges. Each 2D level is based on one of Oswald's original cartoons, and you have to master them to pass the guards and get an audience with him. Don't forget about the secret passage in the throne room floor; there's a whole hidden level under the throne room!

1

You've arrived in Oswald's throne room. Except, there's no Oswald; only his playing card guards. You have to defeat three 2D challenges to pass the guards and speak with Oswald in the next room.

Things to Do

- **Explore the hidden underground level (if you use Gilda's lost axe)**
- **Speak with the Ace of Spades**
- **Beat the "Trolley Trouble" challenge**
- **Beat the "Great Guns" challenge**
- **Beat the "Oh, What a Knight" challenge**
- **Search the area for power-ups and collectibles**
- **Speak with Oswald**
- **Exit back to OsTown**

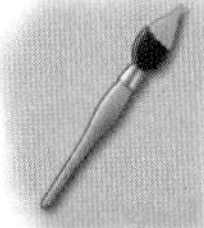

If you spray the floor with Thinner, it opens a secret passage to a whole hidden, underground level.

2

If you can hold off on rushing to Oswald right away, explore the secret level under the throne room first. Spray Thinner on the floor to reveal a ramp down to the underground chambers.

To enter the secret level, you need to remove Gilda's lost axe. If you don't want to remove the axe, you can't enter, but you get a reward from Gilda.

You'll need both your Thinner and Paint skill in the secret level. First, thin out the Oswald faces to prevent toxic gas from blocking your path.

Assuming you remove Gilda's axe, the gate opens and you'll see a series of toxic gas nozzles. Thin out the ears on the first two faces to stop the gas, and erase the face on the third one to halt the green toxins.

After the toxic gas, Paint all the miniature representations of Wasteland around the castle.

Double-jump over to the next platform and paint both sides of the translucent objects. Miniature representations

of Wasteland appear and activate the machinery in the area. The more things you paint in around the castle high above you, the closer you get to the castle as the islands rise.

Continue to double-jump from island to island and spray Paint on the various Wasteland places. When you get to the Tomorrow City platform, jump up on top and turn to face the castle.

Leap off the Tomorrow City platform and double-jump to the castle platform.

Thin out all castle parts so you can climb to the top and jump off for the first pin.

Blast the castle turrets with Thinner. You now have a gap to jump through and access the castle's upper level.

Remove the castle rooftop and jump up on the flattened area.

Double-jump off the rooftop and land on the Mickey statue ear. From the ear, double-jump again to reach the upper platform with the Gold Pin.

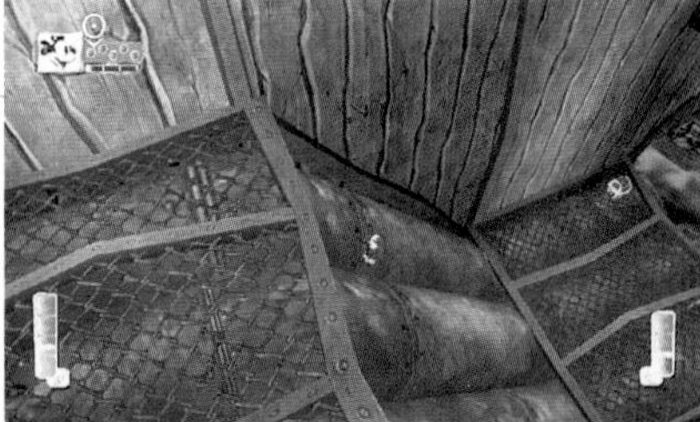

Drop below the Gold Pin platform and slide down to the bottom platform. While riding the Thinner stream, thin out any objects you can to make passage safer.

Thin out the gate on the right side of the Thinner stream. Jump on the next piece of floating garbage and follow the stream out of the room.

Double-jump up on the first overhang and land atop it. If you don't jump, the overhang will knock you into the Thinner. Wait for the next garbage barge and drop down onto it.

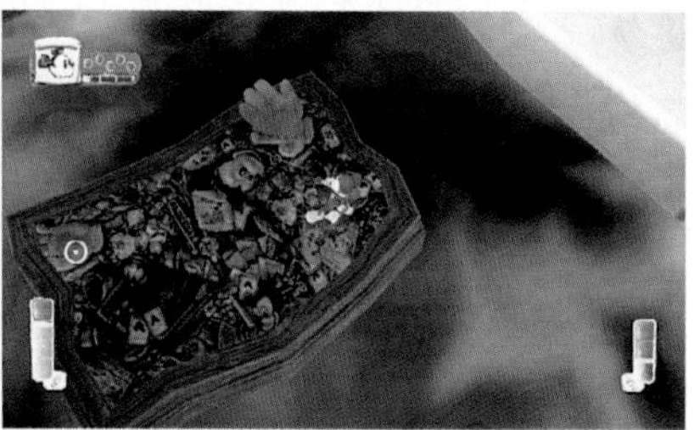

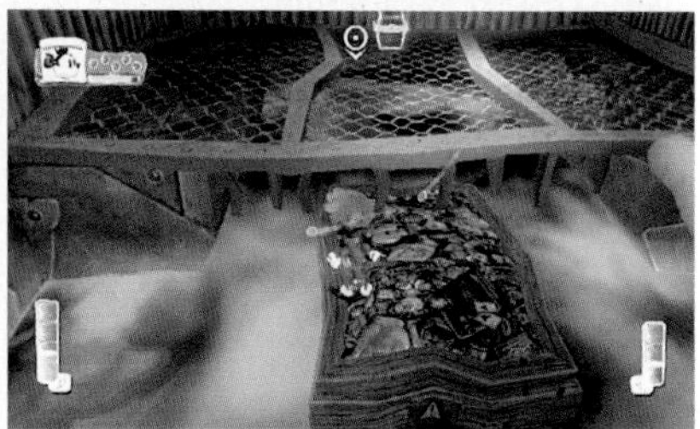

Repeat the process until you land successfully on the steel grate with the final treasure chest.

Open the chest for the Mickeyjunk Mountain Pin. The nearby gate rises and you're back in the original passage that leads back up to Oswald's throne room.

Speak with the Ace of Spades. He only lets you talk to Oswald after you've completed the three challenges. After he gives you one, look for the green traffic light and head through that projector screen.

Extra Content: Oswald's Throne

This is an easy one to find, but easily missed if you rush in to speak with Oswald. Before you enter, or before you embark on any of the three challenges, climb up on the upper balcony with Oswald's throne. The concept art floats behind the throne.

Complete all three challenges and the Ace of Spades opens the door into Oswald's inner sanctum. After you grab the Oswald's Throne concept art, enter and finally get some answers from Oswald.

NOTE

The following three 2D levels represent the challenges the Ace of Spades gives you in Oswald's throne room. Complete them to advance and speak with Oswald.

Trolley Trouble

You arrive near the tracks of a trolley car. Watch out for elevated platforms, lingering cattle, and damaged sections of track as you cross over the mountaintops.

Hop onto the trolley car's roof to set it in motion.

As the trolley rolls along the tracks, it stretches and shrinks at predetermined locations. Wait for the trolley to stretch up, and collect the e-ticket on your way to the first obstacle.

When the trolley shrinks back down, jump over the wooden beams to the right. Grab the e-ticket above the beams, and land on the trolley as it follows the tracks below you.

Wait for the trolley to stretch back up, and hop onto the platform ahead of you. Stay put, and allow the trolley to stop at the nearby signal.

A stray cow blocks the tracks near the signal. Drop onto the trolley car, and move to the edge of the roof.

Jump over to the lever on the next platform. Use the spin move to activate the lever and clear the cow from the tracks. If you've taken any damage, grab the health power-up above the lever. Wait for the trolley to pass under the platform.

Hop onto the trolley as it stretches back up, and leap across to the next platform before the trolley shrinks again.

Jump onto the trolley as it continues up the hill. Collect the e-tickets above the tracks, and hop onto the next platform.

Jump over to the lever ahead of you, and grab the health power-up to recover from any injuries.

Use the spin move on the lever to open the gate below you. Hop back to the trolley before it continues down the tracks.

When the trolley passes through the gate, it quickly picks up speed. To collect the film reel, stay on the trolley until you reach the end of the tracks.

If you choose to collect the e-tickets above the tracks, make sure you land safely on the trolley between each jump.

Watch for the damaged section of track near the end of the slope. As the trolley car rolls toward the drop, prepare to leap over to the right.

When the trolley begins to fall, double-jump over to the platform ahead of you. Collect the film reel when you land.

Drop from the platform's right side to grab an e-ticket, You can activate the exit screen right away, but consider collecting one final e-ticket first. Move left, and follow the tracks to the edge of the water.

Jump over to grab the e-ticket and land on the roof of the trolley. With the extra weight, the trolley quickly sinks. Turn around and jump back to the right before the trolley disappears.

Run along the tracks to find the exit screen to the right. When you're ready, activate the projector to complete the Ace of Spade's first challenge.

Great Guns

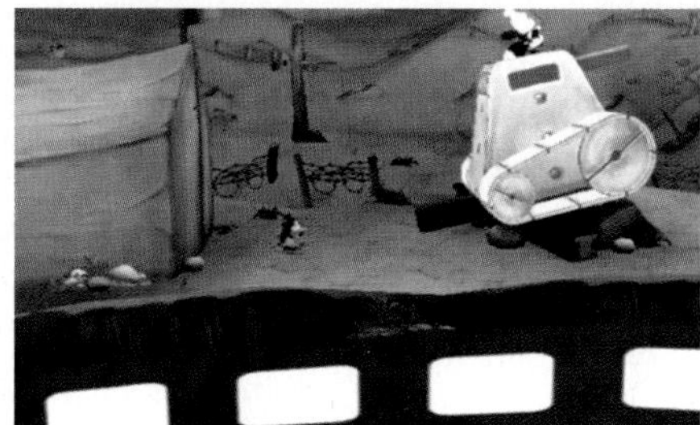

You enter a battlefield cartoon, full of tanks, barbed wire, enemy machine guns, and the occasional bomb to shake you up.

Jump up on the first tank's tread.

Use the first tank to spring up and land on the dead tree branch overhead. Either use the second branch to jump on the flying plane (the upper path) or jump down to the trench (the lower path).

If you take the upper path, leap over to the circling plane and stand in the middle near the cockpit.

When enemy bullets shoot toward you, jump to avoid them. Double-jump to reach the e-tickets in the clouds. Time your jumps to avoid falling off the plane and landing on the lower path.

A second plane appears as the first plane starts to circle back. Jump from the first plane to the second. Grab a health power-up in the sky near where the planes intersect if you need it.

Ride the second plane as it dives, then make the final leap to the dead tree with the film reel. This is the only way to reach the film reel, and it's a great shortcut to the exit projector.

If you stick to the ground (the main lower path), leave the first tank behind and jump down to the first trench. Pick up all red e-tickets as you dodge the various obstacles along the battlefield.

There are two cannons ahead. Wait until the first one fires, hop up on the ledge, and jump atop the first cannon's barrel.

Wait for the second cannon to fire, then leap over the barrel to avoid a cannonball to the gut. You can pick up a health power-up above the broken wall behind the twin cannons.

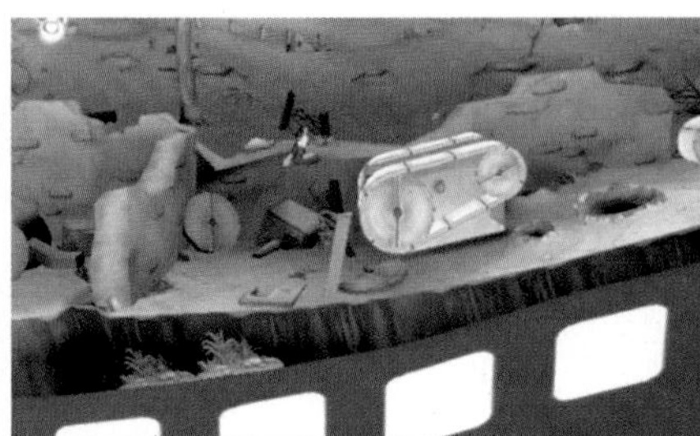
Skip over the broken wall, and jump over the barbed wire to the downed tank on the far side. If you hit barbed wire, it bounces you back and removes one health pip.

Stand on the downed tank and wait for the overhead plane to drop its bomb into the crater just past the tank. Double-jump up to snatch the next e-ticket and carry on.

Hop up on the tread of the next friendly tank. Wait a few seconds and it drives forward.

From the friendly tank, leap over the next barbed wire fence, then double-jump up on the broken wall. Jump to reach a health power-up or slide down to grab an e-ticket as you land behind the next cannon.

Vault over the cannon after it fires and drop down into the lower trench.

Double-jump out of the trench and land in front of the next cannon.

After the cannon fires, double-jump over the barrel and land behind it.

You've now reached the dead tree with the film reel floating above the left branch. The tree's right branch holds a machine gunner. Wait for the bullets to rain down and then run behind them as they spray to the right.

Approach the final cannon. Perform a spin move to lower the barrel and point it at the nearby building.

The exit projector is hidden inside the building. The lowered cannon blasts through the wall and opens the area.

Leap off the cannon barrel and pull the skyward e-tickets toward you as you drop into the building.

You've made it to the end and completed the Ace of Spade's second challenge.

Oh, What a Knight

You appear on a road leading to a medieval castle. Crocodiles protect the moat outside the walls, while mechanical guards patrol the castle. It's up to you to face the castle's mighty knight and rescue the damsel in distress.

Move to the right and double-jump over the donkey. Grab the e-ticket, and land near the edge of the moat.

The moat is filled with crocodiles that dive under the water at regular intervals. Wait for the first crocodile to burst through the water's surface, and stay away from its snapping jaws.

When the first crocodile settles on the water, jump across and land on its head. Hop across the three crocodiles before they dive back down, and grab the e-tickets on the way to the castle.

Enter the castle and double-jump over the guard to the right. Be sure to avoid the tip of the guard's sword. When you land, slowly approach the door to the right.

Stop moving when the door begins to shake. Wait for the lion to pop out from behind the door, and jump on its head. Double-jump up to the left and land by the lever.

Spin move near the lever to lower the drawbridge. Grab the health power-up if you've suffered any damage. Collect the e-tickets on the drawbridge and return to the lever.

Face the guard to the right. Wait for the guard to march away, then jump across the gap.

Hop over the guard and continue through the hole in the wall.

When you land, use your spin move to activate the lever. Jump across the platforms as they move out from the wall. Grab the e-ticket and health power-up above the first platform, but continue up before the platforms retract into the wall.

When you reach the ledge, the knight charges in with his lance. Stand on the elevated section of the ledge to avoid the knight's attack.

Face back to the left. Wait for the guard to turn its back, and double-jump up to the next ledge.

Wait for the guard to march toward you, and jump over to the lever. Use the spin move on the lever to activate another group of moving platforms.

When the guard turns around, double-jump over to the elevated section at the end of the ledge. Wait for the first platform to move out from the wall, and jump up to the right.

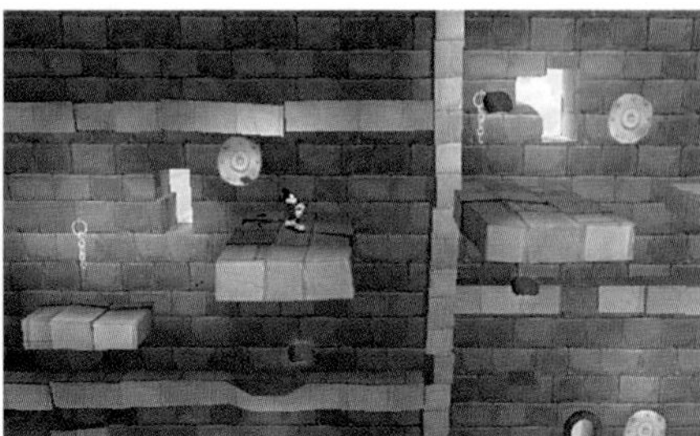

Jump across the moving platforms to collect some e-tickets and proceed to the balcony ahead of you.

The damsel on the opposite balcony is expressing her affection with floating hearts. Wait for a heart to float under the e-ticket to the right.

Hop onto the heart and grab the e-ticket, then double-jump over to the damsel's balcony.

Continue to the right and pass through the door. Jump across the gap to collect the film reel, then drop down to reach the exit screen.

You can activate the projector right away, or pass through the door to the left for two more e-tickets. Jump over the patrolling guards, and use the health power-up if you've suffered any damage.

When you're ready, activate the exit projector to complete the Ace of Spade's third and final challenge. Return to Oswald's throne room to finally speak with the toon in charge.

Return to OsTown

After your trying adventures on Mickeyjunk Mountain, you return to scenic OsTown. You'll see all your favorite toons here, plus a few new ones. Note that Moody won't be around if you accidentally dropped the safe on him earlier, and Telephone won't be around if you had him disassembled by a certain vengeful gremlin.

Gilda is a new face in OsTown. She's migrated from Mean Street and offers you a power spark if you returned her lost axe. She also has a new race for you, which takes you in a circle around OsTown before ending on the thin strip of land behind the Old Gag Factory and alongside the Thinner pool. You earn a power spark for completing the race.

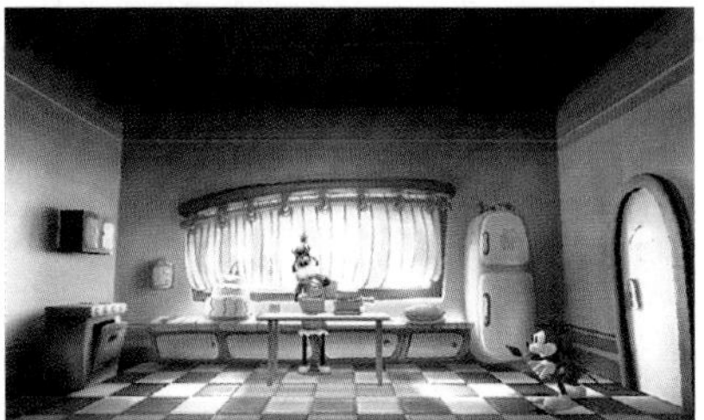

Don't forget to continue any quests you may be on, such as seeing Clarabelle for the pie and/or cake optional quests. When you're finished visiting OsTown again, jump through the projector screen and return to Mean Street.

NOTE

Going back and forth to Mean Street and OsTown takes you through the same 2D level: "Thru the Mirror." See the walkthrough in the "Mean Street and OsTown" chapter for complete details on heading from Mean Street to OsTown. When you return to Mean Street, simply reverse the instructions.

OsTown Continuing Quests

- Back to Mean Street

Go back to Mean Street to see what's happened while you were away.

- Deliver the Cake to Horace

Take the cake to Horace at the Detective Agency in Mean Street. With the ice cream you provided, Clarabelle created a wonderful confection for Horace.

- Deliver the Pie to Horace

Take the pie Clarabelle baked and deliver it to Horace Horsecollar in Mean Street.

Return to Mean Street

You meet Oswald back in Mean Street. He reminds you to go to Tomorrow City to rendezvous with him at the rocket. First, though you must fix the projector screen to Tomorrow City.

Optional Mean Street Quests

- Bunny Roundup I

Round up the Bunny Children by luring them to the pipe sitting next to the City Hall.

- Confront Petetronic

Big Bad Pete wants Petetronic to get with the program.

- Detective Mickey I

Look for clues as to the whereabouts of Horace's lost book. Shifty characters always leave behind clues. Sometimes toon footprints can be revealed with Paint.

- Find Dog Tags

Help Horace solve the case of the missing dog. Horace wants you to find dog tags in Tomorrow City, where the missing dog was seen last.

- Tomorrow City Projector Screen

Talk to Gremlin Markus about fixing the Tomorrow City projector screen.

Speak with Gremlin Markus in front of the Penny Arcade. He can fix the Tomorrow City screen if you can gather five power sparks for him. Once you do, you're free to head to Tomorrow City whenever you like.

Depending on how many optional quests you've completed, you may already have the five power sparks. If not, you can buy power sparks in the Emporium, beginning at 50 e-tickets. The Usher gives you one as a reward if you turn in enough film reels.

To have some fun in Mean Street or pocket some more power sparks, complete more optional quests. First, speak with Big Bad Pete in the City Hall to pick up the "Bunny Roundup I" quest. Head outside to the courtyard, and you'll have Bunny Children on you in no time. Slowly wade over to the pipe between the City Hall and the Fire Station. Get close enough and the pipe sucks up the Bunny Children. Return to Big Bad Pete for the power spark and the "Confront Petetronic" quest (which you can't do until Tomorrow City).

Go talk to Horace in the Detective Agency. Give him the cake or pie if you're working on Clarabelle's quests, and graciously accept the rewards.

Horace also gives you the "Detective Mickey I" quest. When you exit the Agency, you see blue footprints leaving the doorway and traveling down to the Cinema. The footprints go up the Cinema wall and lead to the roof.

Jump up the Cinema facade to gain the rooftop. Speak with Shifty and offer him 50 e-tickets to buy Horace's book back. Return to Horace for your reward. Horace also gives you the "Find Dog Tags" quest for later use.

When you've had your fill on this visit on Mean Street, return to the projector area. You see the new screen flickering for a trip to Tomorrow City. Journey through the Plutopia: Part 1 2D level to reach Tomorrow City.

Plutopia: Part I

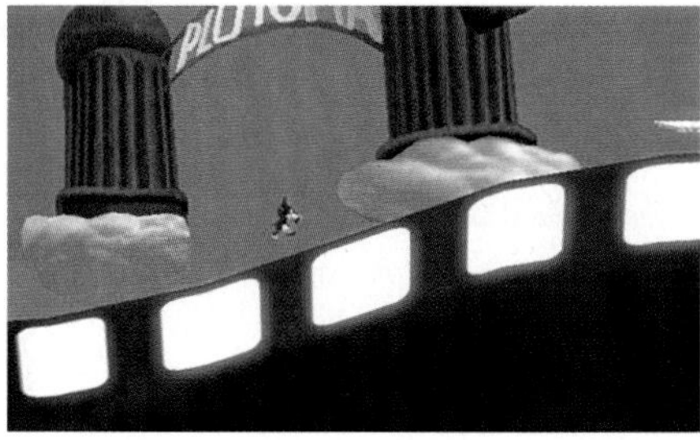
You arrive at the gates of a doggie paradise. Bones and fire hydrants stretch as far as the eye can see, and cleavers stand at the ready to chop fresh meat.

Move to the right, and approach the floating doormat past the gates.

Hop onto the doormat, and ride up along the front of the house. When you're within range, jump onto the rooftop.

Drop down the chimney to collect the e-tickets inside the house.

Exit to the left and hop onto the doormat. Use the doormat to return to the rooftop.

When the hydrant erupts, jump over the chimney and land on the stream of water. If you've taken any damage, jump straight up to grab the health power-up.

Jump along the bones and grab the e-tickets above the stairs. If you fall to the ground, simply use the hydrant to return to the bones.

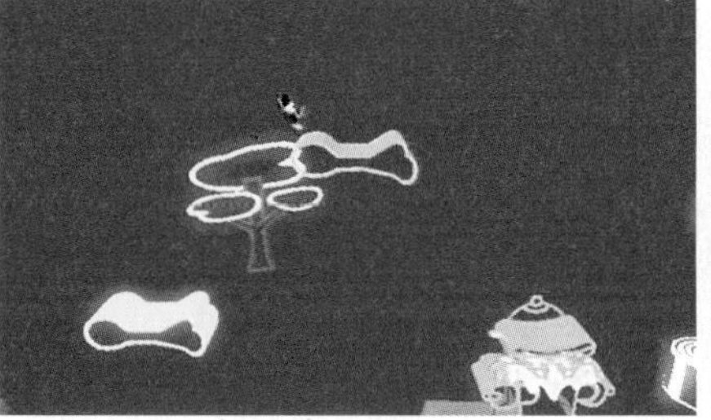
When you reach the third bone, jump onto the hydrant at the top of the stairs. Grab the e-ticket and health power-up above you, and wait for the water to die down. You can continue to the right, or drop to the left for an extra e-ticket.

If you like, head back to the left. Grab the e-ticket in the doorway, and return to the fire hydrant at the top of the stairs.

Hop onto the hydrant, and wait for the cleaver to chop down. Double-jump over the cleaver to collect the e-tickets, and land safely on the other side of the stump.

Move to the cat just past the cleaver. You can see the film reel above the tree to the right, and the cat is holding a sausage link. Grab the nearby health power-up if needed.

Use the spin move on the cat to free the sausage link, and jump back over to the fire hydrant.

Wait for the hydrant to erupt, and ride to the top of the stream. Hop to the bone on the right, and double-jump over to the sausage link.

Jump to the right, and collect the film reel above the tree.

Drop to the ground, and jump over the cleaver to the right. Continue onto the row of hydrants.

Jump across the hydrants to collect the e-tickets above you. If you're running low on health, drop down to collect the two health power-ups between the hydrants.

Continue to the right to find the exit screen.

When you're ready, activate the exit projector to complete the level.

TOMORROW CITY

Notilus

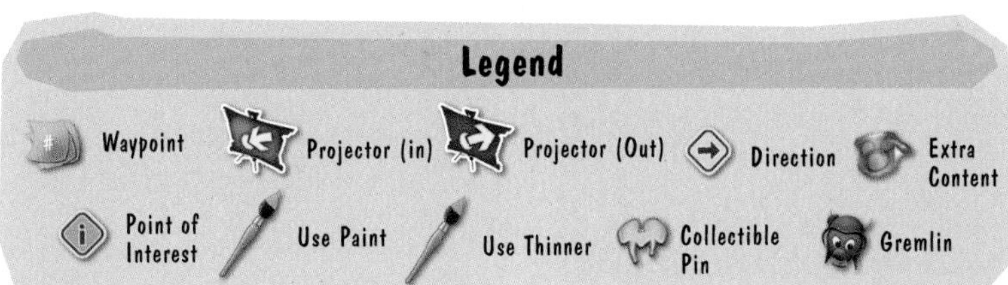

Things to Do

- Paint the gears hidden around the temple
- Repair the first crane
- Collect Goofy's Right Leg
- Repair the second crane
- Free Gremlin Starr
- Take the Notilus to Tomorrow City Lagoon

Level Overview

The Notilus, a submarine needed to reach Tomorrow City, is submerged in the center of an ancient temple. Two cranes were erected to pull the Notilus above what used to be water, but the project was abandoned after the Thinner Disaster. Repair the cranes and pull the Notilus to the surface to continue your travels. Search the area for the temple's hidden treasures.

Gremlin Gus explains that before you can reach Tomorrow City, you'll have to raise the Notilus above the Thinner. Two cranes have been erected for just this purpose. Unfortunately, the Thinner Disaster struck before the cranes were completed, and it's up to you to get them running.

Tomorrow City Quests

- Collect All Rocket Parts

Collect all of the rocket parts scattered all over Wasteland by the Mad Doctor.

- Defeat the Slobber

Defeat the Slobber and move through the Carousel of Progress and onward to Tomorrow Square!

- Enter Space Voyage

Enter Space Voyage. Repairing the rocket ride is one step in clearing a path to Space Voyage.

- Find the Elevator

Confront Petetronic. Find the elevator that leads to Petetronic's arena.

- Open the path to the Great Big Tomorrow

Disable the Thinnerfall to enter the Great Big Tomorrow. Fix the valve system to shut down the Thinnerfall. Once it's stopped, the door to Great Big Tomorrow can open.

- Raise the Notilus

Figure out how to raise the Notilus. Get the two cranes operational again by using your Paint and Thinner abilities.

Tomorrow City Quests (cont'd)

- Redeem or Defeat Petetronic

Use your spin move to deflect Petetronic's discs. Deflect Petetronic's discs back at him. Then, when the moment is right, fill him with Paint or Thinner!

- Repair the Rocket Ride

Find the mechanisms that prevent the rocket ride from functioning and repair them.

- Restore the Pipes

Restore the pipe system. Restoring the pipes will repair the pistons, giving you access to the launchpad.

- Shut Down the Valves

Turn the valves here to shut off the Thinnerfall. Find the valves that control the steam pressure and turn them off. Follow the pipes to locate them.

- Talk to Mister Rover

Move to Tomorrow Square! Mister Rover opens the way for you to move to Tomorrow Square.

- UFO Challenge

Investigate the UFO. Go check out that downed UFO in the sea of Thinner.

2

Thinner has flooded much of the temple floor, so first you must find a way across to the cranes. Move out of the hallway and hop to the column segment on your right. Two Spatters patrol the area ahead. Spatters may not be the toughest enemies, but the pool of Thinner makes the encounter a bit more dangerous; a single head butt can send you flying for double the damage.

The column segment provides a safe path across the Thinner, and also serves as a great perch when dealing with the Spatters. Use Paint or Thinner to take out both Spatters, then hop down to the floor.

3

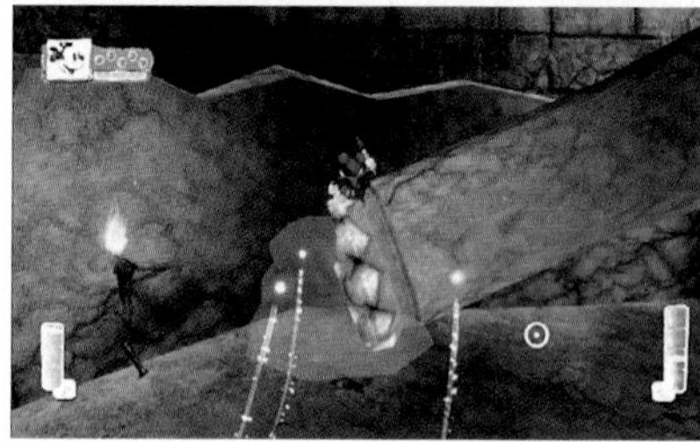

You've managed to reach the base of the first crane, but don't be so quick to head up. Examine the columns along the temple wall; one of them sits atop a painted base. Spray Thinner at the base to topple the column. After the crash, jump onto the column and run to the top.

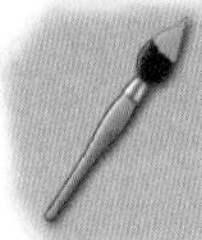

Thin the base of the column near the first crane to create a path to a hidden gear.

Jump across the columns to reach the gear hidden up high on the temple wall. Stand on the platform below the gear, and use Paint to get things moving. As the gears rotate, Gus notices a welcome addition to the environment. Two pillars emerge from the Thinner, opening a path to the second crane.

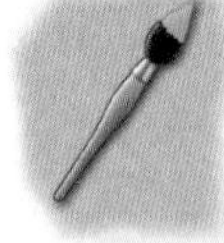

Paint the hidden gear near the temple entrance to open new paths across the Thinner.

Before you drop from the platform, look for the golden ticket above the temple entrance. The ticket is on the far side of the entrance, atop a narrow column. Double-jump toward the ticket, then use your spin move to land on the first column. Double-jump over to the golden ticket and drop back to the first crane.

Move to the base of the first crane and examine the attached platforms. Each platform is connected to a gear, but most of the gears are missing. The first few platforms are already in place, so jump on and continue up the side of the crane. The fourth platform blocks your path, so use your Paint and Thinner to continue. Paint the gear to get the platform moving; when the platform is nearly level, splash the gear with some Thinner to lock the platform in place. Repeat the process on the next platform.

Near the top of the crane, two platforms are attached to a single gear. Wait for both platforms to circle around, then use some Thinner to lock them flat. With the final platforms in position, Gus instructs you to spray Paint on the gear on the end of the crane. Jump to the top of the crane, and paint the gear.

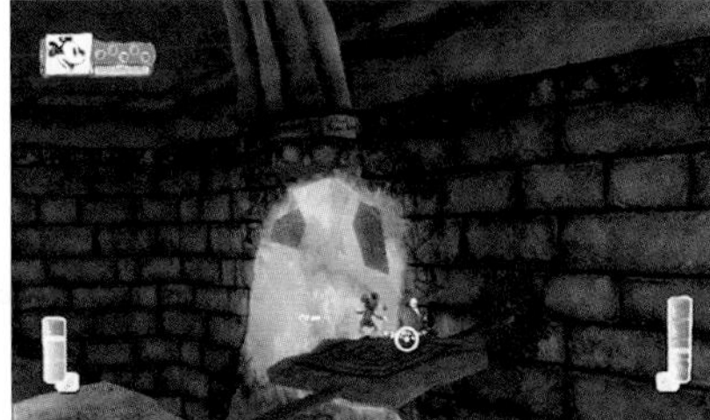

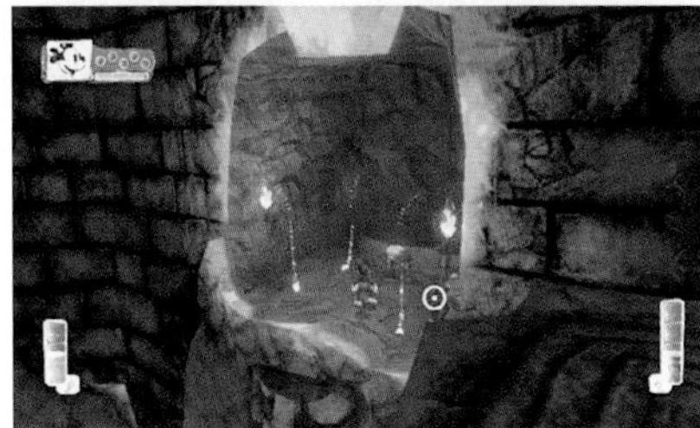

You've got the first crane running, and you're well on your way to raising the Notilus. Before you climb back to the ground, hop back to the two platforms near the top of the crane. Jump across to the second platform to find the crumbling spot on the wall. Spray Thinner on the wall to reveal a hidden chest, then jump down and land in the alcove.

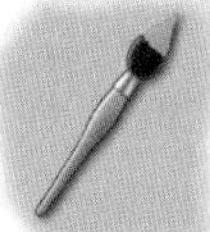

Spray the blue spot on the wall to recover Goofy's Right Leg from the hidden chest.

Goofy's Right Leg

Before his abduction, Animatronic Goofy had been trying to repair the cranes in the temple. Now you can help Goofy pull himself together. Goofy's Right Leg is hidden in a chest behind the removable section of the temple wall. Why not make a quick detour to help a friend in need?

Drop onto the plant below the alcove, then jump to your right and deal with the last remaining Spatter. The nearby column sits atop a painted base, and a stray blast of Thinner can be a real hazard. Use Paint for this encounter, or lead the Spatter away from the column and unleash your Thinner.

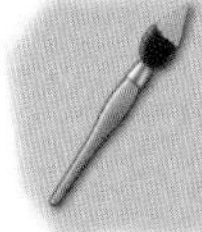

Paint the wall left of the column to reveal a path to the second hidden gear.

Paint the wall near the column to reveal a ledge. If the column is still standing, spray it with some Thinner to create a convenient ramp. If the column has fallen, double-jump to grab onto the ledge's right side and continue up.

When you reach the small rooftop, paint the hidden gear on the temple wall. When the gears begin to turn, two platforms emerge from the giant stone head in the corner.

A tram has somehow crashed into the stone head, and a large piece of the wreckage runs right under the first platform. Hop down to the tram near the wall, then jump up along the platforms. Use Thinner to remove the platform past the next tram section. When a chunk of the sculpture falls to the ground, use some Paint to replace the platform.

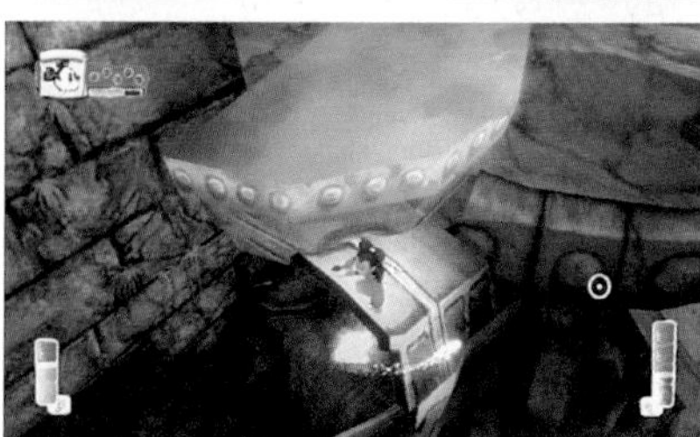

Jump over to the platform and squirt Paint on the temple's third hidden gear to reveal two new pillars. When the gear starts moving, Gus points out the two new pillars near the small structure in the corner. Hop down from the platform and move to the edge of the tram wreckage. Walk over the edge and double-jump to grab the golden ticket inside the tram, then drop to the ground below.

You've landed near the base of the second crane, compete with a familiar set of platforms. If you'd like to make the repairs yourself, use Paint and Thinner just as you did on the first crane. Reposition troublesome platforms, jump up to the top of the crane, and spray the missing gear with a bit of Paint. However, the gremlin trapped in the nearby structure will handle the job in exchange for a timely rescue.

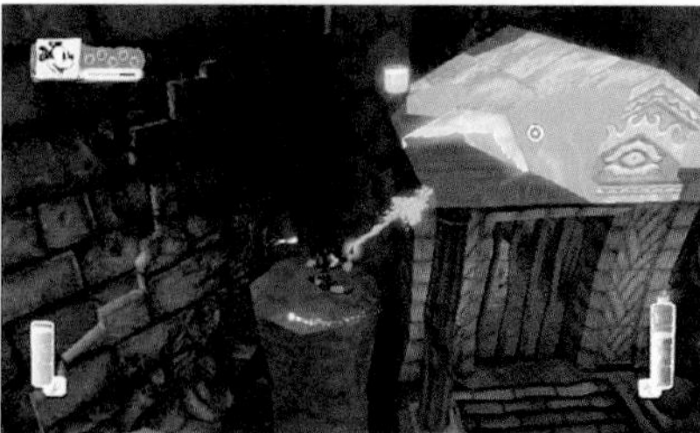

If you'd rather leave the task for faster hands, leap to the stairs in front of the structure. Jump over the Thinner and across to the pillars ahead. Climb up and spray the rooftop with some Thinner, then jump down into the structure to free Gremlin Starr.

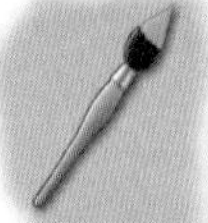

Reach the top of the small structure, and spray Thinner to remove the rooftop.

Gremlin Starr

Gremlin Starr is locked in the small structure in the corner of the temple. Activate the three hidden gears in the temple walls to reveal the two pillars, or climb to the top of the nearby crane. Once you've chosen a path to the structure's rooftop, a little Thinner is all it takes to gain entry. As a show of gratitude, Gremlin Starr completes any repairs on the Notilus raising machine.

Once the second crane has been repaired, the Notilus is pulled to the surface of the Thinner. You can climb aboard for the journey ahead, but you might want to take care of one more piece of business. Paint the fourth hidden gear, located inside the structure with Gremlin Starr to unlock the chamber across the temple. Head to the steps along the temple's north wall to collect another golden ticket, then climb onto the Notilus and activate the onboard projector screen.

Mickey's Mechanical Man: Part 1

You arrive in a makeshift gym. The town has gathered for a boxing match, but one of the fighters can't seem to pull himself together. Dodge surging electricity as you follow the mechanical boxer to the big event.

Jump to the right, and collect the e-ticket above the safe.

Double-jump through the hole in the wall, and drop to the car parked outside. The mechanical man is banging its head against a nearby utility pole.

When you land, the car's horn sends the mechanical man on a rampage through the yard.

Hop over to the downed pole, and continue to the right. Watch for electricity moving along the loose wires. Wait for the surge to die down, and double-jump through the e-tickets.

Make sure you clear the electricity as it travels along the wires. Grab the e-ticket and health power-up while the electricity surges harmlessly behind you.

Stand on the next downed pole and wait for a break in the electricity. When it's safe, double-jump over the exposed wires.

Wait for the electricity to reach the top of the wires, then jump up to grab the e-ticket.

Continue to the right and jump up to grab the e-tickets behind the poster, then jump onto the windowsill.

Hop up and collect the e-tickets to the left. If you need to grab the health power-up above the utility pole, wait for the electricity to die down first.

Continue into the building, and double-jump onto the gorilla.

Hop onto the mechanical man's head, and wait for the gorilla to throw an uppercut. Collect the e-ticket above you, and ride up to the rafters.

When the mechanical man's head pauses at the top of its path, double-jump to reach the rafters on the right.

Move to the right, and jump across the gap in the rafters.

Hop onto the bricks at the end of the rafters. Grab the health power-up if you've taken any damage, and face the lamp to the left. Jump onto the lamp when it swings toward you.

When the lamp swings back to the left, jump toward the gap in the rafters. When you get close to the gap, double-jump to land on the ledge ahead of you.

Hop onto the next lamp and swing over to the left. Leap from the lamp to collect the film reel near the wall.

Hop down to the rafters below you, and drop back down to the ring.

Jump over the fighters, and follow the ring to the right.

Jump onto the bleachers next to the ring, and activate the projector screen to arrive at the Tomorrow City Lagoon.

Tomorrow City Lagoon See map on the following page

Level Overview

High-pressure steam holds the main gate closed, and the overflowing Thinner cascades down to the Lagoon. While Blotlings patrol the walls above, two Beetleworx Spinners keep watch on the docks. Find and activate at least four valves to relieve the pressure on the gate and open the path to Tomorrow Square.

When you arrive at the Lagoon, Gremlin Gus instructs you to find the valves spread across the city walls. Each valve is attached to a steam pipe, and venting excess steam is the only way to open the gate. Follow the pipes to track down every valve and clear the path ahead.

Things to Do

- Defeat a Spinner
- Release the steam valves
- Free Gremlin Wilco
- Stop the flow of Thinner
- Free Gremlin Roger
- Defeat the Blotlings on the UFO
- Enter Great Big Tomorrow

The valves are spread around the area, and you can see two of them as you step off the submarine. When you approach the first valve, Gremlin Gus warns you about the Beetleworx Spinner guarding the docks.

Enemy: Spinner

Spinners are nasty contraptions. These heavily armored and ill-tempered foes use a flurry of whirling blades for a nonstop slicing attack. If a Spinner hits you, it costs you one health pip and knocks you back several feet. Spinners cannot be converted to allies, but you can use a quick burst of Paint to slow one down in an emergency. Use Thinner to melt a Spinner's armor, then move in close for a damaging spin move on the target that's revealed. Vulnerable Spinners recover quickly, so retreat after a successful spin move, then repeat the process to defeat this resilient enemy.

When the Spinner moves in to attack, spray its armor with Thinner until it melts away. With the armor gone, the Spinner flips onto its back. Run in and use a spin move to damage your vulnerable enemy. If your attack hits, the Spinner surges with electricity and knocks you back while it recovers. If you don't land a spin move within a few seconds, the Spinner regenerates its armor and resumes the chase.

If you find yourself cornered by the Spinner, use a blast of Paint to gum up its works. Paint also replenishes any armor you've managed to melt away, so use this technique only when escape is otherwise impossible. Use Thinner to flip a Spinner, and connect with two spin moves to finish it off.

After you deal with the Spinner, return to the valve near the pipe outlet. Spin move near the valve to vent some steam, and slow the flow of Thinner into the Lagoon. Follow the wall past the outlet to search for the next two valves.

The second valve is on the exposed pipe in the wall. Spray the light blue strip running across the ground to reveal the third valve. When you activate the valve on the ground, a large block falls from the wall and floats on the venting steam. Activate the valve on the wall to vent some steam on the wall's first level. The steam melts the bottom half of a large pillar, and the top half comes crashing down next to you. Climb the pillar and jump up to deal with the two Spatters on the wall above you.

Once the Spatters have been either recruited or liquefied, spray some Paint to replace the bottom section of the pillar. Use the pillar to reach the walkway above the wall's first level. Follow the wall to find the Sweeper patrolling the walkway. Move up to the partially painted section in the walkway, and attack the Sweeper from a distance. The Sweeper's Thinner attacks make short work of this removable platform, so stay back until you've won the exchange.

After you've dealt with the Sweeper, spray some Paint to replace any bits of the walkway lost during the encounter. Run to the far end of the painted section, and make a running leap along the walkway. When the trap doors below you fall away, double-jump to land safely on the other side.

Use Paint to restore the entire walkway section. The trap doors ahead leave little room for error, but a smooth approach makes a successful double-jump that much easier to land.

Fill in the next painted section, then double-jump across the second set of trap doors.

When you reach the end of the walkway, hop onto the platform attached to the wall. Jump along the wall to find Gremlin Wilco on the third platform.

Gremlin Wilco

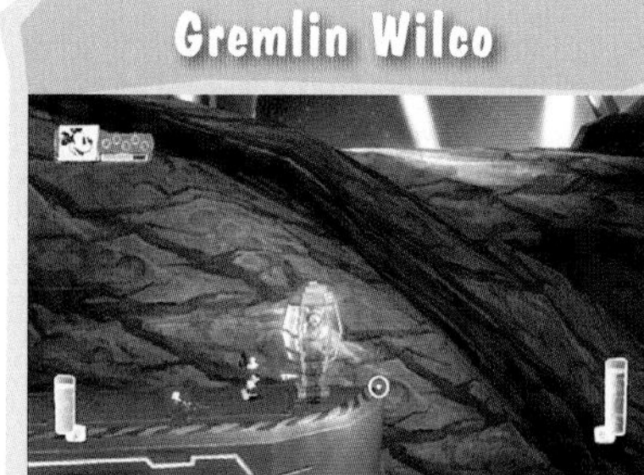

Gremlin Wilco is trapped on a platform high above the Lagoon. When you set him free, he shuts down all the remaining valves, completely stops the flowing Thinner, and opens the gate to Great Big Tomorrow. Freeing Gremlin Wilco is an optional route, but by opening the gate, he gives you a speedy way out of the level, so it is well worth going out of your way to find him. If you eliminate the platform below him, though, you won't be able to reach him, so take care!

When you set Gremlin Wilco free, he uses the control panel to open the path out. Head back across and drop to the wall's first level. Take care of the patrolling Spatter, and look down to find another Spinner guarding the docks. With the gate open, you can leave the Lagoon at any time, but there are few loose ends to wrap up. If you'd like to stay, drop down to the block below you and take out the second Spinner.

You can spray Thinner at the brackets to break the giant hammer loose from the wall. This reveals one of the steam valves, but it also eliminates the path to Gremlin Wilco. Consider your options and plan accordingly.

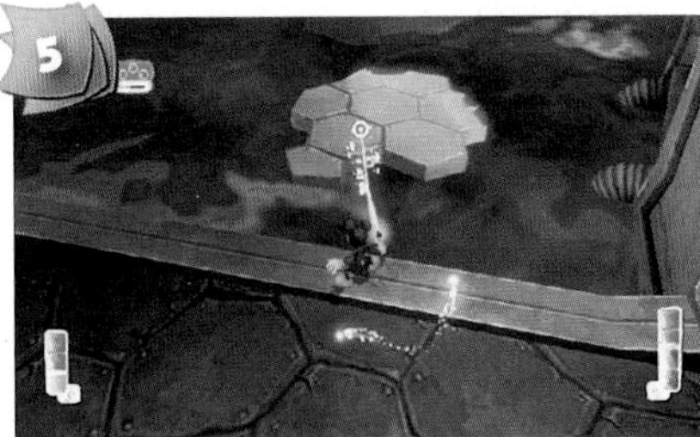

After you defeat the second spinner, find the alcove below the gate. Spray Paint on the platforms near the alcove, then jump over to free Gremlin Roger.

Gremlin Roger

Gremlin Roger is just above the water, behind the sheet of flowing Thinner. Shut down the steam valves to clear a path to Roger and free this grateful gremlin. As a reward, Gremlin Roger offers the "UFO Challenge" optional quest.

When you free Gremlin Roger, he gives you to the "UFO Challenge" optional quest. Hop back up to the dock and paint the platforms leading to the UFO. Spray fresh Paint as needed, and jump to each platform to move across the water. To clear the larger gaps, add a spin move to the end of a double-jump. Cross the platforms all the way to the UFO.

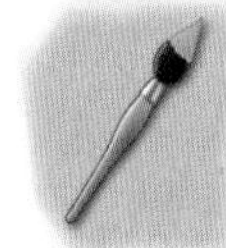

Spray Paint on the platforms above the water, and jump across to the UFO.

Hidden Valves

If you're not interested in freeing Gremlin Wilco, take care of the four remaining valves yourself. Remove the light blue patches on both sides of the gate to find two more valves.

The last two valves are near the second Spinner. One valve is in the pipe on the ground, the other valve is behind the giant hammer. Coat the brackets with Thinner and jump up to the last valve when the hammer falls away. Activate any four valves to open the gate. Activate all seven valves to completely stop the flowing Thinner.

Before you jump over to the UFO, consider a plan of attack. The UFO spawns three Spatters and three Sweepers; this is a lot to handle in such a small area. Because you used a good deal of Paint to reach the UFO, you likely have at least one blue guardian circling you. Jump onto the UFO to begin the challenge. Unleash any guardians you've collected, and defeat all six Blotlings to complete the challenge.

When the battle is over, a chest appears in the middle of the UFO. Open the chest and collect the Bronze Pin.

Bronze Pin

Free Gremlin Roger and complete the "UFO Challenge" optional quest. When you defeat the six Blotlings on the UFO, you're rewarded with this Bronze Pin.

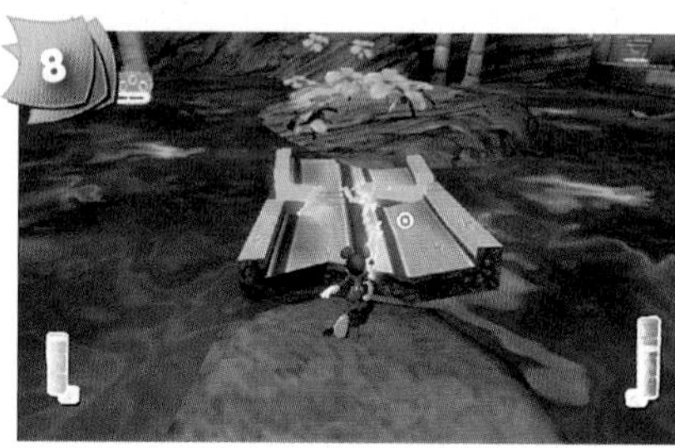

Jump to the rocks near the UFO. Spray Paint on any missing platforms, and follow the path to the edge of the Lagoon.

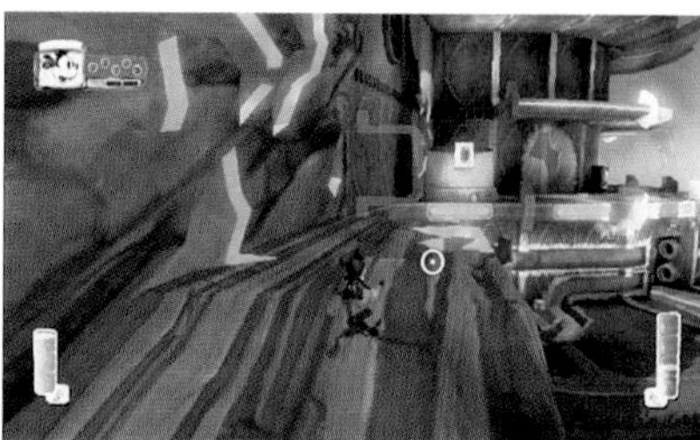

Head up the ramp to return to the dock. Climb up to the wall's first level, and follow it around to the gate.

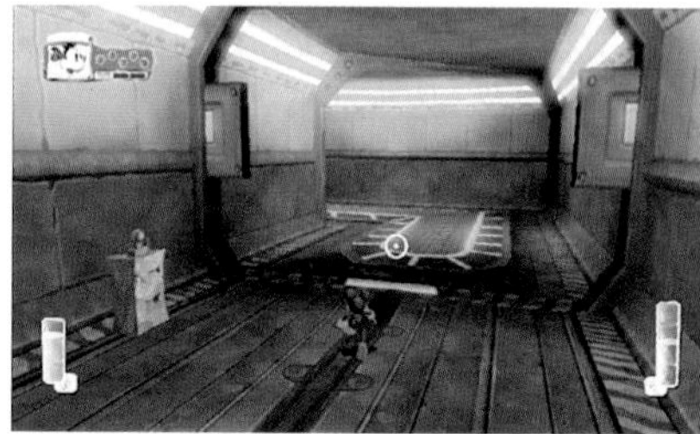

When you're ready to leave, pass through the gate and enter Great Big Tomorrow.

Great Big Tomorrow

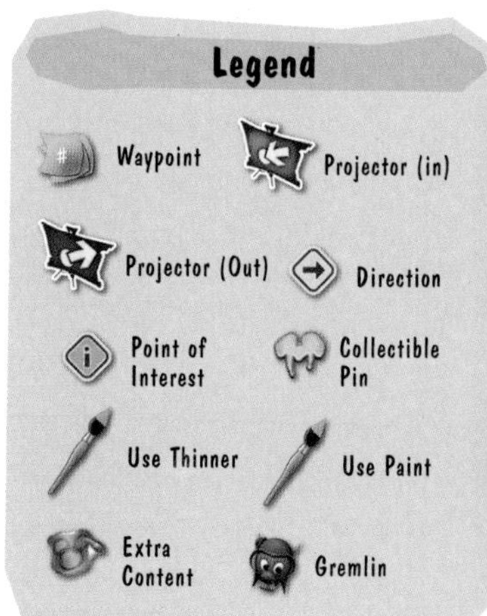

Level Overview

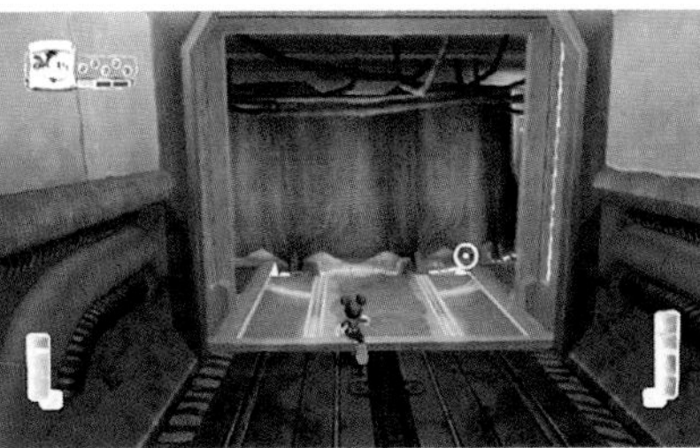

Great Big Tomorrow was designed to show glimpses of the future, but the exhibit has been broken for some time. Mister Rover had nearly repaired the carousel when a Slobber appeared. Use Paint or Thinner to take care of this massive Blotling, and help Mister Rover restore power to the Great Big Tomorrow exhibit.

Gus is excited to see the Great Big Tomorrow exhibit back in action, but the curtains reveal a great big Blotling. This dripping mass is a monstrous foe, and Mister Rover has fled to safety.

Things to Do

- Defeat the Slobber
- Learn about the TV sketch
- Power the carousel
- Talk to Mister Rover
- Take the carousel to Tomorrow Square

NOTE

If you choose to defeat the Slobber with Thinner, you can purchase Goofy's Torso from the Emporium for the hefty fee of 1,000 e-tickets. If you use Paint, you won't be able to collect the Gold Pin.

The Slobber doesn't notice you right away, so take a moment to search the auditorium for Paint, Thinner, and health power-ups.

When you're ready, jump onto the stage to engage the Slobber.

Enemy: Slobber

This extremely tough Blotling has a variety of powerful attacks. The Slobber's fist pound can send you flying, and even cost you a health pip if you're too close to the impact. Its Thinner claws deal double the damage, costing you two health pips and knocking you back with every swipe that connects. When the Slobber attempts to inhale you, spray Paint or Thinner into its mouth.

The Slobber has several attacks and is extremely dangerous in close combat. Keep moving to stay clear of the Slobber's fist pound and claw swipe. The Slobber isn't as slow as it looks; jump over its short-range attacks whenever it catches up to you. Remember to use your lock-on to always keep this nasty enemy in sight.

Dodge the Slobber's attacks and keep moving. When the Slobber spits out puddles of Thinner, it's almost time to

Junction Point: Great Big Slobber

When you battle the Slobber, your choice of Paint or Thinner affects your reward. If you choose Paint, the Great Big Tomorrow carousel rotates to show a pleasant future and presents you with Goofy's Torso. If you use Thinner to defeat the Slobber, the carousel rotates to show a chaotic landscape, and presents you with a Gold Pin for your collection.

fight back. Find a clear path through the Thinner puddles, and wait for the Slobber inhale. Let the Slobber pull you between the Thinner puddles, and aim a stream of Paint or Thinner straight into its mouth.

When the Slobber inhales enough of your Paint/Thinner, it starts to gag and takes a moment to recover. If you reach the Slobber before it gags, jump away to avoid its fist pound. Keep moving and dodge the Slobbers attacks, then continue to blast it with Paint/Thinner any time it inhales.

When the Slobber has consumed enough of your Paint/Thinner, the battle ends and the carousel comes online.

When the carousel rotates, Mister Rover appears and offers you a glimpse of Wasteland's future based on your playstyle. To reward your

victory, Mister Rover presents you with a TV sketch, and Gus instructs you about its uses.

4

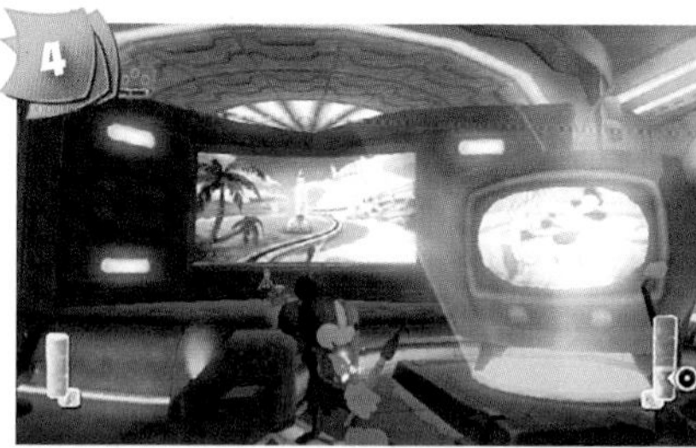

After the tutorial, you appear on a small pad away from the stage. Mister Rover used the last of his energy to reactivate the carousel, and there's not enough power to get it moving again. Use Mister Rover's sketch to drop a TV on the pad. The carousel roars to life, and you're free to continue.

TV Pin

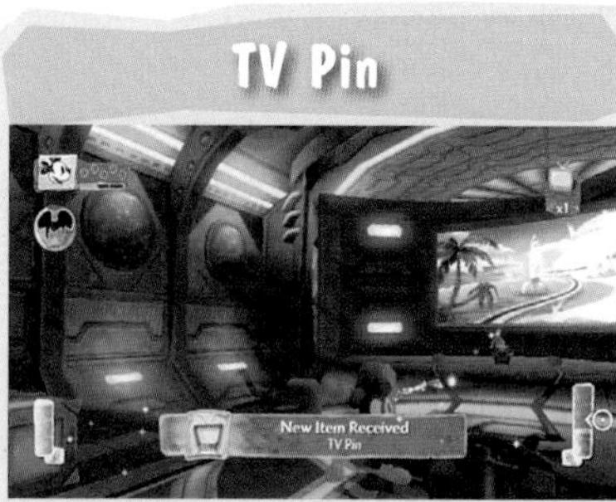

Defeat the Slobber and learn the proper uses of a TV sketch to automatically receive the TV Pin.

5

Head back to the stage and open the chest on the carousel. Depending on your tactics during the Slobber battle, you receive either Goofy's Torso, or a Gold Pin.

Goofy's Torso

If you use Paint to defeat the Slobber, you're rewarded with Goofy's Torso. Animatronic Goofy is sure to appreciate its return.

Gold Pin

Use Thinner to defeat the Slobber and you're rewarded with another Gold Pin for your collection.

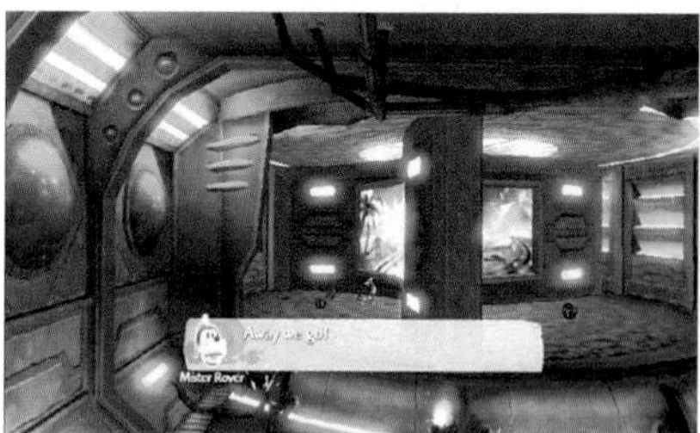

The Slobber has been defeated and the carousel is almost back online. Use a TV sketch to power up the pad and start the carousel, then you're ready to continue your journey. Speak to Mister Rover to rotate the carousel, and follow the corridor to the projector screen.

Plutopia: Part 2

You return to a crazy land of sausage links and fire hydrants. Swinging doors reveal precious items, but falling bones make this visit a little more hazardous.

Move to the right, and wait for the blue door to swing open. Grab the e-tickets and continue up the hill.

Stand on the cracked patch in the ground and wait for the water to shoot up from below.

Jump up to collect the e-tickets above you, then drop to the right. When the green door swings open, grab the e-tickets and move to the top of the hill. Use the health power-up to recover from any damage you might have suffered.

The cat is bouncing on a shovel near another cracked patch in the ground. Use the spin move on the cat to knock the patch loose.

Stand on the patch and wait for the water to shoot up from the ground. Jump up to the red door on the right.

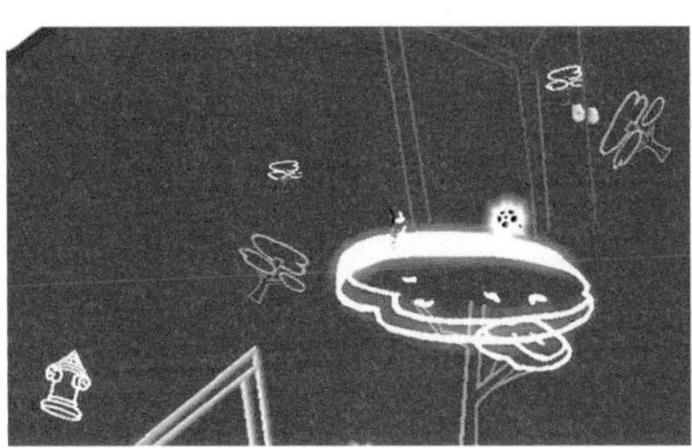

Wait for the red door to swing open, and collect the film reel. Drop to the ground and continue to the right.

When you reach the orange strip on the ground, look for puffs of smoke above you. Each puff of smoke drops two dog bones down the hill. Stay clear of the cracked spots on the ground and let the bones bounce right over you.

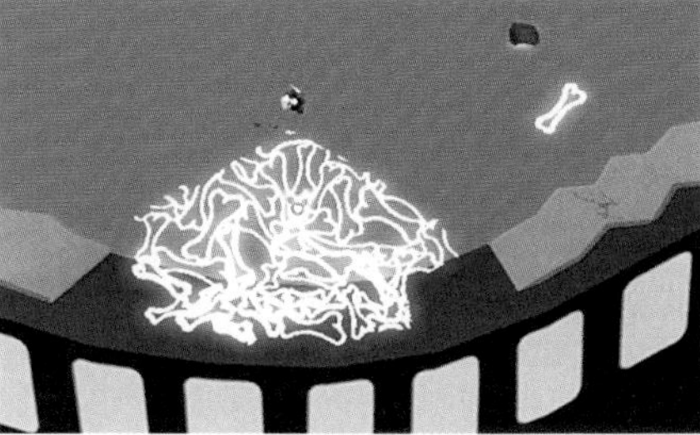

Collect the e-tickets around the bone pile, and grab the health power-up if you've suffered any damage.

Continue right and dodge the bones bouncing down along the next hill.

Wait for the water to drop, and jump over the health power-up under the tree. The cat stands nearby, with a handy sausage link on display.

Use a spin move to knock the cat into the tree. Hop onto the stream of water, and jump up to meet the cat in the tree.

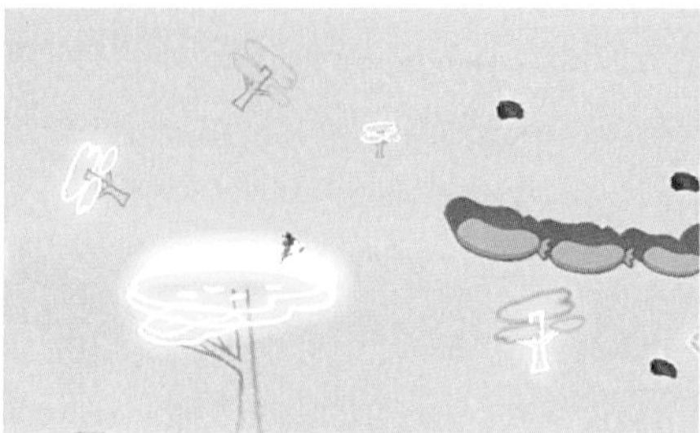

Use another spin move on the cat. The sausage link gets knocked loose, creating a series of platforms.

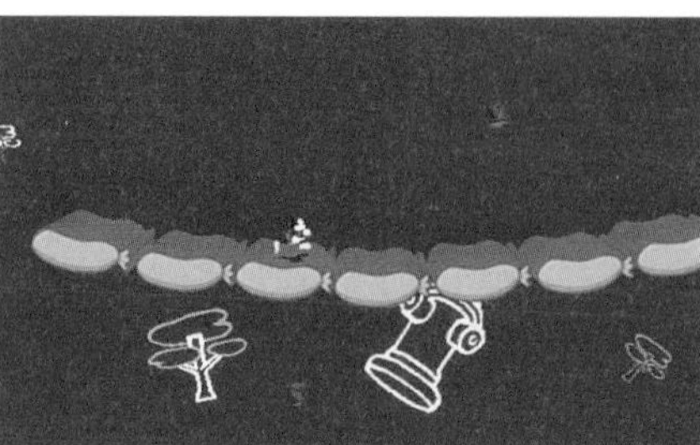

Jump over to the left, and collect the e-tickets along the sausage links.

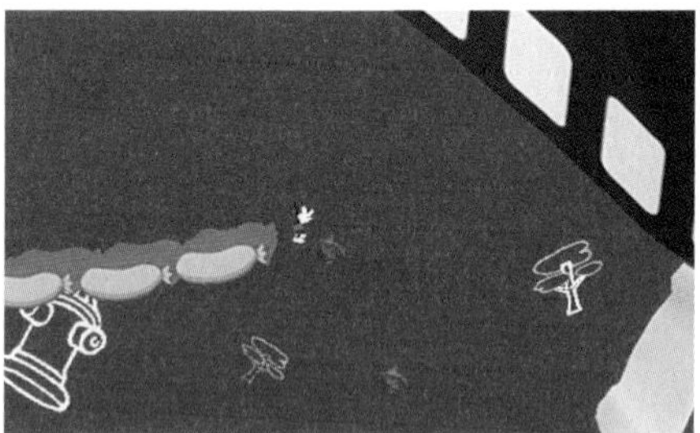

When you reach the end of the sausage links, drop down through the e-tickets.

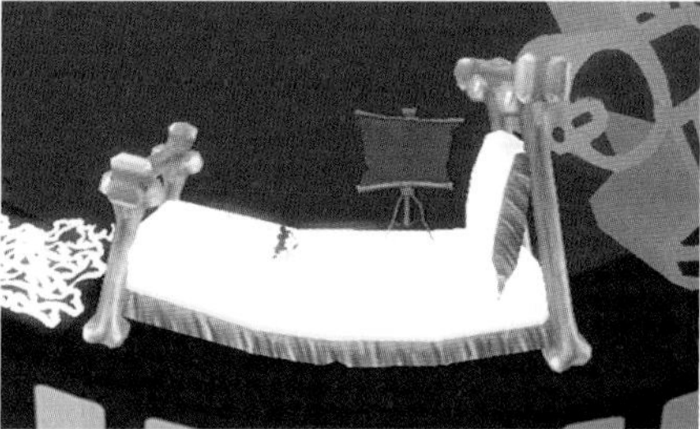

When you land, you bounce off a giant bed. The exit projector is just to the right, and an e-ticket is on the small bone pile to the left.

Jump down and grab the e-ticket, then hop onto the cracked patch in the ground.

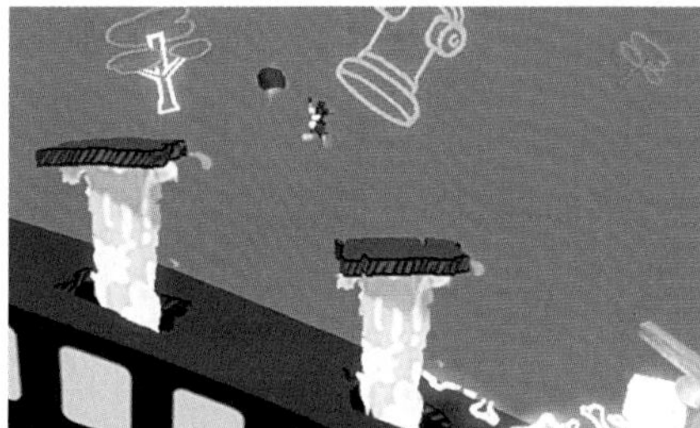

When the water shoots up, jump over and collect the e-ticket and health power-up to the left.

When you're ready, move back to the right and return to the bed. Activate the exit screen to complete the level.

Tomorrow Square

See map on the following page

Level Overview

Reactivate the broken attractions of Tomorrow Square. The rocket ride, sky tram, and people mover are all shut down, and it's up to you to get them running. Fight through the Hoppers, Spinners, and Spatters, and enlist the help of a few gremlins to open the path to Space Voyage.

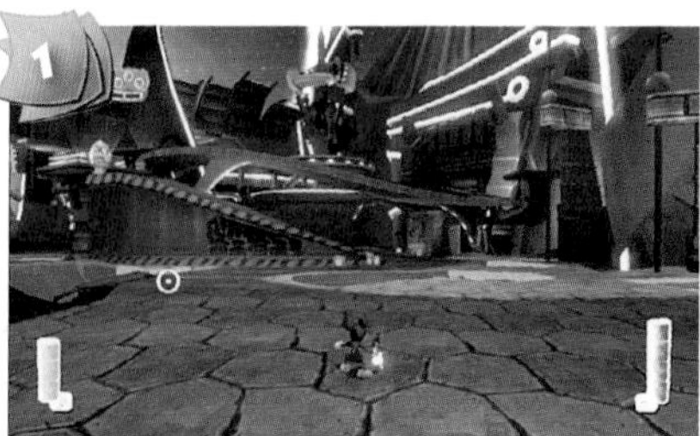

Gremlin Gus tells you to repair the people mover, which opens the path to Space Voyage. He also asks you to try to fix the rocket ride, and suggests you look around for some help. A gremlin's trapped on the ramp just ahead of you.

As you head to the ramp, look out for the Hoppers and Spinners patrolling the area. Any Spinners you defeat are quickly replaced, but consider taking

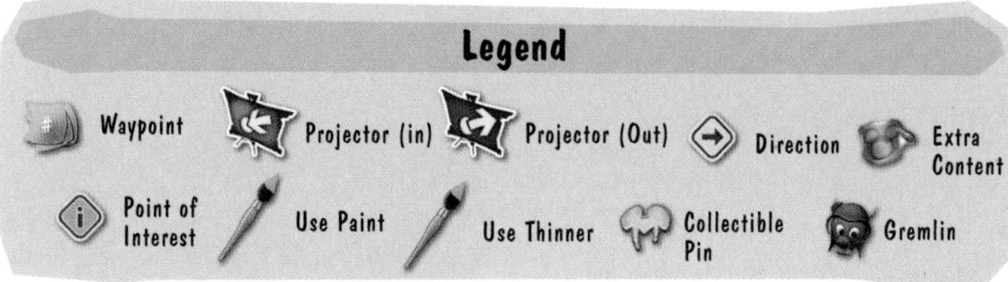

out the Hoppers when they attack. When you're ready, head up the ramp and free Gremlin Apollo.

Things to Do

- Free Gremlin Apollo
- Power the people mover
- Repair the sky tram
- Repair the rocket ride
- Free Gremlin Sparks
- Collect Goofy's Left Leg
- Free Gremlin Nova
- Follow the tracks to Space Voyage

Gremlin Apollo

Gremlin Apollo is at the top of the ramp near the Tomorrow Square entrance. When you free Gremlin Apollo, he tells you how to repair the people mover.

Gremlin Apollo tells you to place a TV on each of the pads along the people mover. When all three pads have

been powered up, the path to Space Voyage will open. Smash the chest near the first pad to collect a sketch, then place a TV on the pad. After you place the first TV, electricity starts moving around the track.

You can see the next pad just across the track. Wait for the electricity to pass by, then hop onto the track and run toward the second pad. Double-jump up to the platform, and smash the chest for a fresh TV sketch. Place a TV on the pad, and jump back down to the ramp.

You can reach the third pad by dodging the electricity on the track (or take a shortcut across the rocket ride's base), but it's best to leave the last TV for later. Head down the ramp, and look for the golden ticket near the Tomorrow Square entrance.

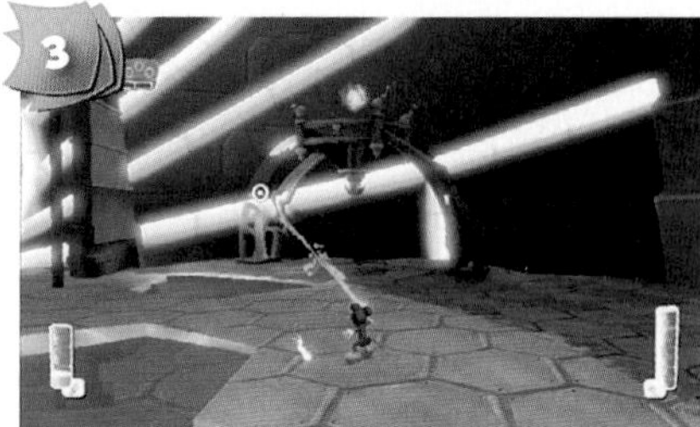

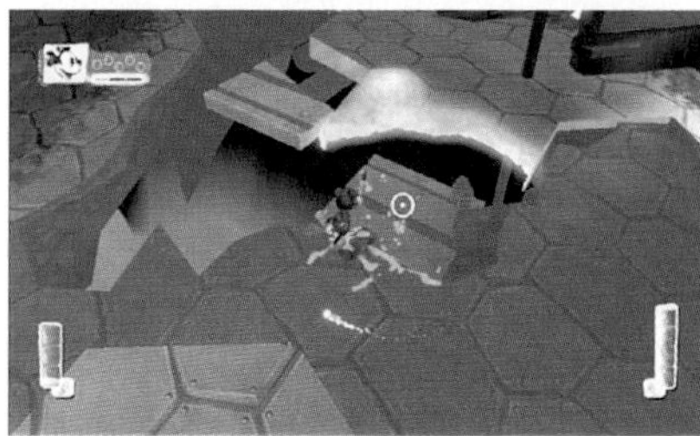

The golden ticket sits atop a small platform near the entrance. Stand on the painted purple tiles and face the structure. Hit the support beams on the left with some Thinner to bring the platform crashing down.

Carefully spray some Thinner to remove the purple tiles, then jump down to the platforms below you. Smash open the treasure chests to collect two more TV sketches, and grab the gold ticket as a bonus. Follow the platforms back up to the surface.

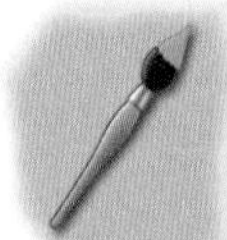

Use Thinner to topple the structure under the golden ticket and expose the platforms under the tiles.

Head under the people mover tracks, and circle around the rocket ride's base. Avoid the Spinners, or use one of your extra TV sketches to distract them when you run past. Look for the pink patch of painted tiles, and spray some Thinner to clear them away.

Run down to the bottom of the ramp, and use some Paint to fill in the missing gears. Hop on the main gear in the center of the device, and use a spin move to bring the sky tram back online. Head up the next ramp, and clear the tiles above you to return to the surface.

Run over to the drop-off near the sky tram. Before you head up the path in front of the building, look for the hidden platform around the corner.

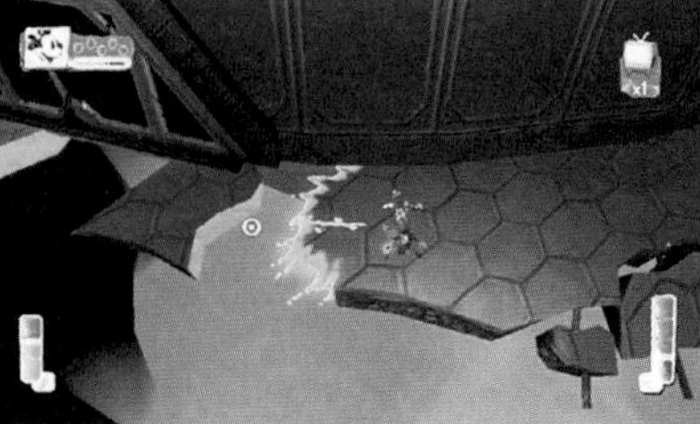

Double-jump over the gap to reach the first platform, then use some Paint to lay down a walkway.

Extra Content: Tomorrow City

Follow the hidden walkway until you reach the large grate on the wall. Use a spin move to take out the grate, and collect the extra content in the alcove.

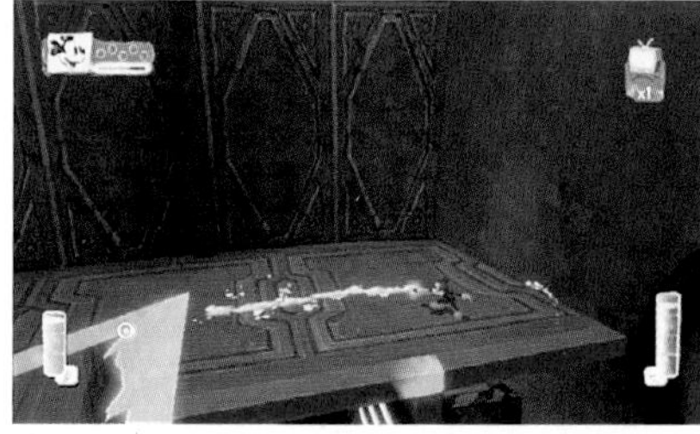

After you've explored the hidden path, return to the platforms in front of the building. Use Thinner to remove any barriers blocking your path. When you reach the top of the platforms, lay down some Paint to repair the walkway.

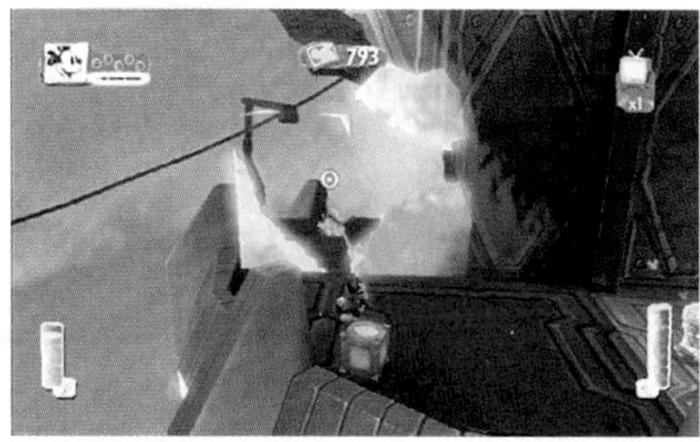

Deal with the Spatter on the walkway, then clear away the wall to continue along the path.

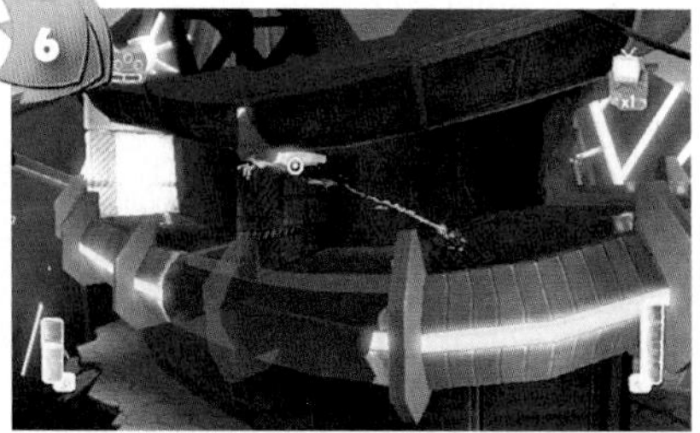

Two more barriers along the walkway are guarded by Spatters. Use your preferred method to deal with each Spatter you find. When you reach the gap in the walkway, spray some Thinner near the top of the barrier to drop it out of the way, then patch up the gap with some Paint.

Blast the next barrier with Thinner, then use a spin move to break through the exposed framework. Jump over to the door ahead, and hit it with another blast of Thinner.

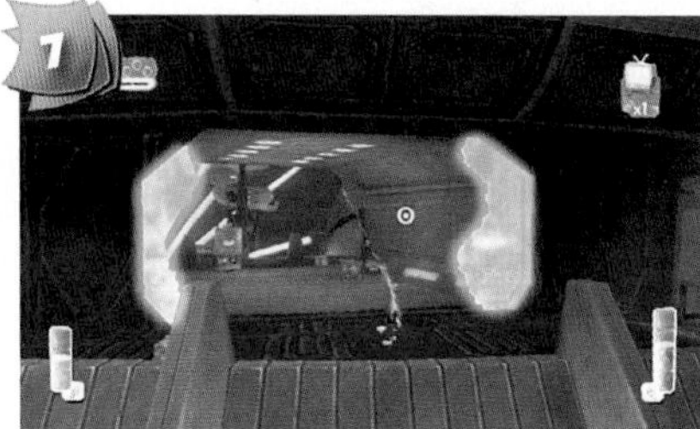

Move to the control box near the ledge, and spin move the stuck gear near the top. After a moment, the rocket ride unfolds and begins spinning around. Before you leave, follow the ledge to the left to discover another gremlin.

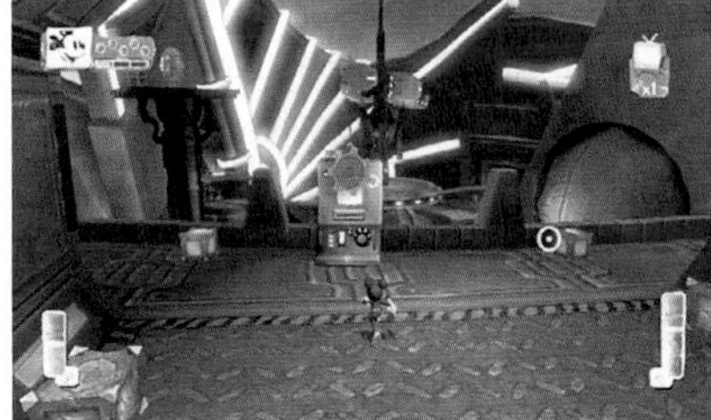

Gremlin Sparks

When you free Gremlin Sparks, he suggests you do the same for his friend, who's trapped on a tall platform near the rocket ride. Sparks says Gremlin Nova is an expert with people movers and could easily fix the ride for you.

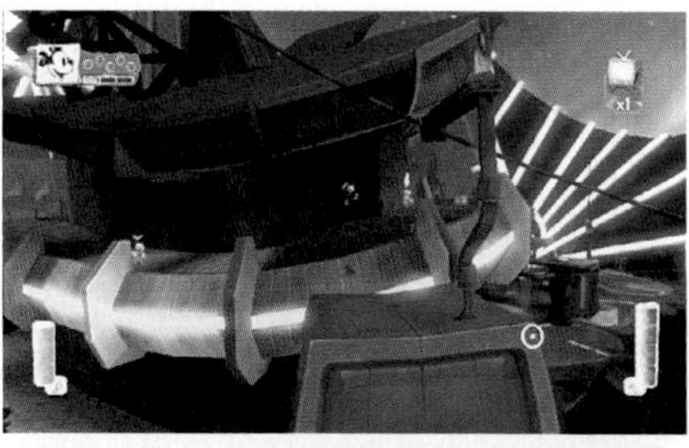

Return to the walkway, and retrace your steps. When the walkway curves around the building, stay put and wait for a sky tram car to pull up. Jump over and ride the car down the cable. Jump from car to car to reach the end of the sky tram.

Hop down and take care of the two Hoppers, then open the chest at the edge of the tiles.

Goofy's Left Leg

You've repaired the sky tram, scaled a building, and made quite a few risky jumps to find Goofy's Left Leg. It may have been a little out of the way, but Animatronic Goofy is sure to appreciate the effort.

After you've collected Goofy's Left Leg, hop down to the Tomorrow Square entrance. Run up the ramp and head back onto the second power pad.

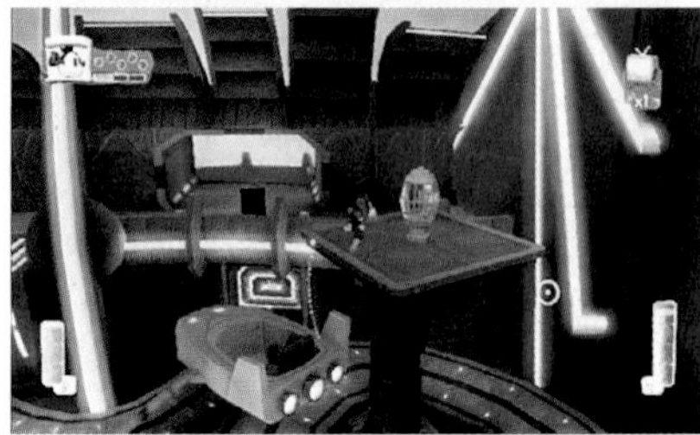

Wait for a rocket to approach, and jump on. If you want to repair the people mover yourself, you can jump from the rocket and place a TV on the third pad. Gremlin Nova, however, presents a much better option. Skip the third power pad, and ride up to the next platform.

Gremlin Nova

When you free Gremlin Nova, he restores power to the people mover whether or not you've placed any TVs. Additionally, this handy little fellow clears the cars from the tracks, giving you a safe and easy path to Space Voyage.

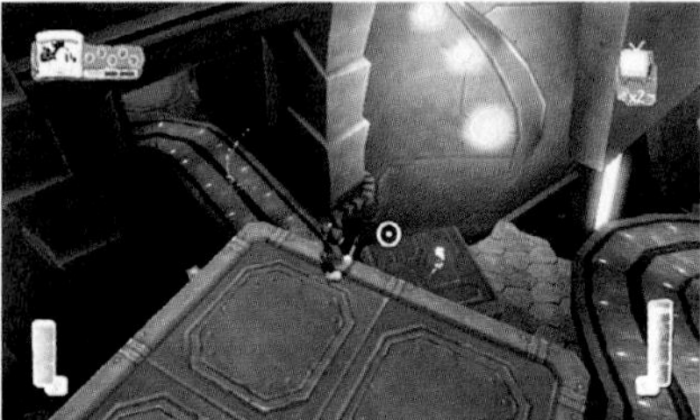

The path to Space Voyage is just below you. Drop to the track and follow it through the door. Follow the corridor to the exit projector to leave Tomorrow Square.

Gold Pin

When you enter the corridor to Space Voyage, turn left at the intersection. Open the chest in the short hallway, and add a new Gold Pin to your collection.

Mickey's Mechanical Man: Part 2

You arrive to find the mechanical man preparing for a rematch. The gorilla has already proved to be a tough opponent, but another horn-induced rampage might be just what the mechanical man needs.

Run across the piano and jump over to grab the e-tickets above the shelf.

Jump over the stacked safes, and hop onto the safe hanging to the right.

Stand on the safe to pull the stack off the ground. Drop to collect the exposed e-tickets, then jump back on the safe to the right.

When the safe touches the ground, double-jump onto the stacked safes.

Jump to the small shelf on the left before the stacked safes drop too low, and grab the e-ticket.

Double-jump back to the right, and collect the e-tickets on the shelf above the safes.

Drop from the shelf's right side and land on the counter near the window. While the mechanical man is training for the fight, a car pulls up outside.

Jump onto the safe in front of the window. When the car horn honks, the mechanical man begins another rampage to the boxing ring.

Double-jump up to the shelf on the right. Grab the e-ticket, then jump across the gap to collect a few more.

Drop down and exit through the hole in the wall. The top of a broken utility pole is suspended by connected wires.

Wait for the top of the utility pole to touch down, and jump onto it. When the wires spring you up, jump to the left and grab the film reel on the ledge.

Hop back to the broken utility pole, and jump over to the bent pole on the right.

Continue across to the next utility pole, or jump down to collect the e-tickets from the car below you. If you've taken any damage, drop and grab the health power-up on the ground.

Jump to the next car, and hop on its hood to spring into the air.

Drop straight down to receive an even bigger boost from the car's hood. Collect the e-tickets on the platform to the right. If you've skipped any e-tickets on the utility poles, use the car's hood to bounce back up to the left.

Grab the e-tickets behind the fight poster, and continue to the boxing ring.

Jump across the cheering fans and collect the e-tickets near the ring. When you reach the third fan, drop and grab the health power-up and e-ticket below the dazed gorilla.

The mechanical man is jumping on and off the gorilla's back. Wait for the mechanical man to hop off, then jump across the gorilla. Drop to the right before the mechanical man resumes its attack.

Jump up along the cheering fans to the right. Collect the e-tickets above you and hop over to the exit projector. When you're ready to leave, activate the projector screen to arrive in Space Voyage.

Space Voyage

Level Overview

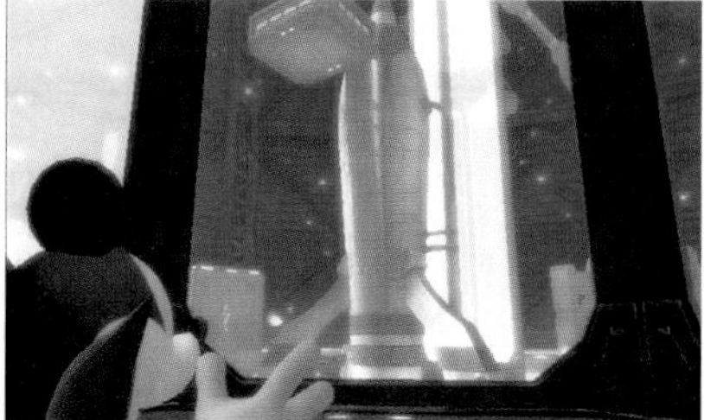

The Moonliner Rocket sits atop its launchpad, but you're not quite ready to blast off. Dodge the trams circling the launchpad and stay clear of the surging electricity. A Beetleworx Tanker guards the launchpad, and two Beetleworx spawners provide a steady flow of reinforcements. Find a way to reach the rocket, and meet Oswald at the boarding elevator.

1

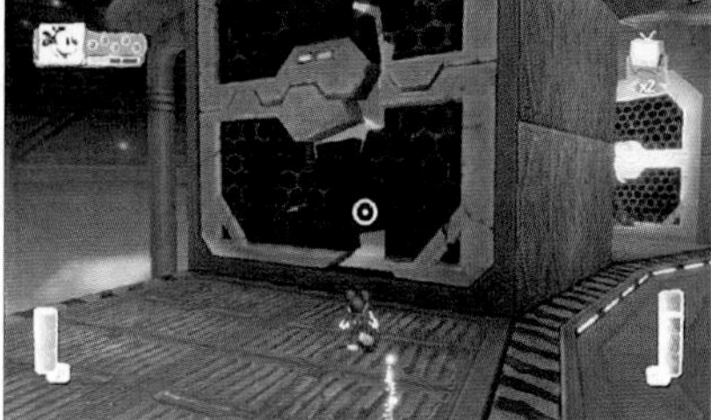

When you arrive, the launchpad rotates and rises out of the ground. Gus doesn't know what to make of it, but he suggests you find a way to fix the pistons near the tram track. Follow the track to the left. Dodge the moving trams and surging electricity to reach the next alcove. Take out the Spladoosh, and move to the broken wall.

Use a spin move to break through the wall and expose the panel behind it. Spray the panel with a bit of Thinner to find a TV sketch and Gremlin Epsilon.

Things to Do

- Free Gremlin Epsilon
- Use a TV sketch to power the crane
- Collect the dog tags
- Free Gremlin Delta
- Free Gremlin Omega
- Defeat the Tanker
- Collect Goofy's Arm
- Find the elevator and meet with Oswald

Gremlin Epsilon

When you free Gremlin Epsilon, he fixes the pistons needed to reach the launchpad. As a bonus, Epsilon offers to stop either the trams or electricity circling the launchpad. If you choose to stop the trams, use Paint the missing sections of track to absorb some of the electricity. If you choose to stop the electricity, use Thinner on the existing track to slow the moving trams.

2

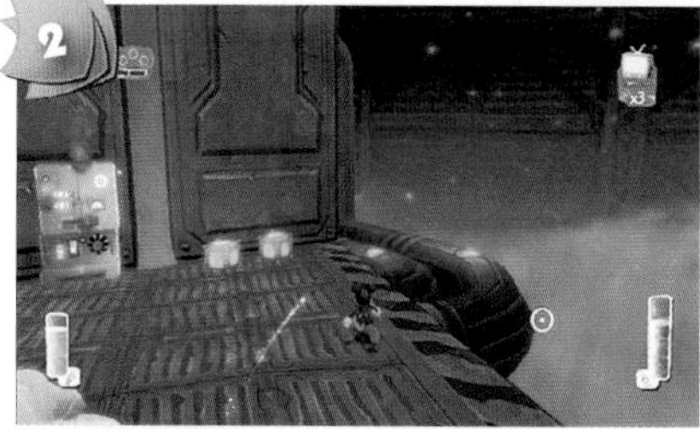

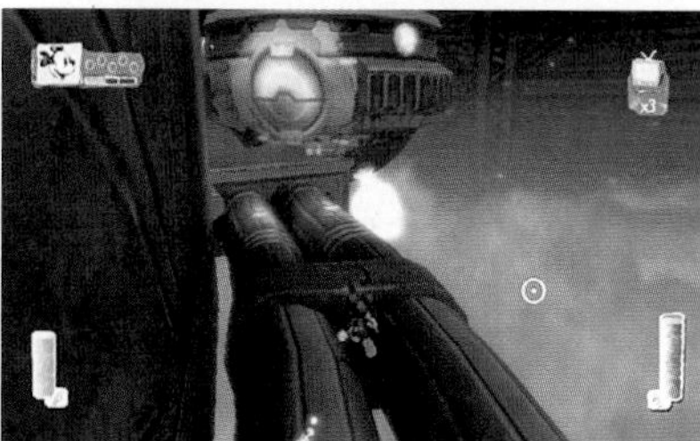

After Gremlin Epsilon fixes the pistons, find the large cables attached to the ledge, just right of the control box. Hop on, and run to the pod at the end of the cables.

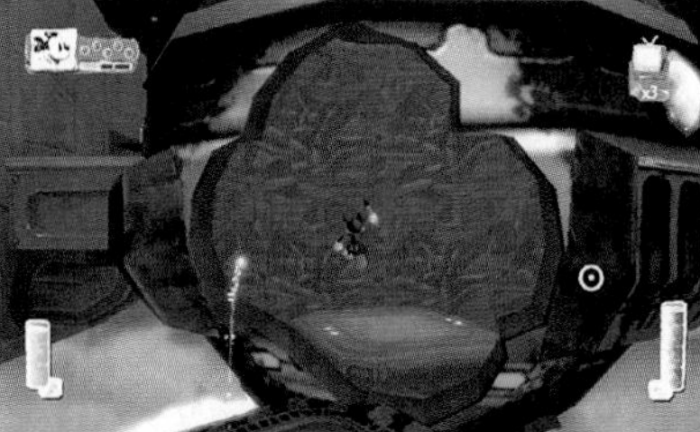

Spray the hatch with some Thinner, then jump inside to activate the pod. When the pod stops, hop out and jump up along the cables. Follow the ramp up to the top of the Beetleworx generator. Grab the golden ticket, and use the TV sketch you found near Gremlin Epsilon to power up the pad.

With the TV in place, the crane comes online. Head back down the ramp and locate the small glass room past the floating pod.

When you activated the pod, it triggered some new platforms. When you reach the end of the cables, jump down to the black platform near the glass room. Hop in through the window and grab the dog tags for Horace, then jump back out and return to the tram tracks.

Dog Tags

Collect the dog tags in the glass room for Horace's "Find Dog Tags" optional quest. If you haven't accepted the quest, you can grab the tags and speak to Horace next time you visit Mean Street. If you leave Space Voyage without collecting the dog tags, you can't complete Horace's quest.

3

Follow the tracks around the launchpad and take care of the Spladoosh near the pistons.

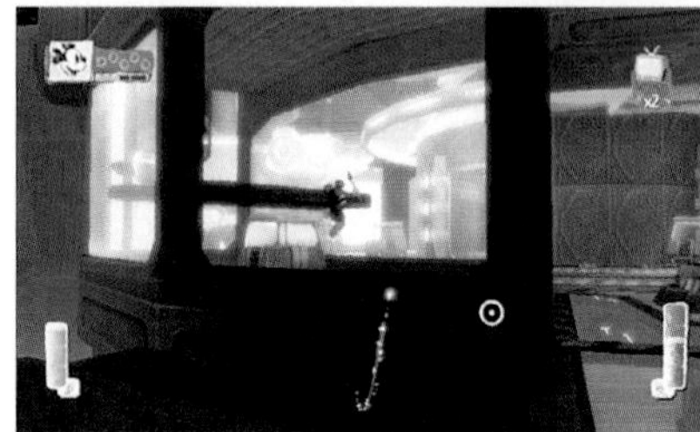

Move past the pistons and look for the platform near the ledge. Hop onto the platform and head into the long glass room. Jump along the platforms to find Gremlin Delta.

Gremlin Delta

When you free Gremlin Delta, he offers you a choice of rewards. Gremlin Delta can shut down one of the two Beetleworx generators near the launchpad, or he can give you three TV sketches.

After you free Gremlin Delta, jump through the window at the top of the platforms. When you land, spin move through the broken wall panel ahead of you.

Extra Content: Petetronic

Grab the extra content hidden near the long glass room along the tram tracks. Look for the cracked panel in the wall, and use a spin move to smash through it.

After you grab the extra content, return to the pistons on the other side of the glass room. Time your jumps to cross the moving pistons, and hop onto the walkway above you.

4

Toss some Paint down on the platform above the pistons, and cross over to the next section of the walkway. When the crane swings the platform down to the walkway, jump on and ride up to the rocket.

As the crane swings up, move to the edge of the platform. When you reach the rocket, spray some Paint to reveal a hidden platform, and jump across before the crane swings back down. Walk to the edge of the blue platform to find Gremlin Omega trapped at the side of the rocket.

Gremlin Omega

When you free Gremlin Omega, he offers you a choice of rewards. Gremlin Omega can shut down the second Beetleworx generator, or he can give you three TV sketches.

After you free Gremlin Omega, use the crane to return to the walkway below.

5

Head over to the launchpad to take on the Beetleworx Tanker.

Enemy: Tanker

The Tanker has powerful short-range attacks, but its true strength lies in its mounted blasters. With each shot, a Tanker fires rounds of Paint and Thinner. If a Paint round hits you, it knocks you to the ground. Thinner rounds deal direct damage for one health pip. Use your own Thinner to melt a Tanker's armor, then spin move into its green weak spot. Damage a Tanker three times to decommission this mobile turret. The Tanker counters any attempts to repair the elevator. If you want to leave Space Voyage without defeating the Tanker, you'll need to move quickly. Paint in the missing power box and run into the elevator before the Tanker can fire off another shot of Thinner. Just be sure to collect any desired objects before you leave the area.

As far as ranged attacks, the Tanker definitely has the advantage. Run in to close the distance, dodging any incoming fire. When you're close enough, the Tanker moves in to engage in close combat. Back off, and blast the Tanker's armor with Thinner as it chases you.

When the Tanker gets close, jump away to dodge its swing attack, then hit it with another blast of Thinner. Lead the Tanker around the launchpad; spray Thinner from a short distance, then jump away from its swing attack. When its armor is gone, the Tanker squats low, spreads its blasters, and unleashes a storm of Paint and Thinner. When the Tanker begins the devastating attack, double-jump to avoid the first blast.

The Tanker rotates its torso and continues to fire. When you land, spin move into the green weak spot on the Tanker's back.

Back away as the Tanker regenerates its armor, and repeat the process to deliver a second spin move to the green weak spot. The next time you melt the armor, the Tanker extends its torso for a slightly higher zone of fire. Dodge around this modified attack, and move in to finish your foe. Run in and jump up to deliver a third spin move to the Tanker's back, and hop away from the impending explosion. Don't forget that you can also use three TV sketches to disable these enemies. Drop them near the Tanker to deliver a jolt to their system!

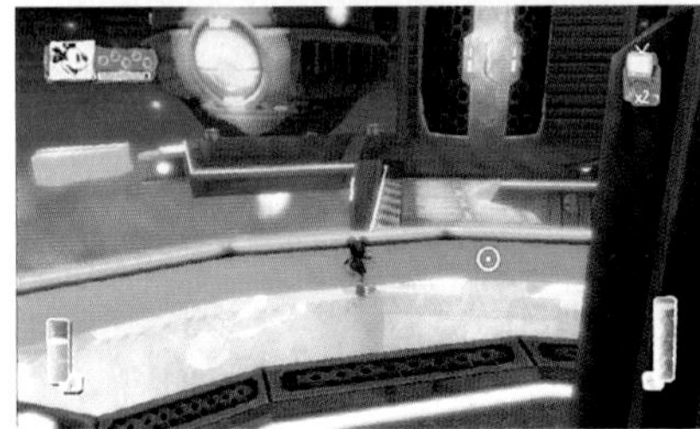

If you've chosen to shut down the Beetleworx generators, the Tanker is the last enemy you have to face. Use some Paint to replace the fuse box and reactivate the elevator. You can leave right away, but a few items are hidden nearby. Look for the floating pod near the Beetleworx generator, and head over to the walkway.

6

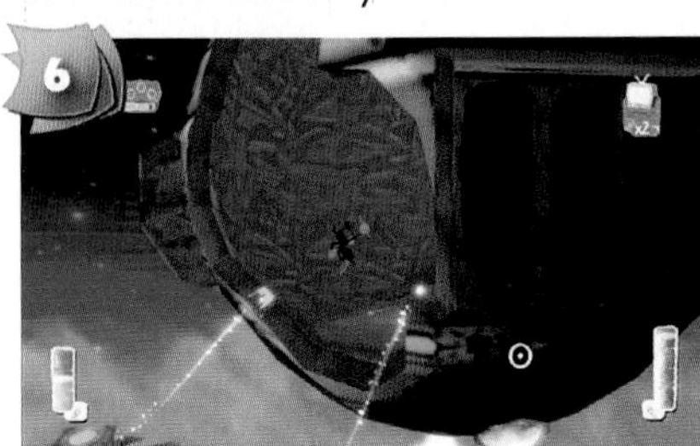

Spray some Thinner on the hatch, and jump inside to activate the pod. When the pod stops moving, hop out and follow the ramp to reach the top of the Beetleworx generator. Find the blue chest at the edge of the generator to collect Goofy's Arm.

Goofy's Arm

Animatronic Goofy's last missing piece is in the chest atop one of the Beetleworx generators. Use the floating pod to reach the ramp at the back of the generator, then head up to collect Goofy's Arm.

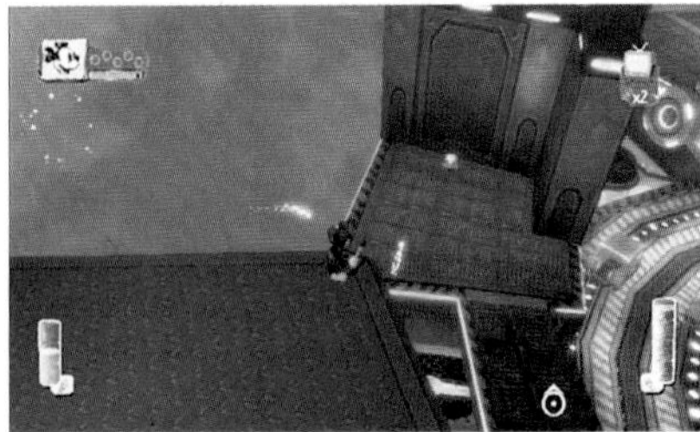

After you grab Goofy's Arm, move left and approach the edge of the building. Look down to find the chest on the walkway. Jump down and collect the Silver Pin from the chest.

Silver Pin

Open the chest near the Beetleworx generator to add this pin to your collection.

7

There's one more piece of business to take care of before you meet Oswald. Jump back to the elevator and continue to the Beetleworx generator across the launchpad.

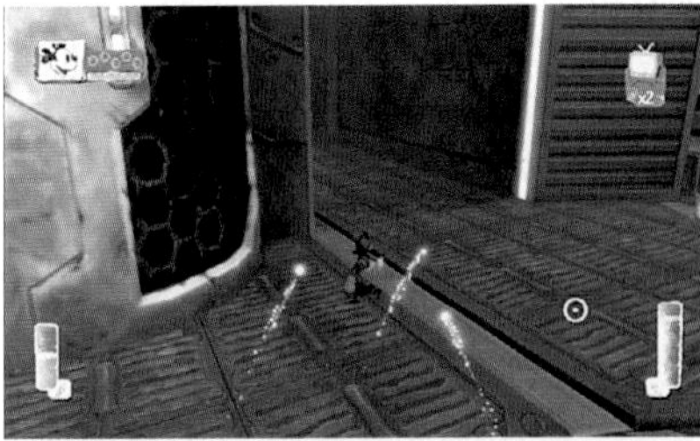

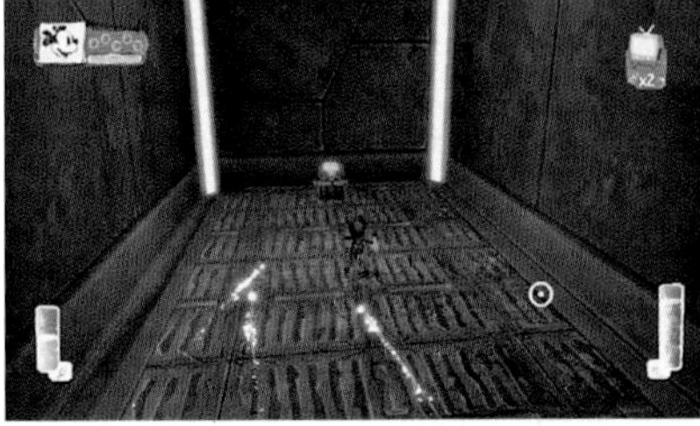

Enter the corridor in the Beetleworx generator to find another chest. Three Hoppers guard the corridor. Consider using a TV sketch to distract your enemies while you open the chest.

Bronze Pin

Before you meet Oswald on the elevator, pop into the Beetleworx generator and add another Bronze Pin to your collection.

When you're ready to leave Space Voyage, head back to the launchpad and enter the elevator. Oswald is waiting with some bad news. The Mad Doctor has taken some crucial pieces of the rocket and used them in his twisted experiments. Until you recover all of the missing parts, the Moonliner Rocket isn't going anywhere. Petetronic is holding one of the rocket parts, and Oswald sends you up to reclaim it.

Petetronic

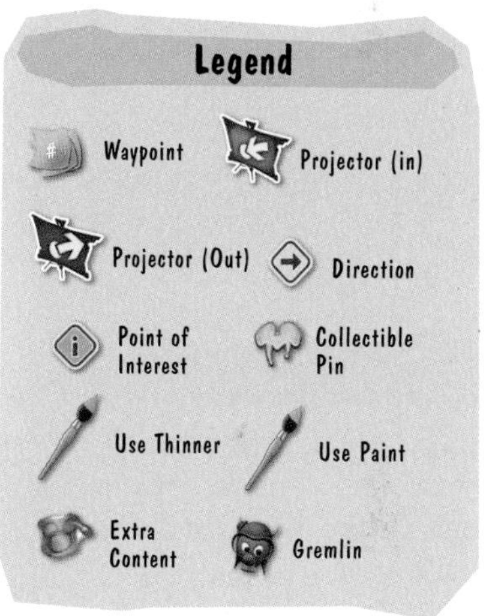

Level Overview

Petetronic has been making trouble throughout Tomorrow City, and he doesn't intend to let up anytime soon. Pete has asked you to talk some sense into his futuristic alter ego, but Petetronic has upgraded himself with some powerful augmentations. Navigate the vanishing platforms and survive Petetronic's attacks to take back his ill-gotten rocket part.

The first rocket part, a large disc, sits on the glowing platform in the center of Petetronic's lair. Run toward the disc as the walkway vanishes behind you.

When you reach the ring at the end of the walkway, Petetronic appears and snatches the disc from the platform. Get ready for some action; Petetronic won't give up the rocket part without a fight.

Things to Do

- Avoid Petetronic's Thinner and stomp attacks
- Turn Petetronic's disc against him
- Fill Petetronic's tanks with Paint or Thinner
- Claim the first rocket part
- Return to Mean Street

Junction Point: Petetronic

If you use Paint to befriend Petetronic, you receive an extra Paint slot, and Wasteland gains a powerful protector. If you fill Petetronic's tank with Thinner, you receive an extra Thinner slot, and rid Wasteland of a blustering bully. Your choice also affects the reward Pete offers when you return to Mean Street, and the movie you see at the end of the game.

When the battle begins, Petetronic opens fire with his first Thinner attack. Move around the ring to dodge the two spurts of Thinner. Any glowing platforms struck in the attack vanish, exposing the ring of Thinner below you. Stand in a safe spot, and use your Paint to replace any lost platforms.

Petetronic throws a small temper tantrum, and leaps into the air for a massive stomp attack. If you're touching any platforms when the tremor hits, it knocks you back several feet. Jump into the air before Petetronic slams down, and wait for his next attack.

Petetronic winds up and sends his disc flying along a curved path. When the disc approaches, use a spin move to smack it back toward Petetronic.

The first time the disc hits him, Petetronic spins around and faces away from you. Aim a stream of Paint or Thinner at the disc on Petetronic's

back. As his tanks fill, Petetronic's armor begins to vanish. Undeterred, Petetronic shakes off your small victory and readies himself for another round.

Move to one of the solid platforms around the ring, and wait for Petetronic to unleash an upgraded Thinner attack. Each wave of the Thinner attack includes three projectiles, and the glowing platforms don't last long. Dodge the falling Thinner, and return to the relative safety of the solid platform whenever possible. Look for health power-ups when the platforms rise out of the ring.

Look for health power-ups on the raised platforms, and repair the ring while Petetronic throws his tantrum. Jump up to avoid his stomp attack, and wait for Petetronic to throw his

disc. Petetronic isn't caught off guard this time, and the impact doesn't faze him. Dodge another round of Thinner and stomp attacks, and replace the glowing platforms whenever possible.

The next time he throws his disc, Petetronic raises a shield around his platform. Fire off a spin move every time the disc bounces back at you, and pick away at the shield until you break through to your overconfident opponent. When Petetronic spins around, blast another shot of Paint or Thinner into his back. The tank on his back is nearly full, but Petetronic still has some fight in him.

Look for fresh health power-ups each time the platforms rise up, and use Paint to lay down a path any time you change positions. Petetronic's Thinner attacks are fully upgraded, and he resists more of your disc deflections, but the same tactics still apply.

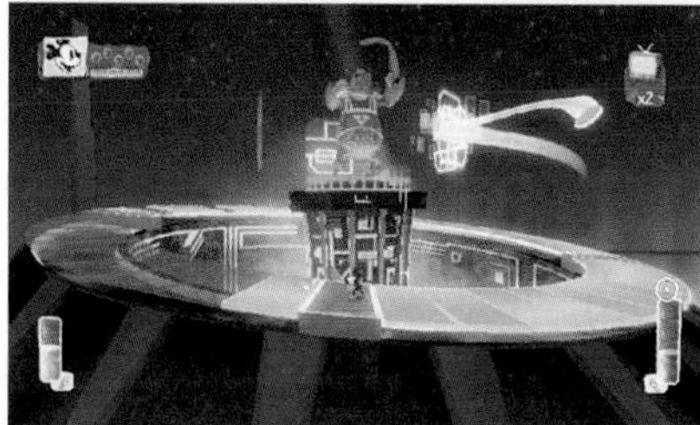

Try to stick to the solid platforms, and repair a bit of the ring after each Thinner attack. Jump up to avoid the impact of his stomps, and spin move whenever the disc is in range.

Use the disc to chip away at Petetronic until he succumbs to your attacks. Top off his tanks with one last blast of Paint/Thinner to end the battle.

When Petetronic falls, you'll gain a Paint capacity upgrade if you defeated him with Paint, or a Thinner capacity upgrade if you beat him with Thinner. After you deal with Petetronic, run over to his platform to collect the first rocket part, and activate the projector screen to head back to Mean Street.

Win the battle against Petetronic to unlock the Space Voyage extra content.

Mean Street

Level Overview

Gremlin Markus has been trapped by a gang of Spatters. Rescue Markus from his captors, and help him fix the projector screen to Ventureland. Look for new quests, swing by OsTown, and collect 10 power sparks to jump start the projector screen.

When you return to Mean Street, Oswald tells you that three Spatters have somehow captured Gremlin Markus and are holding him outside City Hall. The projector screen to Ventureland is broken, and Markus is the only one who can fix it. Oswald wants you to deal with the Spatters personally.

You can clear out the Spatters however you like, but remember that Oswald always expects the worst from you. If

you want to put Oswald in his place, use Paint to befriend all three Spatters, and set Gremlin Markus free.

Things to Do

- **Free Gremlin Markus from the Spatters**
- **Look for new quests**
- **Turn in completed quests**
- **Check the Emporium for new items**
- **Collect 10 power sparks**
- **Enter the projector screen to Ventureland**

Available Quests

- **Ventureland Projector Screen**
- **Detective Mickey II**
- **Bunny Roundup II**
- **Restore Pete Pan**
- **Find the Missing Pirate**
- **Ortensia's Locket**

Befriending the Spatters

If you used Paint to befriend the Spatters in Mean Street, speak to Oswald to receive a power spark. Oswald expected you to blasts the pests with Thinner, and he grudgingly admits you've set a good example for the local toons.

When you free Gremlin Markus, he asks you to collect 10 power sparks to start the projector screen to Ventureland. If you're in a hurry, buy power sparks at the Emporium. Otherwise, head to City Hall and check in with Pete. Speak to Pete to complete the "Confront Petetronic" quest, and pick up the "Restore Pete Pan" and "Bunny Roundup II" quests.

Redeem Petetronic Pin

If you used Paint to befriend Petetronic, return to Pete to receive this special pin. In a show of appreciation, Pete also gives you a power spark.

Defeat Petetronic Pin

If you used Thinner to defeat Petetronic, return to Pete to receive this special pin. He may not approve of your methods, but Pete throws in a few e-tickets for your trouble.

Quest: Restore Pete Pan

Pete Pan has lost his courage and is hiding somewhere in Ventureland. Pete doesn't like the way this makes him look and wants you to do something about it. Head into Ventureland, track down Pete Pan, and convince the coward to toughen up.

The Bunny Children are back on the streets, and Pete isn't happy about it. Lead five Bunny Children to the pipe next to City Hall so Pete can trap them in his jail. Look for the Bunny Children scattered throughout Mean Street.

Round up five Bunny Children and lead them to the pipe near City Hall.

When you've captured five Bunny Children, head back into City Hall. Speak to Pete to receive a power spark, then go back outside to look for more quests.

Stop by the Detective Agency and speak to Horace. Pick up the "Detective Mickey II" and "Find the Lost Pirate" optional quests, and turn in the "Find Dog Tags" quest.

Mystery Solved Pin

Give Horace Horsecollar the dog tags from Space Voyage to collect the Mystery Solved Pin. To thank you for this valuable clue, Horace also presents you with a power spark.

Horace asks you to find out who took Clarabelle's flower, and he suggests you search for clues near her window. Enter the "Thru the Mirror" projector screen and return to OsTown.

OsTown

Locate the footprints below Clarabelle's window, and lay down some Paint to uncover the trail of footprints. Follow the footprints out to the sidewalk, over the fence, and around the back of your house.

Optional Quest: Find the Missing Pirate

Horace has a missing persons case, and needs your help to solve it. When you get to Pirates of the Wasteland, Horace would like you to track down his client's cousin and find out why he didn't return with the other pirates.

When you reach the end of the trail, speak to Ezra. Once faced with the evidence you've uncovered, Ezra pleads ignorance and gives you the flower. Take care of any business you have in OsTown, and return to Horace at the Detective Agency.

Speak to Horace and give him Clarabelle's missing flower. Horace thanks for the good work and rewards you with a special pin and a power spark.

Symphony Sunflower Pin

Complete the "Detective Mickey II" optional quest to earn the Symphony Sunflower Pin.

Animatronic Goofy Pin

While you're back in OsTown, speak to Animatronic Goofy and complete the "Find Goofy's Parts" quest to earn this special pin. Once he's been reassembled, Animatronic Goofy unlocks Ortensia's house in OsTown.

Optional Quest: Ortensia's Locket

Complete the "Find Goofy's Parts" quest to unlock Ortensia's house. Enter the house to collect Ortensia's Locket, then head back to Mean Street.

Sell the locket to the museum for a *lot* of e-tickets, or give the locket to Oswald. If you let Oswald keep the locket, he rewards you with a permanent health upgrade.

If you're short a power spark or two, head over to the Emporium and see if Casey has any for sale. While you're there, you can also purchase new pins and extra content, and pick up any Goofy parts you missed back in Tomorrow City.

When you have at least 10 power sparks, return to Gremlin Markus and reactivate the Ventureland projector screen. Take care of any business you have left in Mean Street, then head to the projector screen and continue to Ventureland.

Jungle Rhythm: Part 1

You arrive in a lush jungle where the plants bob in time with the music. Navigate across the treetops and chimpanzees, and watch out for falling coconuts.

Move to the right and run into the hollow log. While you collect the e-tickets inside the log, coconuts fall from the tree above you.

Exit through the log's right side and jump back to the left. Each time the tree shakes, a fresh coconut drops onto the log. Dodge the falling coconuts and collect the e-tickets above the log.

You can take the lower path along the ground, or you can head into the trees to follow the upper path. If you've taken any damage, jump over and grab the health power-up above the branch.

Hop onto the next branch, and watch the trees to the right. Wait for the tree to swing away from you. After the tree drops a coconut, double-jump to the right. Land on the treetop as it swings back to the left.

Swing over to the right and jump across to the next tree. Grab the health power-up between the trees to recover from any damage.

Continue to the right and jump across to the tree branch.

Drop to the lower branch and jump over to the e-ticket ahead of you.

When you land, you can see the film reel under the log. Continue to the right, or head back to the left and collect the e-tickets along the lower path.

If you decide to explore the lower path, jump onto the tree stump to the left.

The trees are dropping coconuts onto the chimpanzees below them. Wait for the trees to swing away, and jump onto the first chimpanzee.

Dodge the falling coconuts, and jump across the chimpanzees. If you suffer any injuries, grab the health power-ups along the way.

Grab the e-ticket above each chimpanzee, then turn around and jump back to the right.

When you reach the end of the chimpanzees, jump onto the tree stump and continue to the right.

Hop back onto the log, and dodge the falling coconuts as you run to the right.

Drop down into the hollow stump at the end of the log.

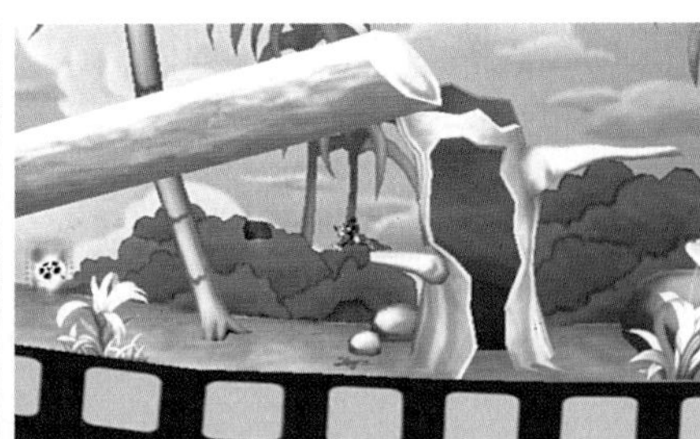

When you land, jump onto the small branch on the stump's left side. Hop down and grab the film reel under the log, then jump back onto the small branch.

Double-jump through the hollow tree stump to reach the next branch. You can see the exit projector to the right.

When you're ready, drop down and activate the exit projector to complete the level.

PIRATES OF THE WASTELAND

Ventureland

Things to Do

- Find Tiki Sam's masks to get the Wheel
- Find Scurvy Pat's treasure to get the Compass
- Help Damien Salt to get the Figurehead
- Bring the three items to Smee
- Speak to Animatronic Daisy
- Enter Tortooga

Level Overview

You arrive in a small village overrun by pirates. When Hook started transforming his crew into mechanical monsters, several of his men fled to Ventureland. The pirates broke the door-locking contraption when they arrived, and a few of the men have wandered off with the pieces. Convince the pirates to hand over the pieces, and open the door to Tortooga.

Find Smee near the village center, and listen to his sad tale. With Hook's mechanical monsters on the loose, the pirates have blocked the only path into Tortooga. Tiki Sam, Scurvy Pat, and Damien Salt are holding bits of the door-locking contraption, but Smee thinks he can repair it if you bring him the missing pieces.

Current Ventureland Quests

- A Pirate's Love

Find a gift for Damien Salt to receive the third piece of the broken contraption.

- Find Daisy's Parts

Help Animatronic Daisy recover her missing parts.

- Find Hook

Hook is hiding the second rocket part on his ship. Before you can recover the part, you have to find a way to reach the pirate ship.

- Gather the Flowers

Collect three flowers in OsTown, and have Clarabelle arrange a bouquet for Henrietta.

- Scurvy Pat's Compass

Recover Scurvy Pat's treasure to receive the second piece of the broken contraption.

- Talk to Smee

Smee is sitting on the ground, sobbing. Find out what's bothering Hook's former right-hand man.

- The Door in Ventureland

The door to Ventureland locked. Find a way to repair the contraption that controls the door.

- Tiki Sam's Masks

Recover Sam's Tiki Masks to receive the first piece of the broken contraption.

CAUTION

If you wish, Thin out the rear wall of the Tiki Shop to access Sam's storeroom. Each mask you deliver can be reclaimed and turned in a second time. This deception can become rather costly, however. Using this tactic forfeits the Tiki Shop discount, and Sam actually raises his prices if you turn in more than the expected three masks.

Head into the Hut Shop near the Ventureland entrance, and ask Tiki Sam about the missing wheel. When the pirates stole his collection of Tiki Masks, Sam returned the favor by swiping the wheel. Tiki Sam agrees to give you the Ship's Wheel if you bring him the three masks scattered around the village.

Head back outside, and find the large tree behind Smee. Jump up along the side of the tree, and use Paint to fill in any missing platforms. When you reach the platform just below the treehouse, jump across to the purple torch on the ledge.

Jump up to the deck, and run around the back of the treehouse to grab the Tiki Mask.

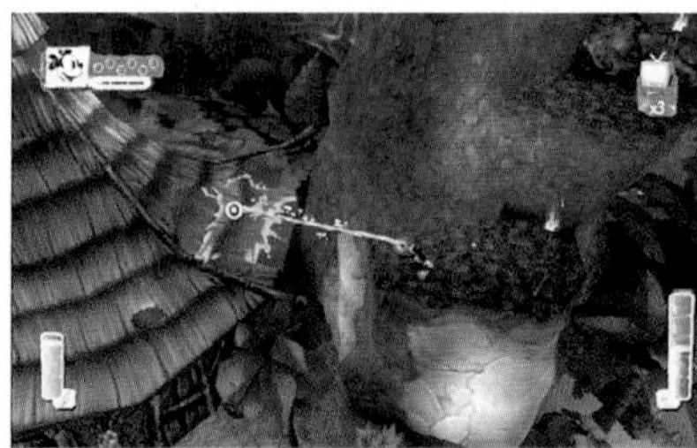

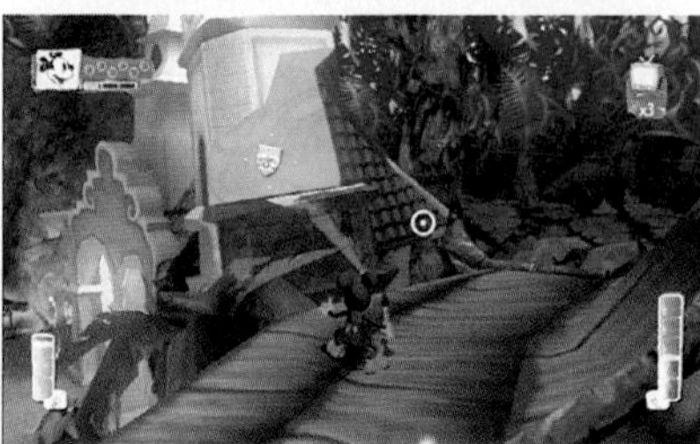

Head back around the treehouse, and drop to the ledge. Follow the purple torches to the nearby hut, and spray some Paint to patch the hole in the roof. Jump onto the hut, and follow the roof to the Tiki Mask on the next building. Jump over to grab the mask, and drop to the ground.

Run across the village, and continue past Sam's Hut Shop. Follow the path behind the shop to find two large, moss-covered stones.

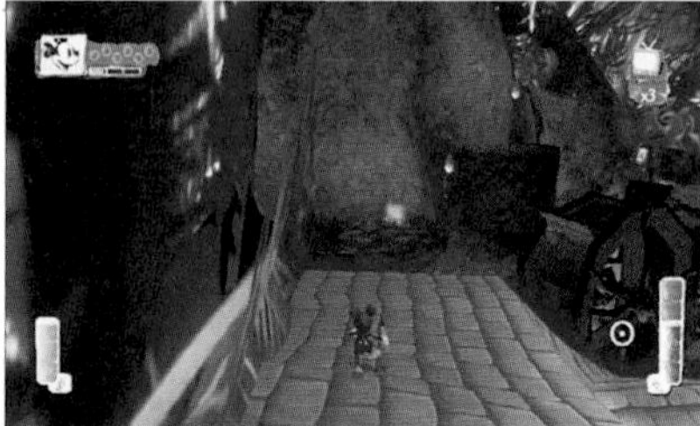

Climb onto the building just past the stones, and run across the rooftop. As you approach the end of the building, you can see the last Tiki Mask floating above the contraption's waterwheel. Jump along the purple torches to reach the top of the wheel, then hop over to grab the mask. Hop down to the ground and return to Tiki Sam's shop.

Tiki Sam is thrilled that you've managed to retrieve all of his masks, and happily gives you the Ship's Wheel.

The Hut Shop

When you return the stolen masks to Sam, he reopens the Hut Shop. The Hut Shop offers a selection of basic power-ups, and a unique piece of extra content.

3

Head over to Scurvy Pat near the center of the village. Buy the compass from him, or convince him to give it to you. In exchange for his compass, Scurvy Pat demands that you recover his stolen treasure. One of the other pirates has hidden the treasure up in the treehouse, and Scurvy Pat wants you to fetch it for him. He gives you the key to the treehouse, and sends you on your way.

Return to the treehouse, and use Scurvy Pat's key to unlock the door.

Enter the house and grab the stuffed bear, then head back outside and return to Scurvy Pat.

With the safe return of his most precious possession, Scurvy Pat hands over the Compass.

4

Damien Salt holds the last piece of the broken contraption. He thinks the Figurehead looks like his beloved Henrietta and isn't willing to part with it. If you could help him win Henrietta's heart, however, Damien Salt would no longer need this pale imitation. The love-struck pirate thinks the proper gift would do the trick, but the wrong gift would surely earn her scorn. He doesn't know if she'd prefer ice cream or flowers, and wants you to find out.

Gus suggests you simply ask Henrietta, who's sitting nearby. Henrietta is happy to chat; she mentions how much she likes flowers, and that she doesn't care for ice cream. When you return to Damien Salt, he asks you to pick out the gift yourself. He tells you to either buy some ice cream in Mean Street, or head into OsTown and ask Clarabelle about flowers.

Head back through the projector screen and return to Mean Street. If you want to bring Damien Salt some ice cream for Henrietta, stop by Ice Cream Parlor and buy some from Paulie.

To track down some flowers, take the projector screen to OsTown, and speak to Clarabelle in her house.

If you choose to purchase some ice cream, you can still accept Clarabelle's "Gather the Flowers" quest in OsTown. Complete the quest to earn three special pins, then choose which gift to deliver when you return to Damien Salt. The gift you choose affects which quests are available on return visits to Ventureland.

Clarabelle won't give you any flowers, but if you find a few on your own, she'll arrange them for you. Head outside to search for three flowers hidden in OsTown.

Spray some Thinner in Clarabelle's garden to reveal a large pit. Drop down and collect the first flower, then collect the e-tickets along the ramp out of the pit.

Use some Paint to cover the pit, and run across to the wall behind Clarabelle's house. When you reach the end of the house, blast the wall with some Thinner to find the second flower in a hidden alcove.

Run past the Gag Factory, and look for the ring of ivy growing on the town wall. Follow the path to the ivy, and stand near the dark green patch of grass. Spray some Thinner to reveal a hidden alcove. Grab the third flower and return to Clarabelle.

There are flowers to find in Mean Street, too. Thin the trees in the roundabout area in front of the train station.

After you give the flowers to Clarabelle, she arranges them into a bouquet, and three special pins appear in the room.

Swamp Iris Pin

After you complete the "Gather the Flowers" quest, you can collect this pin in Clarabelle's House.

Mickey Mum Pin

After you complete the "Gather the Flowers" quest, you can collect this pin in Clarabelle's House.

Sparkle Daisy Pin

After you complete the "Gather the Flowers" quest, you can collect this pin in Clarabelle's House.

Return to Ventureland, and give either the ice cream or the flowers to Damien Salt.

Junction Point: A Pirate's Love

The item you deliver to Damien Salt affects more than his chances of wooing Henrietta. Your choice of gifts determines your reward, the cost of the Figurehead, and which quests are available to you later in the game.

If you miss any of the parts, you can buy them from Tiki Sam once you return to Ventureland.

If you choose to give Damien Salt the flowers, Henrietta is delighted with the gift. Damien abandons his post at the chest to spend a little time with his new sweetheart, and gives you the Figurehead without a second thought.

If you give Damien the ice cream, Henrietta rejects his gift. Damien Salt returns to his post, and offers to sell you the Figurehead for 50 e-tickets. He can't bear to keep the painful reminder of Henrietta, but he's not looking to do you any favors.

Ventureland Romance Pin

If you give the flowers to Damien Salt, you receive this special pin.

Gold Pin

This pin is in Damien Salt's chest. If you bring him some flowers for Henrietta, Damien moves away to be near his new girlfriend. Open the unguarded chest to collect the pin.

5

Bring Smee the three missing pieces, then head over to the doors near the contraption. Be sure to talk to Animatronic Daisy before you leave Ventureland. Her parts are located in the areas past the door, and you need to accept her "Find Daisy's Parts" optional quest before you can collect them.

Junction Point: Animatronic Daisy

Hook's crew of Beetleworx pirates have run off with Animatronic Daisy's parts. Before you can rebuild Daisy, you have to find her missing parts across the pirate waters beyond Ventureland. If you recover all of Daisy's parts, you unlock new quests and rewards, and affect the game's ending.

When you're ready to leave Ventureland, activate the projector screen past the door and set out for Tortooga.

The Castaway: Part 1

You arrive on a small raft bobbing off the coast of an untamed island. Move through the seagulls and swordfish to reach dry land, and overcome the attacks of an angry gorilla.

Move to the right and jump across to the first piece of driftwood. Watch out for the swelling waves; you lose one health pip any time you touch the water.

Jump across the pieces of driftwood and collect the e-tickets above the water. Grab the health power-up to recover from any mistimed jumps.

Continue across the driftwood until you reach the small island.

Jump onto the small island and grab the health power-up. Move to the right until the swordfish jumps out of the water. When the coast is clear, either continue along the surface of the water or take the upper path across the seagulls.

To reach the upper path, jump onto the driftwood on the island's left side. Wait for the seagull to drift into range, then double-jump to the right.

Ride across to the right, and jump over to the next seagull. Collect the e-tickets along the way, and continue to the main island.

Ride along with the seagull, and jump over to the first tree. Jump between the seagulls and trees to collect the e-tickets along the upper path.

When you reach the third tree, jump across to grab the film reel from the treetop. Watch the ground for bouncing rocks, and drop down through the e-tickets.

You land on a large stone near a health power-up. An angry gorilla throws rocks from the right.

If you'd like to grab a few extra e-tickets, head back and explore the lower path to the left. Dodge any rocks coming in from the right.

Grab the health power-up and e-tickets on the next stone, and hop down to the left. Wait for a rock to come rolling down the hill. When the rock bounces over the stone, climb back up the hill.

Stand between the two stones, and wait for the gorilla to throw another rock. Jump over the rock as it falls back to the ground.

Take cover behind the next stone, and wait for the next rock to bounce over you.

When the path is clear, hop onto the stone and wait for the next rock. Jump over the rock and land in front of the gorilla.

Double-jump onto the gorilla's head and run across its back.

Hop down to the large stone past the gorilla. The exit projector is just to the right.

When you're ready to leave, hop down and activate the projector screen to enter Tortooga.

Tortooga

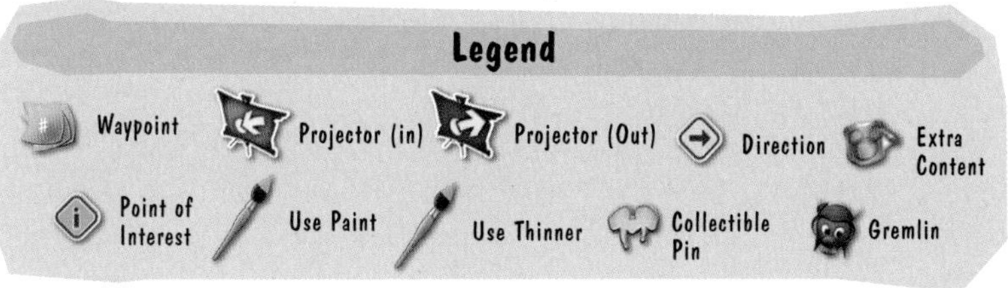

When Hook's men fled Tortooga, a few of the pirates were left behind. Blotlings have taken over the abandoned harbor, and tides of Thinner surge over the docks. Free the pirates in the jail to uncover some of Tortooga's hidden treasures, and convince Beluga Billy to open the path out.

1

Beluga Billy refuses to leave Tortooga until he recovers his stolen bag. The bag is across the docks, but the tide has kept him from reaching it. Beluga Billy agrees to activate one of Tortooga's projector screens in exchange for the safe return of his property.

Things to Do

- Recover Beluga Billy's bag
- Learn about the Watch sketch
- Speak to the pirates in the jail
- Find the three hidden keys
- Free Gremlin Marc
- Recover Billy's belongings
- Complete any optional quests
- Exit to the Jungle

2

Beluga Billy's bag is on the small building across the harbor. Jump across the rowboats to reach the bag. Capsized boats sink when you stand on them; be sure to jump off before they dip too low. The rising tide covers the platform in the middle of the boats. If the tide is too high, stand on the an upright boat and wait for the platform to appear.

Jump along the boats to reach the building across the harbor. There are plenty of barrels around the building, so look for a power-up or two if you've taken any damage. Use some Paint to patch the dock, and spin move into a few of the barrels. Each time the tide rises, it washes over the dock. Keep an eye on the water, and jump up to collect the bag on the roof.

Pirates of the Wasteland Quests

- Billy's Lost Bag

Find and return Billy's bag. Beluga Billy lost his bag while fleeing Tortooga. It is somewhere around the harbor.

- Billy's Lost Belongings

Find the contents of Billy's bag. The pirates locked up in the jail must have looted the contents of Billy's bag. Maybe you can talk some sense into them.

- Find Starkey

Find Starkey somewhere within the Jungle. Gentleman Starkey can help you reach Captain Hook. Locate him to find the answers you seek.

- Find the Jungle Symbols

Find three symbols hidden in the Jungle. Three stones, engraved with ancient symbols, are hidden in the Jungle. Find them and return to Starkey.

- Fix the Pumps

Use Paint or Thinner on the pumps.

- Hook's Machine

Disable or reverse the machine inside Skull Island. Use either Paint or Thinner to disable or reverse the machine inside Skull Island. Look for the four Paint and Thinner Pumps.

- Hostiles in the Jungle

Clear the jungle for Starkey. Eliminate all threats to Gentleman Starkey's well-being. This includes all Beetleworx and Spladooshes in the area.

- Into the Well

A gear inside the well is linked to an old ride. Go down the well, find the gear, and use it. Be careful: the Thinner tide can flood the well.

- Jungle Lanterns

Find all the lanterns in the Jungle and paint them. Hidden in the Jungle are an unknown number of lanterns. It might be rewarding to find and restore them all.

- Mysterious Mystery Gems

Find a use for the gems.

- Open the Skull Gate

Activate the projector screen. Both Beluga Billy and Starkey can activate the projector screen out of Tortooga.

- Paint the Lanterns

Paint in the lanterns to raise the ride from beneath the Thinner. The lanterns are part of an ancient ride system that could be activated by painting them all.

- Save the Sprite

Find a way to save the Sprite! Either defeat Captain Hook or avoid him and save the Sprite from his grasp!

- Smee's Boat

Find and raise Smee's boat to reach the Jolly Roger. Locate the anchors and cut them loose.

When the tide drops below the dock, hop down and follow the boats back to Beluga Billy. When Billy opens his bag, he finds that his belongings have been removed. Billy refuses to activate the projector screen until you recover his belongings, but he gives you a handy Watch sketch for trying to help him.

Speak to Beluga Billy if you want to buy additional Watch sketches; each replacement sketch costs 10 e-tickets.

Billy sends you to interrogate the pirates up at the jail. When the tide drops low, use some Paint to replace missing planks in the dock. Run up to the jail, and deal with the two Seers

patrolling the area. Spray Thinner on the frame around the door; when the door drops out of the wall, head into the jail to speak with the prisoners.

Speak to the three pirates locked in the jail. Ruffian Branderson (in the cell near the stairs) admits that he took Billy's things, and he'll tell you where he's stashed them if you unlock his cell. Three keys are hidden in Tortooga, and each pirate offers a clue to where you might find them.

Exit the jail, and run to the waterwheel past the well. Hop onto the ledge near the ramp, and look down to find the first key sitting on a platform below you. Drop to grab the key, then spray Paint on one of the paddles on the waterwheel. Ride the paddle up to the ledge, then hop across and head up the ramp.

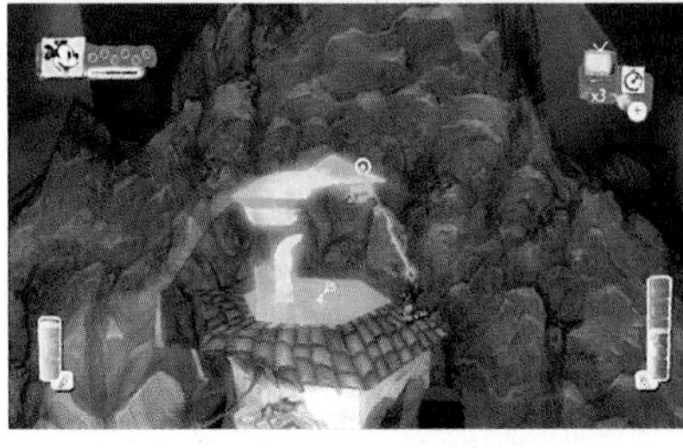

When you reach the top of the ramp, jump up to the ledge at the side of the large building. Double-jump and pull yourself onto the building, then use some Paint to fill in the gaps in the roof. Climb the tower at the center of the building, and use some Thinner to reveal the second key, hidden inside the tallest point of the tower.

Climb down from the building and deal with the Spatters patrolling the walkway. If you used Paint to befriend the Seers, they may already be engaged in combat. Deal with the Spatters, and hop over to the jail roof. Spray the chimney with some Thinner to reveal the last hidden key.

Return to the jail, and let each of the prisoners out of their cells. Ruffian Branderson (in the cell near the stairs) admits that he took Billy's belongings, and tells you where to find them. Cutpurse Tycho offers the "Into the Well" optional quest, and Scallywag Gabe gives you the "Light the Lanterns" optional quest. Head back up the stairs and exit the jail.

Use Thinner to reveal two of the hidden keys. Spray the tower on the large building, and do the same to the chimney on the jail.

If you only want to use Paint, collect the key on the platform near the waterwheel. Use Paint on the waterwheel to ride it back up to the ledge near the ramp.

Optional Quest: Into the Well

Cutpurse Tycho tells you about a gear hidden in the well outside. He's never had the nerve to head down there himself, but knows the gear has something to do with an old ride. He unlocks the well and invites you to go check it out.

Hop on the well and ride the lid down to the gear inside. Spin move the gear to activate the old ride; the well's exit opens up, and some platforms rise to the surface of the Thinner.

Use Paint to reveal a hidden chest on the tall platform. Wait for the tide to drop, then drop to the ground. Make a running leap toward the low platform, double-jump, and throw in a spin move for a little extra distance. If you time it just right, you can reach the low platform and jump up to the chest before the tide rises.

Bronze Pin

This pin is in a hidden chest below the Thinner. Complete Cutpurse Tycho's "Into the Well" quest to raise new platforms above the Thinner, then use Paint to reveal the chest. Open the chest to add another Bronze Pin to your collection.

Optional Quest: Light the Lanterns

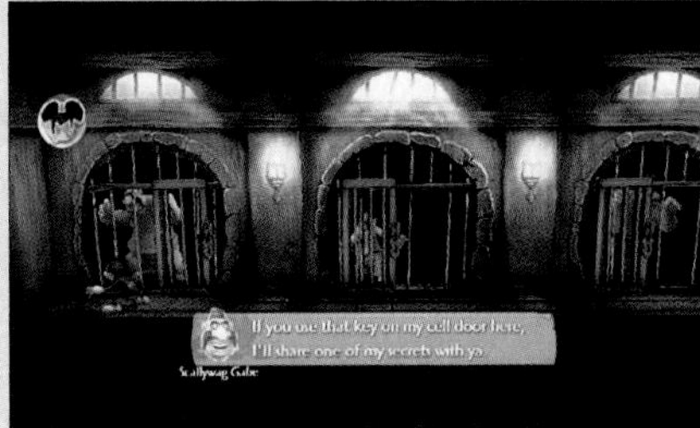

Scallywag Gabe tells you about three hidden lanterns in Tortooga. The lanterns are connected to the old ride under the Thinner, and lighting them should bring sections of the ride up to the surface.

Spray Paint on each of the hidden lanterns in Tortooga. Look for the telltale gnarled post to help you locate each lantern. The first two lamps are near the ramps on either side of the well. The last lantern hangs from the front of the tower at the top of Tortooga.

Light all three lamps to raise some new platforms above the Thinner. Use the rowboats to reach the platforms, and spray some Paint to reveal a hidden chest.

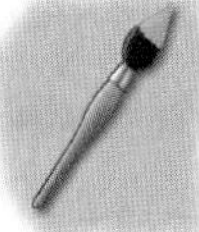

Use Paint to reveal the three lanterns hidden in Tortooga.

Bronze Pin

A hidden chest below the Thinner contains this pin. Complete Scallywag Gabe's "Light the Lanterns" quest to raise new platforms above the Thinner, then use Paint to reveal the chest.

When Ruffian Branderson looted Beluga Billy's bag, he hid the contents in a secret room next to the jail. Head to the well and use Thinner to remove the planks from the nearby arches. Remove all of the planks to reveal the hidden room, a health power-up, and a trapped gremlin.

Gremlin Marc

Gremlin Marc was captured when Hook's Beetleworx attacked, and was forced to watch as Tortooga's pirates were dragged off to Skull Island. After you free him, Gremlin Marc shuts down some pipes, hoping to prevent more abductions by stopping the flow of Spatters into the harbor.

Follow the passage down to the secret room. As you approach, two Spatters appear and spin a gear on the wall; a revolving panel hides Billy's belongings, and the room's columns drop through the floor.

Deal with the Spatters, then look around. Five gears are on the wall. Four of the gears operate the columns, and the fifth rotates the wall panel.

To reveal Billy's belongings, you must raise all four columns, then activate the wall panel before they drop back down. Spin move one of the column gears and use the Watch sketch you received from Beluga Billy. Run around

the room and activate all four columns, then hurry to the last gear at the wall panel. The Watch's effect doesn't last long; spin the gear near the wall panel to reveal Beluga Billy's lost items.

Return to the docks and give Beluga Billy his lost belongings. Now that Billy's free to leave Tortooga, he activates the projector screen past the waterwheel. Check the area for power-ups, take care of any unfinished business, and head into the Jungle to look for Gentleman Starkey.

Jungle Rhythm: Part 2

You arrive back in the jungle. This time, however, the trees aren't the only things caught up in the music; dancing ostriches and a friendly elephant have joined the festivities.

Move right and jump onto the tree stump.

Face the dead tree to the left, and double jump to the branch to grab an e-ticket.

When the tree to the right swings toward you, jump over and land on the treetop.

Each time the large tree swings to the right, it drops a giant coconut. When these coconuts land, they roll through the hollow log on the ground.

Drop to the log to collect several e-tickets. Stay clear of any coconuts.

Wait for the first tree to swing back toward you, and double-jump to return to the treetops.

Jump across to the right, and wait for the large tree to drop another coconut.

When it's safe, jump over to the next tree. Hop over and collect the film reel on the branch to the right.

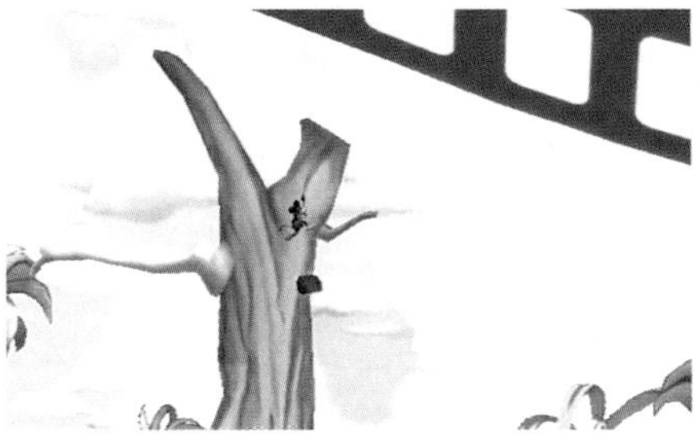

Jump over to the e-ticket and drop down to the branch below you.

Hop across to the dancing ostrich, and ride on its wings to collect two more e-tickets.

When the ostrich lifts its wings, jump onto the tree to the right. Each time the tree swings to the left, it drops a coconut to the ground.

Drop from the tree's right side to land on the next ostrich. Two more e-tickets are under the tree.

Wait for the next coconut to fall, then jump across to grab the e-tickets under the tree.

Turn around, and jump back to the ostrich. Walk across the wings, and wait for the elephant to approach from the right. When the elephant walks into range, jump across and land on its back.

Ride on the elephant, and jump up to collect the e-tickets above you. The exit projector is on the dead tree to the right.

When the elephant reaches the end of its path, jump onto the small tree in front of you.

When you're ready, double jump up to the exit projector. Activate the projector screen to enter the Jungle.

Jungle

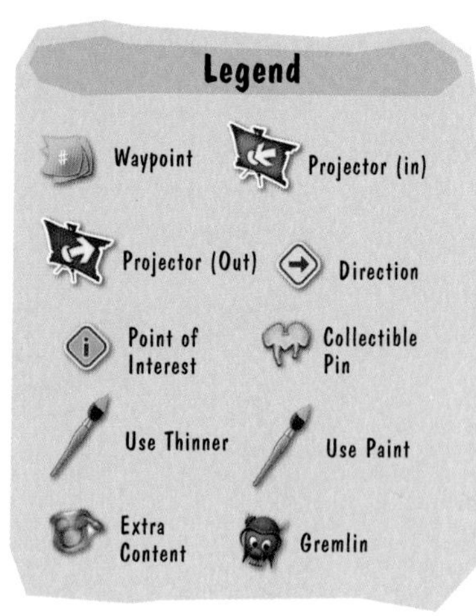

Level Overview

When his shipmates fled to Ventureland, Gentleman Starkey stayed behind to fight Hook's new crew and prevent any more animatronic pirates from invading Tortooga and Ventureland. Search the Jungle for Gentleman Starkey, and unravel the mysteries of this untamed land. Stay on your toes; one of Hook's Beetleworx Bashers has reached the Jungle, and you'll find a sleeping Spladoosh around every corner. Do as Gentleman Starkey asks, and you just might learn the password to Skull Island.

Starkey is hidden somewhere in the area, so start cutting a path through the Jungle. Run straight to the Hoppers ahead of you, and begin your attack. Wear down their armor as usual, or fire off a few spin moves to send them flying into the river of Thinner that cuts through the Jungle.

As you enter the Jungle, you can follow the path on your right to head straight to Starkey. If you wish, you can complete Starkey's "Jungle Symbols" quest and quickly return to Tortooga. If you'd rather discover all of the Jungle's optional quests (and the rewards that come with them), be sure to explore the area before you leave. This walkthrough details a recommended path that uncovers all of the Jungle's hidden treasures.

Use some Paint to replace the missing bridge and prepare for the battle to come.

Things to Do

- Explore the Jungle
- Find Gentleman Starkey
- Find the Jungle symbols
- Clear the Jungle of all hostiles
- Collect five Mysterious Gems
- Find Daisy's Right Arm
- Paint the hidden lanterns
- Free Gremlin Buzz
- Exit through Hangman's Tree

Near the stone heads across the bridge, you see one of the dreaded Beetleworx pirates. Head across the bridge to find out how tough Hook's new crew really is.

Enemy: Basher

The Basher is fast, fearless, and quick with its blade. This brute likes to get in close and spin its torso for a furious slash attack. Use Thinner to melt away its armor, and look for an opportunity to spin move into its weak spot. Even without its armor, the Basher is only vulnerable for a moment; stay clear of that blade until you're sure you have an opening. When the Basher lands a normal attack, it costs you one health pip and knocks you back several feet. When its armor is eliminated, the Basher's attacks deal twice the damage. Land three successful spin moves to the Basher's weak spot to defeat this Beetleworx bully. Remember that sketches come in handy for this fight. A Watch can slow down the Basher's fast attack and allow enough time for Mickey to hit its weak spot, and a TV produces a powerful shock to its system!

With the river of Thinner cutting through the Jungle, a single hit from the Basher might be enough to take you out of the fight. When the Basher charges toward you, jump away from its attacks. Circle around to get clear of the drop-off, then fight back with some of your Thinner.

Each time you dodge its sword, hit the Basher with a quick blast of Thinner. Keep moving and don't try to melt the armor with a single spray. Lead the Basher around in a circle, and chip away at its armor when it stops to attack.

When you've removed its last bits of armor, the Basher winds up for a more powerful attack. It takes a step forward during each of these attacks, so give the Basher plenty of room. When the sword stops moving, the Basher spins its left hand—this is your chance to fight back. Dash in and spin move into the Basher's green weak spot (which has spun around to the front of its body).

You only have time for a single spin move before the sword comes slashing back in the other direction; if your attack failed to connect, jump away and wait for the next opportunity. Each time you damage its weak spot, the Basher regenerates its armor and moves back in to attack. Use the same tactics to hit the weak spot two more times. After three successful spin moves, the fight ends, and the Basher explodes.

3

After you beat the Basher, use some Paint to fill in the log bridge near the stone heads. Cross the bridge and head to the right to find Gentleman Starkey on the other side of the Thinner.

Starkey offers to give you the password to Skull Island if you locate the three symbols hidden in the Jungle. Before you leave, Starkey asks you to clear out all of the hostiles in the Jungle, and promises you a special reward if you can complete both tasks.

4

Head over to Hangman's Tree, just as Starkey suggested. Deal with the Spladoosh in front of the tree, then paint the bridge to head across. Jump over the roots, and take care of the two Spladooshes on the other side of Hangman's Tree.

Jump down and turn back to face the tree. Notice a moss-covered rock between two of the roots. Use some Thinner to remove the moss and discover the first Jungle symbol.

Jump back to the other side of Hangman's Tree, cross the bridge, and past Gentleman Starkey. Another log bridge leads back toward the Jungle entrance. Head across the log bridge, and use some Paint to patch the holes in the ground.

The next symbol is just ahead of you, under the arch to the right. Remove the moss to reveal the Jungle symbol, then follow the path back to the entrance.

Look for the steps near the Jungle entrance, and climb up to the top of the stone. When you reach the top, paint the bridge on your right to continue across the gap. Fill in any missing platforms, and follow the path to the well above the stone heads.

Jump over the well, and spray some Paint to fill in the leaves on the other side. Hop onto the leaves to find the last Jungle symbol just ahead of you. Remove the moss to uncover the symbol, and return to Gentleman Starkey.

After you speak to Starkey, he opens the path to the top of Hangman's Tree. If you wish, you can leave right away. Jump up along the platforms on Hangman's Tree, hop onto the pulley, and enter the door on the front of the tree. However there's plenty left to do in the Jungle, and Starkey won't make it back to Tortooga without your help.

Once you enter Hangman's Tree, you can't return to the Jungle. Make sure you're ready to leave before you head inside.

If you decide to stay, head back to the Jungle entrance. Thin out the wall to the left of the entrance; the wall dissolves to reveal a hidden passage. Head inside and run up to the end of the passage. Take care of the Spladoosh, and grab the jewel floating near the exit.

If you haven't already collected a jewel, you receive the "Mysterious Mystery Gems" quest. To complete the quest, you need to find all five jewels hidden in the Jungle.

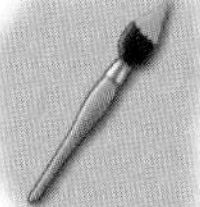

Thin out the wall near the Jungle entrance to reveal a hidden passage.

Move to the ledge past the jewel, and look for the steps running up the side of the arch. Drop to the ground and jump atop the arch. Use some Paint to fill in the top of the arch, then hop across to the trees ahead of you and spray some Paint to reveal the platforms along the wall.

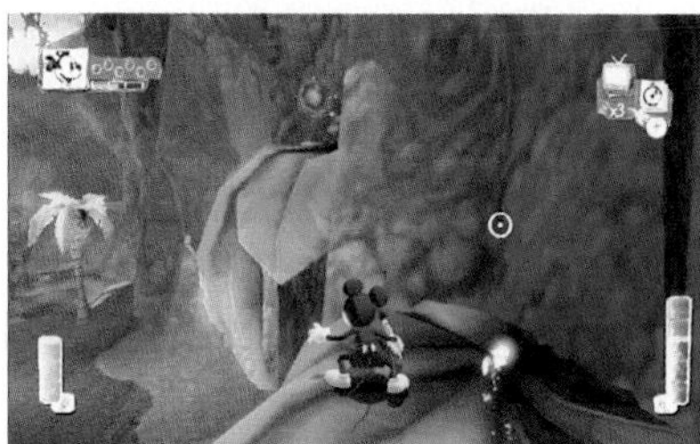

Hop over and follow the platforms across to the next jewel.

Drop from the platforms stand near Gentleman Starkey. Spray some Thinner on the wall to reveal a hidden alcove and recover the jewel inside.

Use Thinner on the Jungle wall to reveal an alcove near Gentlemen Starkey.

Head back to Hangman's Tree. Grab the jewel behind the tree, and take care of the nearby Spladoosh while you're back there.

At this point, you should have at least four of the five jewels. Return to the stone heads, and take out the last Spladoosh. Turn around and approach the Thinner. Look down to find the last jewel on the boat below you. Drop down to grab the jewel, and jump back up to the heads.

Activate each of the heads until you've placed all five of the jewels, then use Paint to fill in any empty slots. The heads spin around and unlock the well on the platform above them. Hop onto the small wooden platform, and climb to the top of the stone heads. Jump onto the lid to enter the well.

When you touch down, head over and open the blue chest to recover Daisy's Right Arm.

Use some Paint to reveal the platform under the wooden door high in the Jungle wall. Jump onto the platform to hear the desperate patter of a trapped gremlin.

Turn to face the Jungle entrance, hop down to the bridge, and run across to the other side. Find the gnarled post on the far ledge, and use some Paint to reveal a hidden lantern. Two more lanterns are hidden in the Jungle.

Daisy's Right Arm

If you've accepted the "Find Daisy's Parts" quest in Ventureland, you can recover the first part in the Jungle. Complete the "Mysterious Mystery Gems" optional quest, and collect Daisy's Right Arm from the chest in the Jungle well. Animatronic Daisy is sure to appreciate it; she always likes to look her best, and recovering her arm is an important part of the process.

Move to the stone heads and face the Jungle entrance. Look for the gnarled post along the ledge, and spray some Paint to reveal the second lantern.

To find the last lantern, head over to Gentleman Starkey and spray the gnarled post near the log bridge.

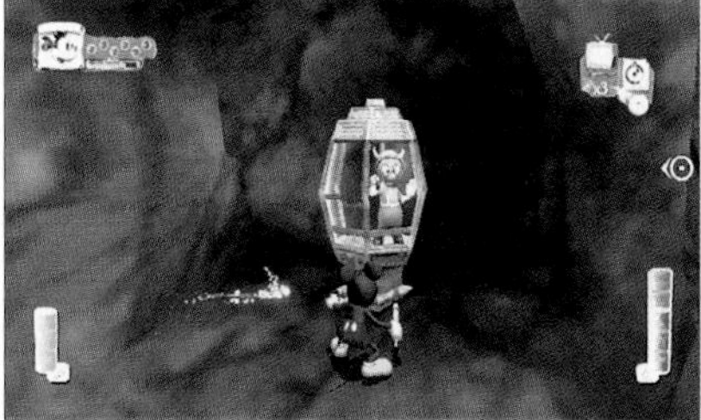

When the door in the Jungle opens, climb back up to find Gremlin Buzz.

Gremlin Buzz

When you free Gremlin Buzz, he shuts the gate on the Jungle wall near Hangman's Tree. When the gate closes, the Thinner drains out of the Jungle, and you're free to explore the dry riverbed.

You've learned the password to Skull Island, recovered Daisy's Right Arm, and freed Gremlin Buzz. There are just a few loose ends to wrap up in the Jungle. If you haven't cleared out all of the hostiles in the area, make a final sweep of the Jungle and return to Gentleman Starkey. Now that the Jungle is secure, Starkey enters the Hangman's Tree and returns to Tortooga.

Junction Point: Hostiles in the Jungle

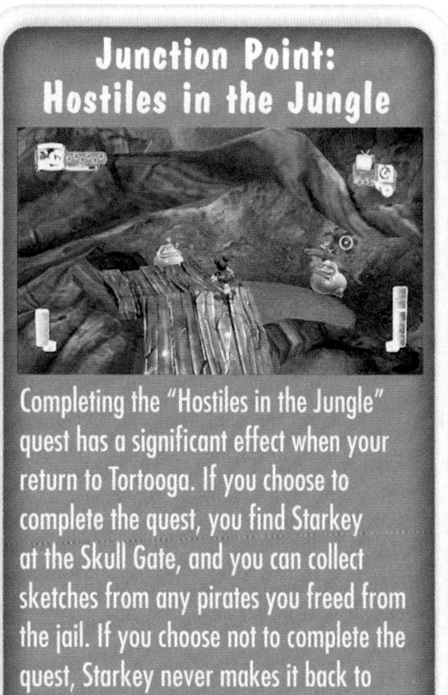

Completing the "Hostiles in the Jungle" quest has a significant effect when your return to Tortooga. If you choose to complete the quest, you find Starkey at the Skull Gate, and you can collect sketches from any pirates you freed from the jail. If you choose not to complete the quest, Starkey never makes it back to Tortooga, and the harbor is overrun with enemies.

Follow Gentleman Starkey to the Hangman's Tree, but check the nearby riverbed before you leave the Jungle. Use Paint to reveal a hidden chest below the tree, and drop to collect a Gold Pin.

Gold Pin

This Gold Pin is in a hidden chest at the bottom of the river. Free Gremlin Buzz to permanently dry the riverbed, or paint the gear on the dam to drain the riverbed for a short time.

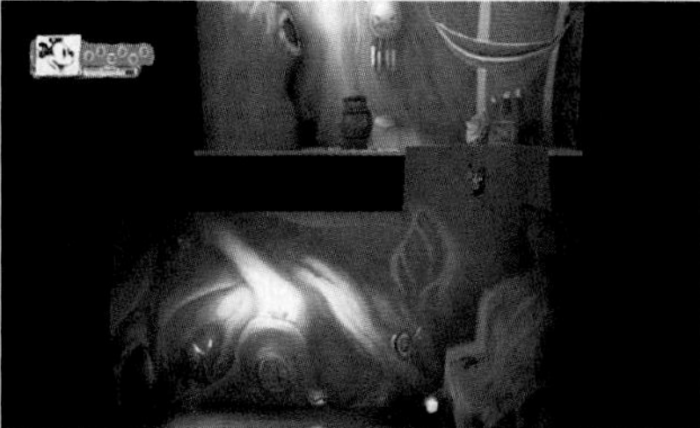

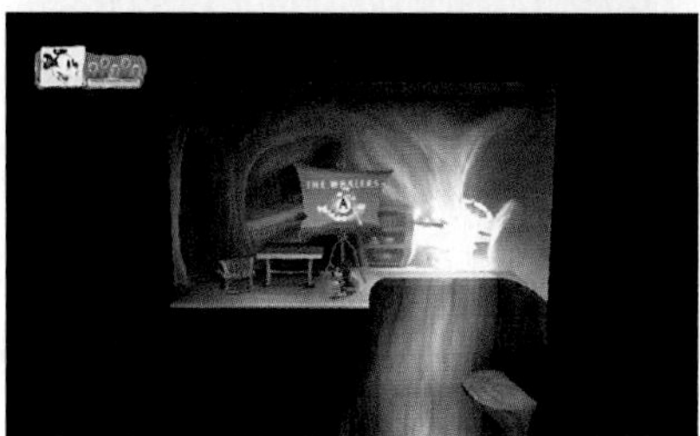

When you're ready to leave the Jungle, enter the door at the base of the Hangman's Tree. Climb along the inside of the tree, and activate the projector screen to return to Tortooga.

The Whalers

You arrive on an old whaling ship, deep in icy waters. The deck is littered with powder kegs, and water spurts from the ship's ventilators. Navigate through the floating ice and flying pelicans to reach the ship's intended prey.

Jump left and grab the e-tickets on the iceberg. When you land, turn around and hop back onto the ship.

Jump up and grab the e-tickets above the first powder keg. When you land on the keg, the fuse begins to burn. Jump onto the pelican before the powder explodes, or continue to the next keg to collect some more e-tickets.

If you choose to continue along the deck, hop onto the powder keg and double-jump over the first ventilator. Land between the two puddles near the ventilators to avoid the spurts of water.

Wait for a break in the water, and grab the e-ticket in front of the first ventilator. Turn around and jump to grab the e-tickets to the right.

Hop up to the smokestack and turn around. Jump across to the crow's nest on the left.

Hop onto the powder keg, and wait for the fuse to burn down. Just before the explosion, double-jump to get clear of the blast. Grab the health power-up if needed, and land back on the crow's nest.

Double-jump to the left and grab the e-tickets above the pelican. Return to the crow's nest, and jump across to the ship's smokestack.

Hop onto the powder kegs and wait for the fuse to burn down.

Jump clear of the explosion. When you land, grab the e-ticket inside the smokestack.

Hop over the next ventilator and drop down near the winch. Land past the puddle to avoid any spurts of water.

Before you activate the winch, collect the rest of the e-tickets on the ship.

Return to the winch, and use a spin move to raise the hinged section of the whaling ship.

Continue to the right before the hinged section drops back down. To collect the film reel, jump across the pelicans to the right. To head directly to the exit projector, jump along the ice in the water.

To take the upper path, jump over to the pelican near the ship and wait for the next pelican to float toward you.

Continue across the pelicans, and collect the e-tickets along the way.

When you reach the last pelican, jump to the right and land on the edge of the whale. Stay clear of the whale's blowhole, and wait for the water to die down.

When the path is clear, continue across the top of the whale and collect the film reel to the right.

Jump back to the left, and move across the pelicans. Position yourself above a piece of ice, and drop down to collect the e-tickets along the lower path.

When you're ready, turn around and move back to the right. Jump across the ice to reach the whale's open mouth.

Jump into the whale's mouth. Wait for a break in the dripping saliva, then run along its tongue. Hop onto the raft and activate the projector screen to return to Tortooga.

Back to Tortooga

Level Overview

You stop by Tortooga on your way to Skull Island. If you cleared out the enemies in the Jungle, you find Starkey near the Pirate Voyage projector screen. If you chose not to deal with the enemies in the Jungle, an invading force has taken control of the harbor. Explore Tortooga to see what's changed since your last visit, then speak to Gentleman Starkey or Beluga Billy near the projector screen.

If chose to leave Starkey in the with the hostiles in the Jungle, the first thing you need to do is clear out some of Tortooga's invaders. When you arrive in Tortooga, Gus points out some of the enemies in the area. One of the Bashers is guarding a blue chest on the docks, and two Spatters have Beluga Billy trapped on a rooftop.

Things to Do

- Take care of the invaders (optional)
- Find Daisy's Right Leg
- Speak with Billy or Starkey to open the Skull Gate
- Enter Pirate Voyage

NOTE

No new quests are available in Tortooga, but look for opportunities to complete or advance existing quests.

Jump across the boats in the Thinner, and start with the Basher across the harbor. You can use standard tactics to chip away at the your enemy, but the environment provides a nice shortcut to victory. Lure the Basher over to the tan patch in the dock, then move away and blast the planks with some Thinner.

When the Basher falls through the dock, the blue chest is left unprotected.

Daisy's Right Leg

Animatronic Daisy's second part is in the blue chest on the docks. After you deal with the Basher, open the chest to collect Daisy's Right Leg.

Head up toward the jail, and take out the Sweeper along the path. A second Basher patrols around the well. Use your Thinner and spin moves to defeat the Basher, and continue toward the Skull Gate.

Deal with the four Blotlings on the ground, then climb onto the rooftop and speak with Beluga Billy. Because Starkey gave you the secret password, Beluga Billy opens the Skull Gate.

If you chose to clear out all the enemies in the Jungle, you don't have to face any invaders. Collect Daisy's Right Leg from the chest on the docks, and speak to the pirates around the well. Each pirate you freed from jail gives you a gift.

Head up to the Skull Gate and talk to Gentleman Starkey. Starkey rewards you with a special pin and opens the Skull Gate for you.

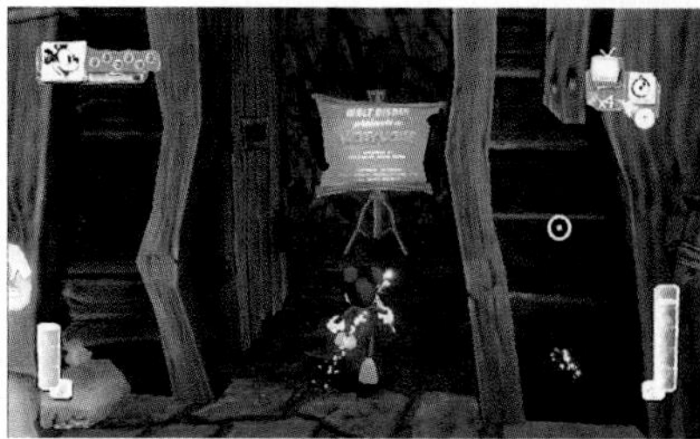

When you're ready leave Tortooga, activate the screen in the Skull Gate to enter Pirate Voyage.

Pirate Hero Pin

If you chose to complete both the "Jungle Symbols" and "Hostiles in the Jungle" quests, Starkey gives you this special pin when you reach the Skull Gate.

The Castaway: Part 2

You return to the makeshift raft, bobbing along with the swelling waves. Follow the driftwood to dry land, and brave your way through spider-infested trees.

Wait for a wave to lift the raft, then jump to the driftwood on the right. Wait for another wave to roll by, then jump across to the next piece of wood.

Jump to the island, and stand near the spiders to the right.

Wait for the spiders to bounce down, then run under them as they spring back up.

When you pass the second spider, jump over the pit to the right.

The next spider doesn't move until you approach it. Walk slowly toward the spider to coax it down from its web.

When the spider springs back up, continue to the right. Stand at the edge of the next pit. When the spider drops down, jump up and collect the e-tickets above the pit.

Land on the spider and wait for it to spring back up. When the spider reaches the top of its path, double-jump to the left. Grab the e-ticket, and drop to the tree below you.

Face the web to the right and double-jump onto the treetop. When you land, watch the spider swinging from the next tree.

When the spider moves toward you, jump on and swing through the e-tickets. Hop down to the right, and grab the film reel on the next tree.

Move to the left, and drop back down to the ground.

Dodge the spider to the right, and jump onto the stone in the water.

When the turtles to the right pull into their shells, they sink into the water. Two of the turtles dive at regular intervals. The turtle in the middle only dives when you touch it.

Stand on the stone and wait for the first turtle to dip under the surface of the water. When the turtle resurfaces, jump to the right and land on its shell.

When the first turtle prepares to dive again, jump across to the second turtle.

When you land, the second turtle begins to pull into its shell. Jump across to the third turtle before it can dive underwater, and hop across to the exit projector on the right.

Run past the projector and grab the last few e-tickets.

You've traversed the island, collected the film reel, and picked up a nice stash of e-tickets. When you're ready to move on, activate the projector screen to enter Pirate Voyage.

Pirate Voyage

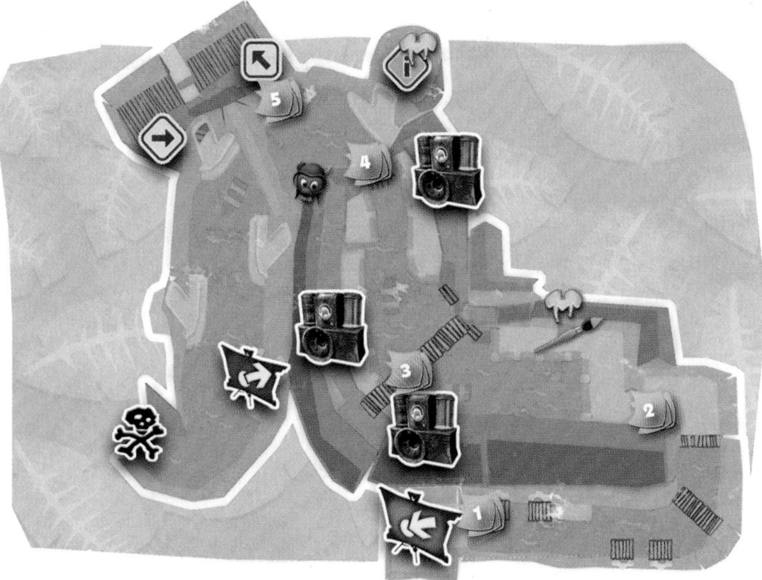

Things to Do

- Reach the boat ride
- Find the three pumps
- Fill each pump with Paint or Thinner
- Ride the boats through the gate
- Free Gremlin Erik
- Find Rigger Greene
- Enter Skull Island

Level Overview

The Pirate Voyage ride is flooded with Thinner, and the boats are barely scraping under the gate at the end of the ride. To reach Skull Island, you must fight past the Blotlings, track down three pumps, and find a way to pass through the gate.

You arrive behind the scenes of Pirate Voyage. Large gears slowly turn above a stream of flowing Thinner. As each paddle rotates into position, spray its gear with Thinner to stop the paddle in a horizontal position and create a safe platform. Jump along the paddles to reach existing platforms, and head to the end of the corridor.

When you reach the boat ride, Gus notices the pumps aren't working properly, and the excess Thinner has raised the stream too high. The boats can slip under the gate, but any passengers will be knocked into the Thinner. There are three pumps somewhere near the stream, but only one is in plain sight. Move to the end of the walkway and use some Paint to reveal an awning just past the ledge.

Fill in any missing planks and tiles to reach the corner of the building. When you reach the corner, double-jump up to the bridge above you.

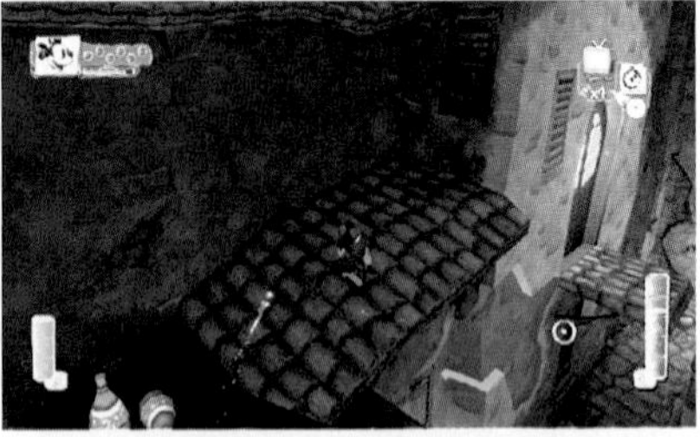

Turn back to face the ride's entrance, and look for the awning above the walkway. Make a running leap across to the awning, then spray the wall with some Thinner to reveal a hidden alcove.

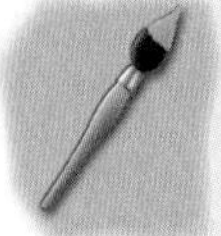

Spray the wall with Thinner to find the chest hidden above the awning.

Bronze Pin

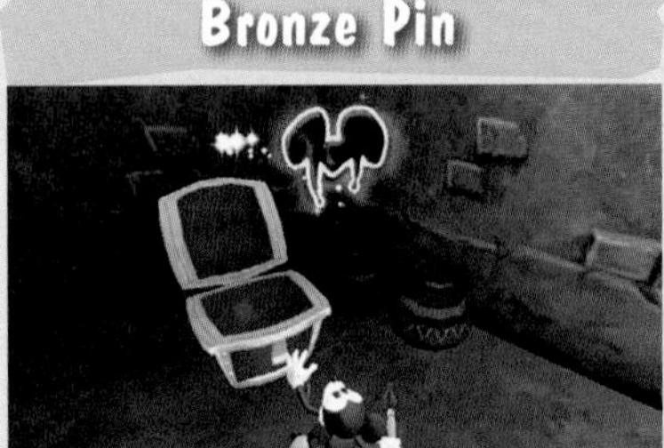

This pin is in a chest near the ride's entrance. Find a way up to the awning, and remove the wall to reveal an alcove.

3

Return to the bridge. Lay down some Paint to patch the bridge, and deal with the Sweeper on the other side. Charge across the bridge and dodge the Sweeper's attacks. Wait until you're safely across the bridge before you fight back, or just use a spin move to knock the Sweeper into the Thinner.

There's a pump hidden in the building across the bridge. Spray some Thinner on the wall above the missing awning to reveal the pump, then head over and blast it with your choice of Paint or Thinner.

Turn right, and cross to the edge of the rooftop. The pump Gus pointed out is in the building below you. Spray the roof of the building with more Thinner, then drop down and fill up the next pump.

When the bars drop down, a Spatter runs into the building to attack. Use Paint/Thinner to deal with the Spatter, or fire off a few spin moves and knock it into the stream.

Hop onto one of the boats, and jump to the ledge on the other side of the stream. Take out the patrolling Spatter, and stand near the large glowing glass door. Spray Thinner around to door to reveal the last pump. Fill the pump with your Paint/Thinner to clear a path through the gate.

Hop onto one of the boats, and ride through the gate. When the boat approaches the whirlpool, jump to the ledge on your left. Spray the bars with some Thinner and free Gremlin Erik from his cage.

Gremlin Erik

When you free Gremlin Erik, he tells you about a pirate trapped in the next cell. Before Erik leaves, he unlocks the cell and suggests you speak to the pirate.

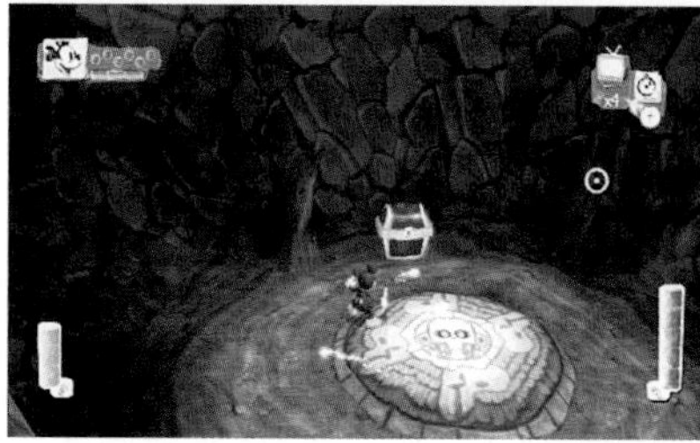

Wait for a boat to come along, then jump across to the open cell. Rigger Greene turns out to be the very pirate Horace is trying to track down. Smash the containers to collect some power-ups or e-tickets, then open the chest at the back of the cell.

Silver Pin

This pin is in a chest, near Rigger Greene. Free Gremlin Erik to unlock Rigger Greene's cell, then open the chest to add another pin to your collection.

Hop back to the boats and jump on the ledge to the right of the whirlpool. Spray the bars with Thinner and enter the corridor.

Take out the Spatter in the corridor and continue to the machinery around the corner. Deal with the Sweeper before you attempt to jump through the spikes. If you have any guardians available, consider firing one off to end the threat quickly.

Follow the corridor to return to the stream. Wait for a boat to surface, then hop on and ride across the Thinner. Take out the Spladooshes and check the cells for power-ups, or continue straight to the projector screen. When you're ready to leave, activate the projector screen and head to Skull Island.

Shanghaied

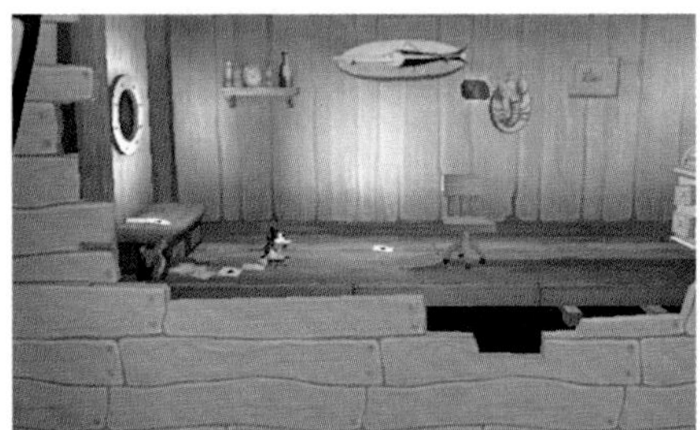

You appear in the lower decks of a pirate ship. Get past the crew of nasty characters, and climb the ship's sails to reach the safety of the crow's nest.

Jump up to grab the e-ticket, then drop down and use your spin move on the chair.

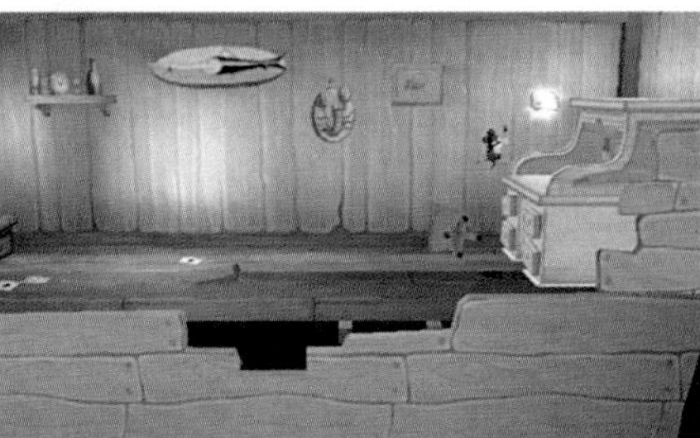

When the chair crashes into the desk, jump up to collect the white e-ticket.

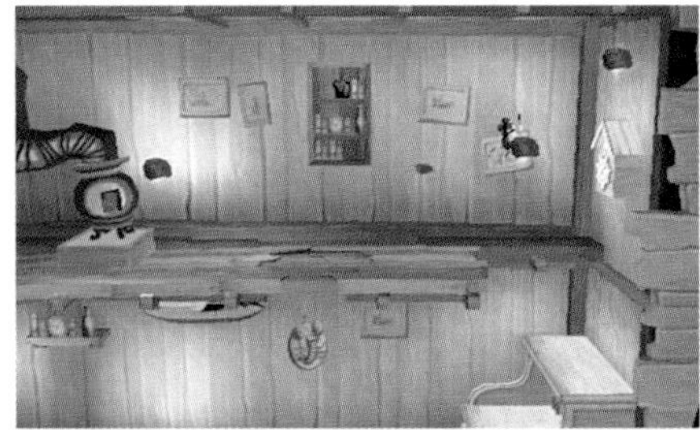

Hop to the top of the desk, and jump to the ledge above you. When you land, jump over and grab the e-tickets near the cuckoo clock to the right.

Return to the ledge and walk toward the stove. As you approach, several of the floorboards give way.

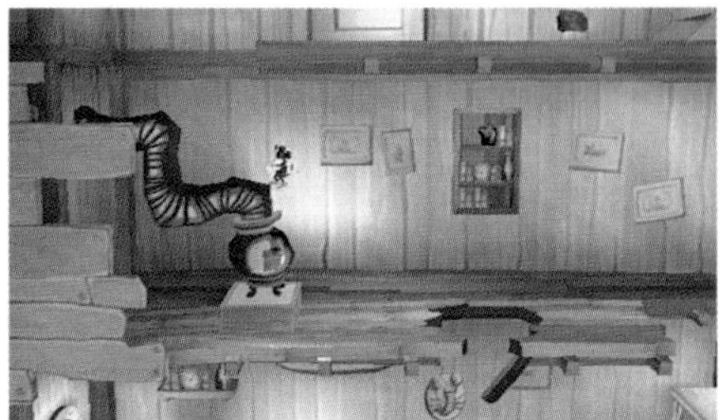

Watch for the flame popping out of the stove. When the stove door slams shut, hop over the gap and jump onto the stovepipe.

Jump up to the door on the right, and wait for the captain to pop out of the porthole. The captain swings a bottle, then disappears back into his cabin.

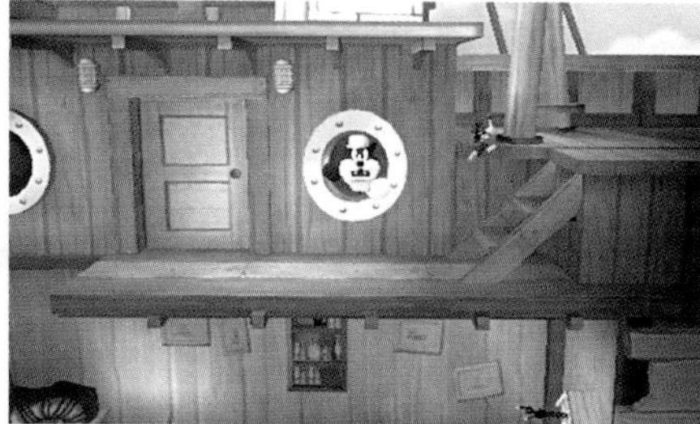

When the path is clear, run to the right and grab the e-tickets around the porthole. When you land, continue up the stairs.

Jump up to the box of signal rockets. A swab leans out from the window to the left, and jabs his mop toward the center of the ship. There are three narrow masts on the deck. Each mast holds a number of rolled-up sails.

Stand on the box of rockets, and wait for the swab to pull back into the window. Use the spin move to ignite a rocket, then hop down and run to the left. The rocket leaves a few puffs of smoke along its path; move quickly to take advantage of these temporary platforms.

Jump up and grab the health power-up near the mast to the left, then jump on the sail to the right.

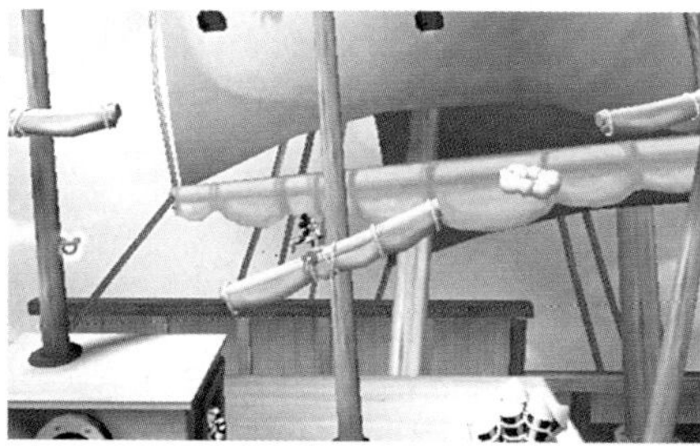

Stand on the sail's left edge to force the other side up a bit, then run over to the right.

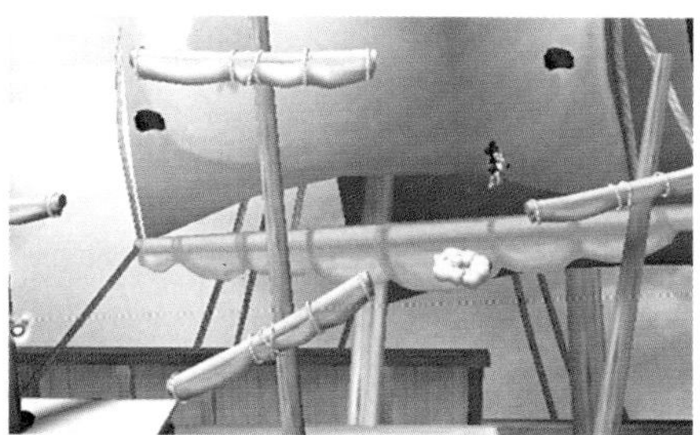

Hop onto the puff of smoke, and continue across to the sail.

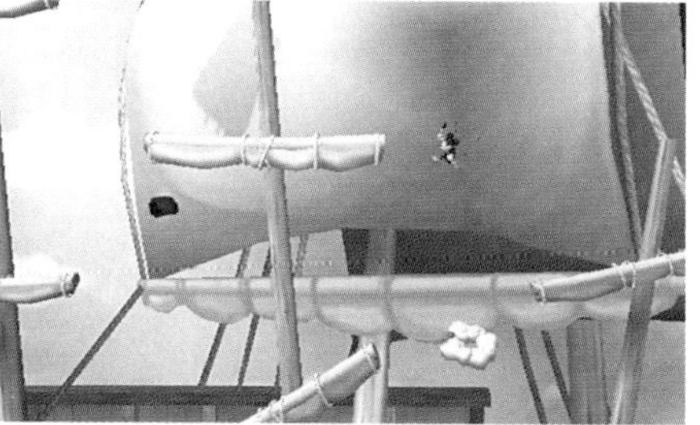

Move to the right just long enough to bring the sail level, then double-jump up to the left.

When you land, stand on the right half of the sail. Ignore the health power-up on the smoke to the right, and make a running leap to the mast on the left.

Double-jump to the projector screen in the crow's nest.

Jump past the screen and land on the large puff of smoke to the right. Jump back to the left, and collect film reel at the top of the mast. If the smoke has disappeared, you can't reach the film reel without firing off a fresh rocket.

When you're ready to leave, return to the crow's nest. Activate the projector screen to enter Skull Island.

Skull Island

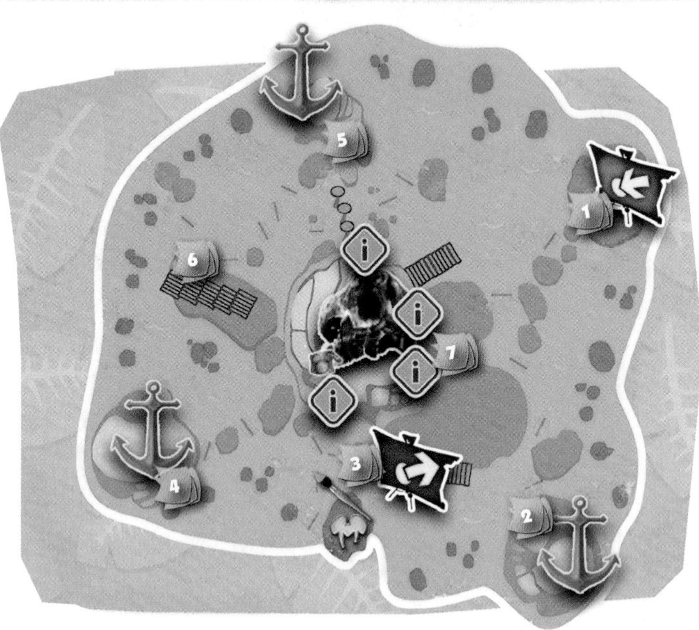

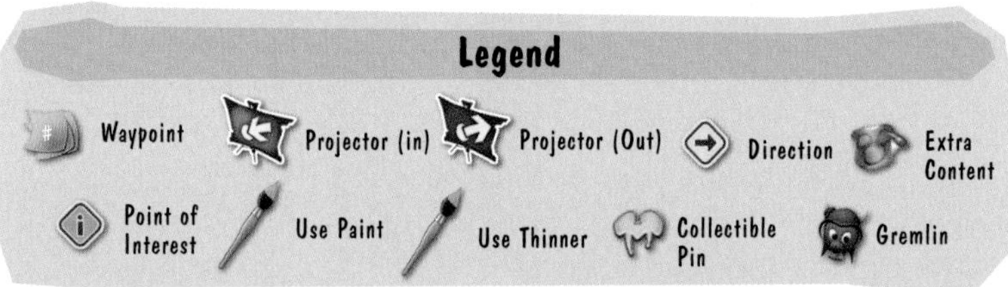

Level Overview

Skull Island is the heart of pirate territory and the source of Hook's mechanical crew. Hook is sailing the Jolly Roger somewhere in the surrounding Thinner; before you can reach him, you need to get your hands on a ship. Smee's boat is docked at the island, but three massive anchors are holding it below the Thinner. Find a way to cut the anchors, and set sail to take back the next rocket part.

1

You arrive on a small island, across the Thinner from Hook's machine. As Blotlings loiter on the shore, the machine cranks out brand new Bashers. Before you charge across to Skull Island, take a moment to uncover some hidden treasure.

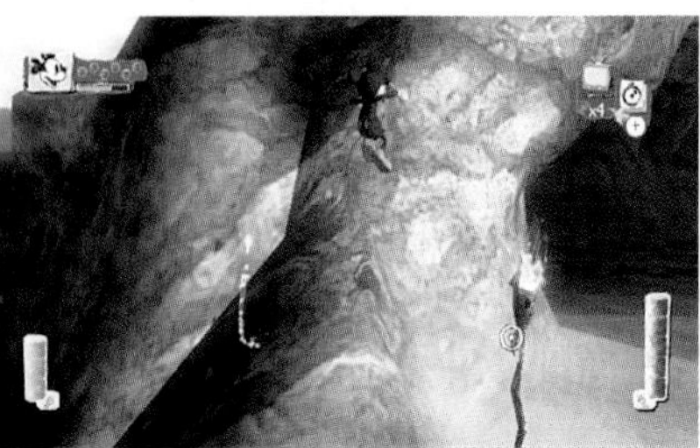

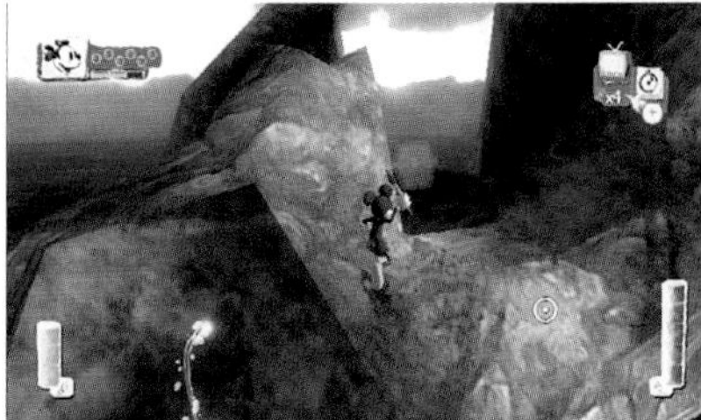

Exit the small cave, and move to the torch on your right. Jump along the steep rocks on the side of the island. There are very few footholds, but a little persistence should see you to the top. Spray some Paint to reveal the hidden chest between the jagged rocks.

Things to Do

- Cut the three anchors to raise Smee's boat
- Find Pete Pan
- Recover Daisy's Right Leg
- Deal with Hook's machine
- Sail to the Jolly Roger

Silver Pin

This pin is located above the Skull Island entrance. Climb to the jagged rocks above the cave to find it inside a hidden chest.

The first anchor is near Smee's boat. Follow the stones to the main island, then jump across the capsized boats to reach a small island. The anchor is guarded by two Spatters, and a set of bars blocks the cave entrance.

Climb the stairs near the cave entrance. When you reach the top, deal with the Sweeper and investigate the jagged rocks.

Thin out the rock near the red flag, then hop onto the gear and perform a spin move.

Head back down the stairs. Take care of the Spatters in the cave, then blast the anchor with your Thinner. Smee's boat rises up a bit, and it's time to track down the next anchor.

Jump across to the main island. Deal with the Blotlings if you wish, but any defeated Bashers are quickly replaced. If you'd rather avoid combat, run past Smee's boat and look for a path off the coast. Jump across the capsized boat and land on the stone ahead of you.

Look to your left and find the large blue rock, then spray it with Thinner.

Jump along the capsized boats to circle around the rock. When you reach the last boat, jump to the ramp on the side of the rock. Follow the ramp up to find another hidden chest.

Gold Pin

This pin is on the large blue rock off the coast of Skull Island. Use Thinner to reveal the chest inside the rock, then climb up and add another pin to your collection.

Climb down and jump back across the boats, then follow the trail around to the second anchor.

When the Sweeper spots you, it raises some bars to keep you from the anchor. Move to your left, and jump across the stones beside the cave. To easily slip into the cave, distract the Sweeper with a TV, or activate a Watch to slow down time.

Climb up to the top of the rocks, and spray some Thinner to create a new opening. Drop into the cave, deal with the Sweeper, and spray the anchor with Thinner. There's just one anchor left! Hop onto the gear, and spin move to drop the bars out of your way.

Exit the cave and jump back onto the trail of stones and capsized boats. Follow the trail all the way back to Smee's boat, and hop to the sand at the front of Skull Island.

Dodge any remaining enemies, and run across to the pier across the sand. Jump onto the pier and look for the metal sheds to your left.

Climb up along the sheds to reach the ledge above the walkway. The last anchor is nearly within reach.

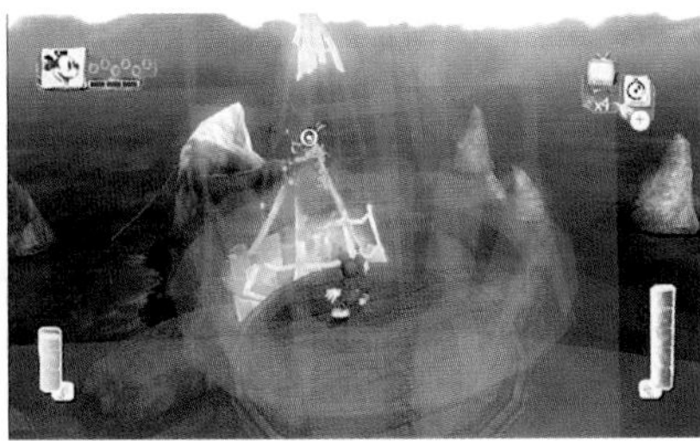

The third anchor is on the small island to the north. Use Thinner to remove the crow's nests, and jump along the masts to reach the stones near the island.

Follow the stones down to the island. Climb up the steps on the side of the island, and take care of the Sweeper near the red flag. Spray the blue stone with Thinner to expose the anchor, then fire off a second blast to cut Smee's boat loose.

After you've taken care of all three anchors, you can sail out to face Hook. If you want to leave right away, jump back along the masts and head over to Smee's boat. However, there's plenty left to do in Skull Island; Smee and the pirates want you to take out Hook's Beetleworx machine, and Pete Pan is hiding somewhere in the area.

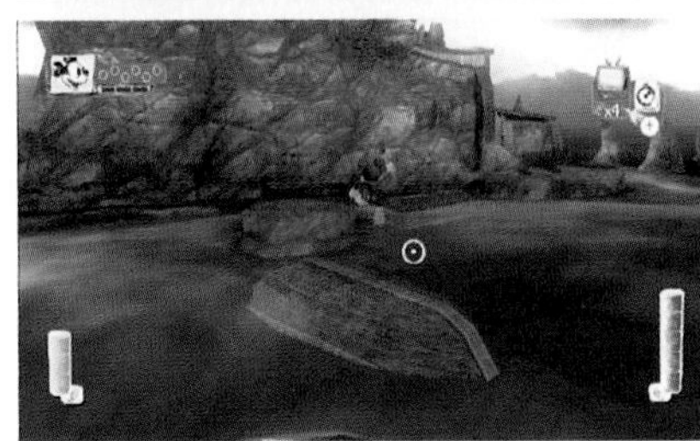

If you choose to stay, take the low path off the small island. Drop down to the torch below the ledge to find a trail of platforms running across the Thinner. Jump along the various platforms to reach the wrecked ship west of Skull Island.

Jump onto the ship's wreckage and use your Thinner to clear away the planks. Climb up along the ship, and jump across the gap to return to Skull Island.

When you land, thin out the planks to the right, and drop through the gap. Face back to the left and clear away the wooden barrier, then take care of the Spatter near the extra content.

Extra Content: Sea Battle

This extra content is on the upper platforms of Skull Island. Climb the wreckage off the coast to reach this area.

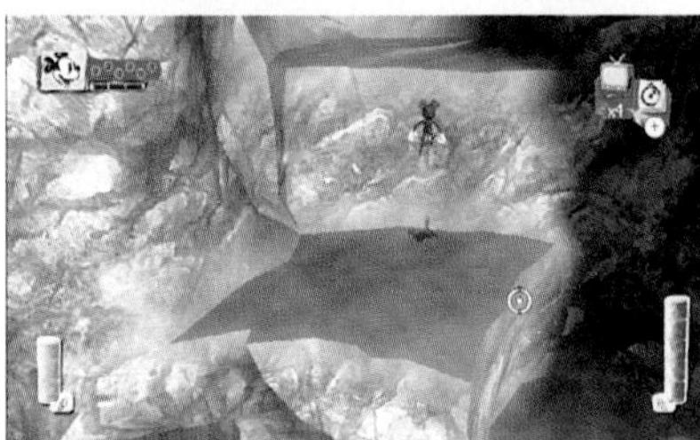

Turn around and follow the walkway around the side of the island. Head up the ramp near the planks, then climb up along the platforms carved into the stone.

When you reach the top of the platforms, you see Pete Pan frolicking near a blue chest. Head over and speak to Pete Pan to accept his "Save the Sprite" quest, then collect Daisy's Left Leg from the blue chest.

Quest: Save the Sprite

When Hook stole his Sprite, Pete Pan lost the ability to fly. It turns out he's more than willing to face Hook, but without his Sprite, Pete Pan is trapped on the top of Skull Island. He promises that if you save the Sprite, he'll come swooping in to personally deal with Hook.

Daisy's Left Leg

Daisy's fourth missing part is near the top of Skull Island. Open the blue chest near Pete Pan to collect Daisy's Left Leg.

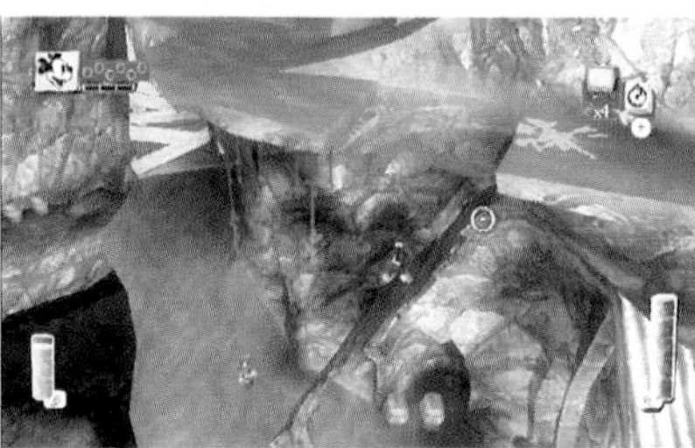

Climb back down the side of Skull Island, and head over to deal with Hook's machine.

Move to the sand at the front of Skull Island, and find the large steps carved into the stone. Jump up along the steps and hop over to the ledge to find the first pump.

Junction Point: Hook's Machine

How (or if) you choose to handle Hook's Machine has a significant effect on your next visit to Ventureland. If you choose to fill the pumps with Paint, you can collect a special pin. If you use Thinner on the pumps, you alter the environment in Skull Mountain. However, if you ignore the pumps, the pirates in Ventureland can't return to Tortooga. When you return to Ventureland, your choice to stop or ignore Hook's Machine determines which quests are available.

If you decide to stop Hook's machine, use your preferred method to take care of the Sweeper, then shoot a stream of Paint or Thinner into the pump.

Continue along the walkway, then jump onto the ledge and fill the second pump. Head back along the walkway and climb down to the sand.

Jump up to the pier and fill the pump just past the metal sheds.

Follow the walkway to circle the island. Use your preferred method to deal with any Spatters, and use Thinner to remove the wooden barrier. When you reach the end of the walkway, fill the last pump to stop Hook's machine.

If you chose to fill the pumps with Paint, return to Hook's machine. Use a blast of Paint to reveal the hidden chest. Open the chest to collect a special pin.

Pirate Friend Pin

This pin is a special reward from the "Hook's Machine" quest. If you choose to fill the three pumps with Paint, the Thinner drains from the machine. Spray some Paint to reveal the chest containing this unique pin.

When you're ready to leave Skull Island, climb aboard Smee's boat. Use some Paint to reveal the helm, then activate the boat to set sail for the Jolly Roger.

The Jolly Roger

See map on the following page

Level Overview

You've reached the Jolly Roger—Hook's infamous pirate ship, and the scourge of Wasteland's seas. The second rocket part is stowed somewhere on the ship, and Pete Pan's Sprite is held captive above the rigging. Outwit Hook in his devious game of hide-and-seek, or take to the tattered sails to stage a daring rescue. Like his ship, the captain is armed to the teeth. Climb aboard the Jolly Roger to put Hook out of commission.

You've made it to the Jolly Roger and must find a way to board the ship. Double-jump across in the crates to stay clear of the animatronic crocodile. Spin move into the winch to lower the lifeboat on the ship's side. Hop up and paint the next lifeboat, then dodge another attack from the crocodile as you jump over the gap. Ride up to the plank and climb aboard the Jolly Roger to confront Hook.

When you reach the deck, Hook springs out and invites you aboard. After eliminating the ship's stairs, he opens fire.

Things to Do

- Survive Hook's attacks
- Defeat Hook or free the Sprite
- Collect the second rocket part
- Check the ship for hidden treasure
- Return to Ventureland

Choose to square off against Captain Hook on the lower deck if you want to take the Thinner path and increase your Thinner capacity at battle's end. Otherwise, climb to the upper deck to free the Sprite and increase your Paint capacity.

Junction Point: Jolly Roger

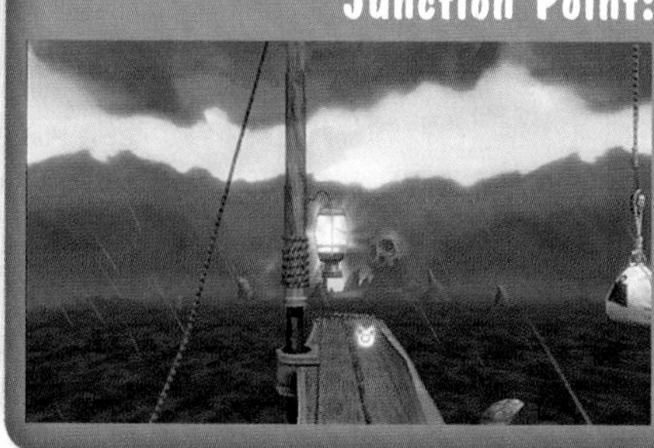

If you choose to battle Hook on the lower deck, you receive an upgrade to your Thinner capacity. If you choose to free the Sprite on the mast, your Paint capacity increases. Each option earns you a unique pin. How you deal with Hook also affects your story's ending.

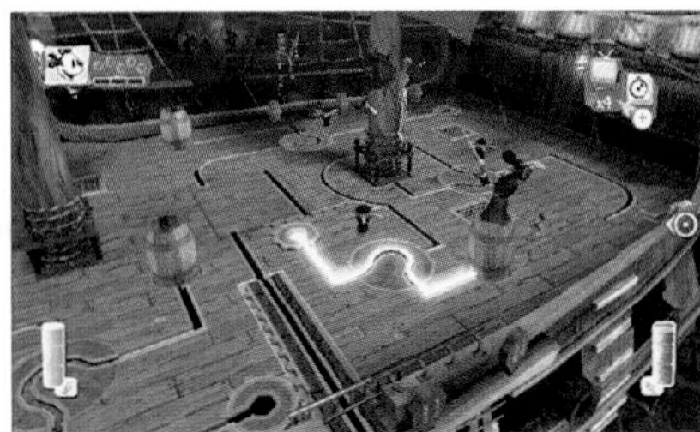

Hook appears in the three barrels on the deck at irregular intervals; keep your guard up for an attack from any of those three directions during the course of the fight. To wound the robot, thin out the barrel, then thin out its armor, before getting in close enough for a spin move. Of course, Hook won't let that happen willingly; watch out for its long blade that can slash you in close combat.

If you stay at range, the captain has even better weaponry at hand. Its pistol fires either a single-shot Thinner stream, or a triple-shot that can catch you with a stream while moving. When you see the triple-shot fired, freeze in between the streams as they fan out.

Hook rolls bombs at you too. The bombs turn red when they're ready to explode, and you'll take damage if you're caught near one when it goes boom. Double-jump over the bombs and keep your distance when they turn red.

You can defeat Captain Hook two different ways. The easier, and more satisfying, method involves having the villain "walk the plank." When Hook appears in a barrel, its current track lights up. Follow where the track goes to see where Hook will ultimately end up on a successful attack.

Each track has two potential destinations. You can change the track destination by using your spin move on the nearby deck wheel.

At the start of the battle, the tracks should all be set to ultimately deliver Hook to the plank. First, though, you need to open the gate across the plank. When Hook appears in the bottom left barrel, charge and stream Thinner to erase the barrel and Hook's outer shell.

When Hook is stripped bare, use your spin move to shoot him down the lit track. The robot spins out of control and smashes the gear at the end of the track. As the gear short-circuits, the plank gate opens.

Next, the long track to the plank must be connected; otherwise, Hook isn't going anywhere.

Wait for Hook to appear in the bottom right barrel. Circle around him to dodge Hook's attacks, and spray Thinner until barrel and armor are gone.

Close in and spin move to send the captain hurtling down the lit track. The second gear shorts out and the missing segment slides over to connect the long track.

Each time you score a hit on Hook, the robot spits out power-ups. If you're low on health, pick up any pink Mickey ears you see before attempting another round against Hook.

When Hook arrives in the top barrel, avoid the robot's attacks and stream Thinner all over barrel and outer armor.

Get in close one last time and use your spin move. With the long track complete, this final spin sends Captain Hook straight off the plank.

Hook's nemesis, a robotic crocodile, champs at the bit for a meal. Captain Hook is forced to flee at top swimming speed, and you've defeated the Jolly Roger boss.

You can also defeat Captain Hook with enough hard knocks. Instead of sending Hook toward the plank, use the three wheels to rotate the tracks and send him to smash against the door (bottom left barrel), the mast (bottom right barrel), and a secret passage (top barrel).

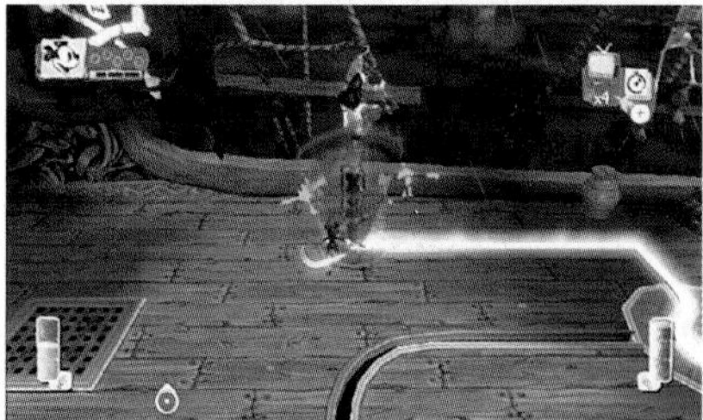

In the alternate track position, the top barrel sends Hook colliding with the ship wall, which in turn opens a secret passage with an extra chest.

In the alternate track position, the bottom left barrel sends Hook colliding with the door and deals more damage to the robot.

In the alternate track position, the bottom right barrel sends Hook colliding with the mast and strikes another blow against the robot.

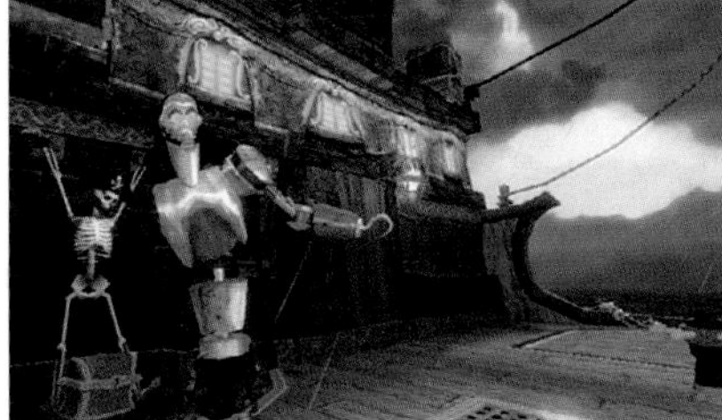

Continue battering Hook around like that and eventually the robot falls to pieces. It's a little more work, but it's worth the effort if the robot knocked you around earlier.

At the end of the battle, you receive the Captain Hook Pin for beating the robot one-on-one. Gus congratulates you with an upgrade to your Thinner capacity.

Captain Hook Pin

Whether you smash robot Hook to bits or send him spinning off the plank, you gain the Captain Hook Pin for defeating Hook on the lower deck.

To follow the Paint path and increase your Paint capacity, you need to find a way to the Sprite. Ignore Hook and run to the stairs. Dodge his ranged attacks and paint the stairs to reach the upper deck. Run around the mast and paint the treasure-packed lifeboat. Climb onto the treasure to find Hook hanging between the sails.

Hook attempts to thwart your rescue by breaking his own sail. Without the sail, the beam rotates away from you. While the captain pats himself on the back, paint the sail to move the beam back into position. Run across the beam and lay down more Paint to counter each of Hook's Thinner shots.

Paint the next sail to continue across the beams. Health power-ups are conveniently placed directly in your path, so you automatically recover from early damage. The next beam is already in position, so hop down and fill in the missing gear with a quick blast of Paint.

When the gears start turning, the beam moves up and rotates around the mast. Hook swings up to meet you and resumes his attacks. At close range, these attacks can be tough to dodge. Luckily, there are several health power-ups along the path to the Sprite. Thin out the barrels on the right. When the platform to the left drops down, hop on and jump across to the next sail.

When you land on the beam, Hook swings over and drops two sandbags on the next sail. The Sprite is just ahead, so keep a cool head to avoid a nasty fall.

Paint the sacks hanging near the mast and run to the right. The sacks have pulled a swinging platform into range. Hook picks up the pace with his Thinner attacks; do your best to dodge them, but watch your step. Jump onto the platform and hop across to the sandbags. Hook swings ahead of you and continues to fire.

Fill in the missing gear on the mast, then aim a short spray of Paint at the next sail. The sandbags prevent your beam from moving, so thin them out with a couple of quick blasts. It takes a while for the next beam to move into position, so hang back and dodge Hook's fire. Stay close to the gears; they don't provide a reliable defense, but they block the occasional shot. Use the health power-ups in the sandbags and wait for the sail to come around.

When you jump to the next sail, Hook swings across your path; time your double-jump to avoid him and fire off a spin move if you need a little extra distance.

When you land on the beam, the Sprite is just out of reach. Thin out the sail to move up the mast. Jump up and use a spin move to free the Sprite.

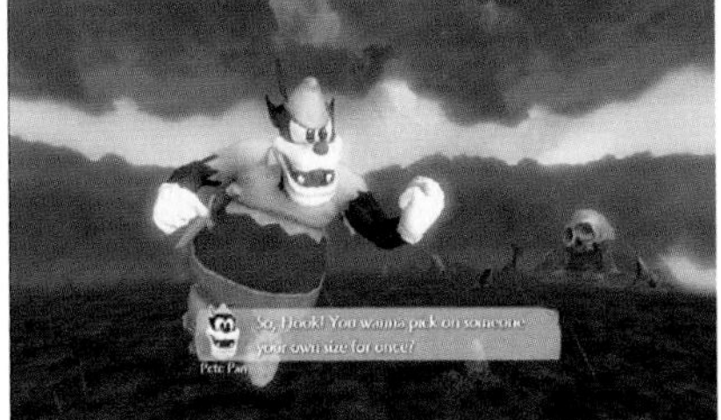

Soon after the Sprite flies off, Pete Pan swoops in to take over the fight.

With Hook distracted by the deceptively agile Pete Pan, you're free to slip back down to the deck. The ship's cabin pops open, you earn a special pin, and Gus presents you with a Paint capacity upgrade.

Whether you defeated or distracted Hook, you still have a few things to take care of before you leave. Move to the crack in the cabin wall and perform a spin move. Open the chest inside to collect a Bronze Pin.

Bronze Pin

This pin is part of Hook's personal stash aboard the Jolly Roger. Spin move through the cabin wall to collect this Bronze Pin from the chest.

Next, head to the upper deck and make your way across the sails. Drop down at the front of the ship to find some extra content.

Extra Content: Animatronic Croc

Wherever you find Hook, that crocodile is sure to be lurking. Cross the sails and grab this extra content at the front of the Jolly Roger.

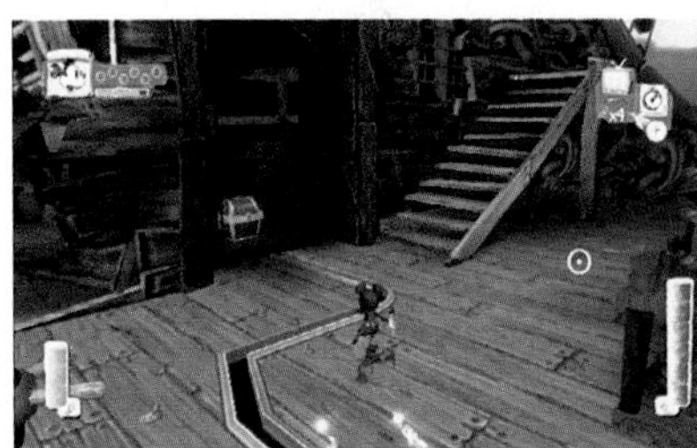

Finally, grab the rocket part from the chest in the doorway. The projector screen appears, and you're one step closer to repairing the Moonliner Rocket. When you're ready to leave, activate the projector screen and return to Ventureland.

Back to Ventureland

Depending on how you handled the machine on Skull Island and Captain Hook, you'll have a different experience when you return to Ventureland. If you eliminated the machine or kicked Hook off the Jolly Roger, the pirates return to the ship and leave Ventureland. If you didn't eliminate the robot-making machine on Skull Island, the pirates are too scared to return to the Jolly Roger and remain in Ventureland.

When you return to Ventureland, Smee rewards you with the last part of Daisy. He then either vacates with the rest of the crew, or sticks around sobbing for better days.

Seek out Animatronic Daisy in town and hand her the rest of the missing parts. She rewards you with the Animatronic Daisy Pin and gives you an optional quest. She lost an album near the train station in Mean Street; ask Big Bad Pete for more info.

Finish up any other quests you may be working on, or pick up a new one. If the pirates are still in town, you might want to try the "Move In" quests.

Jim the Puzzled has three riddles to solve. The first one asks: "I smile upon Ventureland, frozen in time. To seek your help, I ask this rhyme. Hunger is my only complaint. To sate my desire, please feed me some Paint."

The answer to Jim's first riddle is right in Ventureland. The Tiki Mask atop the Tiki Hut has a big grin on it. Shoot a stream

Current Ventureland Quests

- Bosun Blake Moves In (with pirates only)

Bosun Blake needs a place to live. Clear any junk out of the treehouse, so Bosun Blake can move in.

- Damien Salt and Henrietta Move In (with pirates only)

Damien Salt and Henrietta need a nice place. Clear any junk out of the treehouse, so that Damien Salt and Henrietta can move in.

- Find Daisy's Album

Daisy has asked you to find her scrapbook. She lost it near the Train Station in Mean Street. Pete should have more information.

- Gilda's Race in Ventureland

Earn a reward for completing Gilda's race through Ventureland.

- Housewarming (with pirates only)

Damien Salt wants a Tiki Mask for his new home. Find a Tiki Mask for Damien Salt as a housewarming present for his new home.

- Ice Cream For Henrietta (only if Damien left with the other pirates)

Get an ice cream treat for Henrietta. You can find ice cream in the Mean Street Ice Cream Shop.

- Plant Painting (without pirates only)

Paint back in all of the plants and trees in Ventureland. Pirates left a trail of thinned plants behind them when they left. Repaint as many of them as you can.

- Restore Bog Easy Plants (without pirates only)

Botanist Darvin in Ventureland wants you to restore all 20 plants in Bog Easy.

- Solve Jim's Riddle (without pirates only)

Solve a riddle for Jim the Puzzled: "I smile upon Ventureland, frozen in time. To seek your help, I ask this rhyme. Hunger is my only complaint. To sate my desire, please feed me some Paint."

- Solve Another Riddle for Jim (without pirates only)

Solve Jim the Puzzled's second riddle: "My hands, they move about my face. I am the master of every race. Who I am, time will tell. Thin me out for a gift that's swell."

- Jim's Third Riddle (without pirates only)

Solve Jim the Puzzled's third riddle: "My voice carries, near and far. I work in homes, in planes, in cars. I'm rarely hearing, always talking. Turn my dials and I start squawking."

of Paint into to release a sketch. Pick up the sketch and return to Jim for some e-tickets and the second riddle.

The Hut Shop does not open if the pirates are present.

Jim's second riddle reads: "My hands, they move about my face. I am the master of every race. Who I am, time will tell. Thin me out for a gift that's swell."

The answer to the second riddle is train station clock tower in Mean Street. Thin out the clock face and a secret passage opens in the street below it. Grab the candle and e-tickets inside and return to Jim for some more e-tickets and the third riddle.

Jim's third riddle goes: "My voice carries, near and far. I work in homes, in planes, in cars. I'm rarely hearing, always talking. Turn my dials and I start squawking."

You'll have to wait until you visit Bog Easy to solve the third riddle. The radio inside the lonely shack is the answer. Return to Jim for even more e-tickets and a Gold Pin reward.

If you didn't follow the romance quests for Damien Salt and Henrietta, then you can pick up the "Ice Cream for Henrietta" optional quest. Visit the Ice Cream Shop in Mean Street for some ice cream and return to Henrietta for your Ice Cream Pin reward.

Don't forget to visit the shop before you leave Ventureland. Depending on what you purchased earlier, you might still find a valuable health upgrade, the Pirates of the Wasteland Pin, and a wallet upgrade here.

When you're finally ready, set off for Mean Street. You have a few more tasks to accomplish back among familiar faces.

Back to Mean Street

When you return to Mean Street, Gremlin Markus is having a little bit of trouble with the local Bunny Children. Three of them have stolen power sparks from him. To get the Bog Easy screen projector up and operational, Markus asks you to retrieve the three missing power sparks.

If you're in a hurry, buy the power sparks from the Emporium. Or, reclaim them from the Bunny Children.

Current Mean Street Quests

- Bog Easy Projector Screen

Talk to Gremlin Markus about the Bog Easy Projector Screen.

Current Mean Street Quests
(continued)

- Bunny Roundup III

Round up the Bunny Children by luring them to the pipe sitting next to the City Hall.

- Detective Mickey III

Help Horace solve the Missing Mask case. A thief took a Tiki Mask from Tiki Sam in Ventureland. Track down the culprit.

- Find the Hatchet

Find Constance Hatchaway's hatchet in Lonesome Manor. For ages it has been suspected that Constance did away with her husbands, but no evidence has ever been found.

- History of Colonel Pete

Recover the lost cartoon of Colonel Pete. Enter Lonesome Manor, via Bog Easy, and locate the vintage cartoon that features Colonel Pete.

Search for the three Bunny Children around town. When you spot one of the Bunny Children hopping around, charge in close and stream Paint at the Bunny. If you hit a Bunny with Paint, it rolls up into a ball and releases one of Markus's missing power sparks.

Once you have all three missing power sparks, return to Gremlin Markus. He'll fix the Bog Easy screen projector if you have 15 power sparks. If you do, and want to zip straight out of town, you can enter the Bog Easy screen immediately.

If you want to gain more power sparks, or just want to complete the ongoing optional quests in town, talk to your favorite locals. Big Bad Pete offers you "Bunny Roundup III" for some e-tickets and a power spark reward.

This time the Bunny Children are hiding in barrels. Track down barrels around town, and use your spin move to shatter them. When you have four Bunny Children surrounding you, slowly drag them back to the City Hall and suck them up the pipe between the City Hall and the Fire Station.

Check back with Big Bad Pete to see if he has any other rewards for you. Depending on what quests you've completed, he may hand you another power spark for the "Restore Pete Pan" quest. He may also give you the "History of Colonel Pete" optional quest before you head off to Lonesome Manor.

Hook vs. Pete Pan Pin

If you chose to free the Sprite at the top of the Jolly Roger, be sure return to Pete for your promised reward. With Pete Pan back in fighting shape, Big Bad Pete hands over a power spark and this special pin.

Go talk to Horace at the Detective Agency too. Depending on what you've accomplished so far, he may give you the "Detective Mickey III" and "Find the Hatchet" optional quests.

For the third detective quest, head to Ventureland and track the stolen Tiki Mask to Dolly Dalmatian. For the hatchet quest, look for the hatchet in the Library attic.

Horace also gives you a power spark reward if you located Rigger Greene for the "Find the Missing Pirate" optional quest.

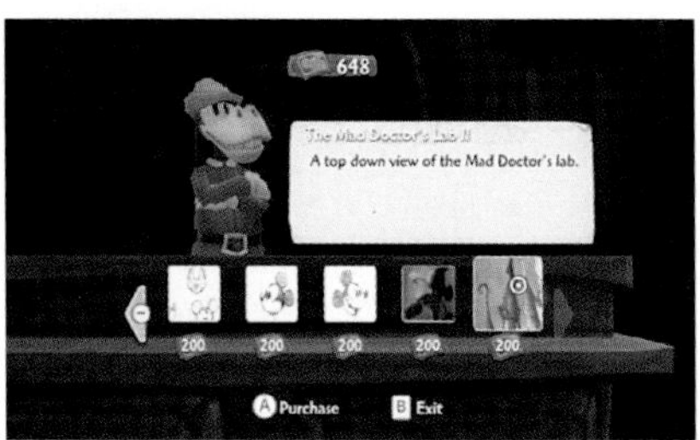

Before leaving Mean Street, visit the Emporium to see what else you might like to purchase. If you have extra e-tickets to spare, collect some more concept art or pins.

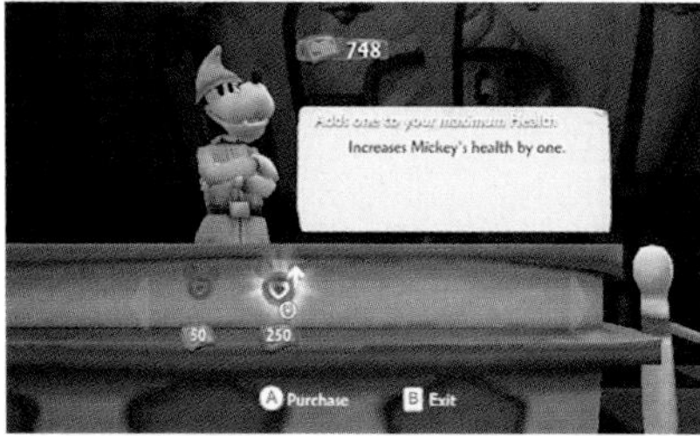

Don't forget to check the Ice Cream Shop and purchase the health upgrade for 250 e-tickets.

See the Usher in front of the Cinema and hand in any film reels you've collected for more rewards.

When you're ready, take the plunge into the Bog Easy screen. First, you'll travel through the Lonesome Ghosts: Part 1 2D level.

Lonesome Ghosts: Part 1

You arrive outside a haunted mansion. Furniture floats through the air, doors and shutters swing on their hinges, and mischievous ghosts are more than happy to stir up some trouble for a new visitor.

Enter the mansion, and jump onto the newspaper at the bottom of the stairs.

Float up on the newspaper, and collect the e-tickets on the way to the ceiling. A ghost appears on the stairs to the right, and starts a little batting practice.

Jump onto the chandelier and swing above the ghost. Hop over to the newspaper on the right, and float up to the ledge above you.

Jump off to the left, and grab the e-tickets above the ledge. Hop back onto the newspaper before it floats back down.

Jump onto the chandelier, and swing across to the dresser on the right.

When you land on the dresser, the top drawer begins to float away. Hop onto the drawer, and ride over to the right.

Jump over the drawer floating toward you, and continue toward the next dresser.

Jump over the dresser and land on the ledge. A line of e-tickets runs above the broken stairs to the right.

Double-jump through the e-tickets, and grab the film reel on the next ledge.

Move back to the left, and drop through the gap in the stairs.

When you land, you can run past the stairs to collect some extra e-tickets, or you can head past the ghost on the right to proceed to the exit projector.

If you choose to collect the e-tickets, run to the top of the stairs. The ghost to the left is throwing dishes onto the ground.

Wait for the ghost to throw a pile of dishes, then drop from the stairs and run to the left. When the window shutters snap shut, jump onto the windowsill.

Jump over and grab the e-ticket on the next windowsill, then wait for the shutters to snap shut again.

Hop along the windowsills, and wait for the ghost to throw another pile of dishes. Jump over to the stairs, and continue to the left.

When you reach the bottom of the stairs, stay put. Wait for the ghost to knock on the door ahead of you.

After the door swings open, run to the left and grab the e-ticket. When you're ready, continue to the right and activate the exit screen to complete the level and head into Bog Easy.

LONESOME MANOR

Bog Easy

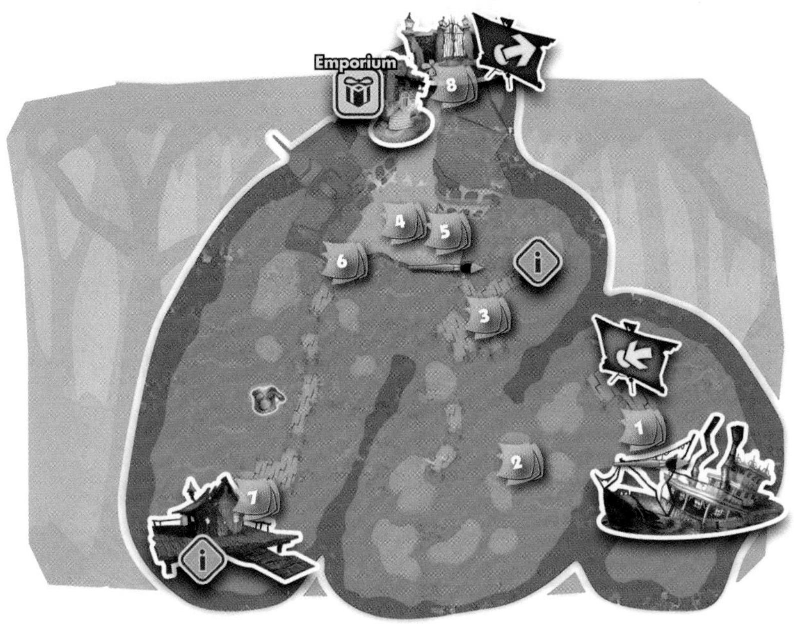

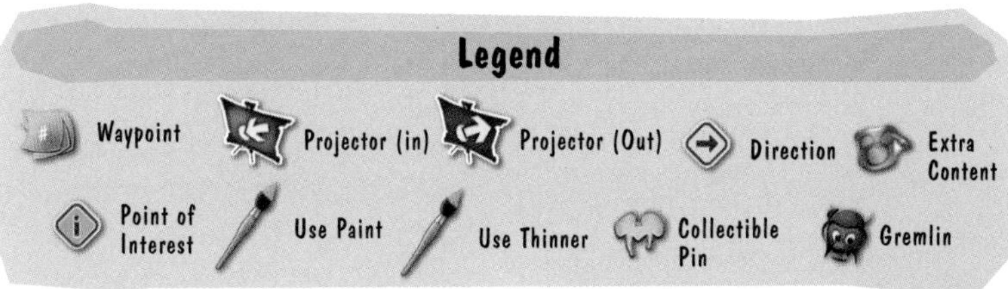

Level Overview

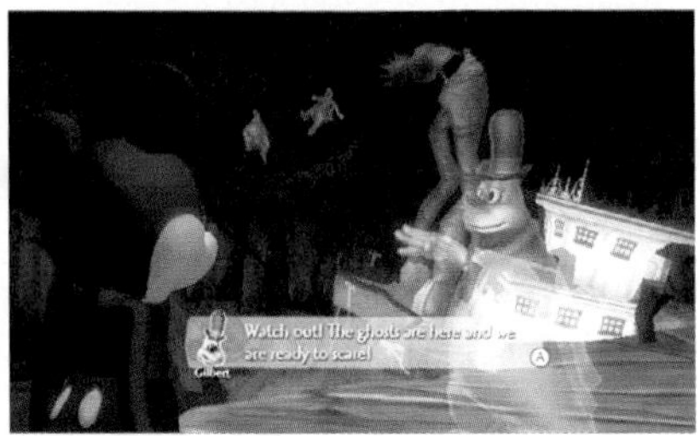

Bog Easy has been overrun by ghosts. You have a choice when you arrive: help the ghosts scare the local inhabitants or aid the townsfolk in driving off the ghosts. One side or the other will open the gate to Lonesome Manor if you complete the necessary tasks. It's the start of a *boo*tiful relationship.

You begin in the swamps outside town, near a sunken steamer. Speak with all the ghosts, and then with Gilbert by the submerged boat.

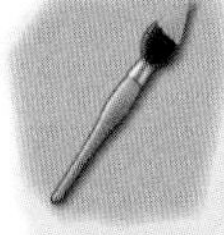

Coat the top of the sunken steamer with Thinner to discover a hidden compartment with the Badge of Courage.

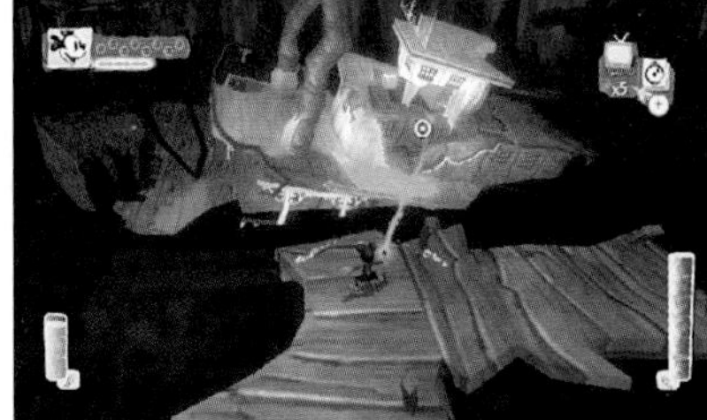

Shoot Thinner on the top level of the steamer to reveal a passage down into the boat. Double-jump off the dock and onto the boat. Enter the steamer and recover the Badge of Courage.

You'll need the Badge of Courage later when you visit Louis out at the lonely shack, or you can give it to Ian for some extra e-tickets if you aid the ghosts in scaring the townsfolk.

Things to Do

- Choose to help the ghosts or the townsfolk
- Retrieve the Badge of Courage from the sunken steamer
- Cross the swamp to town
- Scare or help Bertrand
- Scare or help Louis
- Speak with Metairie or Ian to open the Lonesome Manor gate
- Get Animatronic Donald's quest
- Search the area for power-ups and collectibles
- Exit to the Lonesome Ghost 2 level

Bog Easy Quests

- Help Gilbert Scare Someone

Find Gilbert in the town square. Gilbert has moved to the square and awaits your help in unleashing a new wave of boo scares on the locals.

- Light the Lamps

Bertrand is scared and wants you to light the eight lamps in the area. Bertrand would never admit to being afraid of the dark, but when all the lamps are lit he is undeniably more comfortable.

- Lonesome Manor Gate

Find a way to open the gate to Lonesome Manor. Find the means to open the gate somewhere in Bog Easy. Explore and investigate to figure it out.

- Recover Louis' Courage

Louis wants you to find his courage medal, lost near the partially submerged boat. Louis was bravely exploring the swamp when his courage fell off. He quickly retreated to his cabin and has been afraid to leave it.

- Recover the Runaway Book

Find a lost book somewhere in Bog Easy. Ian the ghost wants you to find the book that ran away from Leona's Library, in Lonesome Manor, as a result of his horseplay.

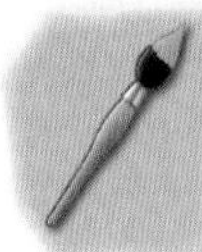

Paint in the docks outside of town to reduce your chances of falling into the Thinner while jumping around.

2

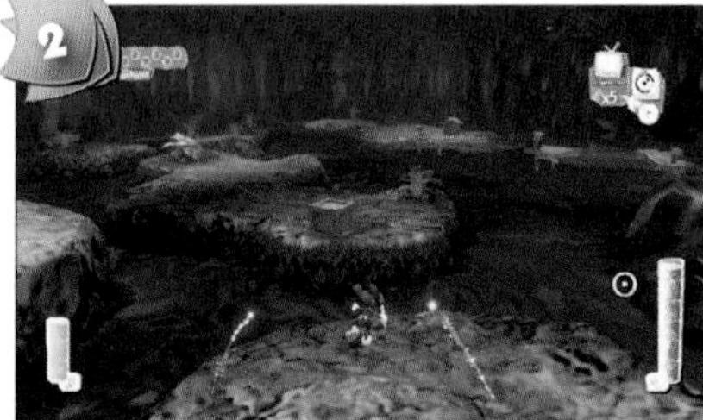

Navigate the swamp to reach the town proper. The Thinner snakes around various raised islands. Double-jump from island to island and pick up any resources along the way. You can Paint in many translucent plants on the islands to gain extra power-ups.

3

Paint in the docks outside of town to increase your safe footing. If you leave the docks translucent, the jumps between islands and docks are much tougher to make. Rather than end up in the Thinner, play it safe with some extra Paint.

Just outside of town, the dock branches off to the right and leads to a small island. Speak with Ian out on this island if you want to pick up the optional quest "Recover the Runaway Book." See the sidebar for more details.

Optional Quest: Recover the Runaway Book

If you visit Ian and accept the "Recover the Runaway Book" quest, he asks you to find one of Madame Leona's missing books. You turn in the quest later in the Lonesome Manor Library, but you can find the book in Bog Easy. Enter town and walk down the main street toward the Lonesome Manor gate. Look left for stairs leading to a blue door. This is the door to the closed Bog Easy Emporium. Enter the blue door and the book is within. If you take the book back to Ian, he insists that you deliver to Madame Leona yourself. If you don't take the book back to Ian, you can claim that you found the book when you meet Madame Leona, but Ian withholds his pin when you return to Bog Easy again. Madame Leona rewards you either way.

If you want to side with the Bog Easy residents against the ghosts, carry out Metairie's quests.

Seek out Metairie in the center of town. She tells you that the ghosts have moved out of Lonesome Manor for some reason and are scaring the townsfolk.

She's not scared, but Bertrand and Louis can't walk down the street without jumping at their own shadows. Metairie sends you to speak with Bertrand and Louis.

Paint the eight lanterns in town to finish Bertrand's quest.

Talk to Bertrand next to the dock entrance. He asks you to run around town and light eight lanterns for him. With the extra light, he won't be scared, and you'll earn favor with Metairie. Two lanterns flank Bertrand near the dock entrance.

Another rests near the exit toward the lonely shack. The rest line the streets all the way down to the Lonesome Manor gate. Paint them all to give Bertrand a dose of courage.

NOTE

Look for a power spark in the back corner of Bog Easy to the left of the Lonesome Manor gate.

TIP

If you want to side with the ghosts and scare some of the locals, carry out all the ghosts' quests. However, Metairie will withhold her Gold Pin.

Near the exit into the swamps toward the lonely shack, speak with Gilbert. He asks you to help him scare Louis.

Regardless of which side you're on, head out to the lonely shack.

Extra Content: Lonesome Manor Passage

As you head to the lonely shack, you pass this piece of extra content on a small island to your right. Double-jump out to the island, collect the concept art, and return to the dock without losing a step toward the lonely shack.

Speak with Louis out at the lonely shack. If you're helping the ghosts, don't return the Badge of Courage to Louis and extinguish all the shack lanterns with Thinner. In the dark, Gilbert can give Louis a good scare. If you're siding with Metairie, return the Badge of Courage to Louis. He thanks you, and you've completed the tasks necessary to have Metairie open the Lonesome Manor gate for you.

Junction Point: Animatronic Donald

Before you head off to Lonesome Manor, speak with Animatronic Donald in the center of town and pick up his "Find Donald's Parts" quest. Most of the parts are inside Lonesome Manor, and you'll receive Donald's Torso from the ghosts when next you return to Bog Easy, if you shut off the organ in the Lonesome Manor Ballroom. If you do restore Animatronic Donald, he becomes your pal and gives you a special pin, and he'll play a more friendly role in the game's ending.

8

Return to town. If you sided with Metairie, she rewards you with a Gold Pin and opens the Lonesome Manor gate on the far side of town. If you sided with the ghosts, they'll open the gate. Journey through the Lonesome Ghost: Part 2 level to reach the Manor House.

Optional Quest: Pipe Organ Madness

Gabriel gives you the "Pipe Organ Madness" quest just before you leave Bog Easy at the Lonesome Manor gate. Complete this quest in the Lonesome Manor Ballroom by playing a special tune on the organ. See the Ballroom section later in the chapter for complete details. If you repair the organ, the ghosts will give you Donald's Torso as a reward and happily depart Bog Easy. If you don't repair the organ, the ghosts will still be hanging around Bog Easy when you return.

Lonesome Ghosts: Part 2

You return to the haunted mansion to give these ghosts a taste of their own medicine. Move through the floating books and slamming doors, and switch on some lights to send these pests into hiding.

Wait for the ghost to open the door to the right. Grab the white e-ticket before the door slams shut.

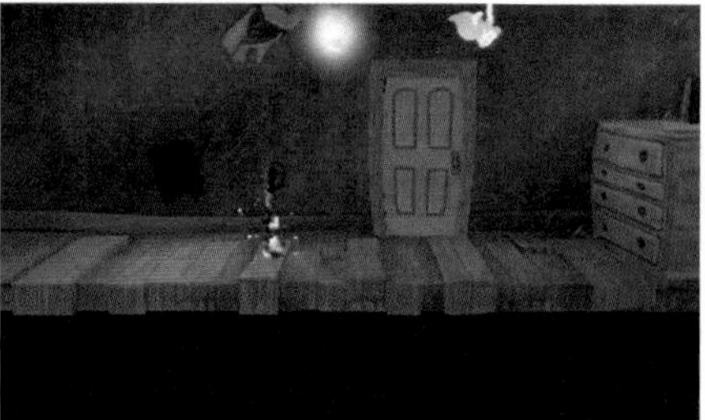

Stand near the switch on the door's left side, and use a spin move to flip on the light. After the ghost disappears, the door no longer opens. Make sure you collect the white e-ticket before you hit the switch.

Move past the door, and jump onto the dresser to the right. Face back to the left, and double-jump to the floating pot on the next floor.

Hop onto the pot, and wait for the window shutters to close. Jump to the right and grab the e-tickets on the sill, then hop across the pot to reach the newspaper to the left.

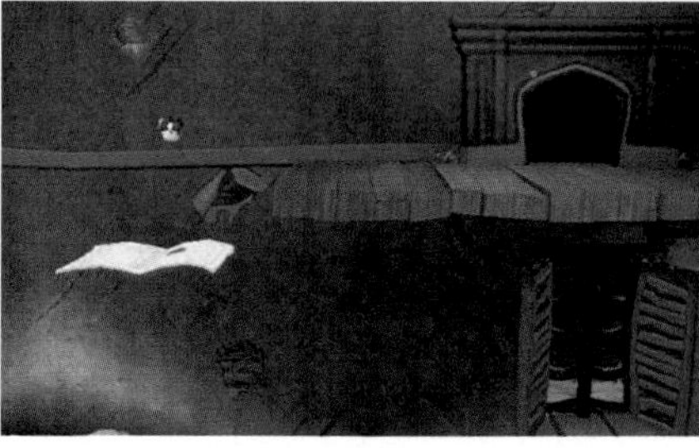

Ride up on the newspaper. Jump up to grab the e-ticket above you, then hop over to the ledge on the right.

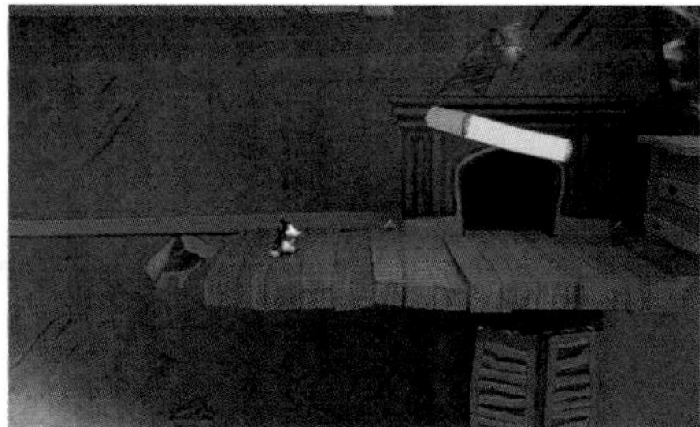

A dresser drawer is floating along a path in front of the fireplace. Wait for the drawer to float down to the dresser.

Hop onto the dresser, and stand on the left edge of the drawer. Ride up to the next floor, and grab the e-tickets to the left. The nearby ghost is taking a nap above a large book.

Stand near the bookcase, and use a spin move on the light switch. When the light comes on, the ghost vanishes into the book.

Hop onto the floating book, and double-jump to the swinging chandelier.

Swing over to the right, and jump down to the dresser. Collect the e-tickets in the area, then hop back up to the chandelier.

Swing back to the left and jump onto the floating book. Ride the book up to the next floor.

Jump off the book, and walk over to the left. The ghost is throwing dishes to the floor, and the shutters above you are springing open.

Wait for the ghost to throw a pile of dishes, then jump onto the dresser. Stand near the switch, and use the spin move to flip on the light.

Wait for the shutters to close, then jump across to the windowsill. Continue up to the next floor before the shutters snap open again.

When you land, a newspaper floats down from above you. Move to the right, and jump up to the switch near the door.

A ghost appears to the left. If left alone, the ghost rolls into a ball, and hits himself straight at you. Use a spin move on the switch to take care of the ghost before he can complete his attack.

Hop onto the newspaper, and ride up to the next floor. The last ghost is holding the door shut. You can see both the film reel and the exit projector to the right.

Jump over and grab the film reel. Stand near the switch and use your spin move to flip on the light. The ghost vanishes, and the door drops to the ground. You've cleared the path to the exit screen.

You can activate the projector right away, or you can collect the remaining e-tickets. Use the floating book to reach the floor below you.

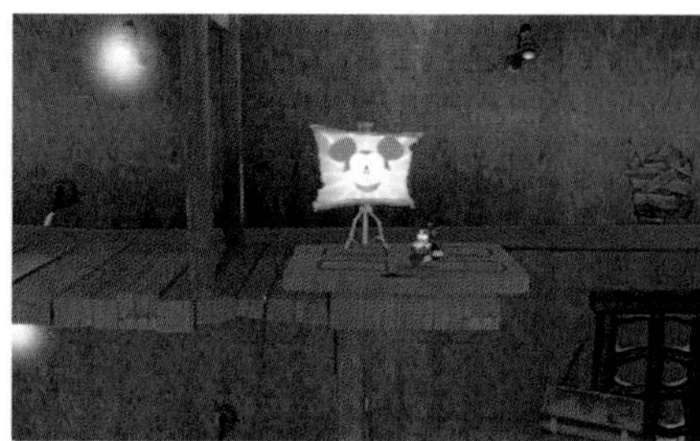

When you're happy with your e-ticket count, return to the exit screen. Activate the projector to complete the level.

Manor House

Level Overview

Lightning flashes from storm clouds when you arrive outside of the Manor House. A Thinner lake spills out into the graveyard, and the house itself is guarded by the Mad Doctor's minions. You must figure out how to climb to the second story balcony, free Gremlin Neville, and open the Manor House door—all without ending up splat at the claws of an enemy or falling off the Manor cliff sides.

Move out from the entrance projector screen and stay to the left on the small path that runs around the Thinner

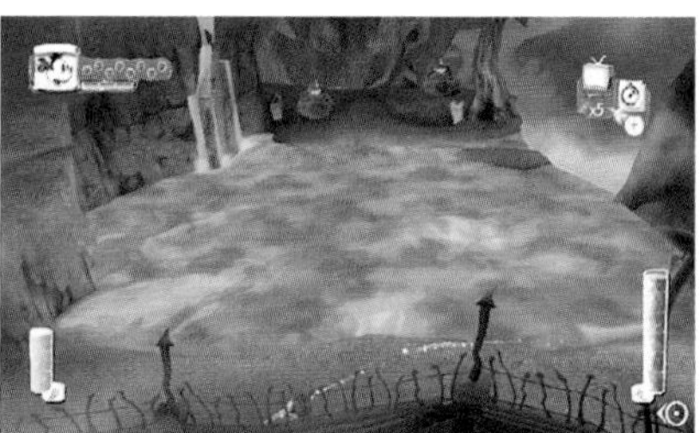

lake. Head straight up to the Manor House if you want to take the shortcut, but you'll miss out on some treasures in the graveyard.

Things to Do

- Recover the graveyard treasures
- Approach the Manor House and speak with the Mad Doctor
- Figure out how to reach the second story balcony
- Free Gremlin Neville
- Beat off the enemy Blotlings
- Drop an anvil on the pressure pad
- Search the area for power-ups and collectibles
- Exit to the Mad Doctor: Part 1 level

Lonesome Manor Quests

- Battle the Beetleworx

Break the three Beetleworx generators in the Attic. Watch for the vulnerable points and use Thinner.

- Catch the Flying Books

Madame Leona asks that you collect the six flying books that are loose in the Library... If you have the time.

- Enter Lonesome Manor

Enter Lonesome Manor just like the quest says.

- Help the Ghost in the Foyer

Free the Lonesome Ghost. The ghost in the bottle needs your help to get free! Activate the two switches in front of his prison to reach him.

- Match the Paintings

Match the paintings in the Stretching Room. Use the spin move on a section of painting to spin it into the correct position. You've got to match them all!

- Oswald in Mean Street

Oswald awaits you in Mean Street. Travel to Mean Street and contact Oswald.

- Play the Pipe Organ

Play the pipe organ's song. Perform along with a demon organist on the keyboard.

Lonesome Manor Quests (cont'd)

- Restore Leona's Paintings

Restore the art collection. Madame Leona asks you to repair and straighten her four paintings around the Library... If you are inclined to do so.

- Retrieve Rocket Part

Find the Mad Doctor's rocket part.

- Return to Ian in Bog Easy

You have aided Leona in the Lonesome Manor. Return to Ian in Bog Easy for your reward.

- Settle the Library Bookcases

Calm the Library spirits. Find the hidden skulls and restore them with Paint. This pacifies the spirits that possess the bookcases.

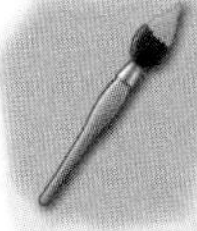

Thin out the brown tree to release an anvil. The anvil lands on a pressure plate and opens the secret area in the graveyard.

2

If you want to explore the graveyard area, stop in front of the tree on the first ledge. Spraying Thinner on the tree drops an anvil onto the nearby pressure plate. This raises islands in the Thinner lake, which you can cross to reach the Spladoosh-guarded graveyard.

3

Double-jump carefully across the three rock islands in the Thinner lake. When you reach the graveyard, tag the closest Spladoosh and double-jump back to the third island. Wait for the Spladoosh explosion, then do the same for the second Spladoosh.

Once the area is clear of enemies, read all the tombstone inscriptions for fun, and shatter the headstones for extra power-ups. Don't forget the Bronze Pin hidden behind the cliff.

Head up to the Manor House. Double-jump over the hazards, such as the Thinner stream and the gap between the lower and upper sections.

The Mad Doctor surprises you in the outer courtyard in front of the Manor House. He brags about his defenses and says they'll stop you cold. Confident in his security measures, he jets off in his flying machine.

Explore the area in front of the Manor House. Beware of the ledge to your right. It holds an attractive chest, but it's a trap. As soon as you step near the chest, the ledge gives way and drops into the gloom below. You don't want to be on that chunk of rock when it plummets.

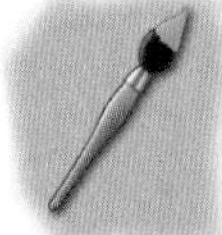

Blast the four columns in front of the house to form a jumping path to the second story balcony.

Reach the second story by thinning out the four front columns. This forms a jumping path up to the balcony. You can even circle up to the front steps and jump off there to reach the third column if you want to cut down on your jumps. From the thinned-out fourth column, double-jump through the gap in the second story railing to land on the balcony.

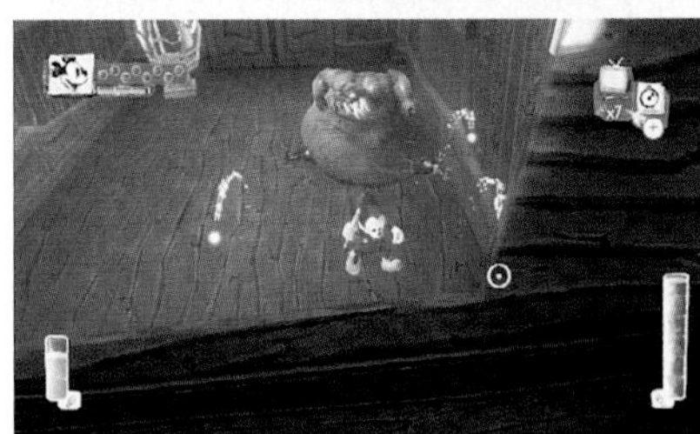

To free Gremlin Neville, splash Thinner on the wall to your left. This opens a secret room with Neville and a Spladoosh guard. Use whatever method you like best to remove the Spladoosh. Neville rewards you with the Anvil Pin and an Anvil sketch.

Pick up another Anvil sketch from the chest in the balcony's bottom left corner.

Gremlin Neville

Find Gremlin Neville tucked into the back corner of the second story. Ascend the thinned-out columns and spray Thinner on the wall to your left. Deal with the Spladoosh guard and free Gremlin Neville with your spin move. He rewards you with an Anvil sketch.

Extra Content: Lonesome Manor II

Instead of going left to rescue Gremlin Neville on the second story balcony, walk over to the right side. Vaporize the toon wall with some Thinner to discover this piece of extra content hidden in a secret room.

8

Of course, the Mad Doctor doesn't want you entering the house, and he's left his minions behind to keep you from the front door. More difficult Spatters and a Sweeper emerge from the house to try to end to your questing.

Take out the Sweeper first. It's easiest to use your spin move and knock the enemies over the side for a long fall. The longer you wait, the more enemies spawn, so take care of business quickly.

Return to the courtyard near the broken ledge. Use an Anvil sketch to drop an anvil onto the pressure plate out there. This opens the front doors and reveals the exit screen.

9

Enter the projector screen before more enemies arrive. Jump through and you pop over to the Mad Doctor: Part 1 level.

The Mad Doctor: Part 1

You arrive at the entrance to the Mad Doctor's lair. This decrepit castle is filled with crumbling walkways, fiendish traps, and reanimated skeletons.

Run to the right, and jump up to grab the e-tickets. Move quickly to reach the ledge before the bridge falls away.

Stand on the ledge and wait for the castle door to slam down. When the door moves back up, slip under the spikes and step into the castle. Walk slowly toward the column to the right.

Wait for the mounted blades to drop from the column, and jump over to the health power-up on the right.

When you land, the walkway begins to crumble. Run through the health power-up, or jump past the cracks in the stone.

Stop just before the next column. Face the e-tickets to the right, and wait for the mounted blades to fall.

Hop over the blades and jump through the line of e-tickets. Before you move onto the stairs, walk back to the left and pass through the coffin-shaped clock.

Jump across the gap in the floor, and grab the e-ticket to the left. Hop back over the gap and return to the stairs past the clock.

Jump onto the stairs and move toward the health power-up to the right. The stair boards flip up to form a ramp.

Double-jump straight into the air to avoid slipping down the stairs. While you're up in the air, the stair boards flip back down.

Continue up the stairs and grab the e-ticket to the right. The stair boards continue to flip up and down at regular intervals. Wait for the boards to flip down, then jump up to the saw blade at the top of the stairs.

When the saw blade moves out of the way, double-jump up to the ledge on the right. When you land, stay clear of the skeleton spider hanging to the right.

Stand in front of the column, and wait for the skeleton spider to spring down.

When the spider bounces back up, jump across the gap to the right. If needed, hop onto the health power-up, then double-jump across the gap.

When you land, approach the skeleton spider above the next gap. Wait for the skeleton to spring back up, then jump across and grab the film reel.

You can drop through the gap to reach the exit projector, but the long fall costs you a health pip. To safely reach the exit, move back to the saw blade at the top of the stairs.

When the saw blade moves out of the way, drop to the stairs and grab the e-tickets to the right.

Stop at the column to the left of the exit projector. A skeleton pops out from the column's right side and throws a stone toward the ground.

After the stone crashes down, run over to the right. When you're ready, activate the exit screen to complete the level and move on to the Foyer.

Foyer

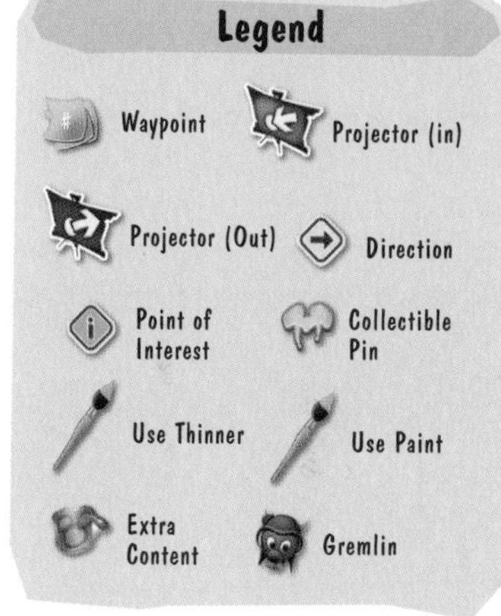

Level Overview

Poltergeists haunt the Foyer and shift tables around through the air. Beetleworx Hoppers patrol the downstairs, and Blotling Sweepers guard the upstairs. A mysterious ghost is trapped inside a vase, and he seems to hold the answer to escaping the puzzling Manor House entrance hall.

You begin in the Foyer with the collapsible stairs in the down position. You need to get them in the up position to reach the exit screen on the upper level balcony.

Things to Do

- Deal with the Beetleworx and Blotling enemies
- Thin the Shadow Blot painting and free Gremlin Haig
- Release Screeching Sam
- Paint the two skull wall reliefs
- Search the area for power-ups and collectibles
- Exit to the Haunted House: Part 1 level

Hoppers roam the first floor, while Sweepers guard the upper level balconies. You have enemies all around you when you begin. Swat the Hoppers away from you, and run up the stairs to either befriend each Sweeper (with Paint) or erase them (with Thinner). Once you thin out the enemies, it's a little less challenging to cross the Foyer.

While the collapsible stairs are down, thin out the toon wall behind them and you'll recover the quest item to complete the "History of Colonel Pete" optional quest for Big Bad Pete. When you return to Mean Street you'll get your reward (See Col. Pete quest).

CAUTION

If you plan to finish the "History of Colonel Pete" optional quest, don't raise the collapsible stairs until you have the quest item.

Gremlin Haig

If you thin out the Shadow Blot painting in the Foyer, you'll uncover a secret room with Gremlin Haig inside. You'll also see the Lonesome Manor I extra content floating right next to him.

Thin out the Shadow Blot painting to reveal a secret room.

Notice the poltergeists floating two tables about the Foyer. One table circles lower than the other. Cross to that balcony and jump on the table as it nears your edge. Thin out the Shadow Blot painting hanging on the wall above the entrance projector screen.

When the two tables come close to each other, jump to the second table. This one floats next to the painting. Double-jump into the secret room when you veer near it. Free Gremlin Haig and pick up the extra content next to his cage.

Gremlin Haig fixes the pressure pad in the secret room. When you step on this pad, it opens the exit gate, but only for 10 seconds. To take this shortcut to the next level, you must jump out of the secret room and onto the tables, then cross and double-jump to the exit screen balcony before the time expires. It's a difficult chore, and if you can't make it, you can always talk with Screeching Sam for the other option to exit the area.

Screeching Sam is trapped in a small cell under the balcony with the collapsible stairs. Two pressure plates flank the cell. Drop an anvil on one of the pressure plates, and then stand on the second one to unlock the cell.

When you release Screeching Sam, he tells you the secret to escaping the Foyer: Paint in the two skull wall reliefs. This calms the poltergeists and raises the collapsible stairs.

Unfortunately, painting in both skulls drops the floating tables, so if you haven't freed Gremlin Haig from behind the Shadow Blot painting before you finish Screeching Sam's quest, you won't be able to reach the gremlin.

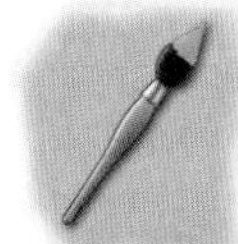

Paint in the first skull from the balcony.

Exit the cell area and take the stairs on your left. Paint the skull on the wall from the balcony, or drop into the area and squirt it from up close. If you drop down, explode each Spladoosh first, defeat any other enemies that may be down there (such as any you swatted over the edge), and then spray Paint on the skull. Don't forget the Silver Pin in the nearby red chest.

Deactivating the first skull forces some of the poltergeists to flee. The tables in the Foyer stop floating after you spray Paint on the first skull.

Cross to the opposite balcony and drop to the back room where the second skull lies. You can also use Thinner to enter the room (and exit the room) through the toon wall leading into the Foyer. Paint in the skull and raise the collapsible stairs into the up position.

Climb up the collapsible stairs and swat the Sweeper out of your way. Enter the projection screen to journey to the Haunted House: Part 1 level.

Silver Pin

It's best to go for the Silver Pin when you're ready to spray Paint on one of the two skulls to calm the spirits. Jump down to ground level, excite one or two of the Spladooshes, and make sure you're on the opposite side of the room when they explode. You might catch other enemies in the goo, which makes cleaning up and nabbing the pin that much easier.

Haunted House: Part 1

You appear on a deserted road. The winds pounds the trees, and the only shelter in the area is a spooky house infested with bats, spiders, and a mysterious robed figure.

Move to the right, and hop across the stones in the road. Jump up to grab the e-tickets above you.

Hop onto the first barrel past the stones. A few bats fly up from the barrels to the right. Wait for the bats to scatter, then jump up and grab the e-ticket.

Jump onto the barrels stacked just outside the house. The front door is nailed shut, so follow the e-tickets to the health power-up in the window.

Jump onto the windowsill, and drop to the awning outside. Wait for the bats to fly out through the window.

When the path is clear, use the window to enter the house. Jump over the hole in the floor and collect the e-tickets above you.

When you land near the bookcase, you can see the film reel on the other side of the wall. Face back to the left, and drop through the hole in the floor.

When you land, approach the table's left edge. Move close enough to collect the e-ticket, but stay clear of the dangling spider.

Move to the right and drop down from the table. Carefully approach the spiderweb. When the bats appear from behind the web, run back to the table and wait for them to pass.

After the bats leave, continue to the right. Jump to grab the health power-up if you've suffered any damage. Approach the dangling spider just past the web.

When the spider moves up, run to the right. You don't have to jump to collect the e-ticket, so stick to the ground and stay clear of the spider.

When you reach the stairs, a mysterious shadow appears on the wall. Jump over the gap to the right, and follow the shadow up the stairs.

When you reach the top of the stairs, enter the room to the right. Carefully approach the exit screen to the right, and wait for the robed figure to appear.

The robed figure jumps out from behind the door and blocks the path to the exit projector. Turn around and run back to the stairs as the robed figure chases you from the room.

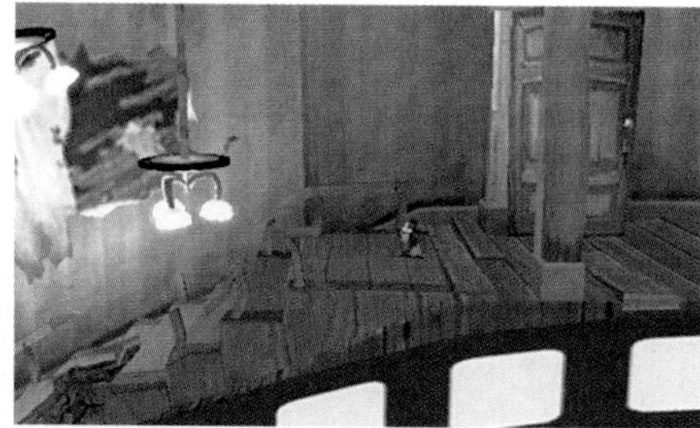

There are two chandeliers above the stairs. Hop across to the chandelier on the left, and let the robed figure continue down the stairs.

When the chandelier swings to the left, jump across to the ledge.

Watch the spider crawling along the floor. When the spider moves toward you, jump up and grab the e-ticket in front of the door.

When you land, continue to the left and grab the film reel under the table. Jump back over the spider, and return to the chandeliers.

Jump across to the chandelier at the top of the stairs. Stand on the chandelier, and ride up to safety as the robed figure approaches.

When the chandelier reaches the top of its path, jump across to the chair on the right. Wait for the spider to crawl toward you, then hop over to the bookcase.

If you need it, grab the health power-up in front of the door. When you're ready, drop through the hole to reach the exit projector.

You've collected the film reel and gathered a nice stack of e-tickets. Hop down from the table and activate the exit screen to jump to the Stretching Room.

Stretching Room

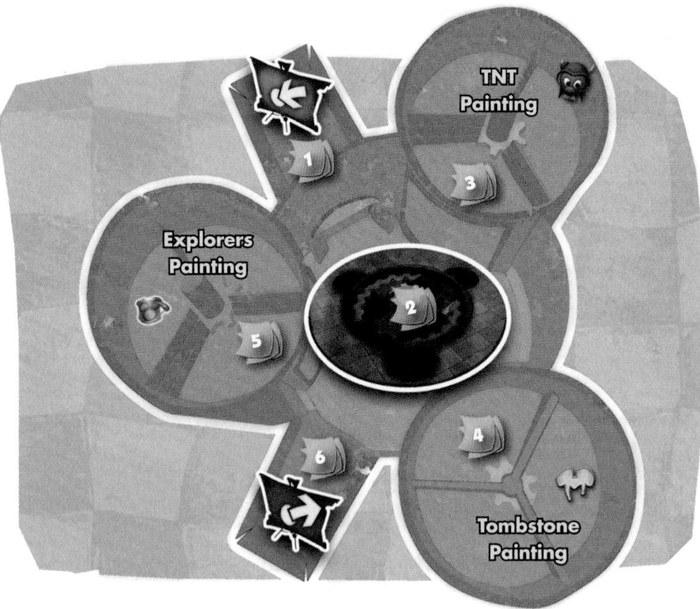

Level Overview

The Stretching Room isn't a torture chamber; it's a room to stretch out and enjoy the tall paintings stretching up to the very high ceiling. It's even more of an eyeful when poltergeists mix up the paintings and create a devious puzzle. Figure out the secrets of the puzzle and the shifting floor to continue through the Manor House.

1

When you enter the Stretching Room, all seems quiet. Alas, several poltergeists want to cause you grief and scramble the tall wall paintings. Each painting has three sections, and the top, middle, and bottom sections in each painting are out of order after

the poltergeist mischief. It's up to you to put them back in order to escape the room.

Things to Do

- Learn how to operate the elevator mechanism
- Solve each wall puzzle
- Free Gremlin Sydney and retrieve collectibles
- Exit to the Mad Doctor: Part 2 level

2

In the center of the room is the elevator mechanism. Three gears form a triangle around a raised gear. One of the outer gears is solid steel, while the other two gears are transparent and can be painted. The raised central gear activates the elevator, and when activated, the entire floor goes up or down.

If none of the transparent gears are painted in, the elevator goes to the ground floor (which it starts on). If you paint in one of the transparent gears

and spin the central gear, the floor moves up to the second story.

If you paint in both transparent gears and spin the central gear, the floor moves up to the third story. If you do everything systematically, you won't have to come back down at any point.

3

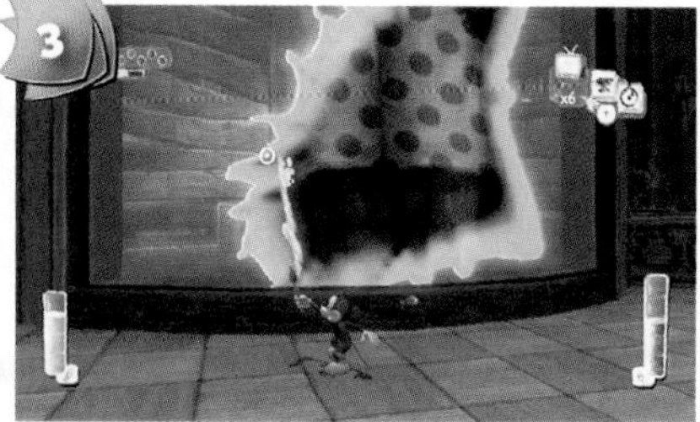

At any point, thin out a painting to gain access to the compartment behind it. If a painting segment is missing, paint it in to bring it back.

To your left is the painting of the man standing on TNT. On the ground level, use your spin move to rotate the painting segment to show the TNT barrel.

On the second level, rotate the painting segment to show the missing trousers.

On the top level, rotate the painting segment to show the man with the moustache and beard.

4

In the middle is the painting of the woman sitting on a tombstone. On the ground level, use your spin move to rotate the painting segment to show the tombstone.

On the second level, rotate the painting segment to show the woman's legs.

On the top level, rotate the painting segment to show the woman holding the rose.

Gold Pin

Find the Gold Pin inside the tombstone painting on the top level. Thin out the painting image and spin the painting until the red chest shows up.

5

To your right is the painting of the three explorers. On the ground level, use your spin move to rotate the painting segment to show the first explorer underwater with piranha.

On the second level, rotate the painting segment to show the second explorer.

On the top level, rotate the painting segment to show the third explorer.

Extra Content: Mad Doctor

Find the Mad Doctor extra content inside the explorers painting on the top level. Thin out the painting image and spin the painting until the concept art shows up.

6

If you want to find Gremlin Sydney, thin out the man with the TNT segment on the second level. Enter the segment and spin the gear in the middle. You'll

rotate with the platform. Keeping turning until you reveal the hidden room inside the wall. Use your spin move to shatter the gremlin's cage.

Gremlin Sydney

One of the toughest gremlins to find if you don't know where to look, Gremlin Sydney is in the wall behind the TNT painting on the second level. You have to enter the painting, turn it from within, enter the secret room and free the gremlin, and then exit the painting and reset it to the proper image.

Spin the gear on the top level with the paintings in the correct order. The exit doors open.

A Spatter and two Sweepers charge through the doors when they open. Battle the three enemies, or bolt for the exit screen before the enemies can line up attacks.

The Mad Doctor: Part 2

You arrive in a laboratory filled with devious experiments. Dodge the roaring fires and arcing electricity to find a way out of this sinister scene.

Jump up to the rods on the right. When the rods begin to crackle, they shoot out a stream of electricity.

Wait for a break in the electricity, then jump up to the conveyor belt on the right. After the next electrical surge, double-jump through the e-tickets on to the left.

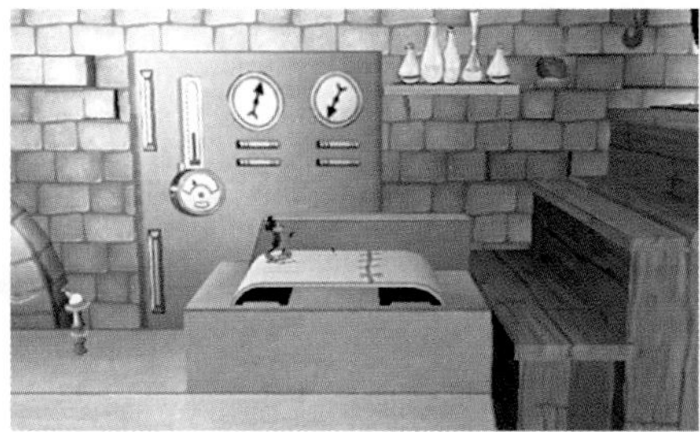

Jump back up to the conveyor belt and continue to the right. Many of the lab's conveyor belts switch directions at regular intervals. To avoid unexpected falls, watch the seam in each belt before you jump on.

Jump up to the top of the stairs. You can see the film reel surrounded by fire and two wicked looking shadows projected on the wall.

Double-jump over the flame and hop up to the burner on the right.

Use your spin move to flip the switch on the burner's left side. Jump into the gas fumes and float through the first few e-tickets, then double-jump to the container on the left.

Use your spin move to knock the container off the shelf and put out the fire. Jump over and grab the e-ticket to the left. Be sure to land on the wooden step to avoid taking damage. Grab the film reel and jump back up to the burner.

Hop into the gas fumes and float toward the ceiling. When you reach the top, jump over to the conveyor belt on the right.

Move to the next conveyor belt. When the seam moves toward the right, hop on and run along the top of the belt. Jump up to grab the e-ticket, then double-jump through the health power-up to reach the ledge to the right.

Continue to the electric rods in the next room. There are two rods on the floor, and several more running along the ceiling. Wait for a break in the electricity and run to the right.

Grab the e-tickets near the ceiling, and stand just left of the health power-up. When the floor gives way, drop to the conveyor belt below you.

Drop to the ground. Grab several e-tickets past the conveyor belt on the left.

Hop onto the belt and continue to the left. Grab the health power-up if needed, then leap across the gap to collect more e-tickets.

Jump along the next two conveyor belts. When the belts switch directions, be mindful of both the gap to the right and the electric rods to the left.

Wait for a break in the electricity, then grab the e-tickets to the left. You've arrived back at the gas fumes. Either jump into the fumes and return to the upper path, or turn around and head back along the lower path.

Take either route back to the right, and continue into the operating room.

Jump onto the operating table. The door slams shut and the saw moves down from the ceiling.

Everything goes dark for a moment, and you appear safely in bed.

Run along the bed and jump through the window on the right. The exit screen is just in front of the doghouse.

Collect the last few e-tickets from the doghouse, and return to the exit screen. When you're ready, activate the screen to complete the level and bounce out to the Library.

Library

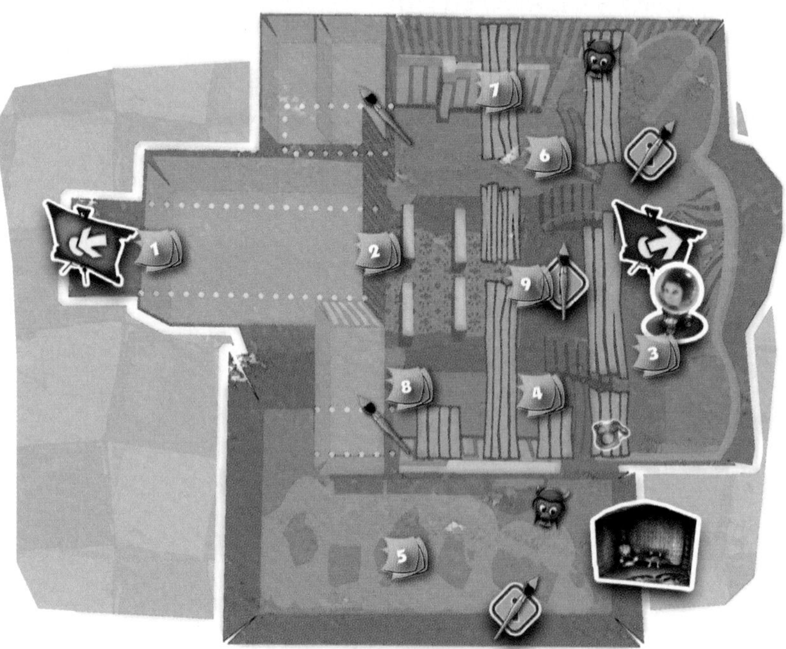

Level Overview

The Library is out of control. Bookcases try to smash whatever moves. Blotlings swarm the rafters. Flying books swoop and buzz you like aggravated birds. Madame Leona, the Library's caretaker, is stuck inside her crystal ball, so she asks you to clean up the meddlesome poltergeists.

1

Chaos reigns when you arrive at the Library. Poltergeists have taken over and have turned the area into a dangerous trap. Bookcases slam together, while other objects whirl about and smash anything in their way.

> **Things to Do**
>
> - Speak with Madame Leona and accept her three quests
> - Paint in the three skulls to complete the first quest
> - Free Gremlin Jumbo
> - Catch the six flying books to complete the second quest (optional)
> - Restore the four paintings to complete the third quest (optional)
> - Explore the rafters and free Gremlin Jarvis
> - Search the area for power-ups and collectibles
> - Defeat the Slobber
> - Exit to the Haunted House: Part 2 level

2

Descend the steps in front of you to the main lobby. Three huge bookcases slam together then draw apart in a perilous pattern. Watch the bookcases until you get the timing down. When you're ready, rush through each open bookcase pair before they crash together again.

3

Run up the steps and speak with Madame Leona in the green crystal ball on the landing. If you picked up Madame Leona's missing book in the Bog Easy Emporium, you can complete the "Recover the Runaway Book" optional quest when you talk to the lady of the Library.

Madame Leona gives you three quests. The first is to drive the poltergeists out of the Library by painting in three skull wall reliefs. The second requires you to catch six flying books loose in the various rooms. The third involves restoring four paintings in Madame Leona's art collection. You only have to complete the first quest to open the exit projector room; the other two quests are optional.

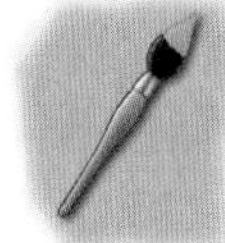

The first skull is below Madame Leona in front of the exit projector room.

Start with the easy skull first. It's just below you on the stone floor in the main lobby. Descend the stairs next to Madame Leona and spray Paint on the skull.

The second skull hides in the long room filled with Thinner. Spot the skull through the hole in the wall behind the first slamming bookcase.

Looking back at the main lobby from Madame Leona's landing, climb the stairs to the left. Three wide bookcases press forward and will squash you against the railing if you get caught in front of them when they extend. Wait till each bookcase retracts and then dash across and stop in the safe zone before the next bookcase.

Repeat for the next two bookcases. Use Thinner on the toon wall at the end to reveal the L-shaped hidden room that wraps around behind the bookcases you just crossed.

Gremlin Jumbo

Gremlin Jumbo stands at the back of the hidden room behind the crashing bookcases. Shatter the cage with your spin move and free him. He offers to help you catch Madame Leona's flying books for 50 e-tickets. It's a great deal, unless you want the fun of tracking them down yourself.

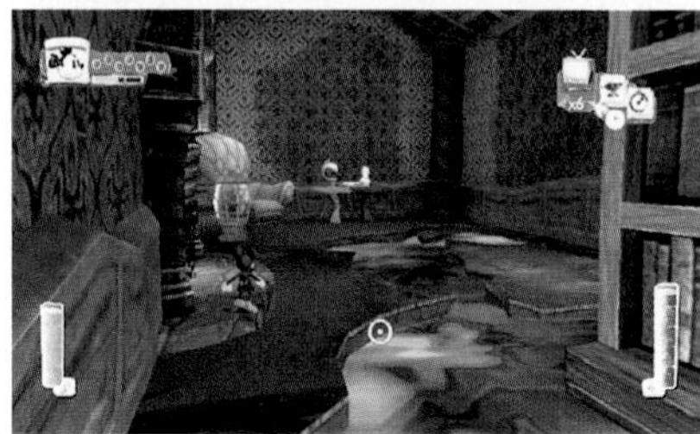

In the Thinner-filled room, double-jump across the fallen stone chunks creating a makeshift "safe" path. Three more smaller bookcases retract and extend in the second half of the room. Time your jumps to hit as the bookcases retract. If you get pushed out into the Thinner by one of the bookcases, immediately double-jump when you strike the Thinner. You take a health pip of damage, but you should be able to catapult to the far side with only that small sting.

When you spray Paint on the second skull, a shortcut secret passage forms in the fireplace next to Gremlin Jumbo.

Fill in the second skull with Paint. It's on the wall behind the bookcases in the Thinner room.

In the back of the Thinner room, free Gremlin Jumbo from his cage. He offers to help you in the flying book quest for 50 e-tickets. If you want to complete the "Catch the Flying Books" optional quest quickly, take Gremlin Jumbo up on his offer. If not, see the optional quest sidebar for details on the exact locations of all six flying books.

Optional Quest: Catch the Flying Books

Madame Leona asks you to retrieve six flying books around the Library. You can either jump into one to catch it, or spray Thinner on it to remove it, but if you use Thinner, Madame Leona won't give you the Silver Pin reward. Find the flying books in the following places:

- The first book floats near the entrance steps
- The second book bobs around the toon wall that holds the pressure plate for the stairs leading up to the rafters
- The third books flies around the Thinner room
- The final three books all dart around the rafters

6

You can only access the third skull by performing a series of maneuvers on the opposite end of the library. Head back to Madame Leona and take the staircase on the right (facing the lobby). Eight bookcases stacked side by side slide out in rapid succession. It's very difficult to time your jumps to bypass them. Luckily, you can use the bookcases out in the lobby to safely jump across.

When the bookcases retract, jump out to the first lobby bookcase and wait for the bookcases to extend then retract again. As soon as the bookcases retract, jump to the space in front of the bookcases, then jump back out to the top of the lobby bookcase. From there you should be able to double-jump over to the toon wall after the bookcases retract again. Thin out the wall to reveal the hidden pressure plate.

The third skull rotates out of the wall after you stand on the hidden pressure plate.

Step on the pressure plate and it reveals the third skull. You now have 10 seconds to race back down the landing and staircase to shoot Paint on the skull before it spins back into the wall. Paint the skull and you complete the quest and send all the bookcase poltergeists packing.

CAUTION

Do not speak with Madame Leona after you finish the skull quest unless you are finished with the Library and want to leave immediately. Once you speak with Madame Leona, she opens the exit room and releases a Slobber, which will stalk you the rest of your time in the Library.

When you paint in the third skull, the bookcases on the nearby landing transform into a staircase leading up. You can now explore the rafters high above the first floor.

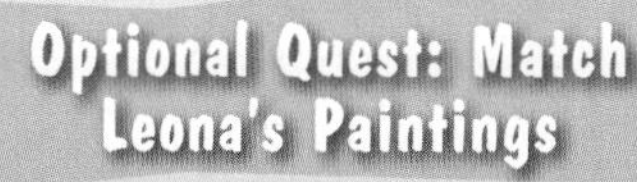

Optional Quest: Match Leona's Paintings

To complete this optional quest, seek out Leona's four painting and straighten them out. Thin each painting to expose a gear inside the frame. Spin the gear to rotate the painting until you get it oriented correctly.

Optional Quest: Match Leona's Paintings (cont'd)

When the frame is set, paint the image back into place and it's ready. Return to Madame Leona for the Art Appreciator Pin reward. Find the four paintings in the following spots:

- The first two paintings are at the entrance steps
- The third painting is between the bookcases in the main lobby
- The fourth painting is in the Thinner room

7

To activate a short staircase up into the rafters, step on the same pressure plate you used to reveal the third skull. You have six seconds to use this staircase to double-jump up to the first rafter. If you fail, return to the pressure plate and try again. Spiderwebs block various spots in the rafters. Before you attempt your jumps, remove the spiderwebs with Thinner.

Land on the first rafter and battle the Sweepers. There's one on each rafter, and they love to toss Thinner on your rafter and dissolve the wood beneath your feet so you go crashing to the ground floor. When you've dealt with the Sweepers, turn right and wipe out any spiderwebs you see.

TIP

If you fall from the rafters, perform a double-jump or spin move as you fall to cushion the drop and avoid losing a health pip from the impact.

Continue straight down the first rafter. At the end, turn left and hop across to the small rafter, then double-jump over to the second long rafter. Turn left and work down toward Gremlin Jarvis. If the Sweeper guard has been removed, jump over to Gremlin Jarvis's platform, and use a spin move to break him out of the cage. He thanks you by offering to help you later on (in the fight against the Mad Doctor in the Attic).

Gremlin Jarvis

Look up in the rafters for Gremlin Jarvis. He's at the end of the second long rafter, guarded by a series of Sweepers. You definitely want to free Jarvis because he'll help you later on in the final battle against the Mad Doctor in the Attic.

On the opposite end of the second rafter lies the Library extra content on the non-thinnable section of the rafters next to the wall. Depending on where you double-jump over to the second rafter, you might run into the concept sketch and its flanking Sweeper on your way to Gremlin Jarvis.

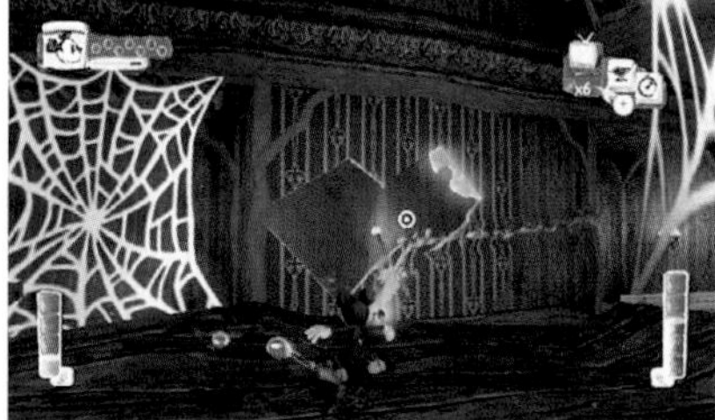

Return to the first rafter and look back toward the entrance. Shoot a long stream of Thinner at the large

toon wall above the entrance foyer. You reveal a secret room with three Spladoosh Blotlings and a red chest.

Remove the spiderweb in front of the room to the left of the secret room. Use the wall-side platform to double-jump into this side room. Spin move to knock the Sweeper over the edge and out of your hair.

Shoot a short Thinner burst at the cartoon wall connecting to the secret room. Try to keep part of the wall intact as a shield. Run into the secret room and tag each Spladoosh one by one. Run back out of the secret room into this side room to avoid the resulting Spladoosh explosion as each goes boom. Grab the hatchet for Horace's "Find the Hatchet" quest from inside the red chest.

After you've finished all your adventuring in the rafters, return to the first floor. In the main lobby, to the right of the bookcases if you're looking in from the entrance, spray the corner wall with Thinner. You'll reveal a small secret room with a blue chest. Open the chest for Animatronic Donald's Left Leg.

Once you've finished all your optional quests and want to leave the Library, speak with Madame Leona. She opens the projector screen room and inadvertently releases a Slobber. You have to take on this lumbering beast to gain the exit (unless you want to chicken out and trick the Slobber to stomp out after you, dodge its attacks, and then escape through the screen).

Whether you choose Paint or Thinner, you'll have to pour a lot of mixture into the Slobber to stop it.

Don't let the Slobber corner you in the Library's many small spaces. Its claws will rake you for serious damage.

When the Slobber inhales, it sucks you dangerously closer. However, it also presents an opportunity to attack. While the Slobber has its mouth open, it's vulnerable to your Paint or Thinner as you chug gallons into its open maw.

Don't forget your other weapons in a tough fight like this. Launch guardians at the Slobber, or drop an anvil on its head to give you a combat advantage. Do enough damage, and you melt the fiend into a puddle.

Advance on the exit screen to continue deeper into the house. Your next stop: the Haunted House: Part 2 level.

Haunted House: Part 2

You return to the haunted house, and things seem to have picked up a bit this time around. While the bats and spiders prowl the hall, spooky skeletons dance along with the music.

Before you move down the hall, head to the left and collect the e-tickets above the organ.

The skeleton to the right is dancing with a cane. Whenever you touch a skeleton, you lose a health pip. Wait for the skeleton to squat low, then jump up to land safely on the cane.

Jump onto the windowsill and hop down to the stool at the end of the gap. When you land on the stool, locate the spider crawling along the ground.

Avoid the spider and grab the e-ticket in front of the fireplace. If you've taken any damage, follow the spider along the floor to grab the health power-up under the table.

If you've managed to hang onto all of your health pips, jump straight onto the table and grab the e-ticket to the right. Avoid the spider below you, and watch out for the gap in the floorboards.

Stand on the edge of the gap. The skeleton puts a bedpan on its head and starts dancing away. Avoid the dangling spider and leap across the gap.

Jump onto the bedpan, and ride the skeleton as it dances to the right. Another skeleton appears ahead of you. Jump up to grab the e-ticket near the light, then drop down to grab another from the floor. Hop onto the next bedpan, and wait for the skeleton to move back to the right.

When the skeleton reaches the end of its path, jump to the clock on the right.

Hop up to the windowsill and wait for the spider to drop down from its web. When the spider moves back up, double-jump over to the next window.

When you land, walk to the end of the windowsill. Bats fly out of the hole in the wall.

Move back to the left and let the bats fly out the window, then continue to the right. Bats continue to emerge from the hole, so jump over to the next windowsill before the next group arrives.

When you land, move to the edge of the sill. Another spider dangles from the web to the right.

When the spider moves out of the way, jump toward the film reel to the right. Even in its web, the spider is dangerously close. Make a short jump to slip under the spider, then double-jump to safely reach the film reel.

Jump to the left and grab the e-ticket, then drop straight down to land on the table. The exit screen is just to the right, but there are still a few e-tickets down the hall to the left. Move to the edge of the table, and face the skeleton playing the accordion.

Wait for the skeleton to spread its accordion, then double-jump over and grab the e-ticket. Double-jump to grab the health power-up above the large gap in the floor to the left, then land on the next skeleton's cane.

Walk across the cane and leap to the table on the left. Hop up to collect the e-ticket, then head back across the skeletons.

Locate the spider crawling under the table before you drop to the floor. A mistimed jump onto the spider costs you a health pip, so make sure the path to the exit screen is clear.

When you're ready to leave, activate the exit screen and jump to the Ballroom.

Ballroom

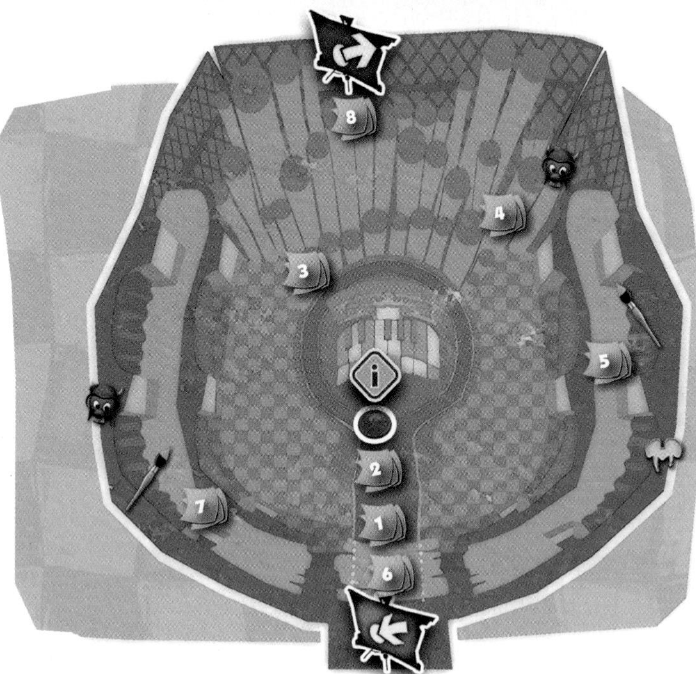

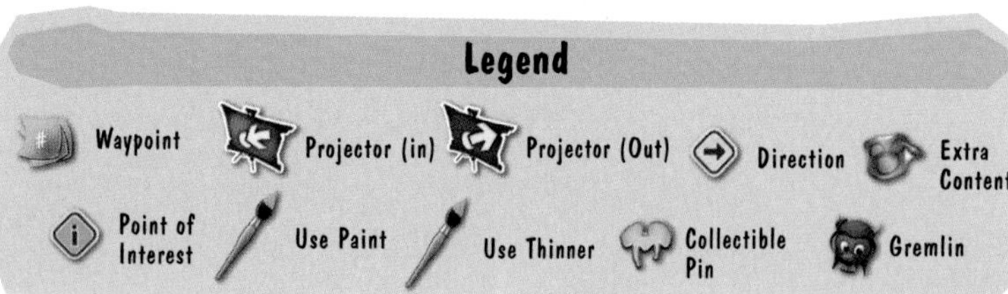

Level Overview

A giant demon organ fills the Ballroom. As you approach, the demon organist asks you to play a musical minigame with him. The demon plays a tune, and it's up to you to jump on the corresponding organ keys to keep up with him. To appease the demon and shut down the organ pipes, you'll have to flex your musical muscles.

Advance toward the large organ directly ahead of you. The demon organists asks you to play a musical minigame. The organist plays a note, which floats above the corresponding organ key, and you have to jump on that key. You only have a short time to reach each key, so follow the notes quickly to beat the music puzzle.

Things to Do

- Play the organ tune to shut down the pipes
- Climb the pipes and explore the balcony level
- Free Gremlins Ferdinand and Stuffus
- Search the area for power-ups and collectibles
- Exit to the Haunted House: Part 3 level

If you're having trouble jumping to any of the organ keys, activate a Watch sketch to give yourself more time to reach your destination.

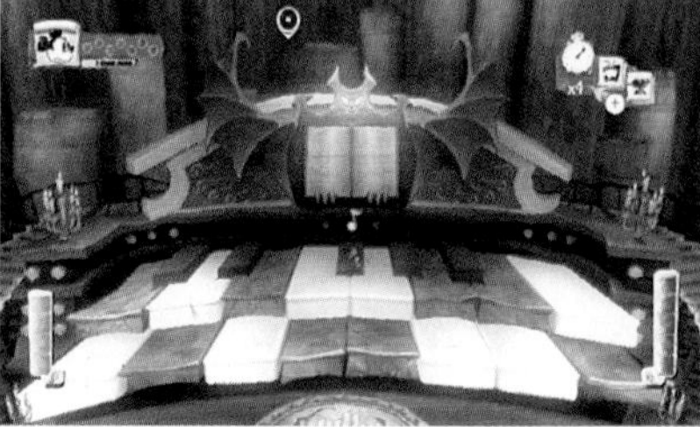

Jump on the second white key in the top row for the first note. Jump on the adjacent black key for the second note.

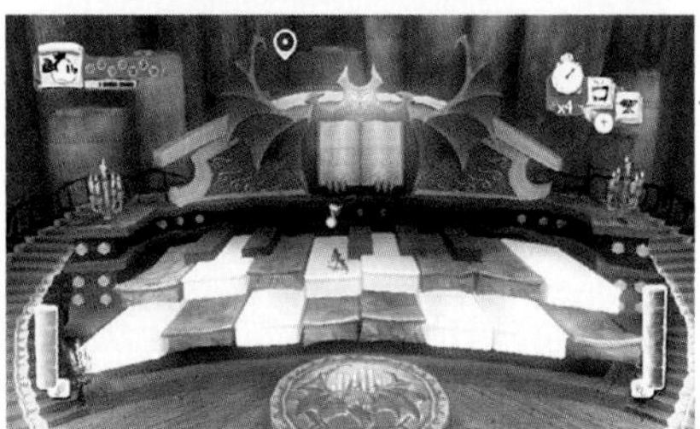

Jump on the third white key on the bottom row for the third note. Return to the original white key for the fourth note.

Jump all the way to the left and land on the first white key in the bottom row for the fifth note. Double-jump across the bottom row to the last white key for the sixth note. This is the hardest note to hit because of the distance you have to travel. If you're having trouble with this note, use a Watch sketch to give yourself extra time.

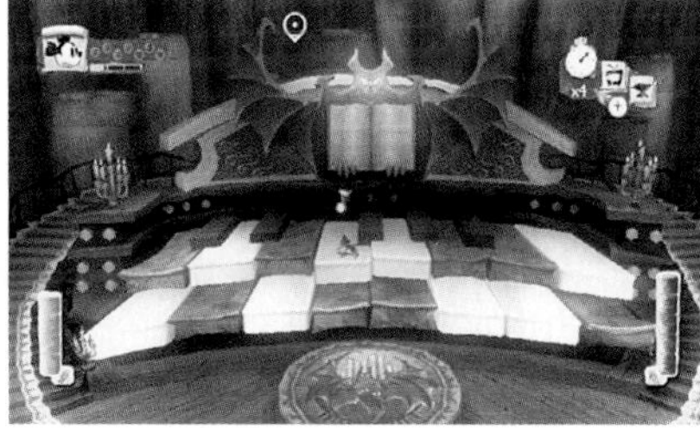

Jump to the left and land on the adjacent white key in the bottom row for the seventh note. Return to the original white key in the top row for the final note.

Hit all eight notes in a timely fashion to complete the "Pipe Organ Madness" quest and earn the Play a Tune Pin. With the organ fixed, the organist lets you continue toward the exit.

It's possible to escape the Ballroom without playing the music minigame. Drop a Watch sketch and, while time slows down, run up the active organ pipes to the exit screen at the top. Unfortunately, you'll won't earn Donald's Torso from the ghosts in Bog Easy if you take this shortcut.

Circle around behind the organ and follow the red carpet up to the green organ pipes. Double-jump up to the shortest one.

The pipes jut up toward the ceiling at different heights. Follow the ascending pipes by double-jumping to each one carefully.

Near the balcony, double-jump off the closest organ pipe to explore the second story.

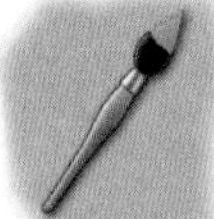

Erase the first curtain on the balcony to reveal the secret room with the Bronze Pin.

Thin out the first curtain on your left. You reveal a long secret room with a Bronze Pin in the back corner.

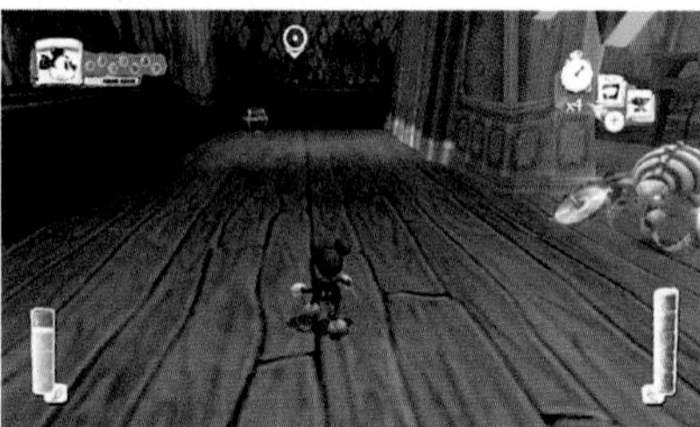

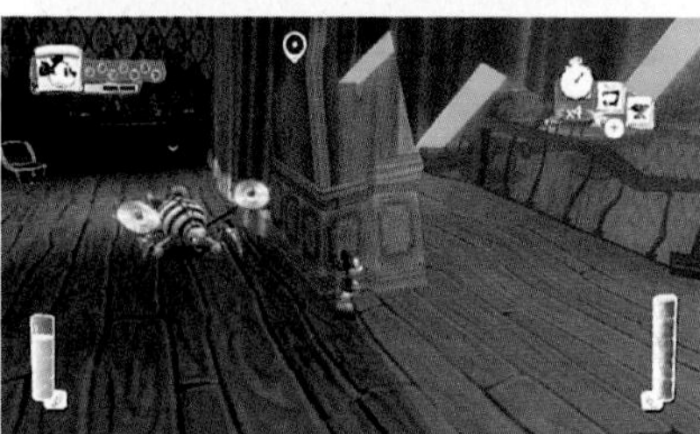

Watch out for the Spinner that patrols the balcony. Its buzz saws can rip you apart. To defeat the Spinner, first coat its armor with Thinner to expose its inner parts, wait for it to flip on its back, and then spin to short-circuit the Beetleworx machine.

You can lure a Spinner behind a curtain and then seal the curtain back up with Paint to trap it inside.

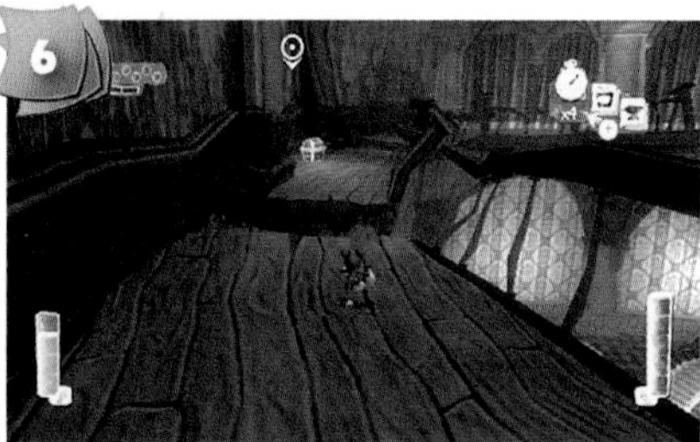

Double-jump across the broken balcony gap to the small balcony piece between the two longer balcony sections. The blue chest holds Animatronic Donald's Arm.

Gremlin Ferdinand

Search for Gremlin Ferdinand on the far side of the balcony. His cage is hidden behind the toon curtain. He gives you two Anvil sketches to help you in future encounters.

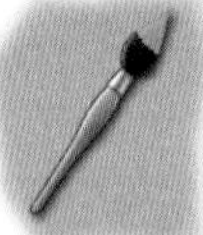

A second secret room behind the curtains on the far balcony contains Gremlin Ferdinand.

Double-jump off the section with Donald's missing arm and onto the last balcony section. Deal with the second Spinner before hunting for Gremlin Ferdinand.

Use Thinner to remove one of the curtains on the far balcony section. Gremlin Ferdinand is trapped inside the secret room. Release him and he gives you two Anvil sketches.

Gremlin Stuffus

Gremlin Stuffus sits up on the top right corner of the organ pipes. You want to free Stuffus. He's a mercenary and asks for 100 e-tickets, but he aids you in the final battle against the Mad Doctor in the Attic, so it's well worth the small investment.

Return to the balcony edge and double-jump back to the organ pipes. To reach Gremlin Stuffus, drop an anvil on the pipes to give you a launching point to reach the higher pipes that hold the gremlin. He'll join you in the fight against the Mad Doctor if you pay him 100 e-tickets.

Continue up the organ pipes on the left side to find the exit screen. Jump in and head off to the Haunted House: Part 3 level.

Haunted House: Part 3

You return to bats, spiders, and skeletons of the haunted house. Everyone has turned in for the night, so try not to disturb any cranky skeletons.

Jump to the left and grab the e-tickets near the organ, then drop to the floor.

Move to the right and stand near the door. When the knob pops loose, the door falls into the hall.

Walk across the door and approach the barrel at the foot of the stairs. When the barrel shakes, a skeleton pops out and waves you on.

Wait for the skeleton to duck back down, then jump onto the barrel. The skeleton pops back out and sends you flying. Aim for the window to the right, and double-jump to land on the sill. If you miss the landing, run up the stairs and hop up from the other side.

Stand on the sill and wait for the bats to emerge from the hole. The bats swoop around the hall and exit through the window to the right.

When the bats fly out of the way, jump up to grab the e-ticket. You can double-jump directly to the next window, but a missed landing can send you straight through the gap in the stairs. For an easier jump, drop to the stairs and hop up to the windowsill.

When the chandelier drops down, hop across to the next window. After the chandelier begins to shake, it breaks loose and drops to the floor. Move quickly to reach the next sill.

Double-jump from the sill to reach the next chandelier. Leap across the chandeliers to continue to the right.

When you reach the last chandelier, jump over and grab the film reel on the windowsill.

Move to the edge of the windowsill. Watch for the bats that appear to the right, and wait for them to fly out the window. Locate the e-ticket near the hole in the wall.

To safely collect the e-ticket, jump in front of the hole and drop toward the table below you. Before you hit the table, use the double-jump to stop your momentum.

Face the skeletons to the left, and move to the edge of the table. Locate the spider crawling on the ground and wait for the skeletons to lean forward.

When the skeletons begin to lean back, double-jump directly to the bed. If you miss the jump, be sure to avoid the spider on the floor. Hop down from the bed and approach the barrels to the left.

Wait for the skeletons to pop out of the barrels. When the path is clear, jump over the barrels and land near the clock.

Stand near the hole in the floor. Wait for a barrel to roll down the stairs, then double-jump to the left as it falls through the floor. Collect the e-ticket at the bottom of the stairs. If you've taken any damage, wait for the next barrel to roll down, then hop over and grab the health power-up.

Turn around and leap back over the hole. Jump across the skeletons and return to the table.

Leap out of the window and land near the exit screen. Approach the shed, and watch out for the skeleton hiding in the hole. When the skeleton takes a swipe at you, jump up and grab the rest of the e-tickets.

When you're ready to leave, activate the exit screen and head to the boss battle in the Mad Doctor's Attic.

Mad Doctor's Attic

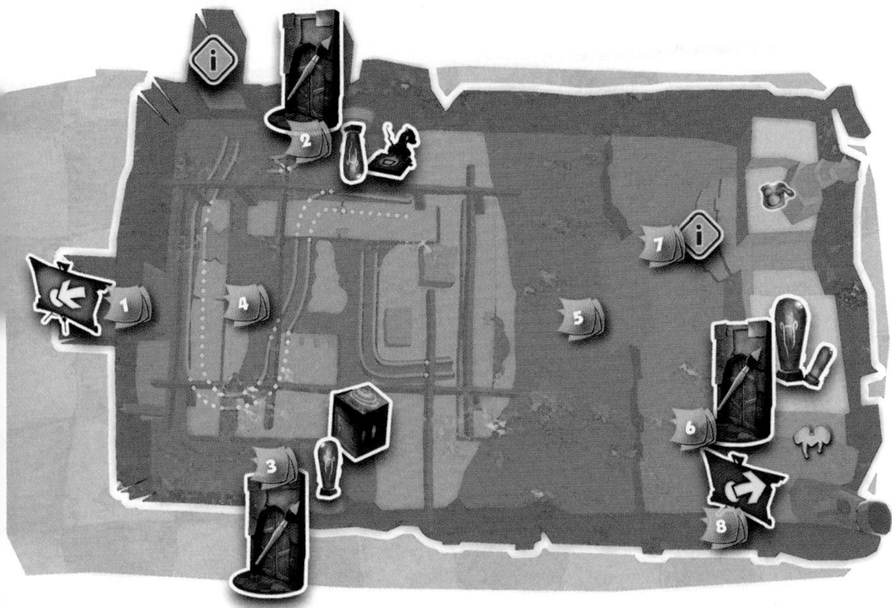

Things to Do

- Battle the Beetleworx enemies
- Defeat the three Beetleworx generators or activate the three generator pads
- Defeat the Mad Doctor
- Search the area for power-ups and collectibles
- Return to Bog Easy

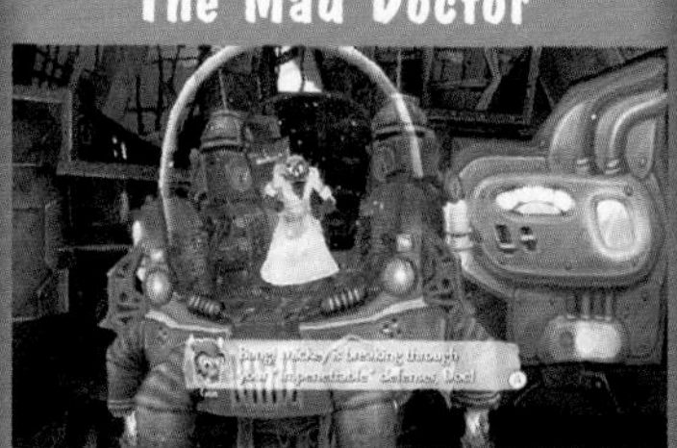

Whether you choose to battle the Mad Doctor with Paint or Thinner affects your reward after the battle. If you wield Thinner against the Mad Doctor's Beetleworx generators, when you defeat the machines you'll gain one permanent extra Thinner slot. Choose to activate the generator pads instead, and you'll gain a permanent Paint slot when you beat the Mad Doctor. Your decision also affects the game's ending.

Level Overview

Finally, you climb to the top of Lonesome Manor and confront the Mad Doctor in his Attic laboratory. The Attic crawls with Beetleworx Tankers, Bashers, and Spinners. Three Beetleworx generators spawn new enemies, and if you can't shut down the machines you'll quickly be overrun. Defeat the Mad Doctor to free Lonesome Manor from his villainy.

1

The Mad Doctor plots his next scheme in his Attic laboratory. To defeat the Mad Doctor, you must battle through the Doctor's Beetleworx guards and shut down the three Beetleworx generators or activate the three generator pads.

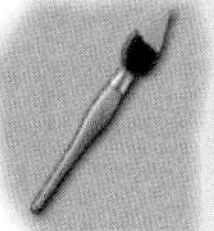

Defeat each Beetleworx generator by spraying Thinner on the machine's red eye.

If you saved Gremlin Jarvis earlier, he shows up to disable the first Beetleworx generator.

If you didn't save Jarvis, you have to defeat the machine yourself. When the generator opens its doors to spawn a new enemy, thin out the glowing red eye to shut down the machine.

If you saved Gremlin Stuffus earlier, he shows up to disable the second Beetleworx generator. If you didn't save Stuffus, you have to defeat the machine yourself. When the generator opens its doors to spawn a new enemy, thin out the glowing red eye to shut down the machine.

To reach the platforms atop the attic, spray Paint on the box near the broken trolley. Double-jump up on the box and look for the broken trolley track.

Double-jump up on the trolley track and follow it to the next wooden platform. Race down the last few steps of the track and double-jump up to the next wooden platform.

Open the blue chest to recover Animatronic Donald's Right Leg.

While you're running around the Mad Doctor's Attic, the Beetleworx generators continue to spawn new Beetleworx. Defeat one and another takes its place. Don't take on multiple machines at once. They will overwhelm you quickly. As long as you keep your distance from the Bashers and Spinners, you can avoid their melee attacks; however, Tankers fire Paint and Thinner missiles, so watch them at all times, even at range.

To eliminate a Beetleworx enemy, isolate it and dump Thinner on its armor to open a vulnerability. Use your spin move to short-circuit the Beetleworx when you see an opening.

Gain sketches by defeating the Beetleworx enemies. Tankers drop Anvil sketches, Bashers drop TV sketches, and Spinners drop Watch sketches.

Mad Doctor's Pod and Gold Pin

To catch your breath from the Mad Doctor battle, jump up on the machinery behind the Beetleworx generator. Besides taking a rest, look for the Mad Doctor's Pod concept art on the first machine and the Gold Pin in the back corner.

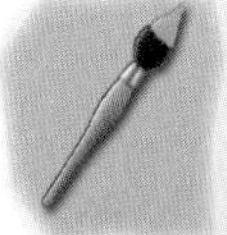

Activating the three generator pads give you the Paint capacity upgrade when you defeat the Mad Doctor.

6

You can defeat the Mad Doctor in one of two ways. The first earns you the Paint capacity upgrade at the end of the fight. You must depress all three generator pads at the same time. Two of the pads accept an anvil or you can stand on it yourself, while the third you must drop a TV on. Fire off a Watch sketch to slow time, drop a TV and anvil, then get on the third pad before either of the other sketches expire. The TV is often eliminated by roaming Beetleworx, so take the enemy patrols into account as well.

The second method to defeat the Mad Doctor involves eliminating the three Beetleworx generators; the most difficult one lies behind the Mad Doctor and his enemy guards at the back of the Attic.

Use your Watch sketches and TV sketches to give you combat advantages against the swarming Beetleworx. The watch slows your enemies down, while the TV shocks any Beetleworx that approaches.

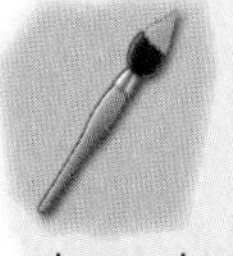

Eliminating the three Beetleworx generators gives you the Thinner capacity upgrade when you defeat the Mad Doctor.

After the first two generators have been eliminated, head for the third generator at the back of the attic. The generator door only opens when it spawns a new enemy, so seize the opportunity when you see that red eye. Slow down time with a Watch sketch, rush toward the generator, and spray Thinner directly into the eye.

With his machines in pieces, the Mad Doctor confronts you directly. You discover that he's actually a Beetleworx machine himself, disguised as a human, ready to conquer Wasteland once the Shadow Blot is victorious. While the Mad Doctor delivers his speech, Gus sneaks behind the flying craft and pulls out the rocket pack. The flying craft launches uncontrollably up into space with the Mad Doctor, and you have the final rocket part you need.

When you're all set, head over to the exit projector to the right of the final Beetleworx generator. It's time to return to Bog Easy. With one major villain defeated, you have one to go: the Shadow Blot.

BEATING THE BLOT

Return to Bog Easy

When you exit Lonesome Manor, you arrive back in Bog Easy. If you didn't repair the Ballroom organ, you'll have some extra ghost quests. If you did repair the organ, you'll have Donald's Torso. Explore Bog Easy thoroughly to see what's changed since your last visit.

Bog Easy Quests

- Fix Donald's Boat (if Animatronic Donald assembled)

Donald wants you to fix his boat by taking his boat gear to Moody in OsTown. Donald's tugboat has been sitting at the bottom of the Thinner lake for a very long time. Moody can use the special gear to raise the old tug.

- Fix the Bridges (townsfolk only)

Metairie wants you to paint in all of the bridges around Bog Easy. Metairie can't stroll through the swamp with the bridges in disrepair.

- Free the Trapped Ghosts (ghost only)

Ghost Ian wants you to free all the ghosts from the candles around the bog. Some of Ian's friends have been trapped inside candlesticks and wander the swamp, unable to free themselves.

- Gilbert Wants to Fish (ghost only)

Gilbert wants you to free the boat that is stuck under the dock. Dropping something solid and heavy on the dock will provide just the shock needed to shake the stuck boat loose.

Bog Easy Quests (cont'd)

- Gilda's Bog Easy Race

Earn a reward for completing Gilda's race through Bog Easy.

- Help Bertrand Open His Store

Bertrand wants to reopen his store but needs his store sign. The sign was last seen near Louis's shack. When replaced, it will remind customers that the store is open for business.

- Investigate Donald's Pains (if Animatronic Donald assembled)

Donald is having mysterious pains and wants you to find out what is causing it. Donald is not in control of his own limbs since being reassembled. The answer to this mystery lies in the swamp.

- Restore the Bell

Louis wants you to find the two pieces of the broken bell. Two segments of the bell were lost when mischievous ghosts broke it and sold the parts.

- Go Back to Mean Street

Return to Mean Street and look for Oswald. Explore Bog Easy along the way, if you wish.

As soon as you exit the Lonesome Manor gate, you meet Ian and the ghostly gang. If you repaired the organ in the Ballroom, the ghosts head back into Lonesome Manor. If you didn't repair the organ, the ghosts remain in Bog Easy, and you'll have optional ghost quests to complete if you like.

Well Read Pin

New Item Received
Well Read Pin

The ghosts hand you the Well Read Pin when you return to Bog Easy, if you returned the missing book to Madame Leona and completed all the other book-related tasks in the Library.

If you ousted the ghosts, speak with Metairie in the main courtyard. The ghosts have ruined the bridges throughout the swamp, and she asks you to paint them all back in.

Optional Quest: Fix the Bridges

Metairie gives you this optional quest if you repaired the Ballroom organ and sent the ghosts back to Lonesome Manor. Paint in all the faded bridges around the swamp and she rewards you with a Bronze Pin.

If you repaired the Ballroom organ, the ghosts hand you Donald's Torso. If you have all the other pieces, you can assemble Animatronic Donald and he becomes a walking, talking NPC and thanks you with the Animatronic Donald Pin. Donald gives you the "Fix Donald's Boat" optional quest and the "Investigate Donald's Pains" optional quest.

Optional Quest: Fix Donald's Boat

Take the gear Donald hands you, and return it to Moody in OsTown. This optional quest is only available if Animatronic Donald has been reassembled.

Look for another power spark up on the Bog Easy rooftops, near the house bordering the swamp in front of the lonely shack.

Bertrand has an optional quest for you too. If you recover his lost shop sign, you help him open the Bog Easy Shop. Once it's open, you can shop for various items, including an Anvil

sketch capacity upgrade and a health upgrade.

You can also brave the outskirts and speak with NPCs, such as Louis who offers you a quest, and Gilda, who offers you another race. Beat her time as you cover the entire Bog Easy map and you win a power spark.

Optional Quest: Restore the Bell

Louis asks you to find the two missing parts of the bell that they use to ward off evil spirits around town. If you do, you automatically defeat one of the Bloticles attacking later in "Battle in Bog Easy" when you first arrive.

When you're ready to leave Bog Easy, return to the exit screen to Mean Street. The next time you're back, you won't like what they've done to the place.

Optional Quest: Investigate Donald's Pains

Someone, or something, has it out for Donald. The poor animatronic duck is suffering from the powers of a voodoo doll. Your job is to search the swamp for the culprit, which you can find on one of the small islands in front of the lonely shack. Dispose of the Spatter on the island and return the voodoo doll to Donald. Once you return the doll to Donald, he'll ask you to keep it somewhere safe. This doll can be given to a couple people with varying rewards. Try giving it to Metairie, Daisy, or Big Bad Pete to see what happens.

Optional Quest: Help Bertrand Open His Store

After speaking with Bertrand and offering to help him out, look for the missing sign behind lonely shack. Return the sign to Bertrand, and he opens the Bog Easy Shop. Besides lots of useful items, you can also find special items in the shop inventory, including the Bog Easy concept art and the Lonesome Manor Pin.

Return to Mean Street

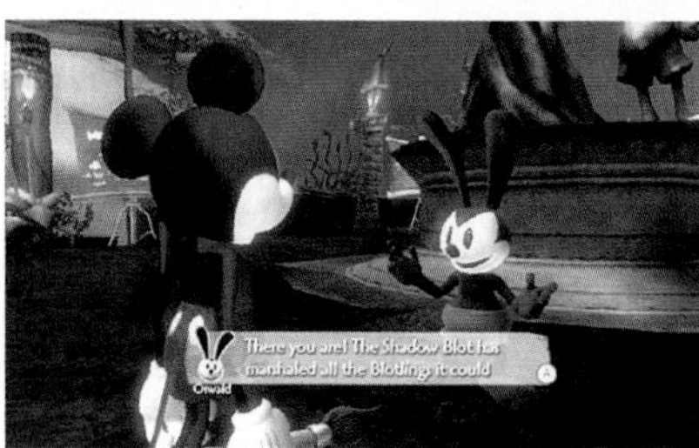

You meet Oswald in Mean Street's upper courtyard in front of the projectors. He informs you that the Shadow Blot has marshalled his forces and it's off to the top of Mickeyjunk Mountain for a confrontation with the creature. Before you head off, however, you may want to reconnect with old friends in Mean Street.

Mean Street Quests

- Secret Door

Gremlin Markus needs 30 power sparks to power the mysterious machine. What does the extra compartment on the projector screen machine unlock? Turn in 30 power sparks to find out.

- Detective Mickey IV

Find the missing candle for Horace. Travel to Bog Easy and search the vicinity of Louis's cabin for clues leading to the missing candle.

- Bunny Roundup IV

Round up the Bunny Children by luring them to the pipe sitting next to the City Hall.

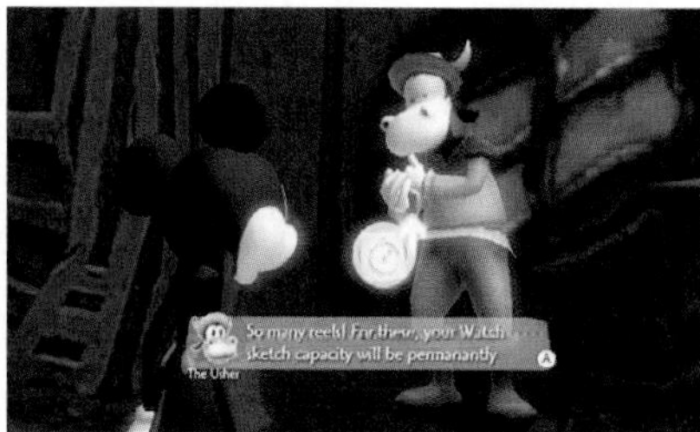

Visit the Usher in front of the Cinema and turn in any new film reels you gained on the 2D levels. Gaining a sketch capacity upgrade or health upgrade before the final battles can be a big help.

Optional Quest: Bunny Roundup IV

Seek out Big Bad Pete at City Hall and get the latest quest of rounding up Bunny Children. You have to collect 13 of them this time, so scour every corner to find them all and earn a power spark.

Make sure you turn in any outstanding quest items, such as the hatchet found in the Lonesome Manor Library for Horace's "Find the Hatchet" optional quest. He'll reward you with a Case Closed Pin and a power spark. Big Bad Pete will also give you a power spark if you complete the "History of Colonel Pete" now that you're back from Lonesome Manor.

If you've been working on Horace's detective quests and/or Pete's bunny roundup quests, finish them off before you head to the final battles against the Blot. By helping Horace and Pete in their bids to look good in Mean Street, you alter the game's ending in favor of these two popular characters.

Optional Quest: Detective Mickey IV

Horace has lost another object: a candle this time. Head back to Bog Easy and search around Louis's lonely shack for clues leading to the missing candle. Return it to Horace for another power spark.

Pick up any of the three new optional quests. See each quest's individual sidebar for details. If you're looking for more power sparks to complete the "Secret Door" optional quest, "Detective Mickey IV" and "Bunny Roundup IV" will help.

Optional Quest: Secret Door

You need 30 power sparks for Gremlin Markus to open the secret door in the Fire Station, but it's worth it. The secret door leads into Walt Disney's apartment, where you can find the Mickey and Oswald concept art.

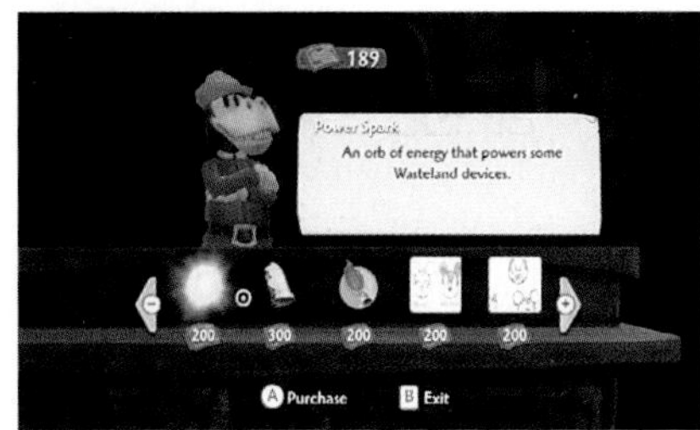

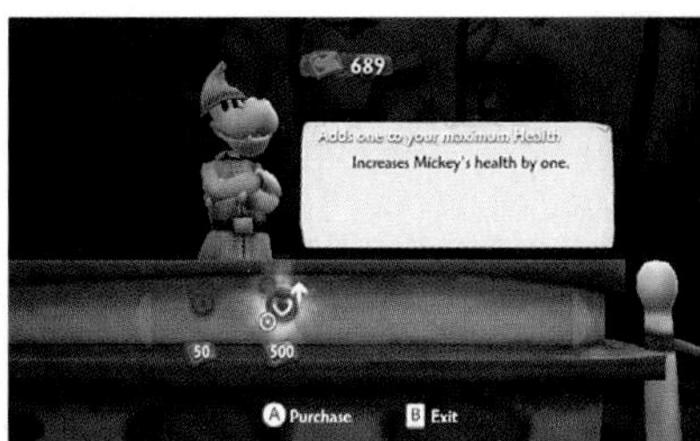

Don't forget to visit the shops before you leave town. The Emporium still holds whatever nifty items you haven't purchased yet, including more power sparks. The Ice Cream Shop offers a valuable health upgrade for 500 e-tickets. If you haven't bought this upgrade yet, do so before leaving for the end battles.

Return to OsTown

Before you can climb up Mickeyjunk Mountain to face off against the Shadow Blot, you first have to scamper through OsTown. As with Bog Easy and Mean Street, make sure you finish off whatever last errands you'd like to do in OsTown, because the next time you come here will be in the middle of a huge battle.

If you put Animatronic Donald together and he gave you the gear to fix his

tugboat, speak with Moody in front of his house. He raises the tugboat, and you're rewarded with a gold e-ticket on the tugboat deck.

Speak to any other of your friends in OsTown before departing for the exit screen to Mt. Osmore Caverns.

Return to Mt. Osmore Caverns

The exit screen from OsTown takes you directly to Mt. Osmore Caverns this time. Cross to the chamber to Oswald's control room.

Extra Content: Oswald Poses

Before you speak with Oswald in his control room, look for this art sketch in the main courtyard in front of the throne. It floats above the hand of the giant Mickey statue to your left. For an easy grab, drop an anvil and double-jump up.

Oswald briefs you on the coming battle: You'll take on the Shadow Blot while he deals directly with the

bottle and cork that holds all the Blot essence.

It's time for the big battle. Enter the projector screen and get ready to face off against the Shadow Blot, after a brief trip into "Ye Olden Days."

Ye Olden Days

You appear in front of a large castle. Maneuver through slamming shutters, diligent guards, and a gluttonous king to reach the top of the castle's massive tower.

A horse and donkey face off at the tower base. Jump onto the horse and grab the e-ticket to the right. When the donkey pushes the horse back to the left, jump up to the awning above the door.

Wait for the chandelier to swing toward you, then double-jump to the right.

Swing on the chandelier and jump to the ledge across the tower. Move onto the castle wall, and hop onto the platform under the tree.

Double-jump back to the tower and stand to the right of the window. When the guard leans out of the window, he thrusts his spear downward. Wait for the guard to jab his spear three times, then run across to the tower's left side.

Hop onto the tree branch. Jump up to grab the e-ticket above you, then leap onto the ledge near the window.

When you land on the ledge, the guard turns his attacks upward. Wait for the guard to lean back inside, and jump to the ledge across the window. Hop onto the tree branch next to the tower.

Double-jump up to the tower. The king is sitting in the window to the left, and there is an e-ticket in the tree to the right. Grab the e-ticket from the tree and drop to the branch, then jump back up to the king.

After the king takes a bite of meat, he spits a bone into each of the piles under the window. Wait for a bone to land in the pile on the right, and follow the bones to the end of the ledge.

Hop onto the tree branch to the left of the tower. If you've taken any damage, grab the nearby health power-up. Watch the window above the king. When the shutters snap open, a guard leans out and thrusts his spear downward.

After the shutters close, hop onto the ledge below the window. Double-jump to the left to reach the next ledge before the shutters snap open.

When the shutters close, leap to the ledge across the window. The castle jail is on the narrow tower to the right.

Jump up to the first cell, then hop over to the ledge on the left. Stand near the lever to the right of the window and use a spin move to unlock the cells.

Drop back down to the right. When the bars move out of the way, grab the e-ticket inside the first cell and wait for the bars to slam down. When the cell opens, jump back up to the lever.

Watch the window near the lever. When the shutter shakes, a guard peeks out of the window. Jump onto the guard's shutter, and locate the e-ticket above you. When the shutter behind the e-ticket closes, double-jump onto the windowsill.

Hop on the nest to the left. When the nest springs into the air, jump up to grab the e-tickets above you. The exit screen is on the ledge to the right, but a set of bars blocks the path to the film reel.

Follow the nest back down and face the tower. When the shutters close, jump back to the windowsill and drop down to the lever. Wait for the bars to lift out of the way, then jump up to the second cell.

Stand clear of the bars and watch the shutter to the left. When the shutter closes, hop onto the windowsill and jump into the third cell. Grab the hidden e-ticket inside the cell and wait for the bars to slam down.

When the bars rise out of the way, jump up and grab the film reel on the tower then stand near the lever to the left.

Use a spin move to clear the bars from your path and run over to the exit screen. When you're ready, activate the screen to complete the level and move on to face the Shadow Blot.

The Shadow Blot

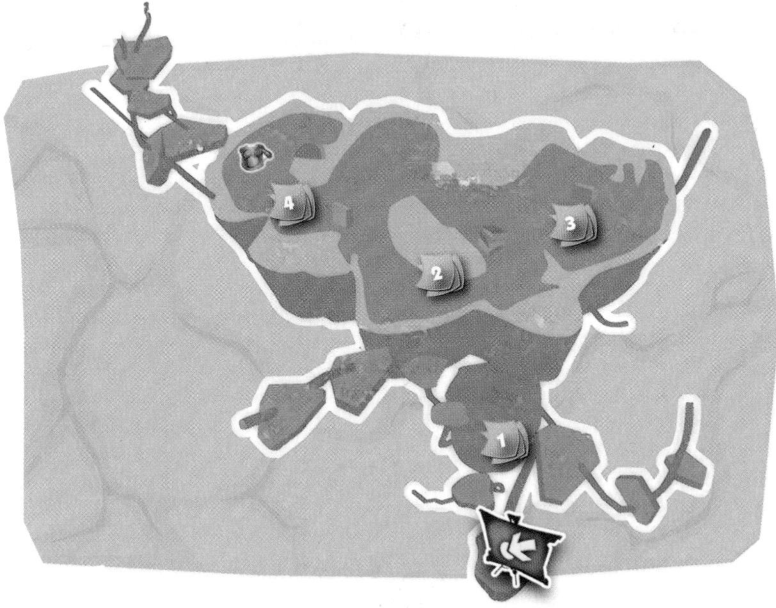

Level Overview

Atop the summit of Mickeyjunk Mountain, the Shadow Blot awaits. It towers overhead and threatens to leave you nothing but an ink smear on the Wasteland mountaintop. Learn to defend against its shadow bolts or perish. Learn to survive its aerial bombardment or perish. Learn to battle its minions at the same time or perish. Basically, you'll perish unless you fight the battle of your life.

Outside the entrance screen, a series of unstable rocks leads up to the mountaintop plateau. Double-jump to each of these rocks, but don't stay on them long; they wobble when you land on them, then plummet down the mountainside a couple of seconds later. Jump across them all without stopping. When you arrive on the plateau, you square off against the Shadow Blot on the far side.

Things to Do

- Grab the Spatter Puddle concept art
- Defeat the Shadow Blot
- Exit to the Battle in OsTown

Study the Shadow Blot's attacks before worrying about any sort of offense. If it raises one arm, it will throw a shadow bolt that strikes for one health pip of damage if it connects. To avoid it, dodge in the same direction as the raised arm, because the shadow bolt curves as it screams toward you.

When the Shadow Blot hovers higher and roars, it will charge. Immediately run to the side and avoid its head-on assault. If the Shadow Blot connects, you lose one health pip and lie stunned on the ground for a couple of seconds.

If the Shadow Blot raises both its arms and forms a ball of shadow energy, it's summoning reinforcements. The shadow ball arcs down to the plateau, usually not more than halfway across the terrain, and spews forth a Spatter. You now have to deal with a Shadow Blot minion while keeping an eye on the master.

Focus your attention on the Shadow Blot, not the minions. If they get too close, swat them aside with your spin move. If you start concentrating on the Spatters, the Shadow Blot will nail you with its attacks.

When the Shadow Blot conjures shadow energy in a ball at its side, it fires a bigger shadow bolt directly ahead. Dodge to the side immediately to avoid more damage.

If the Shadow Blot holds its palms face up and then rockets skyward, it's about to rain shadow bombs down on your head. Sprint across the plateau, keeping one step ahead of the aerial assault.

If you hit the Shadow Blot with Paint or Thinner while it's not attacking, it will try to shake it off. When you see this reaction, you know that the Shadow Blot's aerial attack will come next.

As soon as the Shadow Blot rockets skyward, run to the top right part of the plateau and wait for the Shadow Blot's circular shadow to stray over you. Immediately sprint to the left and continue at a dead run to the far side of the plateau. If you time it properly, you'll stay one step in front of the inky barrage that blows up dirt in your wake.

To damage the Shadow Blot, work the same strategy as attacking a Slobber: aim for the open mouth. Keep your distance so the Shadow Blot doesn't suck you into range of its slashing claws. Circle the Shadow Blot while it climbs out of the puddle. If you stand still, it erupts shadow tentacles out of the ground that damage and upend you. Stay on the move, and dump enough Paint or Thinner in its mouth to strike a blow while avoiding its nasty counterattack.

Junction Point: The Shadow Blot

As with all boss fights, your decision to choose Paint and redeem a boss or choose Thinner and defeat a boss has ramifications at the end of the fight and at the end of the game. If you defeat the Shadow Blot with Paint, you gain the Me and My Shadow Pin with the victory. If you defeat the Shadow Blot with Thinner, you gain the Shadow Boxing Pin. It takes two playthroughs, alternating paintbrush mixtures, to earn both pins. Depending on your paintbrush preference, you get different animations at the end of the fight: an angry Shadow Blot loser with Thinner, and a cuddly Shadow Blot who hugs and tickles Mickey if you used Paint. In the game's final scene, you'll also get different animations depending on whether you used Paint or Thinner.

After the first aerial assault and corresponding counterstrike, reset to the original starting location in the center of the plateau. Continue to dodge the Shadow Blot's attacks and wait patiently for the next aerial assault.

If the Spatters begin to annoy you, wait for the Shadow Blot to charge and step aside. While the Shadow Blot flies back around to its attack position, you have a few free seconds to smack the Spatters over the plateau edge. If they were caught in the Shadow Blot's charge and consequently stunned, it makes your job that much easier.

Also try using Paint on the Spatters. This keeps them off your tail and prevents the Shadow Blot from conjuring additional minions.

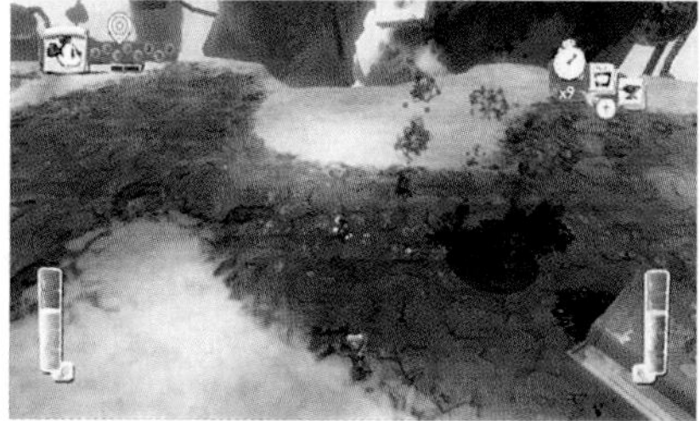

When you spot the next aerial assault, stop whatever else you're doing and sprint for the top right plateau corner again. Run across the battlefield, staying ahead of the shadow barrage, and turn to attack once you reach the far left end.

Your Watch sketches can make a huge difference if you're having trouble. Slow down time just as the Shadow Blot touches down (or any time you're in serious danger). Now you'll have a lot more time to aim into the Shadow Blot's open mouth.

There are precious few resources on the plateau. When a health power-up appears, swoop over and get it unless the Shadow Blot goes into its aerial assault mode.

If you're good, the third aerial assault will be the Shadow Blot's last. If you missed dealing damage on previous attempts, that's fine too. Keep playing defense until you get more opportunities. As before, outrace the aerial assault and position yourself on the far left side.

Repeat your attack pattern with another Watch sketch if you have one available. Fill the Shadow Blot's mouth with Paint or Thinner when it suctions you toward it. If you pour in enough paintbrush mixture for the third time, you finish off the Shadow Blot.

You'll get a different reaction from the defeated boss depending on whether you used Thinner or Paint. And just when you think it's over, Oswald accidentally busts open the corked bottle holding the rest of the shadow essence and the entire Blot oozes out. You have an even bigger mess to clean up now.

Battle in OsTown

Bloticles

The Blot sucks the Paint straight out of Wasteland with its Bloticles, huge tentacles that snake through the main worlds. If you can't defeat the Bloticles, the places you've come to love in Wasteland will thin out of existence. Each Bloticle tentacle has yellow pustules that blister out from its grayish skin. One pustule will be larger than the rest. Start with that pustule and hit it with a stream of either Paint or Thinner. The first pustule pops, and another on the skin bubbles larger. Keep defeating big pustules until the whole tentacle vaporizes in a goo explosion.

OsTown is under siege by Bloticles when you return after defeating the Shadow Blot. Look for the first one to your right as you cross the bridge to the Mickeyjunk Mountain exit screen. Stream a blast at the first pustule, then hit the second pustule farther up the tentacle. Once both pustules rupture, the first Bloticle explodes.

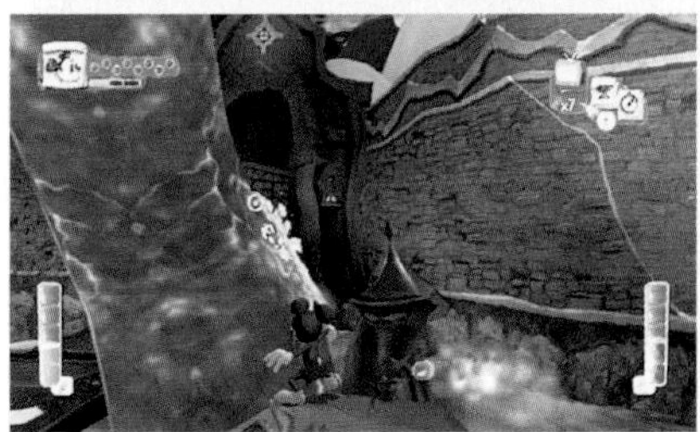

Turn to your left. Spray the first pustule on the next Bloticle flanking the bridge. Continue forward and jump atop Donald's tugboat. Hit the second pustule and defeat the second Bloticle.

When you reach the center of town, Spatters swarm to protect the remaining Bloticle. Use your spin move to knock them around and steer the unfortunate creatures into the Thinner pool.

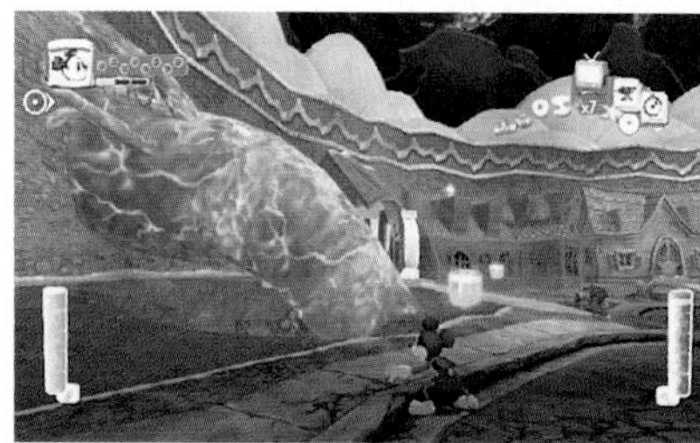

Attack the third Bloticle in Clarabelle's garden. Spray the first pustule on the top, and roll around to the house side to find the second pustule. The final pustule is underground on the back side. If you inch to the lip of the hole, you should be able to hit it; if you're having trouble, drop into the hole to get a better shot.

With the third Bloticle in gooey pieces, Gus appears in front of the exit screen back to Mean Street. He rewards you with a health upgrade, and the extra toughness will certainly help in the coming battles.

Battle in Mean Street

Back on Mean Street, one giant Bloticle tentacle infests the main courtyard. Unlike the battle in OsTown, you have more enemies, including a Slobber, to handle while defeating pustules this time around.

The Slobber is your main concern; explode the Spladoosh when you get a chance, and swat the Spatters away unless you have a chance to isolate them and convert them to your cause with a healthy dose of Paint. On the long Mean Street, you have plenty of space to keep your distance from the Slobber and approach only when you can jam Paint or Thinner down its throat.

Either take out the Slobber first, or lure it high up on Mean Street so you can bypass it and run down to the Bloticle. Shoot the lowest pustule first, and battle back any encroaching enemies.

Circle to the other side of the Bloticle and zap the next pustule. Continuing circling around the Bloticle as you blast the third pustule and keep the Blotlings at bay.

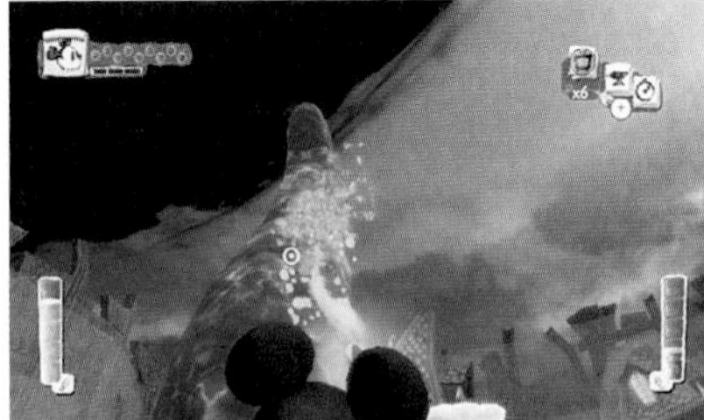

Fire at the highest pustule to finally defeat the Bloticle. When you do, the Blotlings flee and you save Mean Street. But your Bloticle-hunting is far from over. Next stop: Ventureland.

Repair Mean Street Pin

As a reward for your hard-fought victory, you receive the Repair Mean Street Pin where the Bloticle once stood.

Battle in Ventureland

It's time to save Ventureland from the Bloticles. At the entrance arch, confront the first group of Spatters. You can eliminate them with Thinner; however, it's better to drown them in Paint. With three Spatters fighting by your side, the rest of the battle goes easier.

Enter the village square and attack the first Bloticle. Pop the pustules near the base first.

Continuing defeating pustules while you're free from enemy interference. The more you can pop without an enemy hassling your flank, the faster the battle goes.

When a Sweeper shows its face, blast it with Paint or Thinner. Don't worry about the Bloticles until you've dealt with the Sweeper. The fight has no time limit, so take your time and avoid getting blind-sided.

Finish off the last of the pustules to free Ventureland. Now it's off to Bog Easy.

Battle in Bog Easy

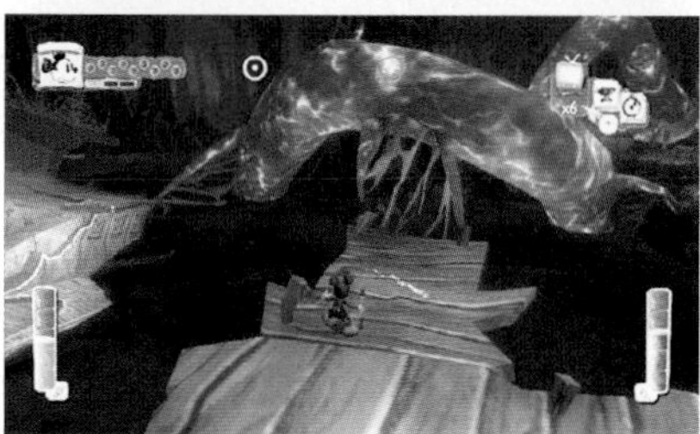

When you arrive in Bog Easy, the first Bloticle worms through the swamp near the entrance dock. Defeat the first pustule near the sunken steamer.

Double-jump over to the first island and ward off the first round of Blotlings. Other than the Spladoosh, it's easiest to spin move your foes off the islands and into the Thinner bog.

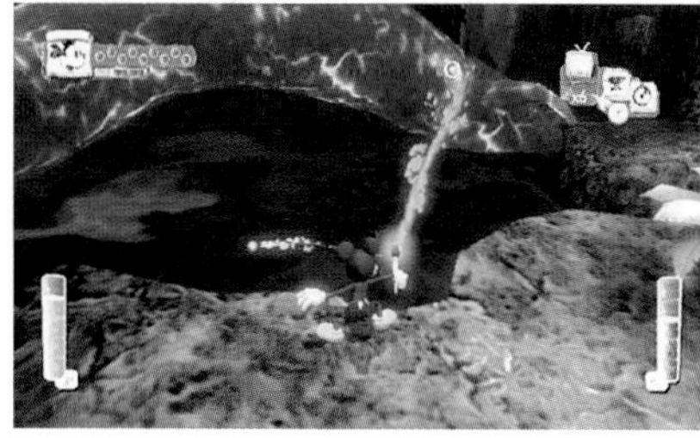

Continue following the long Bloticle tentacle and popping the larger pustules.

Keep clearing enemies and defeating Bloticle pustules until you approach town.

A single Slobber guards the entrance into town. Run across the plank, tag the Slobber, and race back to the docks to avoid the explosion. If you have an anvil to spare, drop that on its head too.

NOTE

If you completed the "Repair the bell" quest for Louis, the entrance will be unguarded.

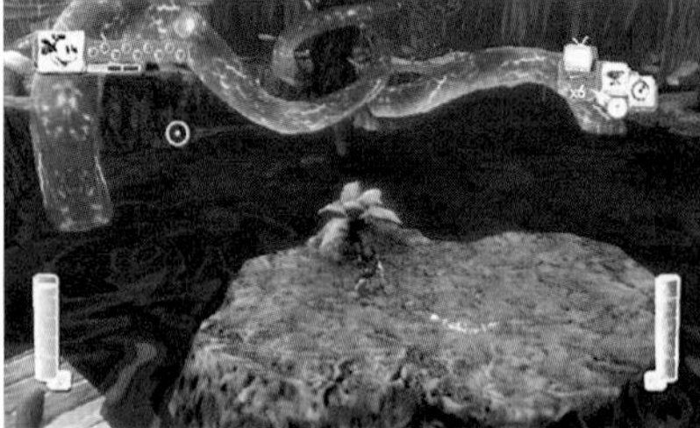

Cross to the swamp entrance toward the lonely shack and look for another Bloticle stretching up out of the bog next to town. Defeat the first pustule near the shore and a second on the other side farther out into the bog.

Continue following the Bloticle tentacle out into the swamp. Paint in the nearby dock so you have a platform to get a better angle on the pustules.

From the dock, you can shoot the remaining two pustules on the back side of the Bloticle and send it to a slimy demise.

Track down the final Bloticle near the lonely shack. Take out the slumbering Spladoosh on the island ahead, and use the islands and the docks to find all the pustules.

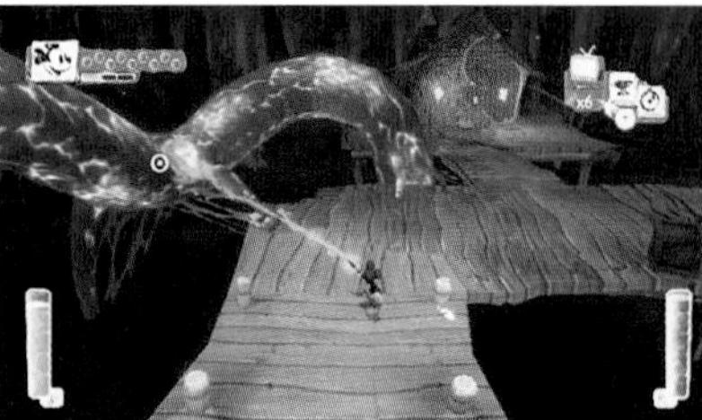

Paint in missing dock sections to defeat more pustules.

You have to get back out into the swamp to reach the final pustules. When you've popped the last one, the Bloticle is dispatched and Bog Easy lives another day.

Return to Mean Street and move on to the next Bloticle battle in Tomorrow City. You'll receive the No More Bloticles Pin at the Tomorrow City projector screen. Even though you've saved your friends's homes, you must clean up more Bloticles on your way to the rocket.

This is your last chance to visit Mean Street, OsTown, Ventureland, and Bog Easy. If you have any unfinished business, take care of it now. Once you enter Tomorrow City, you've set your course for the finale.

Battle in Tomorrow City

Tomorrow City Quest

- Battle in Tomorrow City

Defeat all three Bloticles in Tomorrow City. The Bloticles in Tomorrow City are blocking access to Space Voyage.

With many enemies and obstacles in Tomorrow City Square, it's best to take the high ground. Seek out the first TV platform up the ramp near your starting position. Eliminate the Sweeper.

From the TV platform, defeat the first two pustules on the Bloticle facing you.

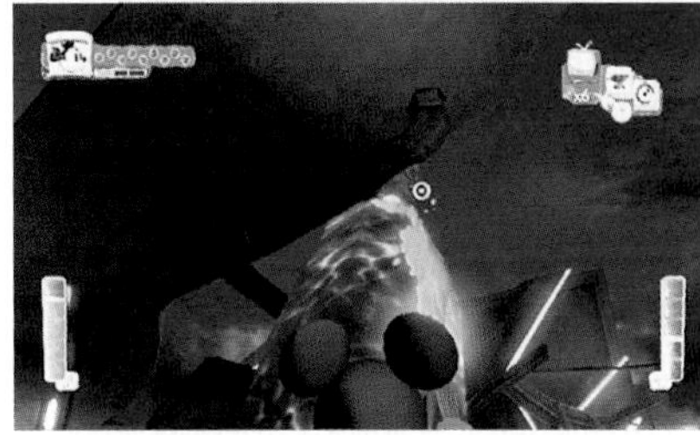

Drop to ground level and defeat the third pustule on the Bloticle's opposite side.

Return to the first TV platform. Double-jump over to tram track, and then up to the second TV platform. Knock off the Sweeper to give yourself breathing room.

Blast away at the larger pustules that grow on the Bloticle skin.

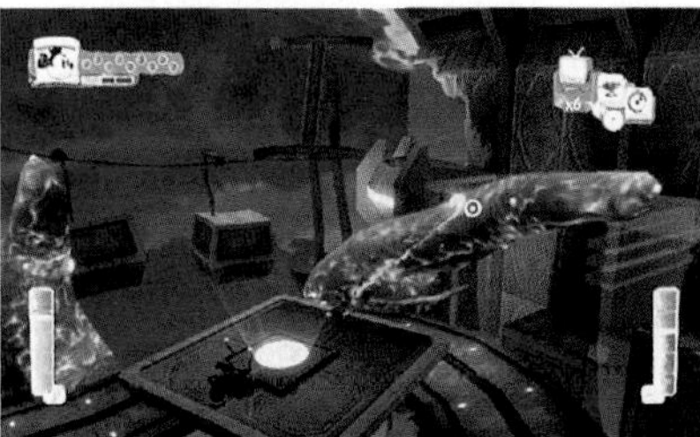

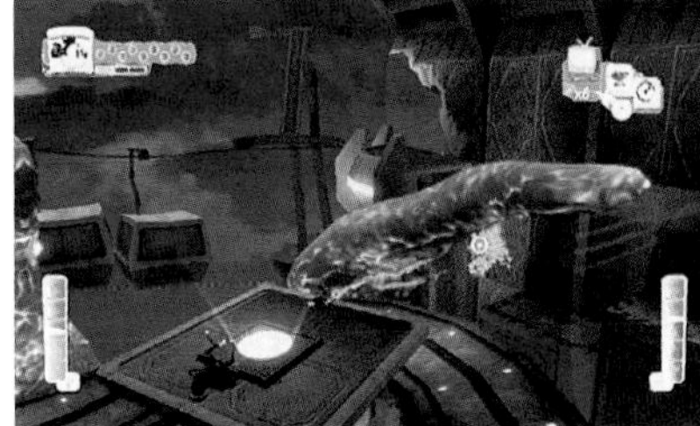

Finish off the three remaining pustules on the first Bloticle tentacle.

Turn to your left. Pop the next two pustules on the second Bloticle.

Jump over to the central circular platform.

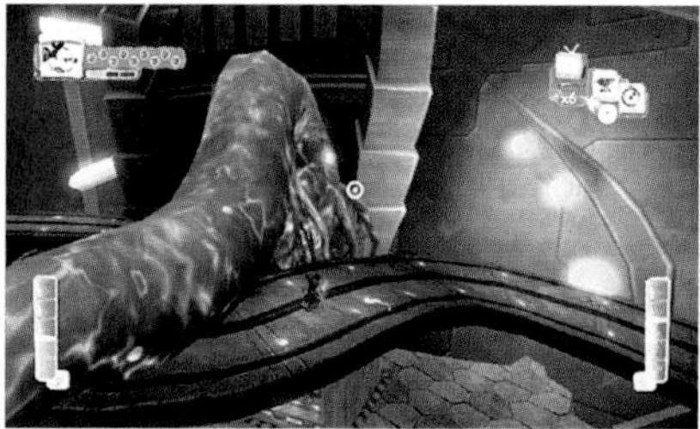

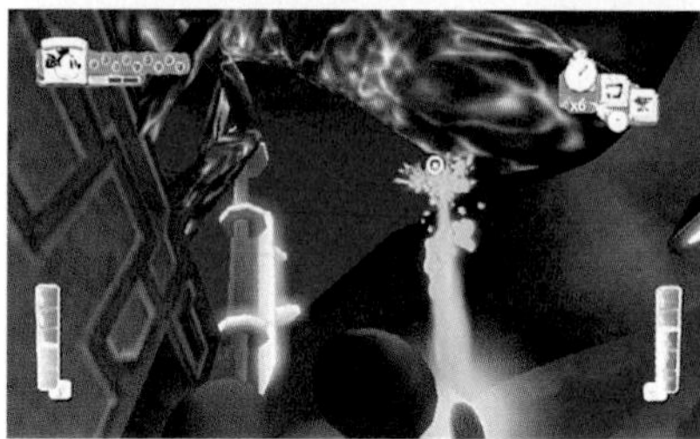

Get down on the tram tracks to pop the next pustule, then drop below to get an angle on the next two.

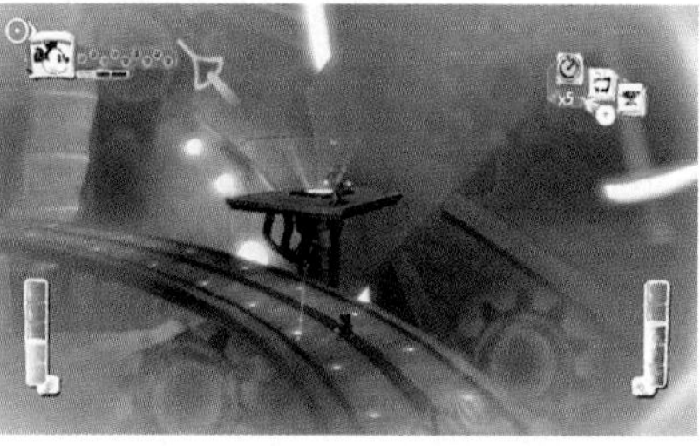

Slow down time with a Watch sketch if you need to cross longer distances with lots of hazards and enemies.

Climb back up to the central circular platform and go after the final two pustules.

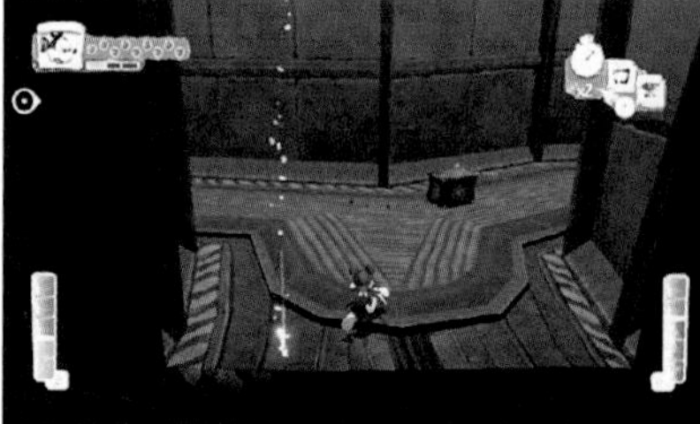

When the final pustules pops, dart into the tunnel leading to Space Voyage. You have one more Bloticle to go in the Tomorrow City complex.

Battle in Space Voyage

Space Voyage Quest

- Battle in Space Voyage

Defeat all three Bloticles attached to the rocket. The rocket cannot lift off until all of the Bloticles have been removed.

You descend in the elevator with Oswald, and he plans to meet you at the rocket after you finish off the remaining Bloticles. Exit the elevator onto the trolley tracks.

You can use the elevated platforms to reach the second floor, but there's a better sneaky way to attack the Bloticles.

Avoid the Tankers and Bashers on the lower floor. You don't have to fight them; it's the Bloticles you want.

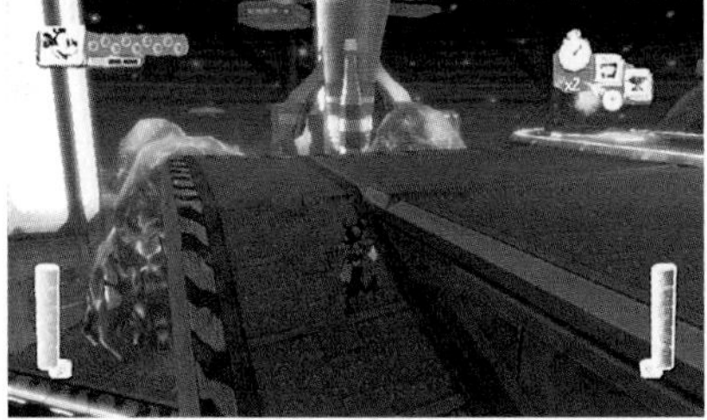

Circle around until you find the pod behind the cubicle with Horace's lost dog tags. Ride the pod to the opposite end, then follow the pipes up to the next terrace and run up the ramp to get an overview of the Bloticles surrounding the rocket.

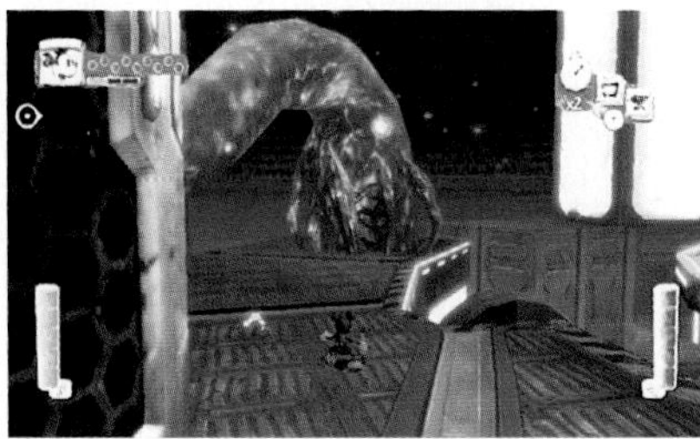

Drop to the platform below and look for the Bloticle on the left. Shoot the first two pustules close to the platform's edge.

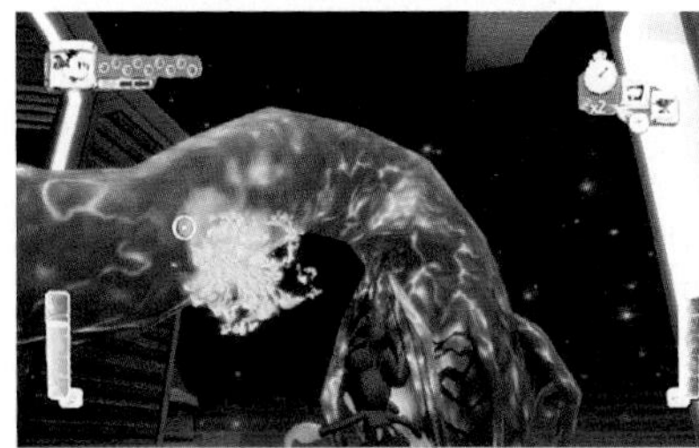

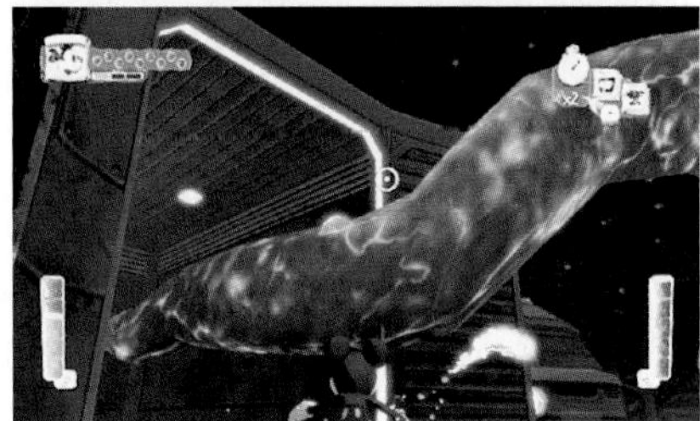

Follow the enlarging pustules down to the Bloticle tip. Defeat the next three to finish off this Bloticle.

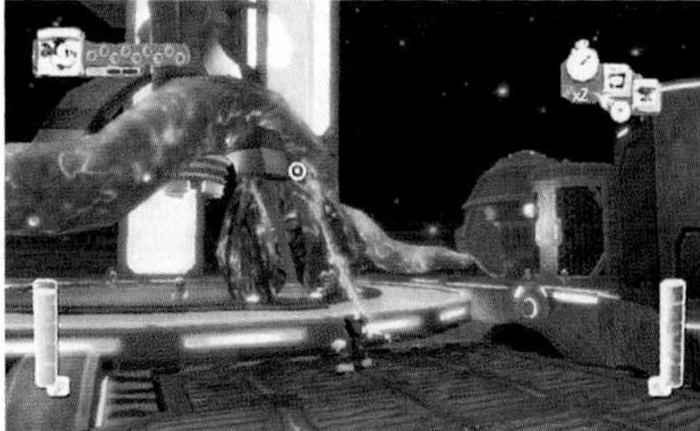

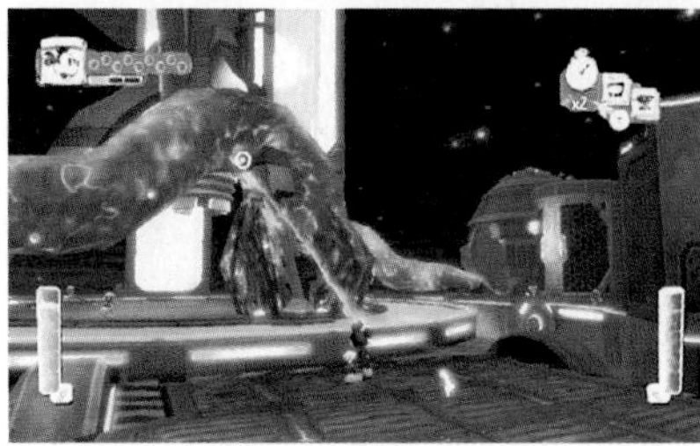

Advance on the central rocket platform, but don't jump over to it yet. From the edge of your current platform, all the pustules on the second Bloticle should be in range.

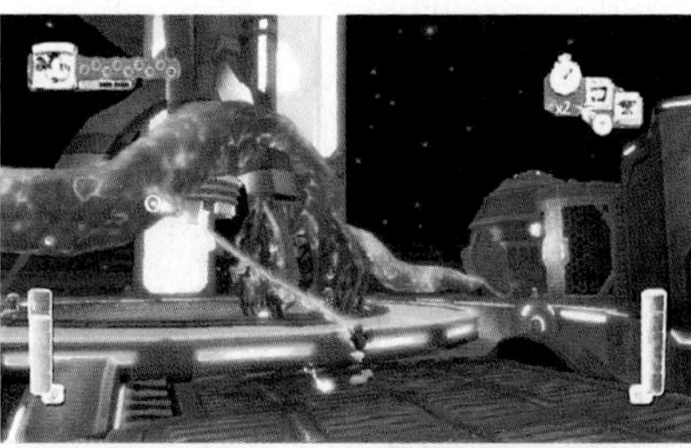

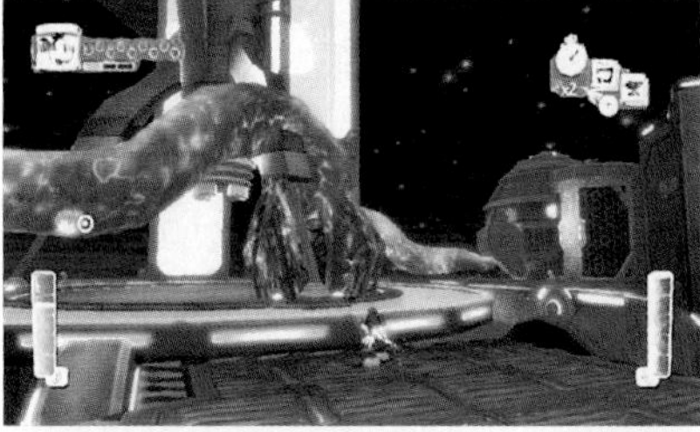

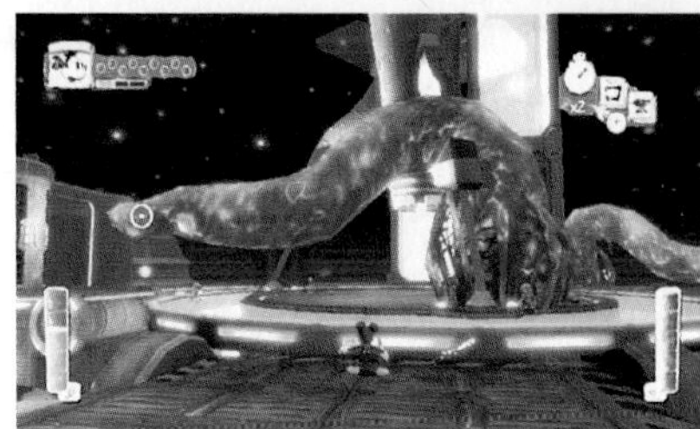

Spray down on the Bloticle and pop each pustule that bulges up. When you defeat the one near the tip, the second Bloticle explodes.

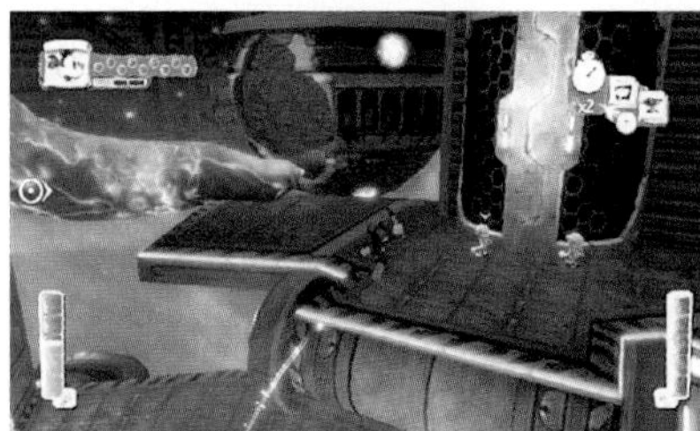

Double-jump over to the platform with the two Spatters. Swat them over the edge with a few spin moves.

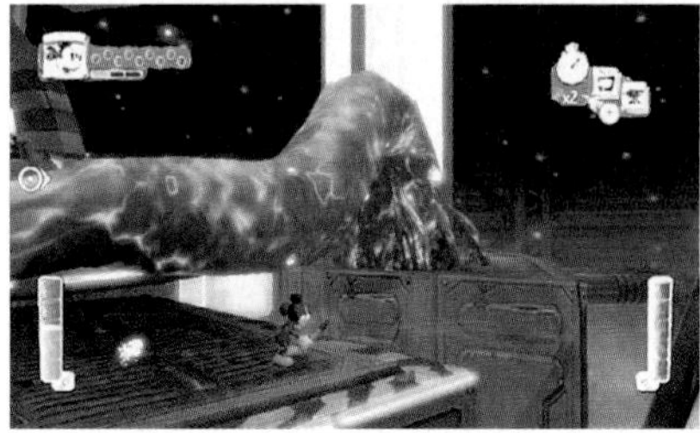

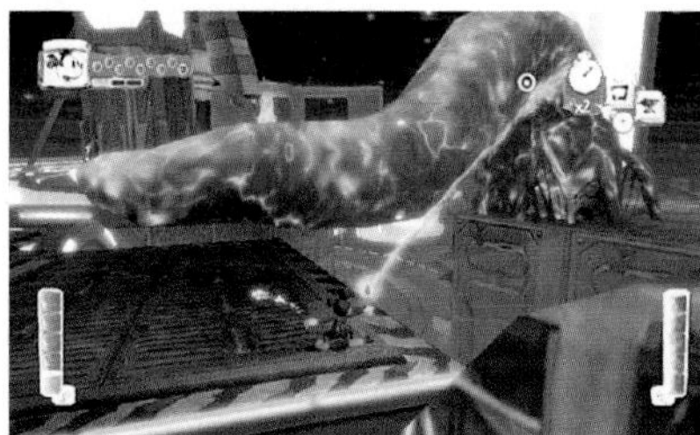

Move out to the edge of the platform and search the back side of the final Bloticle for enlarged pustules. Blast them one by one.

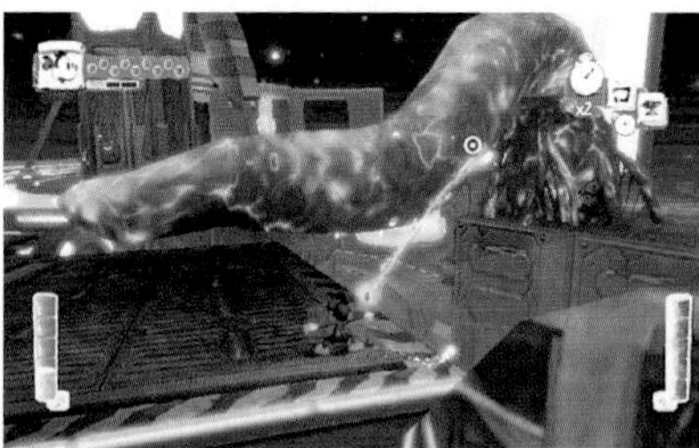

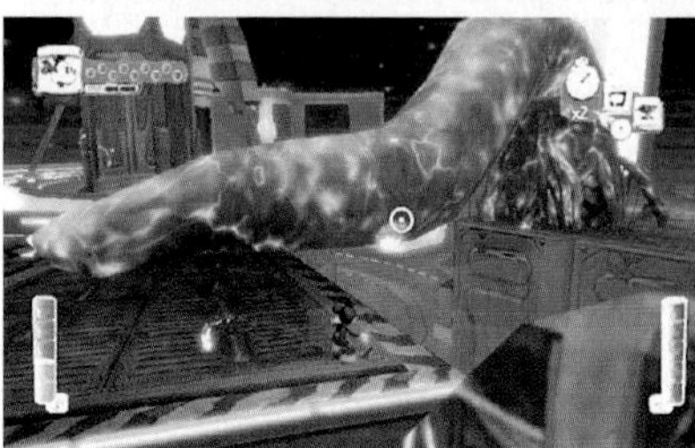

Continue popping pustules down the tentacle.

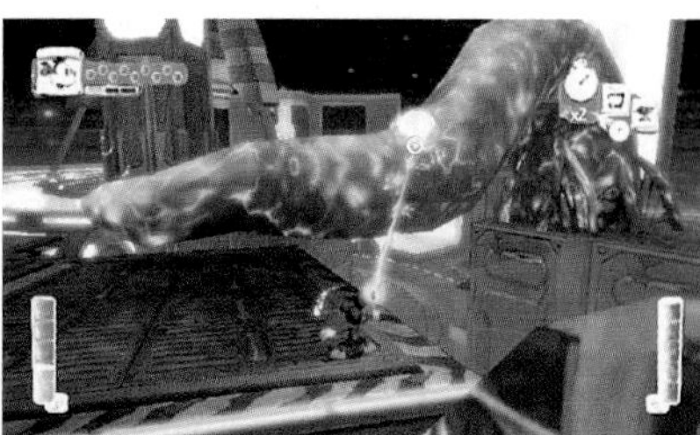

Pick off the last pustule and the Bloticle explodes spectacularly overhead.

Oswald waits for you in the elevator up to the rocket. Alas, the rocket attack against the Blot fails to live up to your expectations. The Blot cripples the rocket en route and forces you to crash land in the next destination: your very first location in Wasteland, Dark Beauty Castle.

Mad Doctor's Lab

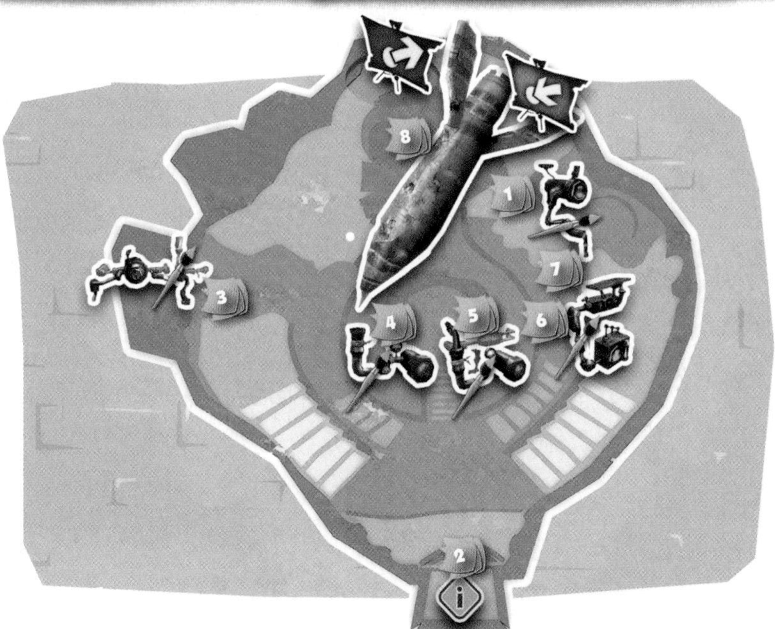

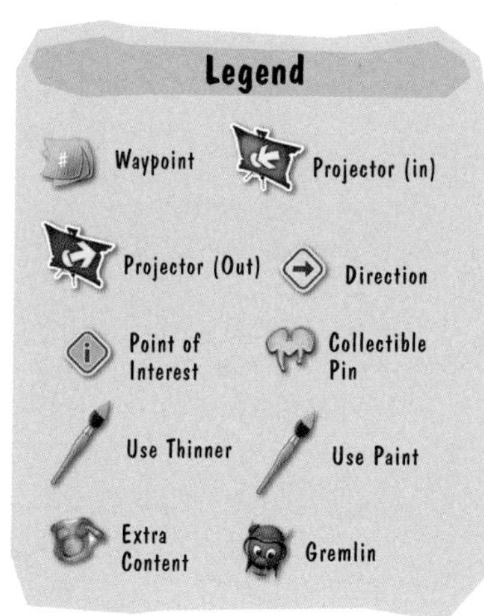

Level Overview

The Mad Doctor's Lab is even more of a disaster than when you left it back in Dark Beauty Castle. Thinner has flooded the chamber; cutting off your escape path. Can you paint in five steam pipes spread about the room in 45 seconds? If not, the returning Thinner flood will consume you.

1

Leave the rocket area and double-jump to the platform with the broken control panel. Spin move to swat the patrolling Sweeper over the edge and into the Thinner flood.

The Mad Doctor's Lab I concept art is on the left side of the crashed rocket. Drain the Thinner in the Lab and then double-jump and spin move to the ledge with the extra content.

Things to Do

- Drain Thinner out of the room
- Patch the steam pipes
- Beat the Slobber for the exit key
- Exit to the Sleeping Beauty 2D level

Continue down the ramp and carefully jump up on the railing to your right. Inch forward until your toes almost touch the Thinner. Double-jump over to the floating debris, and immediately double-jump again to reach the Mad Doctor's stage.

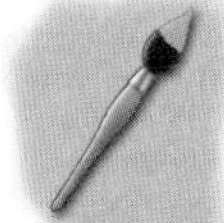

Paint in the thinned-out chest under the wooden staircase by the stage for extra loot.

2

Jump up on the alcove behind the shattered stained glass window. Activate the Thinner pump in the alcove to temporarily remove the Thinner flood.

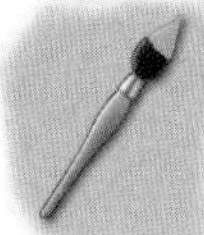

Use Paint on all five steam pipes to get them back in working order. Activate a Watch sketch to make this a lot easier to tackle.

3

Without the steam pipes working, though, the Thinner flood will pour back into the room in 45 seconds. Jump down from the stained glass window and run to your left. Race down the ramp and squirt Paint on the first steam pipe on the left wall near the Oswald statue.

4

Turn around and race toward the room's center. Jump down to the lowest level and look for the second steam pipe in a small alcove behind you.

Double-jump up the wall and then back down to reach the third steam pipe in an alcove on the opposite side of the lowest level.

Continue in the same direction and double-jump up to the higher level. You'll see the last two steam pipes, one outside and one inside the final alcove. Paint the outside steam pipe.

With time winding down, spray Paint on the fifth steam pipe inside the alcove. The Thinner flood won't return now that the machinery is back to normal.

A Bronze Pin is in the room with Thinner canisters behind one of the thinned-out Oswald statues. Paint in the chest and the pin is yours.

The Thinner danger is over, but you have a new one to address: a Slobber and two Sweepers bar the way to the exit screen. Defeat them to retrieve the key that opens the exit door.

Paint the Sweepers first. The Slobber takes longer to defeat, and the Sweepers can pelt you with Thinner while you battle the Slobber, so convert them to your side. Remember that you can also Thin them if you need more health, and activate your guardians if you're having difficulty defeating these challenging foes.

While the Sweepers occupy the Slobber's time, get into position to take

shots at it and high-tail it out of there when the Slobber counterattacks.

Work with the Sweepers to thin out the Slobber. You could use Paint on the Slobber, but the Sweepers fire Thinner and that has a tendency to counteract your Paint attacks. Grab the key when the Slobber drops.

Use the key on the exit door and jump through the projector screen to the Sleeping Beauty 2D level.

Sleeping Beauty

You appear in the jagged landscape outside the castle. Escape from a nasty dragon to reach the safety of the forest.

Hop along the ground to the right, and follow the jagged rocks to the top of the hill.

There is a tree just over the hill. If you need a little boost, drop down and grab the health power-up on the ground.

Hop onto the tree and jump over to the right.

Jump onto the next tree. The film reel is on the ledge to the right.

Hop over and run across the ledge. A dragon swoops down and hovers to the right. Grab the film reel and run back to the left. When the dragon flaps its wings, the force pushes you off the ledge. Jump onto the tree and drop to the ground.

When you land, grab the sketch on the ground and continue to the right.

Move past the jagged rocks to reach a tranquil forest. A small bird is perched on a tree to the right.

Drop to the ground below the tree. Continue to the right to find a hidden passage.

Run through the passage to pop out under the fallen tree. Drop down and grab the sketch on the ground, then back up to the passage.

Exit the passage and jump up to the fallen tree. Run across to the hollow log on the right.

Collect the sketch hidden inside the log. The projector screen is on the ledge to the right.

When you're ready to continue, jump onto the ledge and activate the projector screen to the Throne Room.

Throne Room

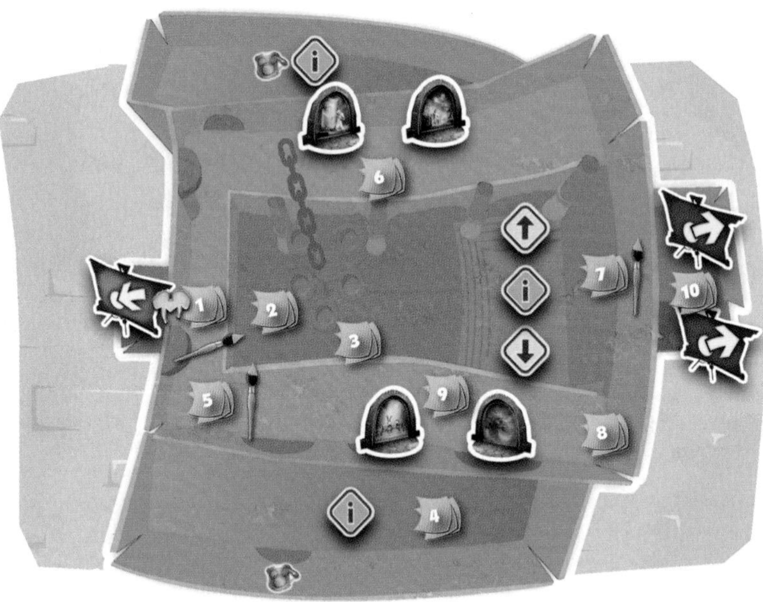

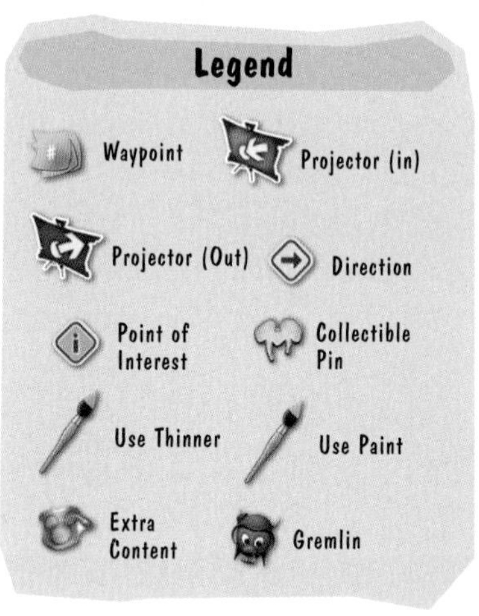

Level Overview

Like the Mad Doctor's Lab before it, the Throne Room lies in ruins. A broken stained glass mural hangs above thinned-out paintings. A Slobber smashes around the lower level, while twin Sweepers terrorize the balcony. A giant boulder has even crashed into the side corridor and created an impromptu trap.

You begin staring down a long red carpet at a Slobber at the far end. This Throne Room has a few squatters: a Slobber on the ground floor and two Sweepers upstairs on the balcony. Before you can make progress with the room's puzzles, you must deal with the enemies.

Things to Do

- **Battle the Slobber and Sweepers**
- **Paint the paintings and mural or use Thinner on the four walls that hide the chain pulleys**
- **Thin all four chain pulleys and enter the broken chamber to exit to Fantasia 1**
- **Spin the gargoyles and activate the gem to exit to Fantasia 2**

Gold Pin

This pin floats above the entrance projector. Either jump down from the balcony to grab it, or drop an anvil and use it to vault up for the pin. You can also jump off the Slobber's head to reach it.

By this point, you should be experienced at battling Slobbers. Stay out of reach of the claws and far enough back that its suction breath doesn't draw you in too close, but close enough that you can flood it with Paint or Thinner.

If you befriend the Slobber with gallons of Paint, it will aid you against any Sweepers that end up on the ground level.

Exit the Throne Room relying on Paint or Thinner. If you use Thinner, you exit via the Fantasia 1 2D level. If you use Paint, you exit via the Fantasia 2 2D level. Oswald also awards you the special Oswald Pin in the Fireworks Control Tower if you use Paint to escape the Throne Room. Assuming you choose the Paint option, coat the paintings along the wall with Paint until you reveal all of each painting.

If you attempt to Paint the walls with Sweepers present, they will frustrate you by throwing buckets of Thinner on the paintings to undo your work.

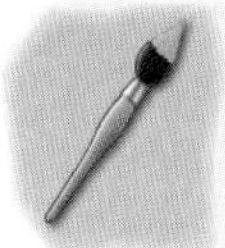

Use Paint to befriend the Sweepers and easily complete the Paint option.

The Thinner Solution

Instead of using Paint, use Thinner to break the four walls around the Throne Room. Inside each broken wall is a chain pulley. Thin out all four chain pulleys.

When the last chain pulley thins, the chandelier breaks and opens a hole into a secret chamber. This chamber holds the exit screen to Fantasia 1. Once you trigger the broken chandelier, it's impossible to solve the Throne Room with Paint and you must exit via the Fantasia 1 screen.

Don't forget about the little paintings if you're pursuing the path toward the Fantasia 2 screen. Find the little paintings hidden in the corners.

Extra Content: Throne Room

Paint the wall left of the throne to reveal a secret corridor. Brave this tentacle-filled corridor to reach the top section. Thin out the floor in this location and drop down to get the concept art.

4

When you first enter the side corridor, a giant boulder rolls down at you when you step just short of the halfway point. Turn around and race back down the corridor and out the ground level doorway. Once the boulder crashes, you can scoot by it and continue up the side corridor.

Convert the Sweepers to your side with Paint. Thinner is difficult to control on the balcony, and eliminated Sweepers respawn quickly anyway.

5

Break out your Paint on the balcony and turn both Sweepers to your cause. You can use Thinner to erase them, but the Sweepers respawn quickly if you do. If you befriend them with Paint, new Sweepers don't respawn. Plus, much of the balcony is made of toon material, and a stray Thinner stream will send you crashing to the ground level.

6

If you're pursuing the Paint path, restore the paintings to full detail with streams of Paint.

Make sure you reveal each piece of a painting so that you don't have to double-check everything later for a missed spot.

7

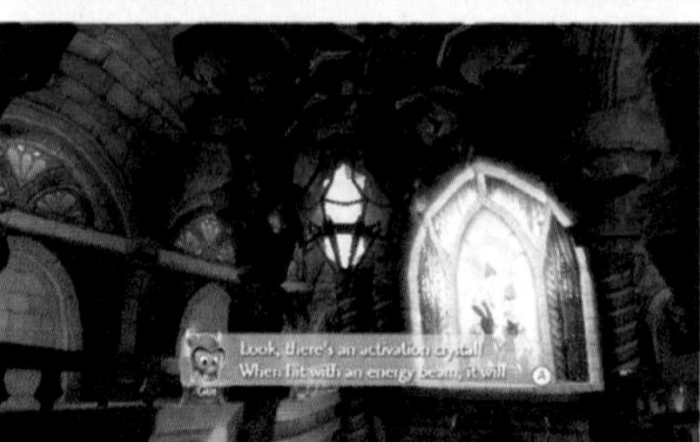

Extra Content: Oswald and Ortensia

On the left wall in the side corridor, notice a toon spot about three quarters up to the balcony. Thin out the wall to see this concept art in a small alcove.

Paint in the stained glass mural of Oswald and Ortensia. A huge gem lowers from the ceiling and light radiates out of the mural.

If you've painted everything correctly, a gargoyle spins out of the wall on either end of the balcony. Spin each gargoyle so that it emits a beam of white light.

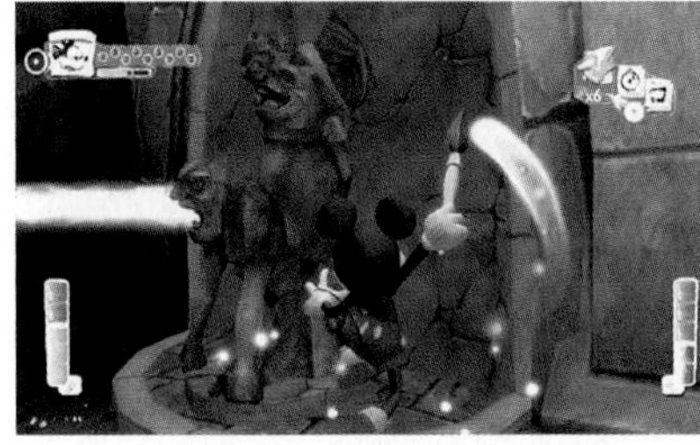

Now you have to reflect the light beams to strike the gem. Spin each gargoyle on the balcony to direct the gargoyle mouths so that they bounce the light onto the gem.

Once the gem lights up, the mural drops to reveal the secret chamber that holds the exit screen for Fantasia 2. Enter the screen to visit the 2D level and then onto the Fireworks Control Tower.

If you escaped the Throne Room using Thinner, you exit to Fantasia 1. If you escaped the Throne Room using Paint, you exit to Fantasia 2. You cannot open both Fantasia 1 and Fantasia 2 in the same playthrough.

Fantasia: Part 1

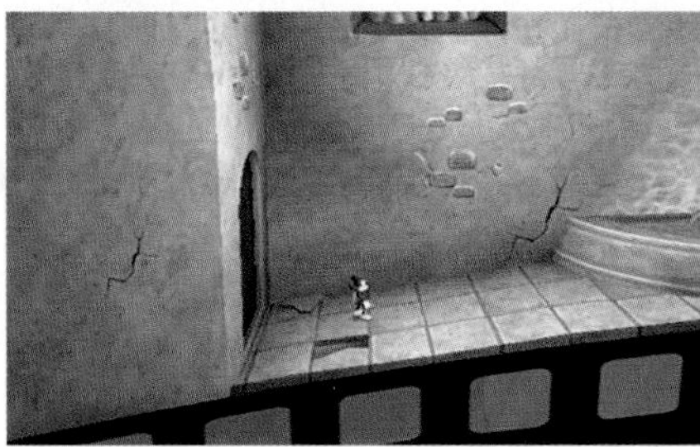

You appear in a wizard's workshop. Borrow a little magic to bring everyday objects to life. Avoid streams of water, hovering butterflies, and busy brooms as you maneuver through the hallway.

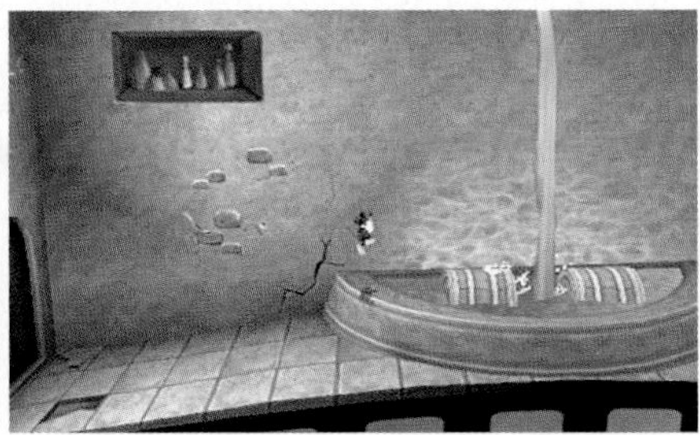

Move to the right and hop on the fountain edge. Two barrels float in the pool, and a fixture on the wall pours fresh water at regular intervals.

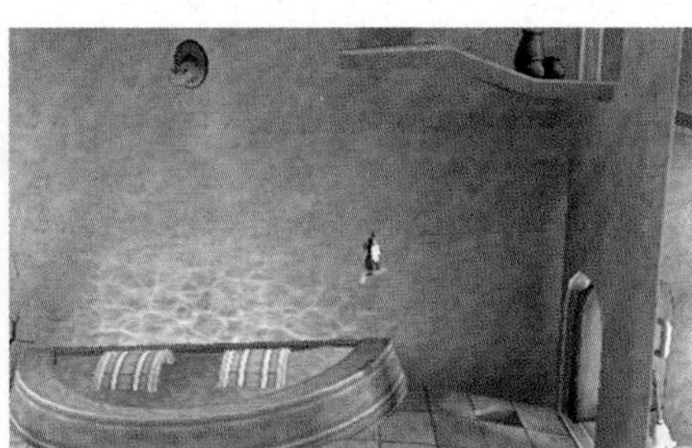

Wait for a break in the stream and hop across the barrels. When you land, continue through the door on the right.

Run down toward the table. If needed, hop up and grab the health power-up above the stairs. A broom leans against the door on the left. Jump onto the table and move across the book.

Grab the wizard hat to enchant the objects in the area. The book to the left floats into the air and the vase to the right shoots out a stream of water. A butterfly appears near the crack in the wall and the brooms in the hallway spring to life.

Wait for a break in the water, then jump over the vase. Avoid the broom marching on the floor to the right, and drop down to grab the sketch near the table.

Jump back over the vase and hop onto the book. Wait for the broom to reach the table, then jump over to the stairs.

Stay ahead of the broom and hop up to the edge of the fountain. Jump onto the nearest barrel when it touches down on the water.

Ride the barrel into the air. A ledge runs through the door on the right, and a sketch floats near the fixture on the wall. Jump onto the ledge before the barrel heads back down.

To collect the sketch, hop over the fixture and drop to the barrel on the fountain's left side. Use the barrels to return to the ledge, and continue through the door on the right.

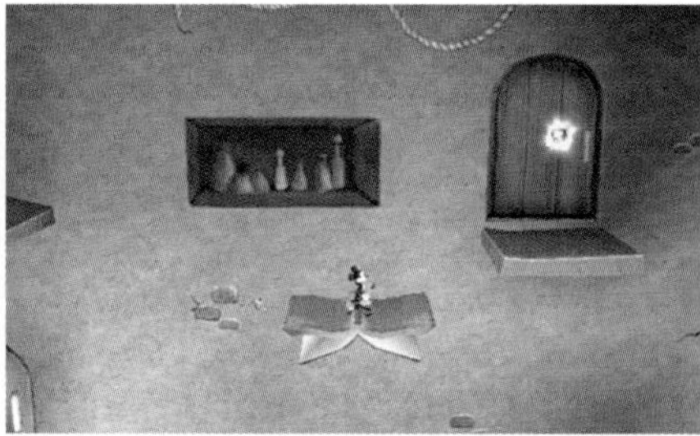

Wait for the book to float up, then double-jump to the right. Hop over to the sketch on the next ledge.

The film reel is on the ledge to the right, but keep a few obstacles in mind. Stand in front of the small door and wait for the vase below you to blast another stream of water. Locate the butterfly near the ceiling and prepare to jump across.

When the water dies down, jump over the butterfly and grab the film reel.

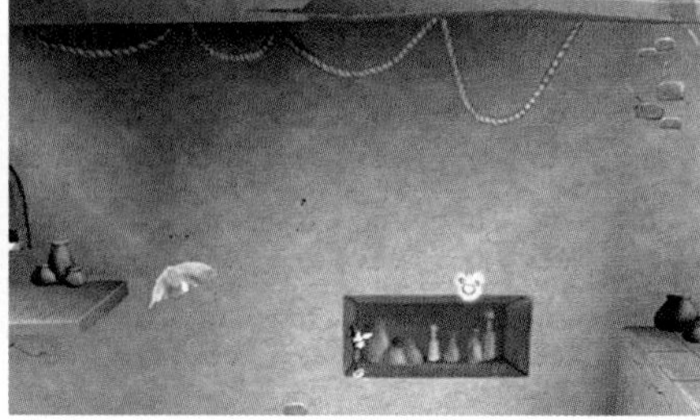

Move to the right and stand on the edge of the shelf. Watch for the barrels blasting up below the health power-up. Jump over the butterfly to the right and land on the nearest barrel.

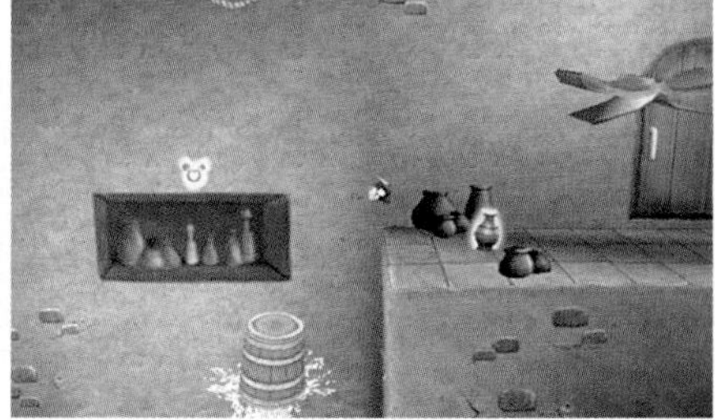

Hop onto the next barrel and jump on the ledge to the right. When you land, wait for the vase to blast out a stream of water.

When the water dies down, hop onto the book. If you need it, grab the health power-up to the right. Stand on the book as it floats up to the next ledge.

Watch out for the butterfly above you and wait for a break in the water. Jump across to the projector screen on the left.

When you're ready to leave, activate the projector screen and complete the level to exit to the Fireworks Control Tower.

Fantasia: Part 2

You appear on a narrow mountaintop, under the sparkling stars of the night sky.

Jump onto the star to the right and watch for its distinctive twinkle. The two stars on the left emit an even glow. Glowing stars vanish at regular intervals, while twinkling stars remain visible at all times.

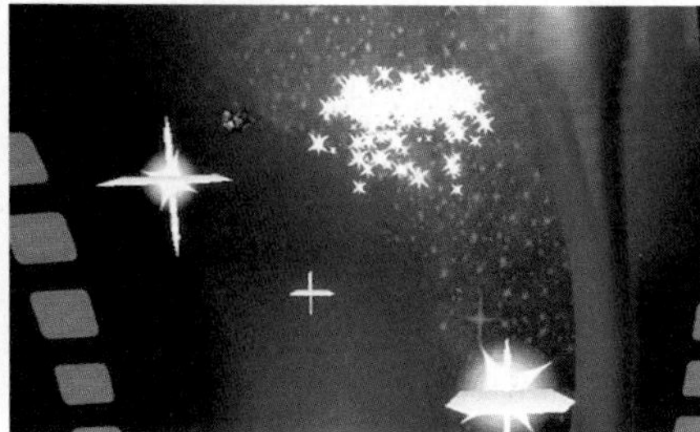

Jump across the glowing stars before they vanish, and leap to the star cluster near the ledge to the right.

When a star cluster appears, it burns brightly and slowly fades away. Jump up to the ledge before the star cluster vanishes.

Hop to the twinkling star near the ledge. Wait for the glowing star to appear, then continue to the left.

Jump up to the ledge before the glowing star vanishes.

Hop up to the next ledge. Grab the health power-up and wait for the glowing star to appear to the right.

Jump onto the glowing star, then jump across the two twinkling stars to the right.

A star cluster appears to the left. Above you, clouds float across to the right. To collect the sketch near the twinkling star, use the star cluster to hop onto the clouds, then ride over to the right. Drop through the sketch and double-jump back to the twinkling star.

Hop onto the star cluster and wait for a fresh cloud to appear. Jump over to the cloud before the star cluster vanishes.

When you land on the cloud, jump up to the twinkling star on the right.

Hop across the twinkling stars to reach the ledge on the right. If needed, collect the health power-up below the star to the right.

Hop back down across the twinkling stars. Another sketch is high to the left.

When the glowing star appears, jump up to collect the sketch. Hop over to the right and land on the next glowing star.

Jump up to the glowing star on the left. The film reel and projector screen are both to the right. Jump up and collect the film reel on the giant star.

To collect another sketch, wait for the glowing star to appear on the left. Hop up to grab the sketch, then double-jump back to the glowing star.

Double-jump over the giant star to reach the projector screen.

When you're ready to continue, activate the projector screen and complete the level to exit to the Fireworks Control Tower.

Fireworks Control Tower

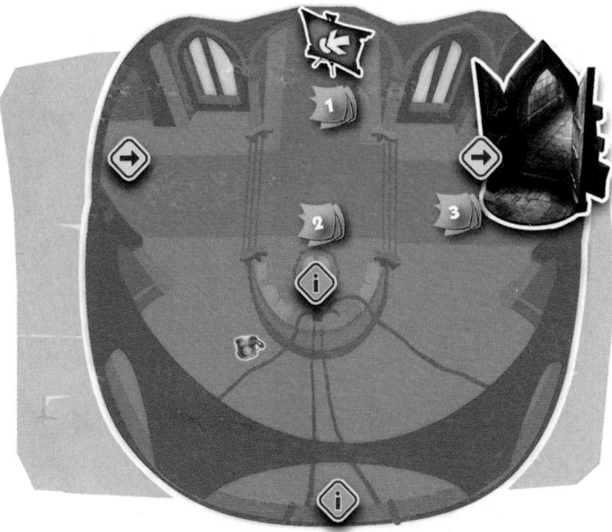

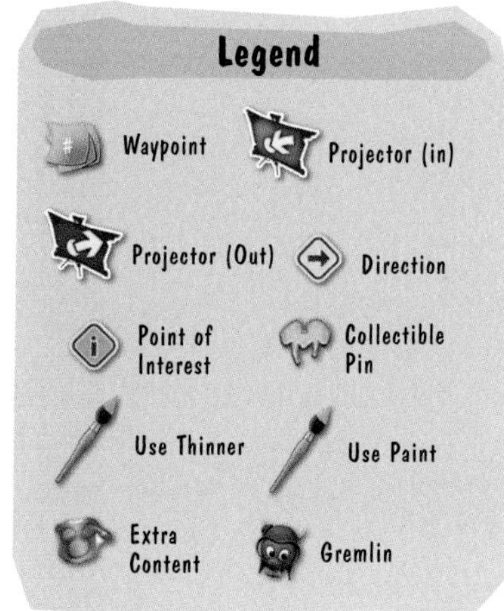

Level Overview

You've caught up with Oswald again. This time he has a plan to arm the three main towers with fireworks to blast off at the Blot and take the thing out once and for all. Oswald needs you to climb each tower and activate the fireworks while he makes the final preparations.

Enter the Fireworks Control Tower. Get your new marching orders from Oswald: climb three towers and activate the fireworks atop each one.

Things to Do

- Speak with Oswald
- Pick up the Sleeping Ortensia concept art
- Exit to the Utilidor IV corridor

Extra Content: Sleeping Ortensia

This is an easy one. Barely hidden behind Oswald's control panel lies the Sleeping Ortensia extra content. Hop behind the control panel to get it.

If you used Paint to escape the Throne Room, Oswald rewards you with his special Oswald Pin.

Exit directly into the Utilidor IV corridor that links the Fireworks Control Tower with the first fireworks-laden tower: Sorrow Tower.

Utilidor IV

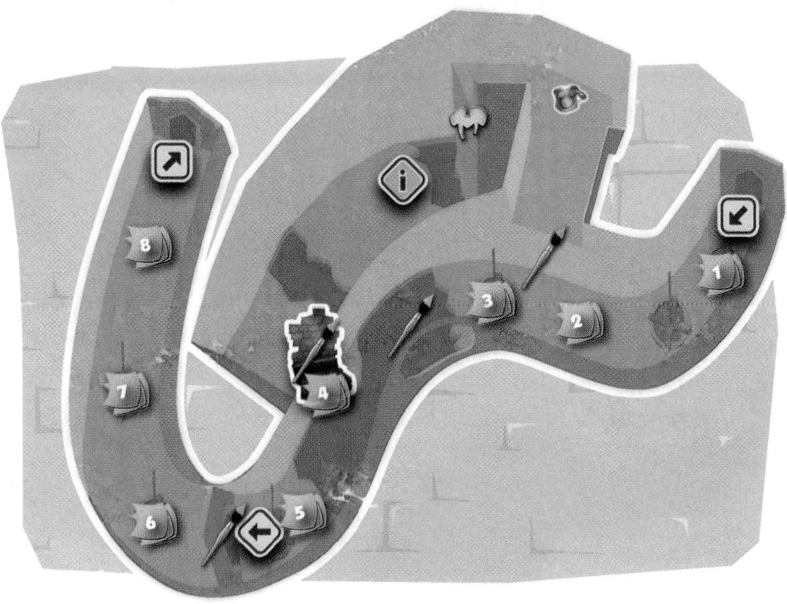

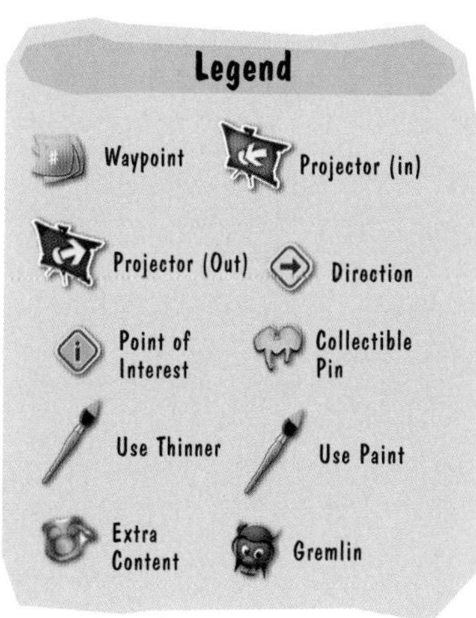

Level Overview

Who would have thought the corridor next to Oswald's Fireworks Control Tower was so fraught with peril? The Blot extends its shadowy tentacles through the walls to grab you. The crumbling floor gives way to dangerous drops in inconvenient spots. Luckily these towers have a lot of chandeliers to jump along.

1

Watch out for the crumbling corridor in front of you. Rather than cross most of this corridor on the stone floor, you're going to use the hanging chandeliers. Jump over to the first one.

Look to your left and spot the translucent gear. Paint in the gear to raise your current chandelier and lower the next one. Double-jump over to the second chandelier.

Things to Do

- Use the hanging chandeliers to bypass tentacles and reach the end of the corridor
- Exit to Sorrow Tower

2

Shadow tentacles clog the next stretch of corridor. Stand on the chandelier and watch the tentacle pattern as they extend and retract. Begin your double-jump off the chandelier and down to the stone corridor floor while the tentacles are still out but are about to retract. Race past them and stop in front of the second chandelier set, far enough away that you don't fall through the collapsing floor.

Extra Content: Dark Beauty Castle II

To get this piece of concept art, go to the second chandelier set and raise it. Turn around and thin out the wall on your left. Double-jump to the hidden alcove and recover the extra content.

Paint in the second chandelier and the translucent shield on the wall for extra defense against the invading shadow tentacles.

3

Double-jump up on the first chandelier. Paint in the second chandelier and the gear on the wall to raise your current chandelier.

Double-jump off the second chandelier onto the small ledge next to the toon wall patch. Either time the jump to avoid the shadow tentacle that oozes through the right wall, or spray Paint on the translucent shield hanging on the wall, which slows the tentacle down and prevents it from jutting all the way into the corridor.

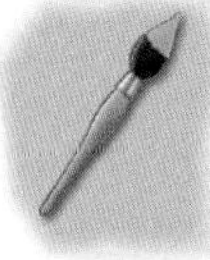

Erase the toon wall past the second chandelier set to reveal a secret corridor branch to the Silver Pin.

4

Thin out the wall behind you. Enter the secret corridor and stay near the entrance. Watch out for the crumbling stone in front of you, and pay attention to the tentacles that swarm the landing beyond the gap. Take a running start and double-jump over the gap and run to the other side of the landing near the toon wall. You have to time it perfectly; start your jump while the tentacles are still at full extension, and they should be retracting while you're in midair.

From your safe spot at the end of the landing, stream Thinner up at the toon wall and evaporate it. Double-jump up to the hidden alcove and recover the Silver Pin in the red chest.

5

Return to the main corridor. Double-jump up on the swinging chandelier. The landing around the door falls apart as you approach; you can't use it. Instead, thin the door and surrounding wall so you can jump through.

6

Double-jump through the thinned-out doorway and land on the next chandelier as it swings closer to you. Time your jumps on the swinging chandeliers or you'll have a painful fall. The double-jump to the next stationary chandelier is easier; however, that chandelier begins to descend when you land on it.

7

Immediately jump off the chandelier to your right and into the alcove high up on the wall. There's a chest inside, but more importantly, it gives you time to plan your next move.

8

The final stretch of corridor before the exit door looks deserted, but it's not. Shadow tentacles gush out of the wall at a regular interval. Jump out of the alcove and onto the descending chandelier when the tentacles are fully extended. Double-jump over to the corridor and run for the exit doorway to escape multiple hits.

Sorrow Tower

Level Overview

As soon as you set foot in Sorrow Tower, it falls apart around you. Only a thin strip of stone circles up around the outer wall; the rest drops into the abyss below. Spiral up the tower to the top and square off against the Blot. Oswald is counting on you to get those fireworks operational.

Work your way up the Sorrow Tower outer edge. Go slowly because pieces of the stone ledge shake and drop

loose as you approach. Double-jump over the first gap to the solid stone beyond.

Things to Do

- Circle up the Sorrow Tower
- Battle the giant Blot
- Focus the four gargoyles on the gem
- Activate the fireworks
- Exit to Fantasia: Part 3

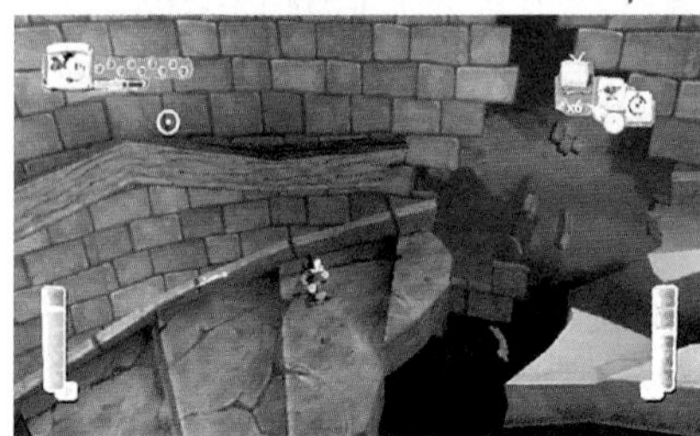

Continue to the next gap. Don't jump across right away. Fire a Paint stream over to fill in the translucent sections of ledge so you have somewhere safe to land.

Tread slowly in the next section and watch for shadow tentacles to thrash through the wall to your left. Time your double-jump to clear the tentacles and find safe stone past them.

When you run out of ledge, double-jump onto the hanging chandelier.

Look up and paint the higher section of stairs. Double-jump up to the new section.

Watch for more tentacles. Wait until they retract, then run across and paint in any translucent footing. Keeping climbing until you exit out top on the tower.

The Blot waits for you outside on Sorrow Tower. If it spews forth a blast of shadow essence, dodge right or left to avoid taking damage.

When it roars, retreat to the back of the tower to negate the effects of the air blast.

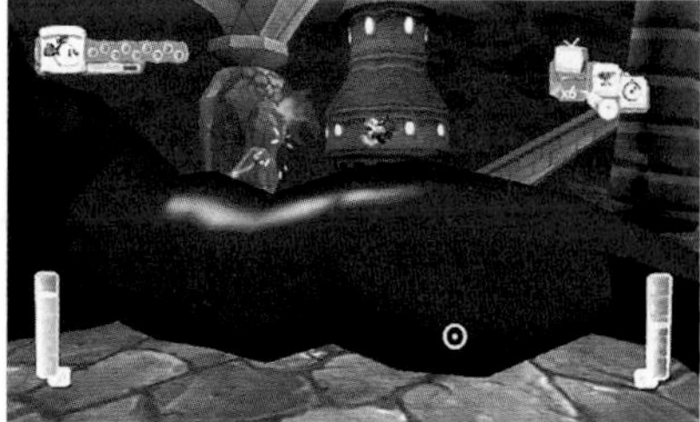

The Blot also reaches in with its arm and tries to rake you with its shadow claws. Watch where it's going to stretch and jump over to the opposite side of the tower. Its arm covers a lot of real estate, so move quickly if you anticipate the attack.

To activate the gem and the fireworks, spray Paint on the gargoyle head and then use your spin move to rotate the gargoyle so that it fires its beam at the gem.

If you need a health boost, look in a single chest at the back of the tower.

Paint all four gargoyle heads and rotate them in toward the gem, all while avoiding the Blot's potent attacks.

Once all four gargoyles hit the gem with beams, the gem powers up and drives off the Blot.

Prime the fireworks on the Sorrow Tower rooftop. Go through the doors in the side tower under the glowing purple gemstone and be sure to pick up Horned Blot concept art in the exit chamber. The projector screen takes you to Fantasia: Part 3.

Fantasia: Part 3

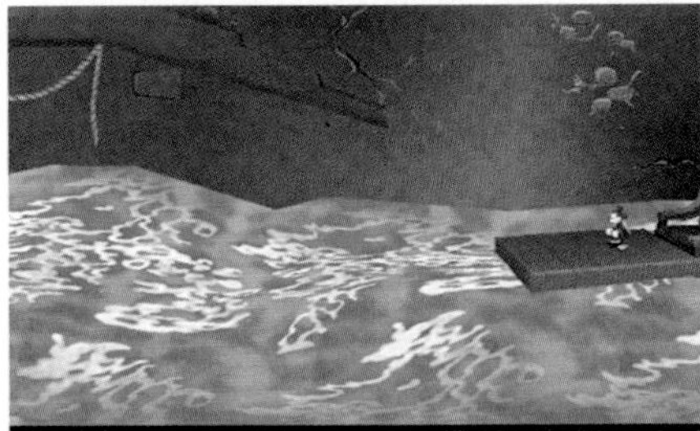

You appear on a table floating in a large pool of water. Jump across floating books as enchanted brooms empty their buckets into the flooding room.

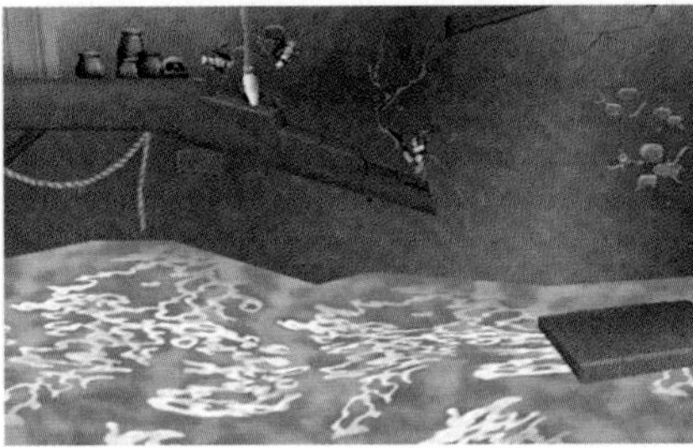

Hop to the steps on the left and double-jump over the broom as it marches toward you.

Jump back over the broom and land on the steps to the right. Stay clear of the brooms and jump up to the stairs on the left.

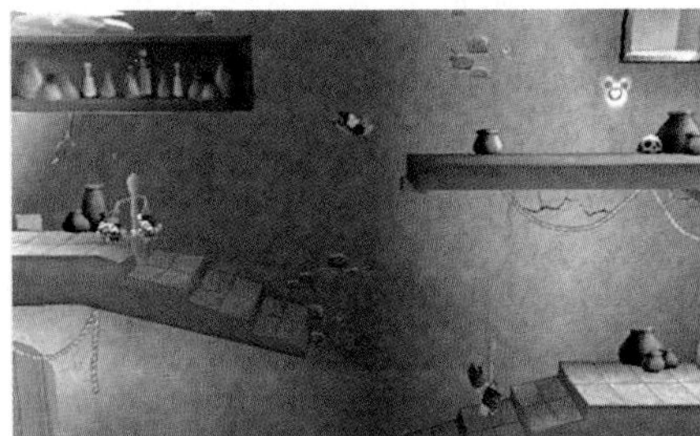

If needed, hop over to grab the health power-up to the right. When you're ready to continue, jump over the boom near the floating book.

Hop onto the book and ride up to the ledge above you.

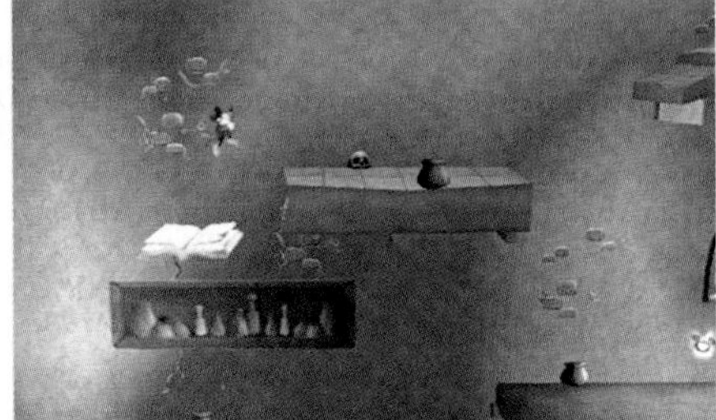

When the book reaches the top of its path, hop across the ledge and jump to the steps on the right.

Double-jump up to the ledge on the left. Take care to land to the right of the blue vase.

Two brooms pour water from the platform above you. Stay put and wait for the broom on the right to dump its bucket.

Move past the vases and stand on the ledge's left side. Wait for the next broom to pour out its water, then jump over and run up the steps. Pass under the floating book to grab the health power-up near the door.

Jump onto the book and float to the next set of steps. The broom above you pours two streams in rapid succession. After the second stream lands, hop over and run to the right. Drop down to grab the sketch, then hop onto the book above you.

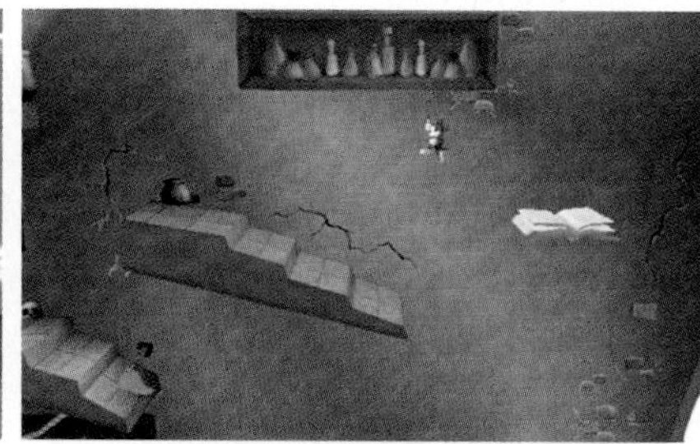
When the book floats up, jump over to the steps on the left. Continue to the left and grab the sketch, then jump back to the right and return to the steps.

Hop up to the ledge on the left. Wait for a book to slide under the small platform, then jump over to the right.

Ride the book up and around to the barrier to the right. When the broom pours out its bucket, reposition yourself to avoid the water.

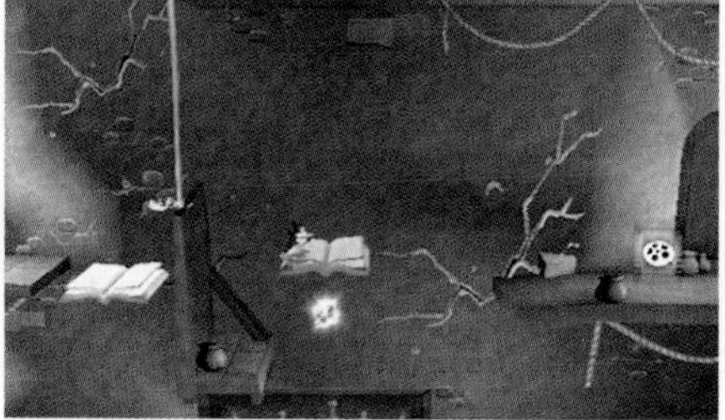
Ride the book down along the barrier. Grab the sketch, then jump over and collect the film reel on the right.

Jump past the floating book and land on the small platform near the barrier.

After the broom above you pours a fresh bucket of water, double-jump over the barrier. Touch down on a floating book and ride back up.

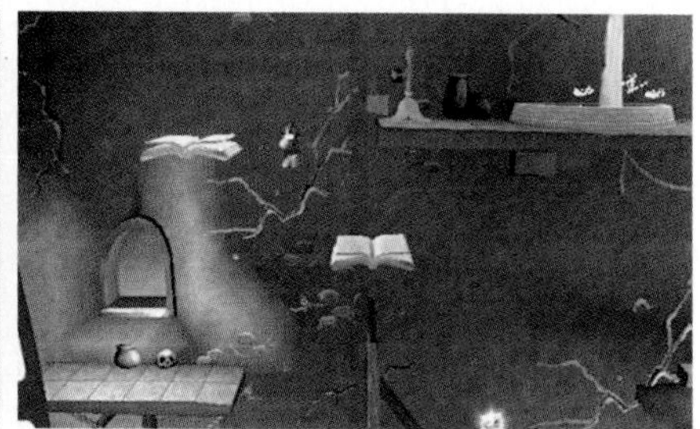
When you begin to float back to the right, jump to the book on the left.

Double-jump over the broom and land on the floor near the fountain.

When you're ready to leave the area, activate the projector screen and complete the level to move on to Grief Tower.

Grief Tower

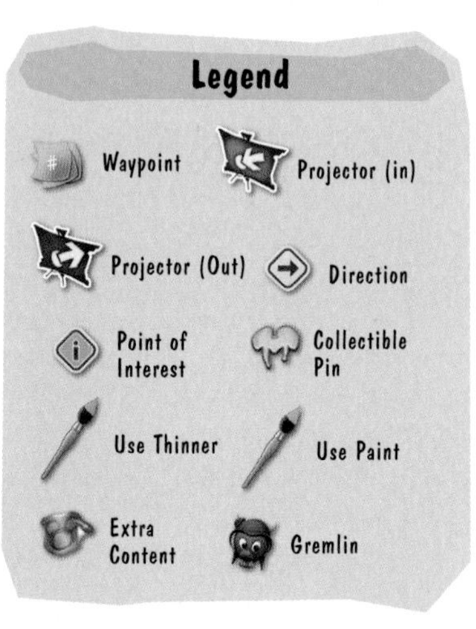

Level Overview

As you circle up Grief Tower, you have more corridor footing than Sorrow Tower; however, the Blot takes more of an interest in your ascent. Shadow tentacles pour through the walls, and the Blot rips open a section of the tower as you climb. Prepare for lots of surprises.

At the base of Grief Tower, it's quiet. Take a moment to compose yourself, because the rest of the trip up the tower will definitely stress your nerves.

Things to Do

- Circle up Grief Tower
- Battle the giant Blot
- Focus the four gargoyles on the gem
- Activate the fireworks
- Exit to Fantasia: Part 4

Inside the tower at the first big curve, look for a translucent shield on the left wall. These shields are a dead giveaway that shadow tentacles lurk behind the wall. Paint in the translucent shield to temporarily barricade the area and slow down tentacle attacks. You can also time your run to pass a tentacle area after they retract.

Gold Pin

Paint the translucent chest in the small side room at the start of Grief Tower. Open the red chest for another Gold Pin.

Put on the brakes immediately after the first tentacles. The Blot crashes into the tower ahead and rips a huge hole in the floor. After the Blot retreats, double-jump across the gap.

Dodge more tentacles and leap over the next gap in the corridor floor.

Slow down and survey the next torn hole in the floor and wall. You can't make the jump without spraying Paint on the far side to make more ledge to land on.

The Blot gets in your face in the next part of the tower. It roars and tears open the space around you. Wait until the dust settles, paint the far ledge, and then double-jump over.

Continue circling up the tower. Avoid the shadow tentacles and stop between attacks to scan ahead. When you see crumbling stone, wait for it to collapse so you can see exactly where to jump. When you see translucent stone, paint it in to rebuild the tower.

Up ahead, you'll see a short ledge to your left and a floating art concept sketch to the right. You can pick up the sketch, if you're careful, or keep going.

Extra Content: Blot Attack I

You pass this extra content on the main path up the tower. It floats to the right of the short ledge. Jump out to the right, snatch the extra content, and quickly jump back to the left and land safely on the ledge.

Use a Watch sketch to slow down time to gain an advantage against the tentacles and get farther up the tower.

Take the final big jump and rush to the top.

2

The Blot has the same complement of attacks on Grief Tower as it had on Sorrow Tower. Watch its movements carefully and avoid the attacks as they come.

Paint the first two gargoyles and spin them toward the gem.

Paint the third and fourth gargoyles and spin them toward the gem.

This time you have to deal with some Blotling enemies as well as the Blot's major attacks. Retreat to the bridge between the Grief Tower and the nearby smaller tower to spin move the Blotlings over the edge. Befriending them with Paint makes this battle a lot easier, too.

3

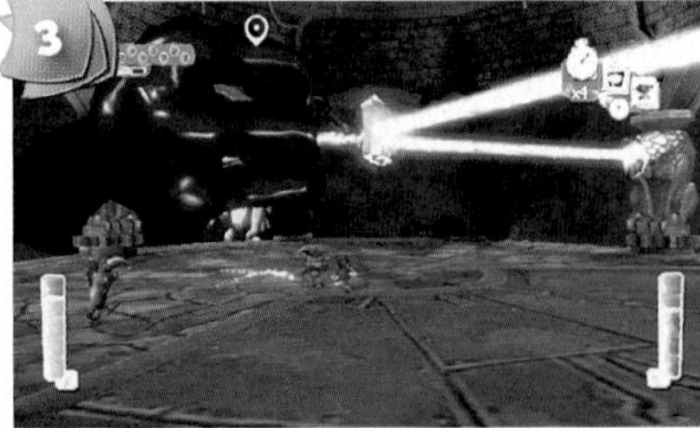

As soon as all four beams strike the gem, the concentrated blast repels the Blot. Proceed to the exit chamber. Pick up the Slobber Charge extra content above the barrels in the corner opposite the exit screen. Jump through the screen to journey to Fantasia: Part 4.

Fantasia: Part 4

You arrive at the bottom of the wizard's tower. Use barrels, books, and some well-timed jumps to stay ahead of the rising water.

Run up the stairs and hop onto the barrel. Stand on the barrel until a stream of water pours down to the right.

When the path is clear, hop to the right and grab the sketch. Quickly return to the barrel before the water reaches you.

Stand on the barrel and float up with the water. Face the steps to the right and wait for another stream of water to pour down.

Hop over to the barrel on the steps. When the book floats down, jump on to gain some distance from the water.

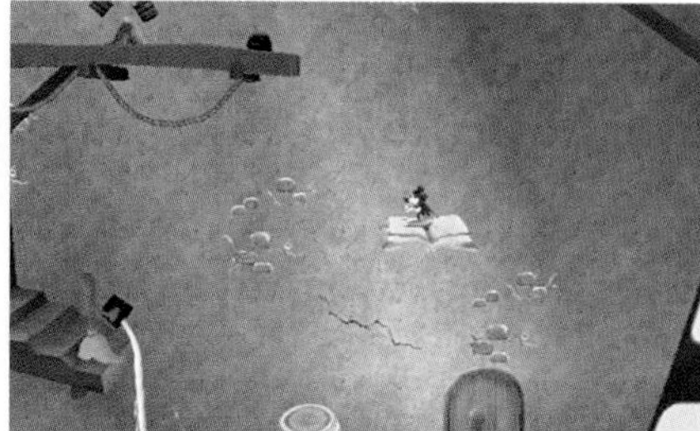

As the book floats up, locate the marching broom on the ledge to the left.

Jump to the left and avoid the marching broom, then hop up to the ledge on the right. Face back to the left and locate the book above the marching broom.

When the book moves into range, jump on. Float toward the sketch on the left and hop to the ledge.

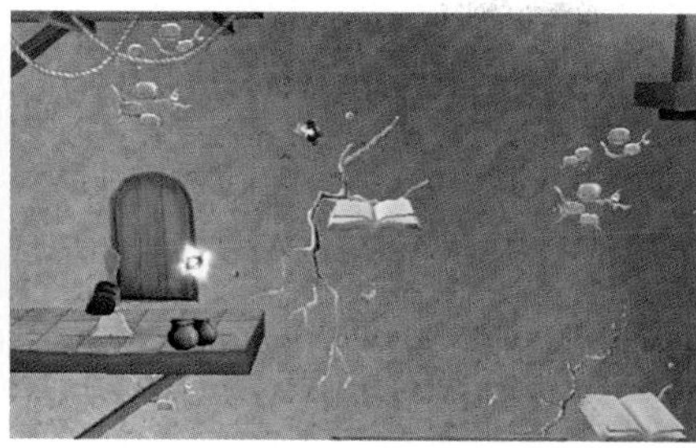

Wait for the next book to float down, then jump on to take another ride.

When the book reaches the top of its path, jump to the barrel on the ledge. Hop onto the floating book to the left.

Ride the book up and jump to the ledge on the left.

Double-jump up to the barrels on the next ledge.

Hop onto the barrel near the broom. You can see the film reel on the ledge above you. You can't reach the film reel until the water lifts the barrel into range. If you've moved quickly, the water is still far below you. Jump over the broom and drop down to the right.

When you land, grab the sketch and hop onto the barrel. Stand on the barrel and wait for the water to catch up to you.

Float up with the water, then jump over the broom and land on the barrel to the left.

Ride the barrel up and grab the film reel on the ledge. Move quickly to stay above the water and jump back to the barrel.

Hop to the left and land on the next barrel. Wait for the broom above you to empty its bucket.

Hop onto the next barrel. When the barrel shakes, it sinks into the water. Jump to the ledge on the left, then double-jump over the broom to the right.

When you land, continue to the right. Activate the projector screen to complete the level and jump into the start of Loss Tower.

Loss Tower See map on the following page

Level Overview

The final fireworks tower has more surprises for you than the other two combined. Wind up the outside of the tower to reach three enemy arenas. Each one locks as soon as you enter to force a winner-take-all battle against Blotling foes. When you get to the top, activating the gem is a snap, but the Blot smashes the entire tower and you fall down through the center floor by floor.

Enter Loss Tower and follow the ramp up to the right.

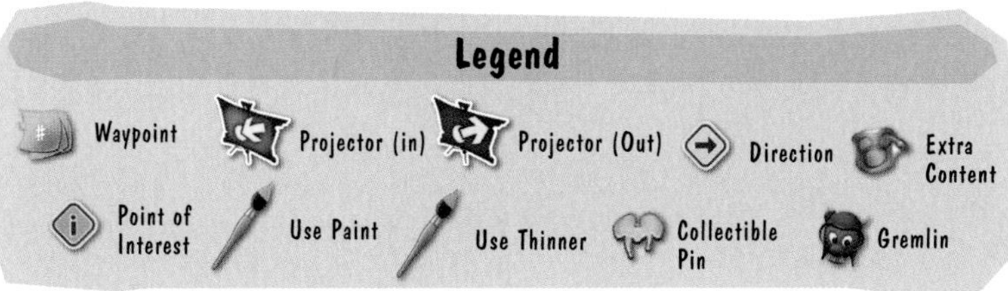

Things to Do

- Circle up Loss Tower
- Win the first enemy arena
- Win the second enemy arena
- Win the third enemy arena
- Focus the four gargoyles on the gem
- Fall through the tower
- Exit to Utilidor VII

Stop in front of the translucent section of stone. Paint in the stone and wait for the tentacles to extend and then retract before you race to the other side.

Make the next long jump after the tentacles withdraw into the wall.

The Blot rips apart the outside of Loss Tower. You have nowhere to go forward.

Turn around and spray Paint on the translucent ledge high overhead. Double-jump up to the new ledge.

When you enter the tower again, a gate slides down behind you and locks you into the arena.

Your first arena battle pits you against two Spatters and a Sweeper. In the small space, it's difficult to maneuver. Go with Paint and convert the two Spatters immediately when they charge at you.

Let your new allies attack the Sweeper. Sit back and use either Paint or Thinner to aid the Spatters against the Sweeper.

Don't forget to pick up all the power-ups before you leave the arena. Exit to the outside of the tower and climb again.

Paint in the first ledge and double-jump up to the new platform.

Continue up the tower ledge by ledge. Near the second arena entrance, spray Paint on the final ledge and wait for the tentacles to retreat before jumping onto the arena platform.

The second arena adds another Sweeper to the mix. As with the first battle, use Paint to convert some allies early in the fight to help you out.

Concentrate on one of the Sweepers first, and don't get caught in a crossfire between the two Sweepers. If you run low on health, start shattering resources and looking for health power-ups, or use Thinner on the Sweepers and collect the health power-ups they leave behind.

Once you've defeated all the enemies, the final gate to the outside part of the tower opens. Paint in the first ledge and continue your ascent.

Paint the next ledge and double-jump up. Either drop to the lower ledge with the chest, or double-jump up to the arena platform.

Gold Pin

The Gold Pin is out on the ledge below the third enemy arena. Double-jump down to the ledge, retrieve the pin, and jump back up the ledges on the opposite side.

The third arena holds two Spatters and a Slobber. It's tough to avoid the Slobber in the tight space, so give it a distraction: convert the two Spatters with Paint and send them at the Slobber first.

Feed Paint or Thinner into the Slobber's mouth to gradually defeat it. If it traps you against a wall, double-jump over the Slobber.

Finish off the Slobber with one more stream from your paintbrush.

Ascend the final few ledges to the top of the tower.

2

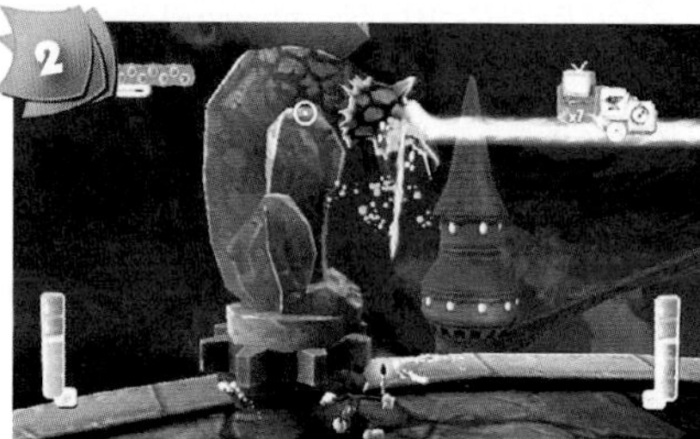

Something is wrong when you arrive at the tower top. The Blot is nowhere

to be found, and you can set up all the gargoyles with ease.

3

As you try to exit, the gem falls to the floor. You walk over to figure out what's wrong, and the Blot springs its trap. It shatters the tower floor and sends you cascading down through the center of the tower.

You land on the tower floor below. A few seconds later, the whole floor crumbles and drops out from under you. If you hurry, you can pick up a sketch before you fall.

The second floor holds Paint power-ups. If you hurry before the floor drops out, you can scoop up extra Paint.

The third floor holds Paint and Thinner power-ups. If you hurry before the floor drops out, you can gather extra Paint and Thinner.

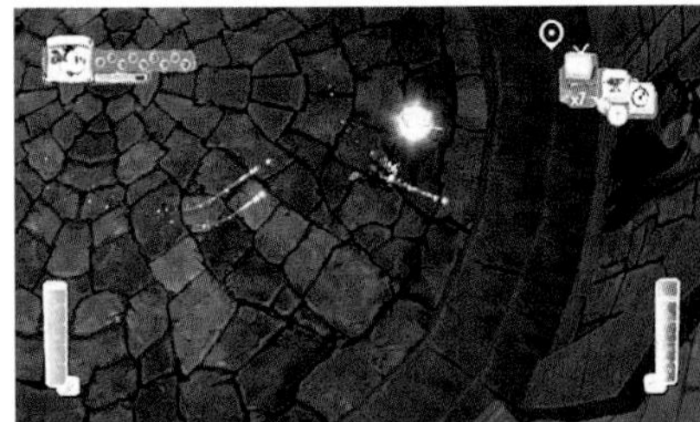

The fourth floor holds the Blot extra content. If you hurry before the floor drops out, you get this concept sketch; otherwise, you don't get a second chance.

Extra Content: The Blot

When falling down the Loss Tower, this concept art is in the lower right corner of the fourth floor down. You only have a couple of seconds to grab it or else it's gone for good.

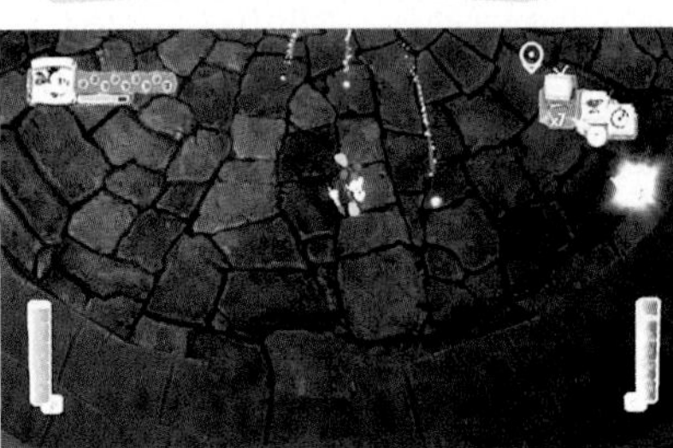

The fifth floor holds a Watch sketch. If you hurry before the floor drops out, you can add it to your arsenal.

The sixth floor ends your fall. You've finally made it to the bottom and survived. As a reward for finishing Loss Tower, open the red chest for the Skydiver Pin.

Utilidor VII

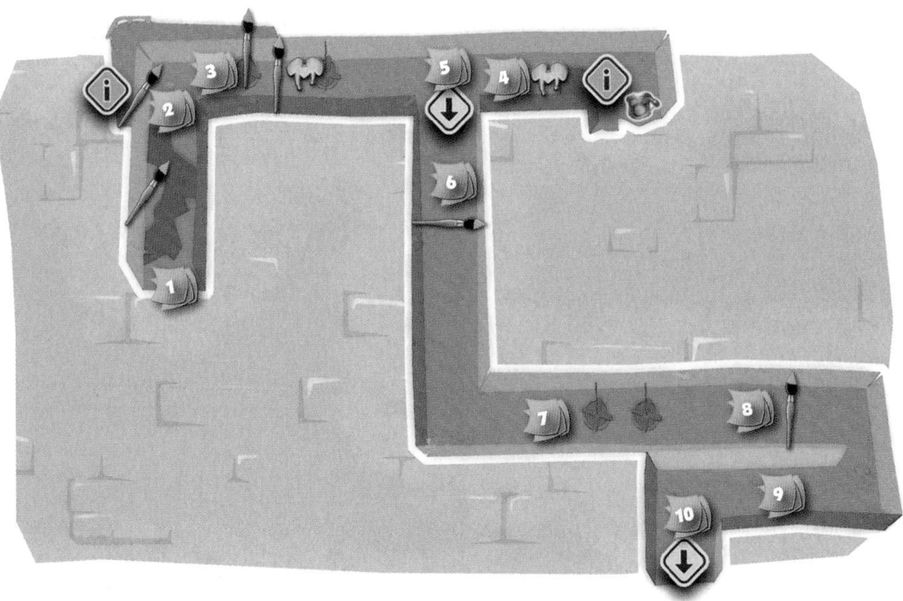

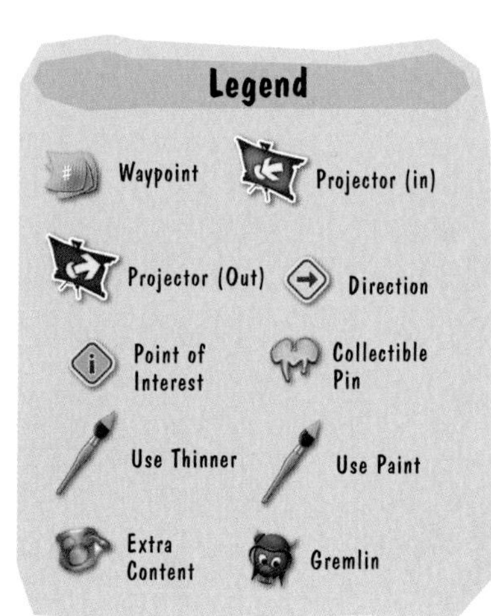

Level Overview

The final corridor leading outside has a few challenges to keep you on your yellow-booted toes. Tap into all your navigation skills to outmaneuver the shadow tentacles, swaying chandeliers, and crumbling floors in this corridor.

1

After the floor falls out in chunks ahead, you're faced with a small ledge to bridge the entrance area and the first corner. Tentacles assault the small ledge. Paint in the wall shield and slow down the tentacles.

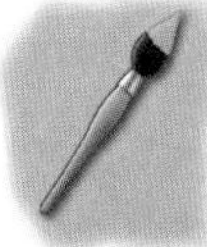

Paint shields on the walls to slow down incoming tentacles.

Double-jump over to the small ledge in front of the shield, and immediately double-jump to the corner and avoid the tentacles as the shield fades away.

Things to Do

- Pass the shadow tentacles
- Exit the corridor and reenter through the toon walls
- Cross the hanging chandeliers
- Traverse the disappearing ledges
- Overcome the obstacles in the last portion of the corridor
- Exit to confront the Blot

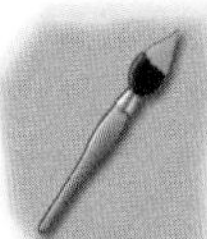

Remove the toon wall in the corner to exit the corridor and return through a second hole in the wall.

2

Look for the toon wall to your right and erase the stone with Thinner. Jump out through the hole to the outside and take the stairs up and around the corner.

3

Thin out a second hole in the toon wall at the top of the stairs. Paint in the gears to the left if you want to manipulate the chandeliers inside the corridor to your

liking. Double-jump through the wall and onto the first chandelier.

Paint in the second chandelier and double-jump over to it. Claim a Silver Pin here.

4

When you jump over to the next chandelier, the corridor ahead collapses and the chandelier farther ahead breaks and drops into the darkness below. Wait for your swaying chandelier to swing as far down the corridor as possible. Double-jump and spin move at your apex to grab hold of the top ledge.

If you make the jump, the upper passage takes you to a Gold Pin and the Blot Attack II extra content. If you miss, you can continue on the lower passage, but you miss out on the rewards above. Regardless, the far end of the corridor collapses and forces you back the way you came.

Gold Pin

Double-jump and spin move off the swinging chandelier and land on the upper passage near the collapsed wall to gain a Gold Pin in the red chest.

Activate a Watch sketch when you approach this corridor. This gives you enough time to simply run to the chest and collect the Gold Pin while the hall is still intact.

Extra Content: Blot Attack II

Continue past the Gold Pin chest and around the corner for this art concept sketch.

Return to the edge of the corridor near the swinging chandelier. Part of the wall collapses and reveals a new corridor branch.

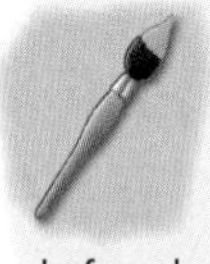

How fast are you on the Paint draw? You have to be quick to cross the disappearing ledges before they fade out.

A series of translucent ledges leads down the new corridor. Paint one in and seconds later a tentacle extends and thins it out. So, you can't paint the ledges in advance; you must paint one, jump to it, then paint the next.

You only have a second or two to stand on the ledge while you squirt Paint at the next one. When the tentacle appears, the ledge disappears under your feet. Stream Paint quickly and double-jump even as the next ledge is fully forming.

Keep going, and when you reach the last ledge, double-jump for the solid ground at the corridor turn.

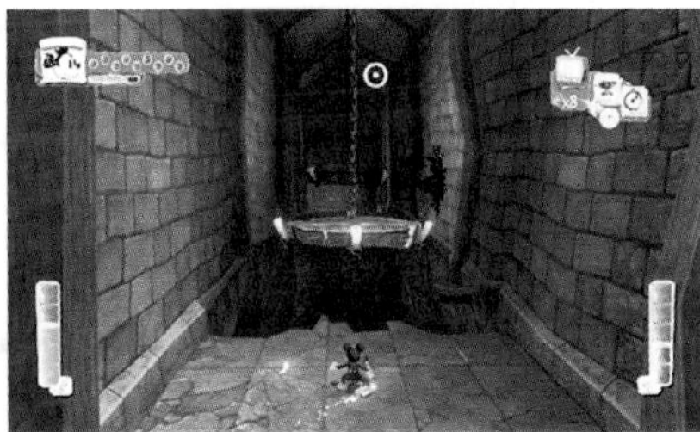

Walk out slowly in the next corridor and wait for the floor to give way. You now need the chandeliers to cross the area.

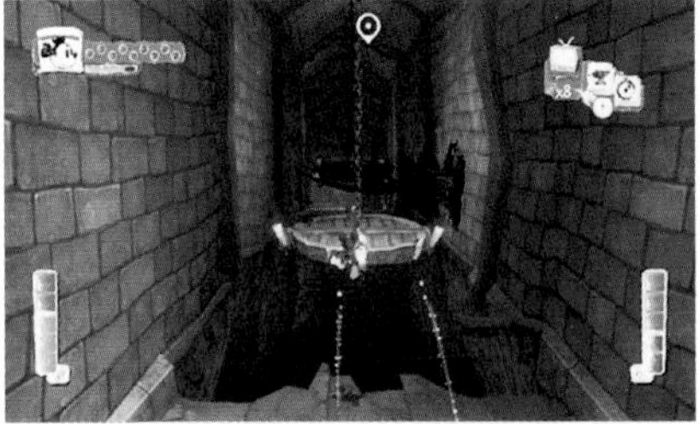

Double-jump to the first chandelier. Immediately Paint in the shield on the wall so that the protruding tentacles don't knock you off.

Double-jump to the next chandelier, and double-jump for the landing below when the chandelier swings fully forward.

Don't leave anything to chance. Paint in any missing platforms to give yourself the most real estate for safe landings.

8

The floor ahead collapses. Paint in the small ledge to your right and the corner ledge to the left. Then paint the wall shield next to the small ledge.

While the tentacle is preoccupied with the new shield, double-jump to the small ledge and then over to the corner ledge.

Advance to the next corner after painting it in.

9

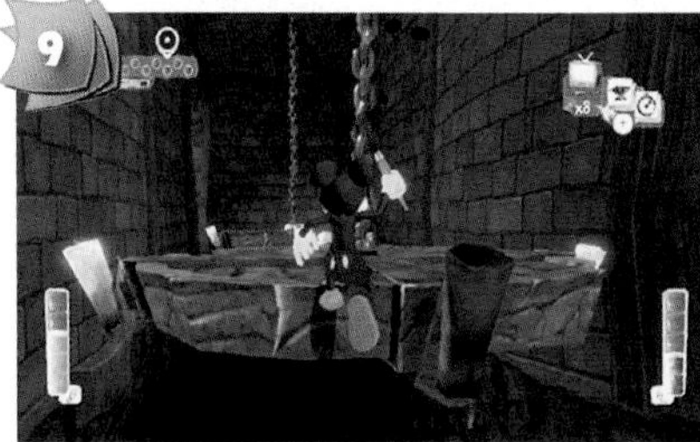

Jump up to the nearby chandelier. Your weight pulls this chandelier down, so before you drop too low, vault off and land on the second chandelier. As that one drops, double-jump over to the right corner where you can land on solid ground.

10

At last, you've found the exit. Now to meet the Blot for the last time.

Inside the Blot

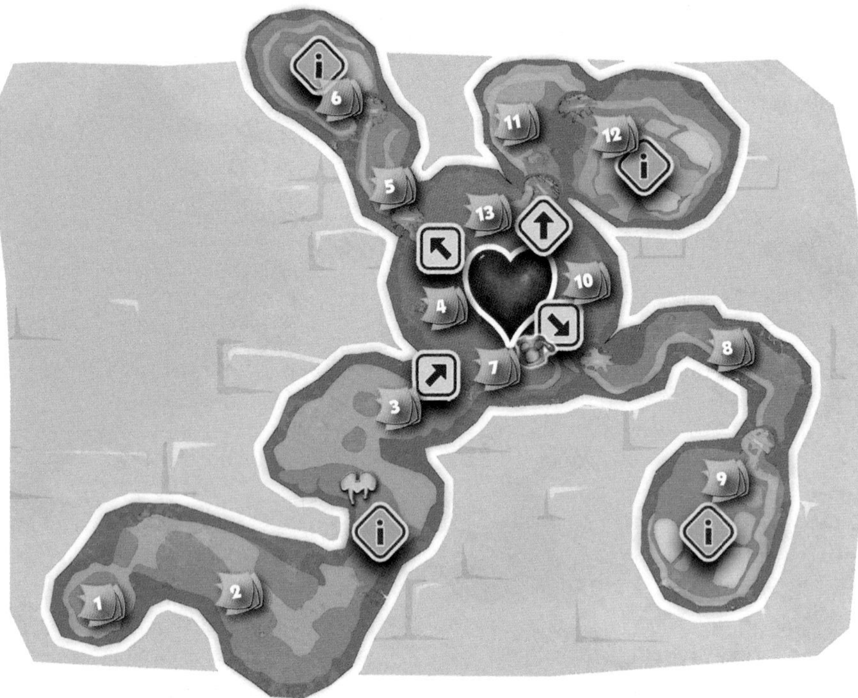

Things to Do

- Find the heart chamber
- Defeat the first Bloticle holding your heart
- Defeat the second Bloticle holding your heart
- Defeat the third Bloticle holding your heart
- Defeat the fourth Bloticle holding your heart
- Regain your heart and defeat the Blot forever

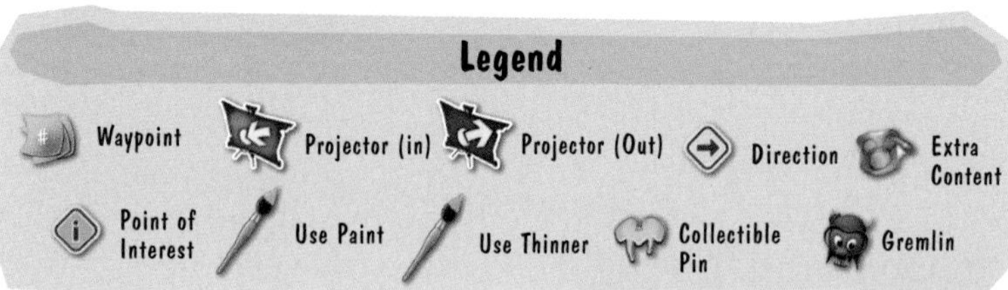

Level Overview

Your plans to eliminate the Blot haven't worked. With Gus and Oswald absorbed by the Blot, and your heart trapped inside its massive body, you decide to fight the monster from within. Diving into the Blot, you must travel through its interior defenses to free your heart so the monster doesn't use it to escape Wasteland and enter the real world.

A Spladoosh guards the entrance area. Pick your favorite method to bypass the threat: walking, tagging and running, painting, thinning, or dropping an anvil on its head.

Jump up the steps by the Thinnerfall and dispatch the second Spladoosh.

Gus meets you before the third Spladoosh. If you've saved all 30 gremlins in the game, he hands you the Gremlin Guardian Pin after you speak with him.

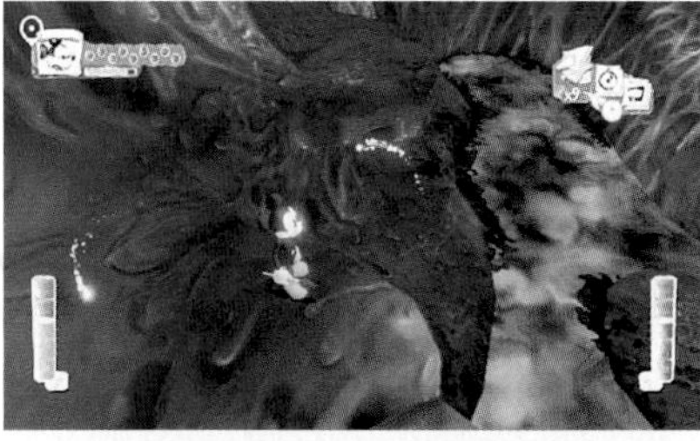

Remove the third Spladoosh and drop next to the Thinner pool. Paint in the red chest in the corner to recover another Bronze Pin.

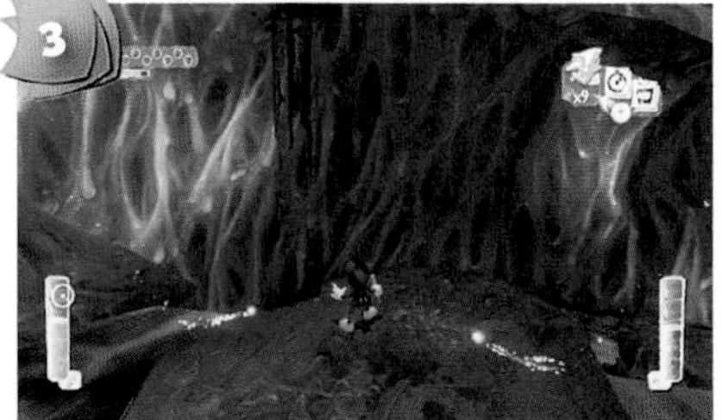

Climb the remaining steps to get your first view of the heart chamber.

Your goal is to defeat all four of the Bloticles imprisoning your heart and retake what you gave up for the sake of others.

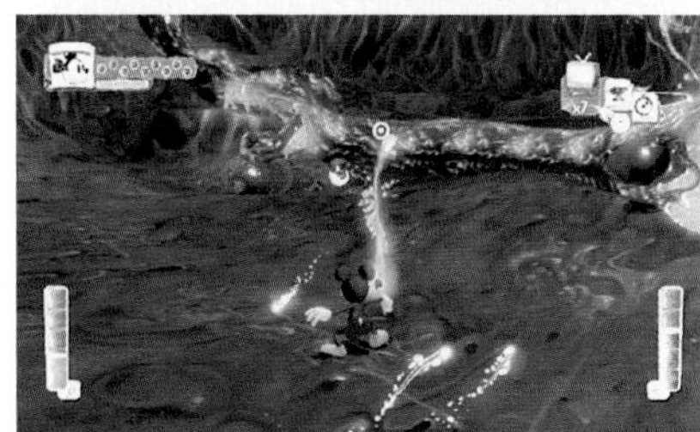

Descend into the heart chamber and battle the first enemy wave. Seers roll around and a Spladoosh sits near the steps leading to the next area. That area remains sealed shut while this part of the Bloticle thrives. Hit the first two pustules with a stream of Paint or Thinner to pop them.

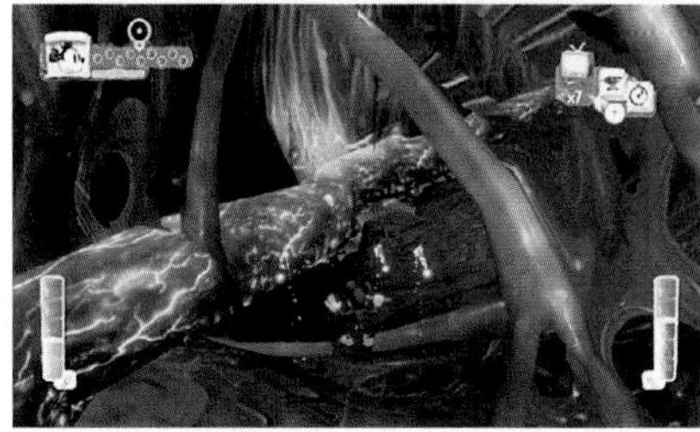

Hop up on the Bloticle to avoid the rolling Seers. Inch along the Bloticle until you're in range to defeat the third pustule. This opens the next area. Climb up the steps behind the Spladoosh and enter through the open orifice.

In this chamber, defeat the pustules while dodging tentacles. Explode the pustule near the entrance and slowly walk forward and watch for tentacle movement. Shoot the second pustule directly ahead and continue forward. Time your runs between pustules to avoid the lashing tentacles.

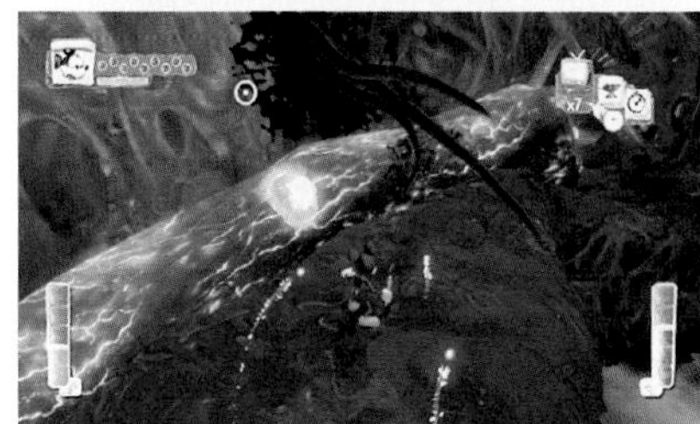

Spray the third pustule and dodge the next set of tentacles. Inch up on the fourth pustule and pop it.

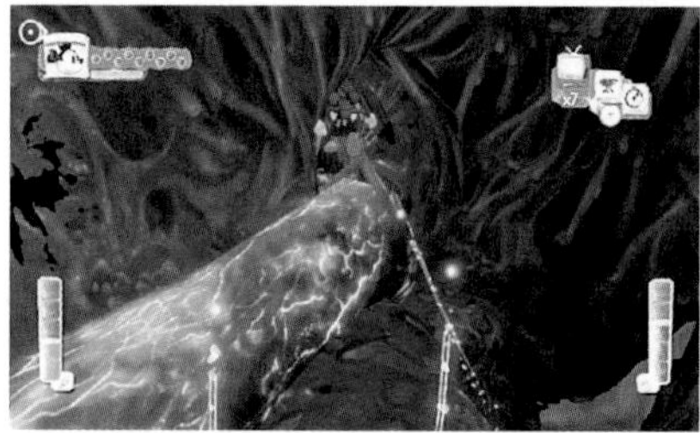

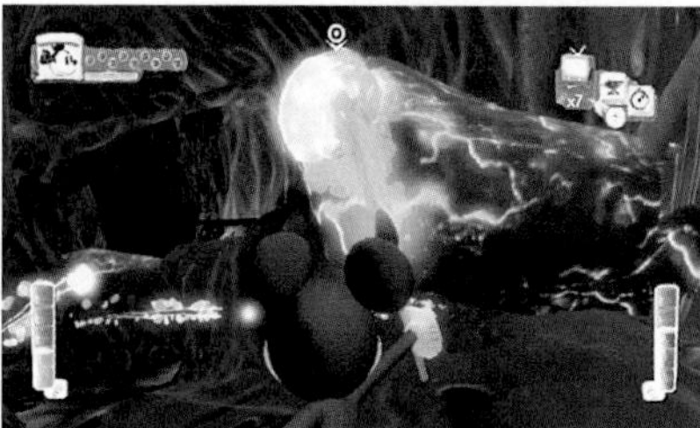

Rather than attempt the ledge to your left guarded by tentacles, wait for the tentacles directly ahead of you to quiet, then double-jump up on the Bloticle and run along its body to the exit. Turn around and blow up the final pustule to open the next orifice.

Aim at the first pustule in the last chamber from your perch at the entrance.

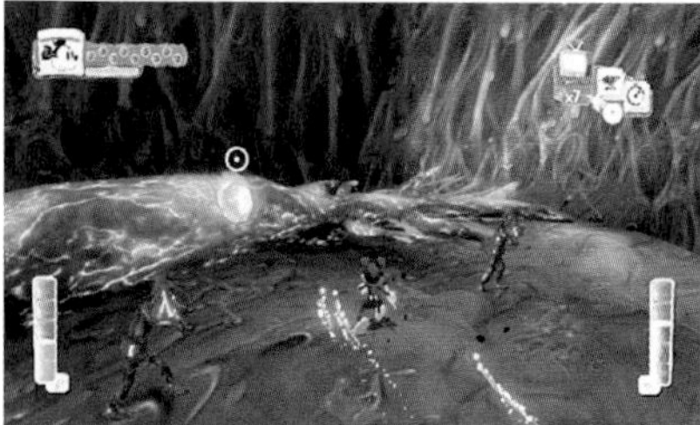

Citizens of Wasteland consumed by the Blot defend the Bloticle. These wayward spirits can materialize out of the Blot at any point, and touching them causes damage. It's best to simply avoid them as much as possible with well-planned routes and double-jumps to get out harm's way.

There will be fewer Citizens here if you redeemed each Pete. His character only shows up in these levels if you defeated him or ignored the Pete request on your way through the game.

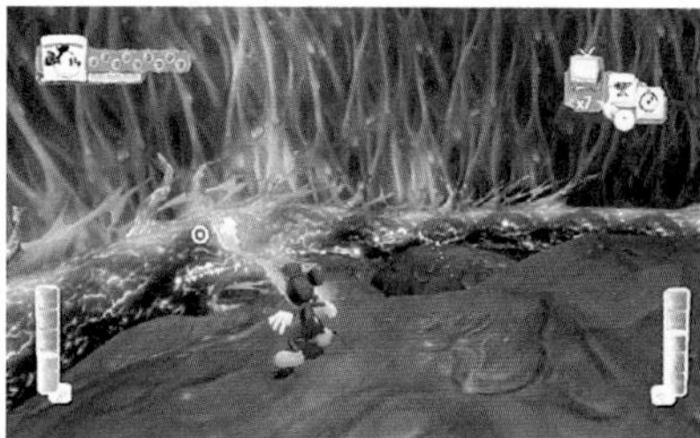

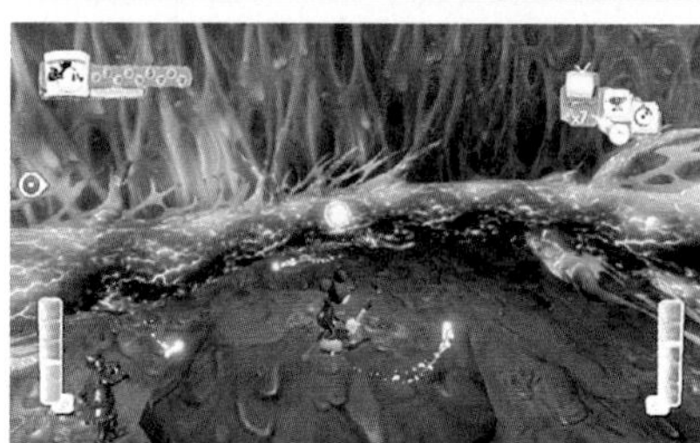

Drop to the lower terrain, and use a double-jump or spin move to break your fall before you hit the bottom. Spray the second pustule and jump up on the rock-like structure to avoid the Blot spirits and hit the third pustule.

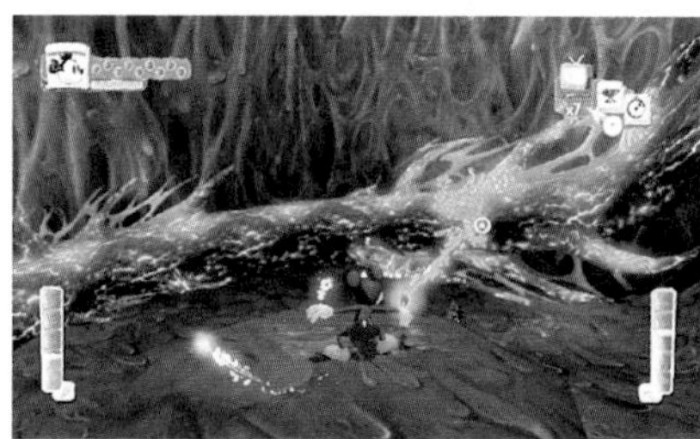

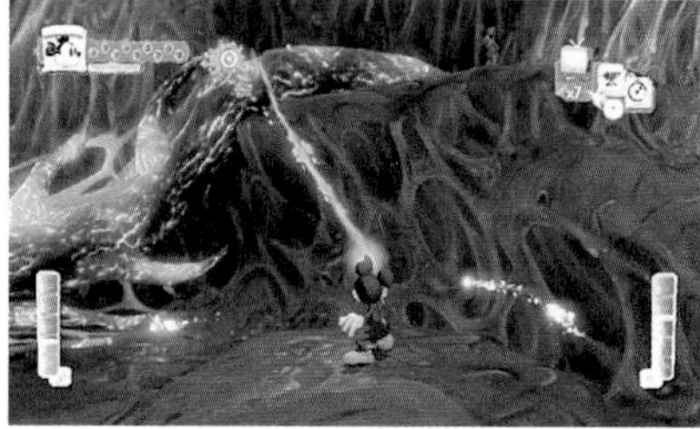

Take out the next two pustules before the spirits catch up with you.

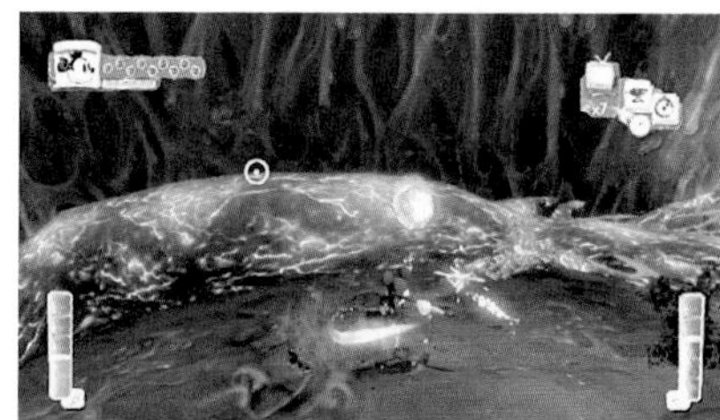

Double-jump up to the higher shelf, and remove the spirits so you can get a clean shot at the final pustule. Defeat it to wipe out the first Bloticle.

Return to the heart chamber. More shadow tentacles show up on the return trip. Dodge those carefully as you retrace your steps.

Back in the heart chamber, Spatters join the fight. Run through the Seers, Spatters, and Spladoosh to the opposite side of the chamber. Jump up on the Bloticle to get out of reach of all enemy attacks.

Look for the Lonesome Manor III concept art during the second fight in the heart chamber. It's on the right behind some Bloticle strands.

Spread Paint around to drown the nearby enemies. Once they've turned to allies, let them go out and attack their fellow Blotlings. If you're low on health, sit back and wait for your new friends to win the battle. Otherwise, convert more to your side and end the battle quickly. After you beat the final Blotling, the next orifice opens into the new area.

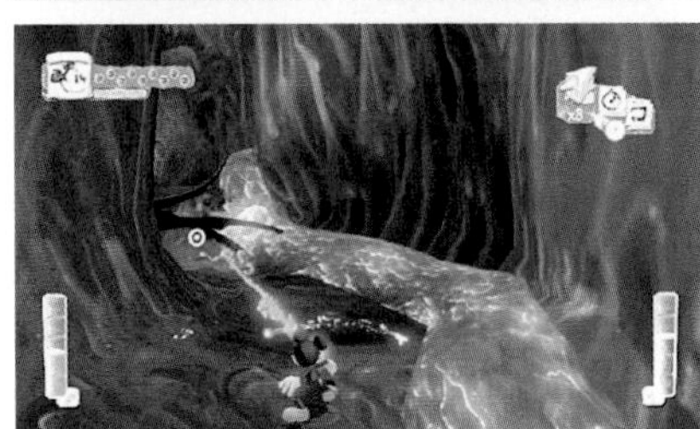

Explode the first Bloticle pustule and advance on the corner. Shoot the second pustule and watch for tentacle movement. If you delay after exploding each pustule, you should pass through the area unscathed.

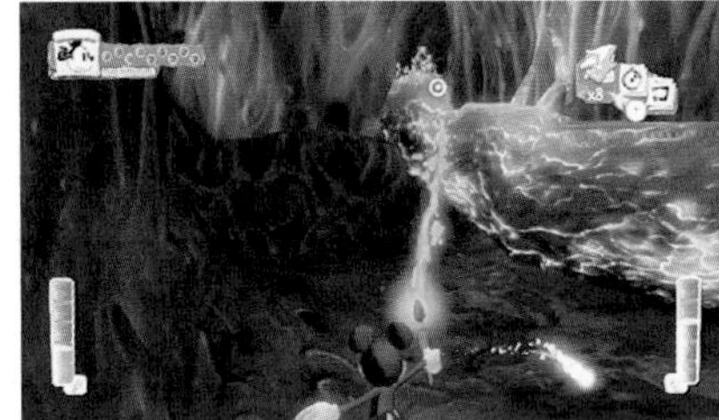

Remove the third and fourth pustules while avoiding tentacles.

With the tentacles behind you, stream your paintbrush mixture at the fifth pustule. When it pops, the orifice opens to the final area.

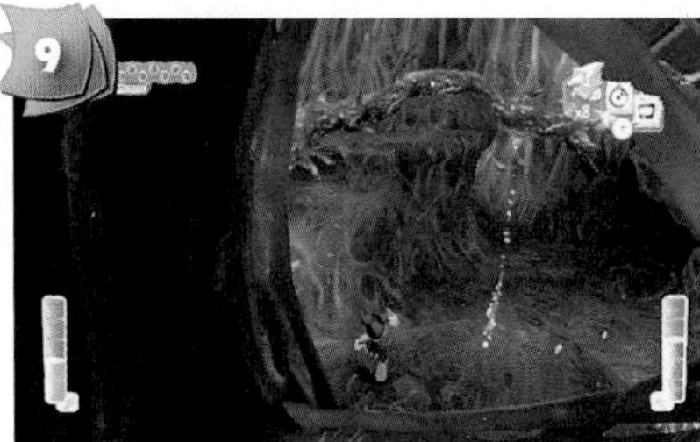

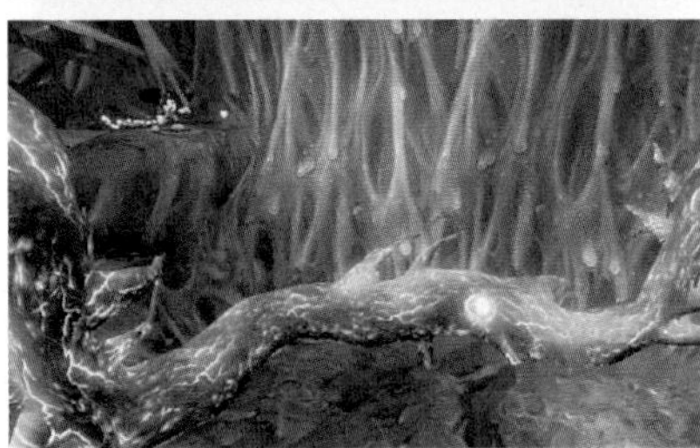

Move out onto the ledge and look for the first Bloticle pustule down below you.

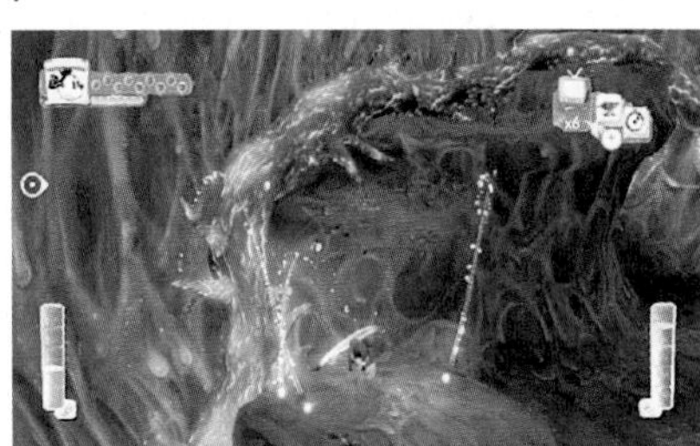

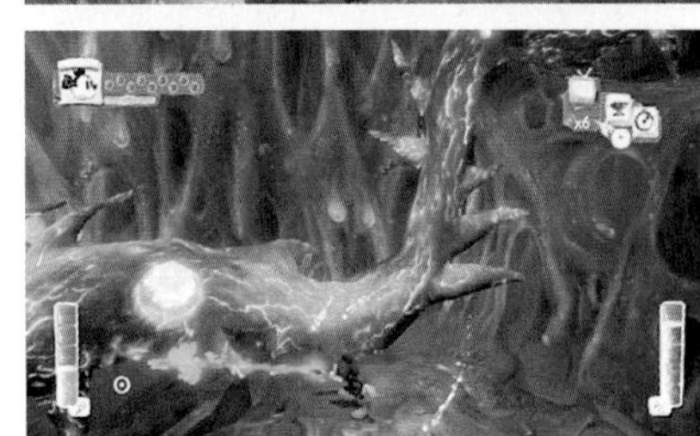

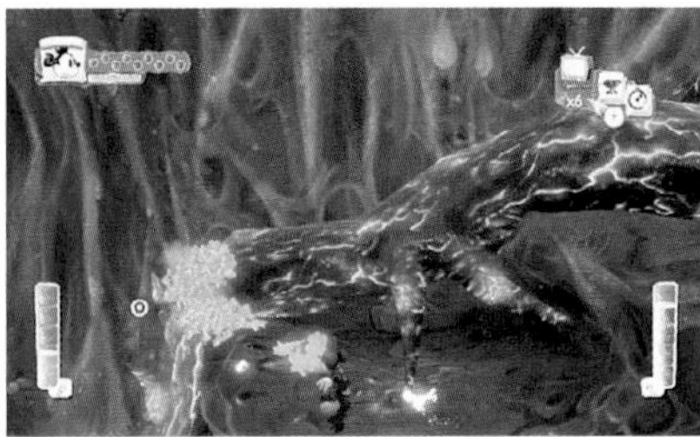

Drop to the bottom level and use a spin move to slow your momentum before you hit the ground. Follow the Bloticle and keep exploding pustules.

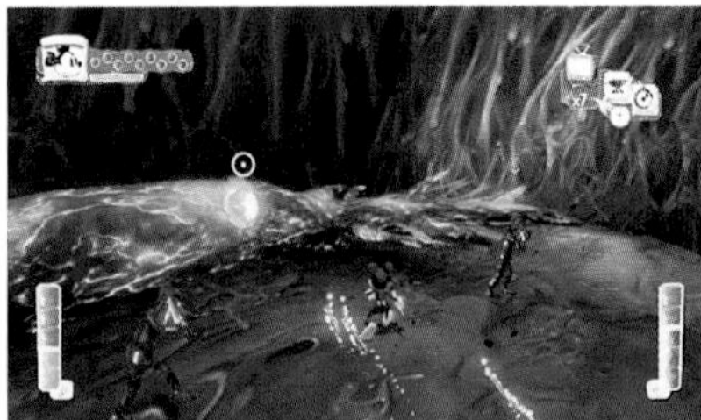

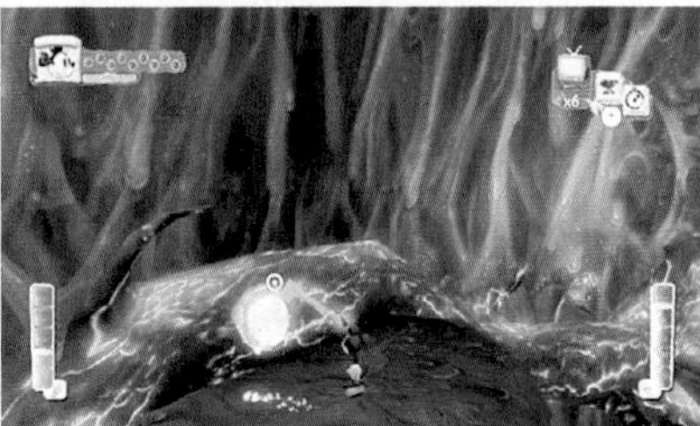

Battle some of the Blot spirits to reach the middle pustules.

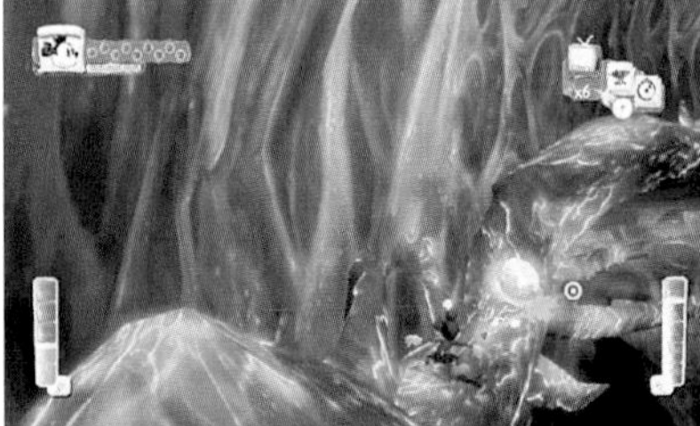

Jump onto the Bloticle to pop another pustule and keep the spirits off you. Then jump off and get the penultimate pustule near the tip.

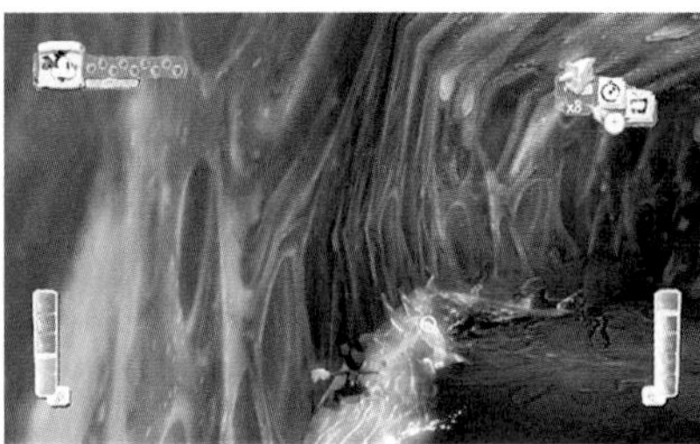

Before the spirits lock onto you, spray the last pustule and defeat the second Bloticle.

Retrace your steps back to the heart chamber. The way is now filled with new shadow tentacles and crushing boulder-like structures. The first one rises up and down. Time your run to pass under the boulder as it rises.

The second boulder pair crushes side to side. Wait patiently to understand the pattern. Dart through when the opening is clear and enter the heart chamber again.

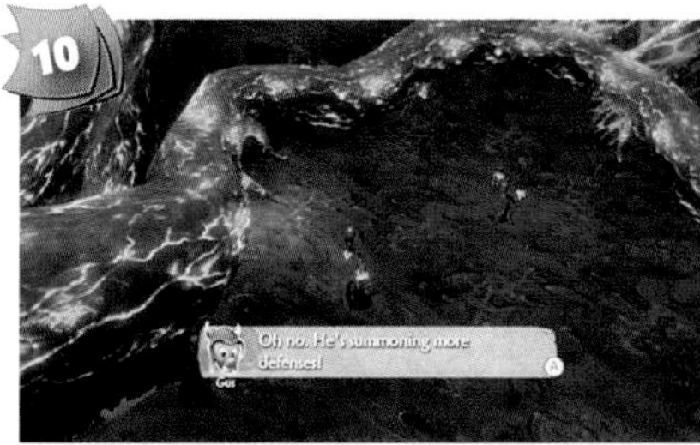

Sweepers join the next heart chamber battle.

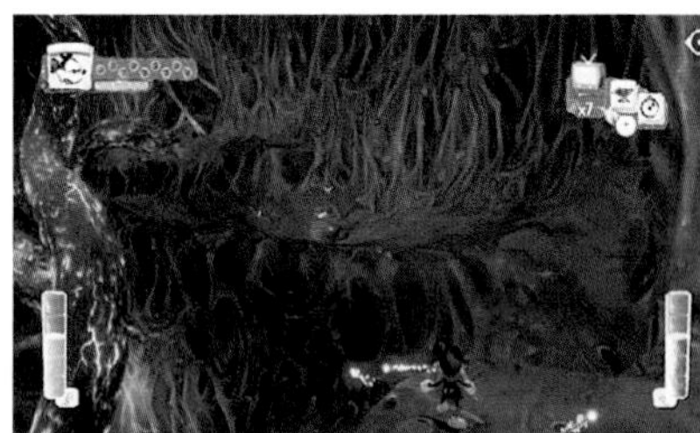

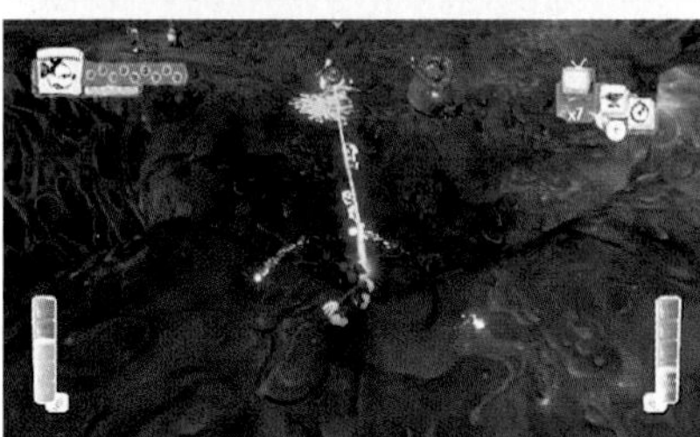

Climb past the Spladoosh and circle around to the other side of the chamber. Drop down to the lower ledge above the enemy's ledge and fire Paint at the closest Sweeper.

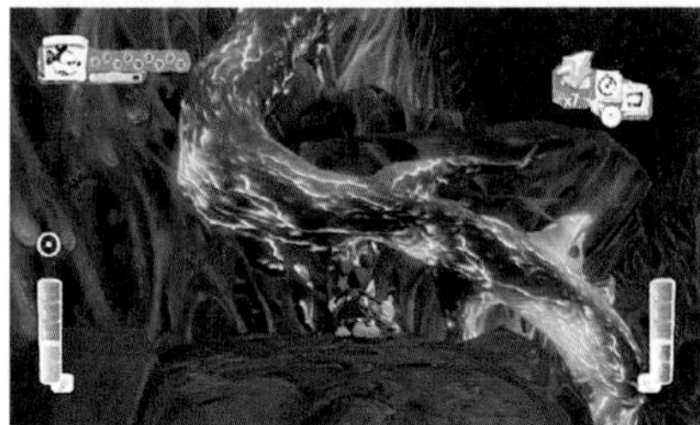

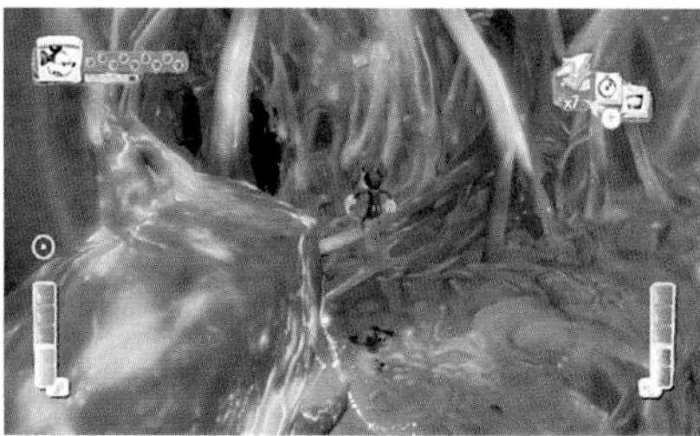

Work with your converted buddy to take out more enemies. Turn another Sweeper and the battlefield slowly becomes yours. When the last enemy is down, the orifice opens to the next area.

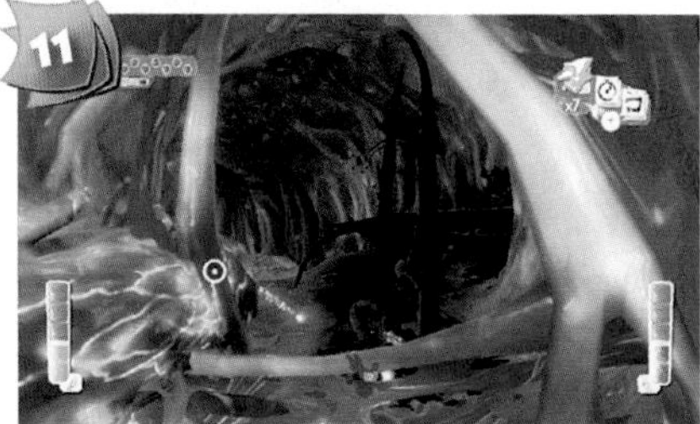

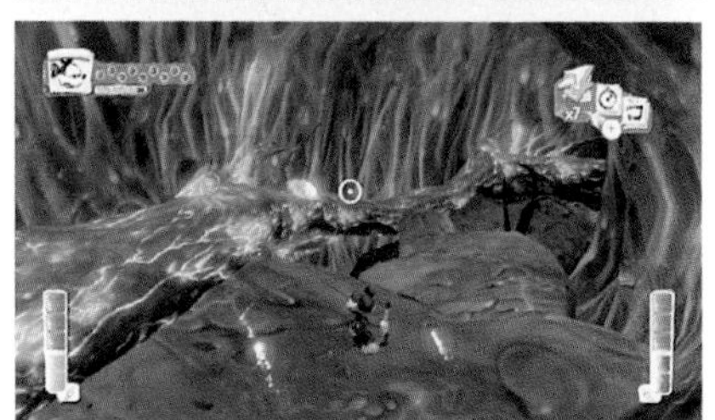

Tentacles ambush you right at the entrance. Fake them out by jumping in and jumping back out again. As they retract, race to the other side. Take out the first pustule and follow the Bloticle as it worms through the passage.

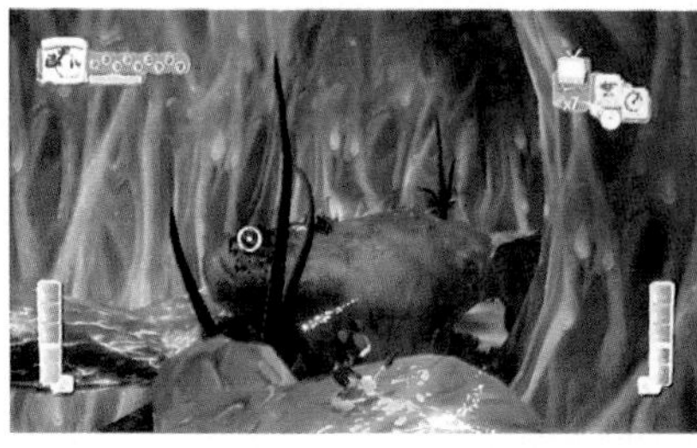

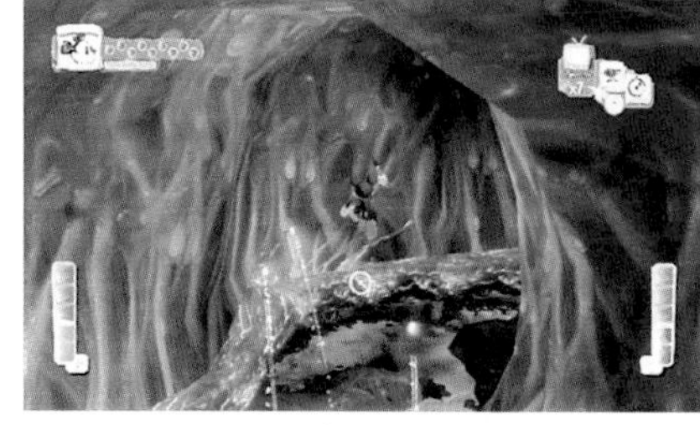

Jump on the two ascending and descending structures and pick off pustules in range. Don't ride the structures to the Thinner below; it's better to jump onto the Bloticle and walk along it.

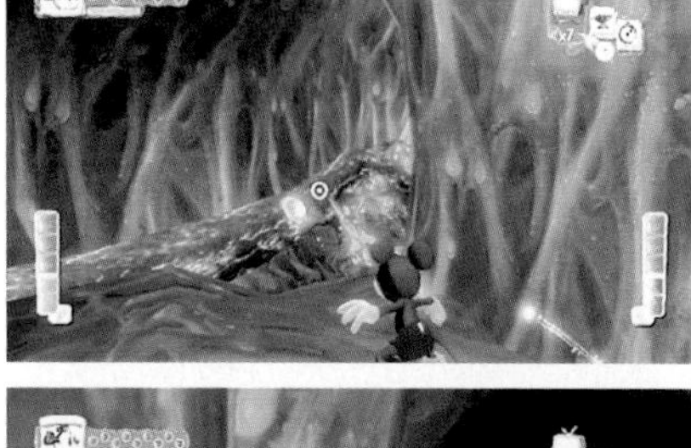

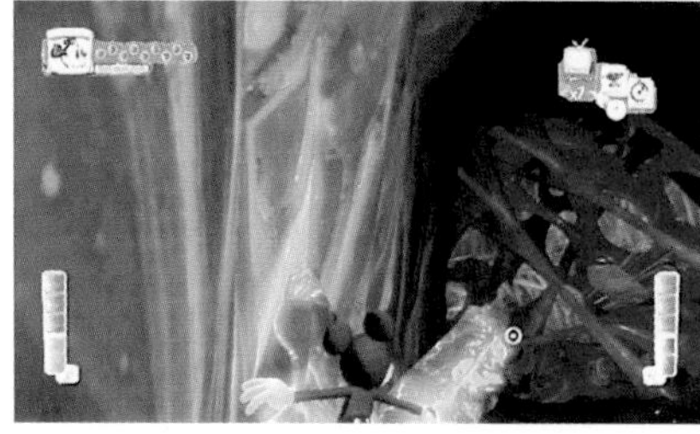

Follow the Bloticle to the end and defeat the last two pustules to open the orifice into the final area.

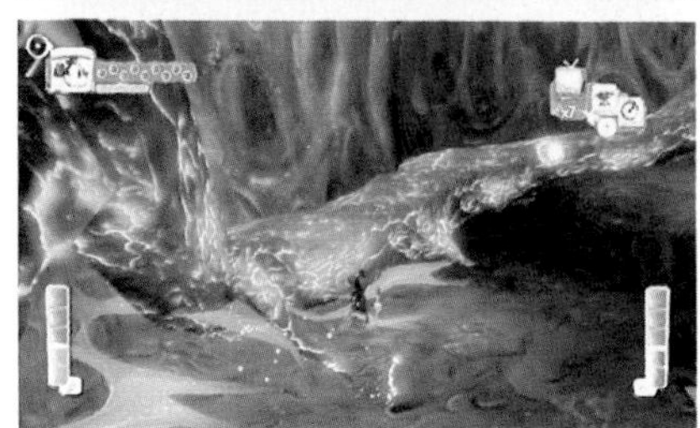

You can't reach the first pustule from your high perch at the entrance. Drop down and break your fall with a double-jump or spin move. Race for the first pustule and pop it before the Blot spirits become alerted.

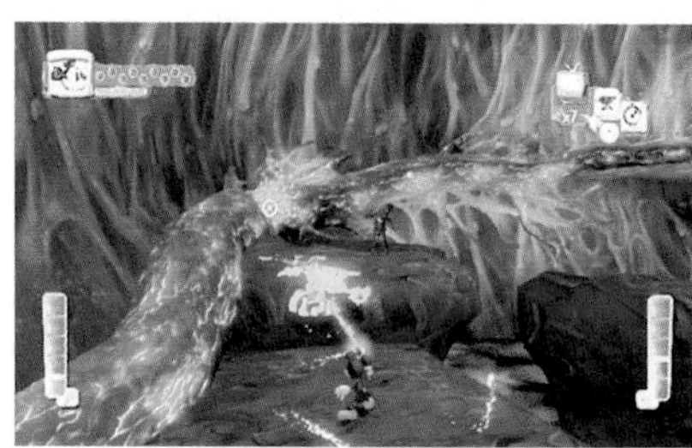

Blast the second pustule from the same perch. A nearby spirit advances on you.

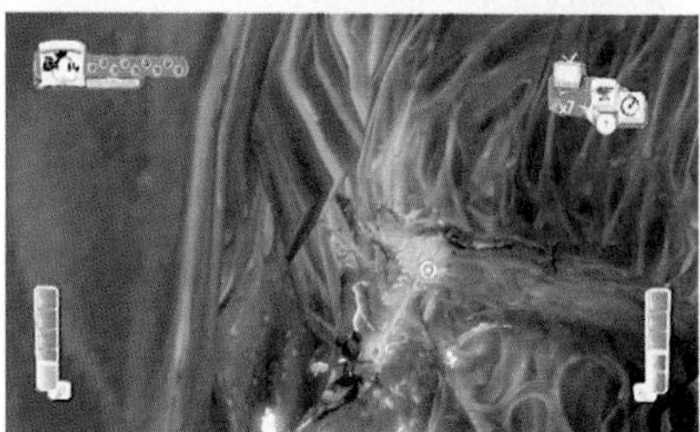

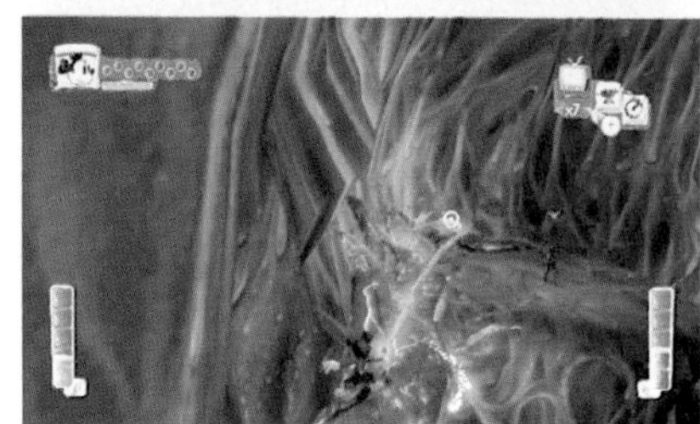

Avoid the spirit by jumping on the Bloticle. Shoot the third pustule and continue along the shaft to defeat the fourth pustule. Another spirit guards the final platform, but you don't have to jump there. Pick off the final pustule from the Bloticle itself and get ready to jump off when it goes boom.

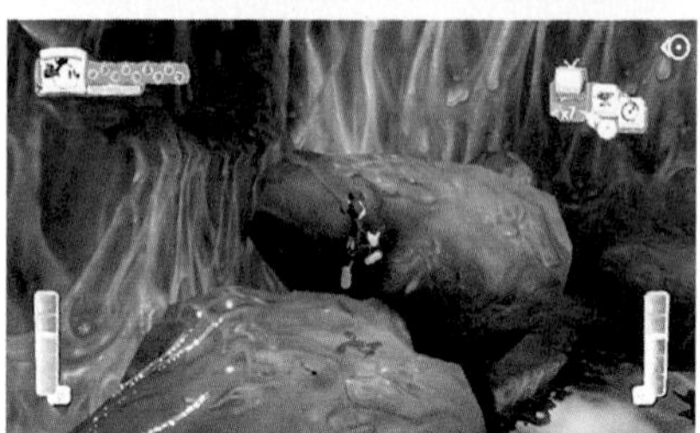

Return to the heart chamber for the last time. Double-jump off the main ledge to the left and circle around the Thinner pool. Climb the rock-like structures to the higher level.

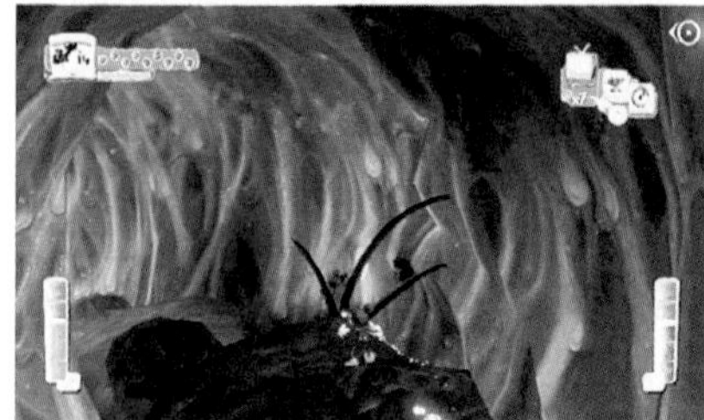

Put on your running shoes for this next section. Tentacles spring out constantly, so you have to sprint as soon as you spot the opening.

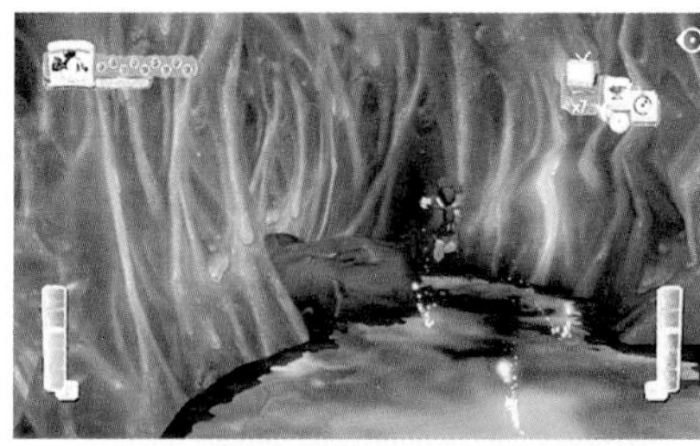

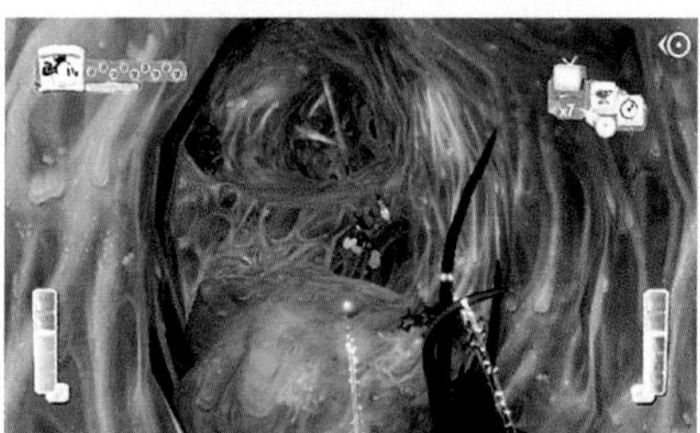

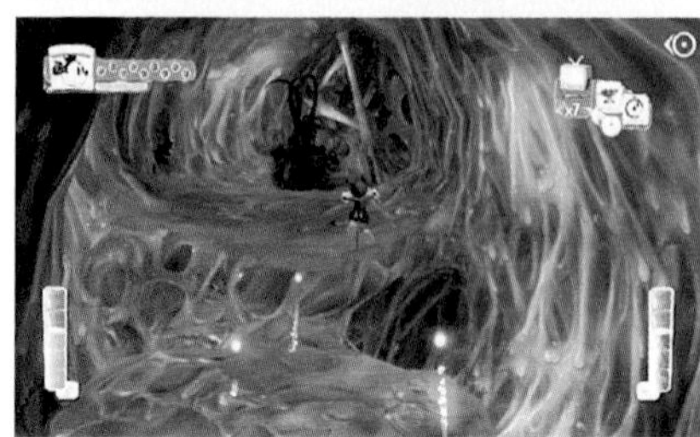

Jump onto the rock-like structure after the tentacles and race to the end as it descends into the Thinner. It will sink all the way under, so double-jump for the shore when you near the Thinner surface. Double-jump up the steps to the heart chamber again.

Search for the largest pustule on the fourth Bloticle and drop to the ledge just above it. Aim for the first pustule and pop it at long range.

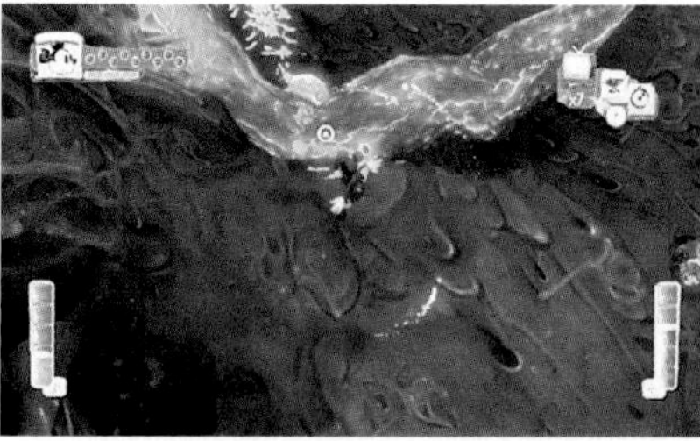

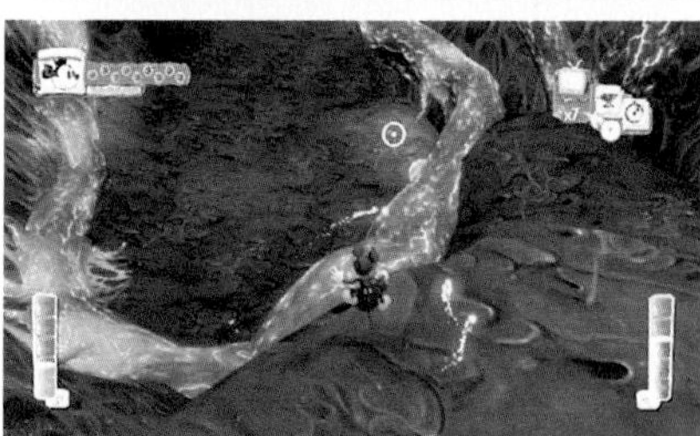

Point down and pop the second pustule under your feet. Then reach the third pustule with another stream.

A Slobber and Sweepers join the battle. This is the last battle, so use up all your resources. Guardians work well in this situation, especially tints, which you can launch at the Slobber and nearby Sweepers to convert them into allies.

Advance with your allies until you're in range of the fourth pustule. Pop it and continue to battle nearby enemies. Remember to snatch up health power-ups and Paint/Thinner power-ups from defeated foes.

Distract enemies with a TV sketch to position yourself for any of the pustules. Throw down a TV when going for the fifth pustule, which forces you out in the open battlefield to defeat it.

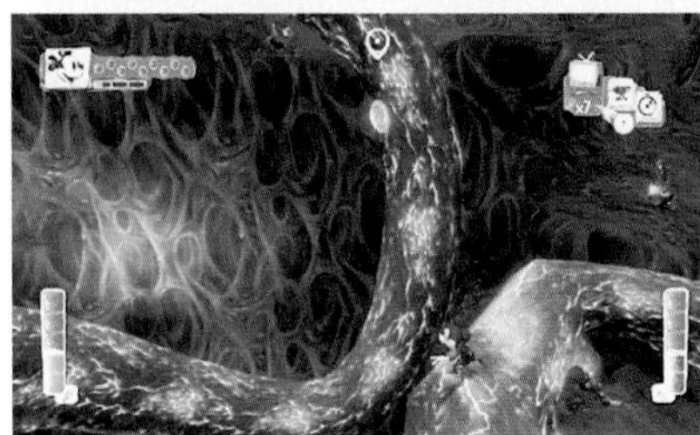

Climb high up on the far ledge to draw a bead on the sixth pustule. Once you have that one, double back to the battlefield and climb up on the Bloticle to aim at the seventh pustule.

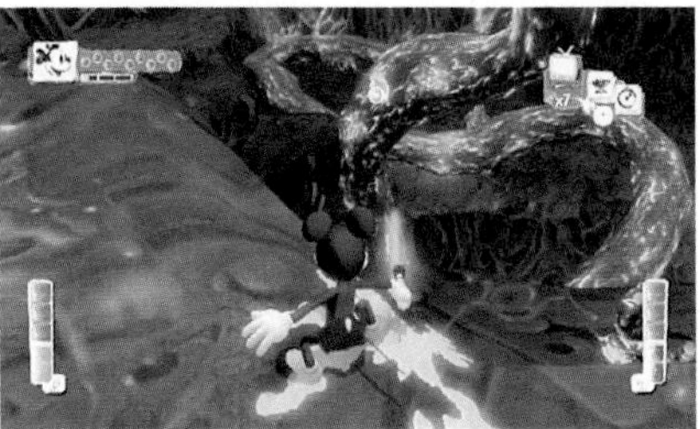

Look for the highest point in the chamber and climb up to the top ledge for the final two pustules. Shoot down at the eighth pustule and pop it.

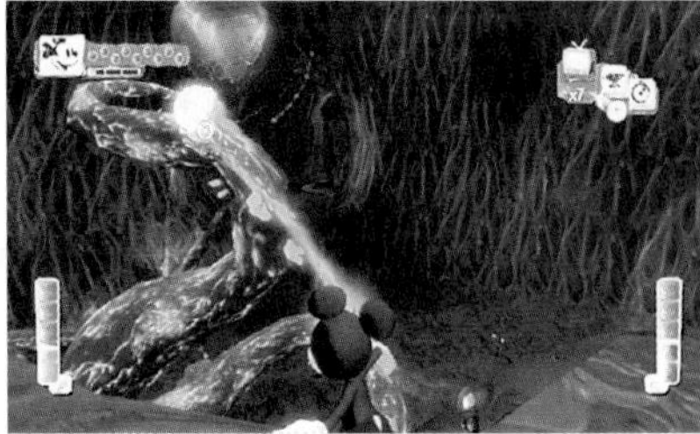

With your heart in sight, let loose your final stream on the ninth pustule. With its explosion, the fourth Bloticle withers and you regain your heart. You and your companions escape the Blot, and Oswald finally launches the fireworks at the creature. Together you've beaten the villain and saved the world.

Congratulations on an epic journey and a mighty accomplishment! One playthrough, though, isn't enough to capture everything in *Disney Epic Mickey*. You'll still need to collect more pins, and possibly extra content and film reels. One game's ending will be different than another game's ending depending on the choices you made. You'll need at least three playthroughs to master the whole world of Wasteland and claim the title of ultimate champion. Go ahead and get back in there...

APPENDIX

Extra Content

Art concept sketches are found floating around various secret spots in *Disney Epic Mickey*. Usually, you'll have to use Thinner to erase a toon wall or floor piece to discover these 50 hidden pieces of extra content. Here's a list of all the extra content in chronological order as you're likely to discover them:

EXTRA CONTENT		
Concept Art	World	Location
Mad Doctor's Lab II	Dark Beauty Castle	Mad Doctor's Lab
Dark Beauty Castle I	Dark Beauty Castle	Courtyard
Tunnels	Gremlin Village	Slalom
Spatters Spring Up	Gremlin Village	Ticket Booth
Pirate Gate	Gremlin Village	Jungle Boat Ride
World of Gremlins II	Gremlin Village	Asian Boat Ride
World of Gremlins I	Gremlin Village	World of Gremlins
Inky Mickey	Gremlin Village	European Boat Ride
Mean Street	Mean Street	Train Station
Mickey Faces I	Mean Street	Emporium
Ortensia's House	OsTown	Hidden alcove behind Clarabelle's house
Bunny Children	Mickeyjunk Mountain	The Heaps
Mickeyjunk Mountain	Mickeyjunk Mountain	The Piles
Epic Mickey	Mickeyjunk Mountain	Mt. Osmore Slopes
Oswald's Throne	Mickeyjunk Mountain	Mt. Osmore Caverns
Mickey Faces II	Mean Street	Emporium
Thinner Falls	Mean Street	Emporium
Tomorrow City	Tomorrow City	Tomorrow City Square
Petetronic	Tomorrow City	Space Voyage
Space Voyage	Tomorrow City	Petetronic
Mickey Faces III	Mean Street	Emporium
Mickey Spill	Ventureland	Hut Shop
Sea Battle	Pirates of the Wasteland	Skull Island
Animatronic Croc	Pirates of the Wasteland	Jolly Roger
Thinner Pump	Ventureland	Hut Shop

EXTRA CONTENT		
Concept Art	World	Location
Fantasyland	Mean Street	Emporium
Mickey Faces IV	Mean Street	Emporium
Blot Roar	Mean Street	Emporium
Lonesome Manor Passage	Bog Easy	Lonely Shack
Lonesome Manor II	Lonesome Manor	Manor House
Lonesome Manor I	Lonesome Manor	Foyer
The Mad Doctor	Lonesome Manor	Stretching Room
Library	Lonesome Manor	Library
The Mad Doctor Pod	Lonesome Manor	Mad Doctor's Attic
Bog Easy	Bog Easy	Bog Easy Shop
Mickey and Oswald	Mean Street	Secret Door
Oswald Poses	Mickeyjunk Mountain	Mt. Osmore Caverns
Spatter Puddle	Mickeyjunk Mountain	The Shadow Blot
Blot Mirror	Mean Street	The Usher
The Mad Doctor's Lab I	Dark Beauty Castle	Mad Doctor's Lab
Throne Room	Dark Beauty Castle	Throne Room
Oswald and Ortensia	Dark Beauty Castle	Throne Room
Sleeping Ortensia	Dark Beauty Castle	Fireworks Control Tower
Dark Beauty Castle II	Dark Beauty Castle	Utilidor IV
Horned Blot	Dark Beauty Castle	Sorrow Tower
Blot Attack I	Dark Beauty Castle	Grief Tower
Slobber Charge	Dark Beauty Castle	Grief Tower
The Blot	Dark Beauty Castle	Loss Tower
Blot Attack II	Dark Beauty Castle	Utilidor VII
Lonesome Manor III	Dark Beauty Castle	Inside the Blot

Film Reels

Each 2D level in the game has a single film reel. Look for the film reel before you leave through the exit screen, and turn them in to the Usher in front of the Mean Street Cinema for extra rewards.

FILM REELS	
Film Reel	**Encountered In**
Alpine Climbers 1	Mickeyjunk Mountain
Alpine Climbers 2	Mickeyjunk Mountain
Castaway 1	Pirates of the Wasteland
Castaway 2	Pirates of the Wasteland
Clock Cleaners 1	Gremlin Village
Clock Cleaners 2	Gremlin Village
Fantasia 1	Beating the Blot
Fantasia 2	Beating the Blot
Fantasia 3	Beating the Blot
Fantasia 4	Beating the Blot
Great Guns	Mickeyjunk Mountain
Haunted House 1	Lonesome Manor
Haunted House 2	Lonesome Manor
Haunted House 3	Lonesome Manor
Jungle Rhythm 1	Tomorrow City
Jungle Rhythm 2	Pirates of the Wasteland
Lonesome Ghost 1	Mean Street/Lonesome Manor
Lonesome Ghost 2	Lonesome Manor

FILM REELS	
Film Reel	**Encountered In**
Mad Doctor 1	Lonesome Manor
Mad Doctor 2	Lonesome Manor
Mickey and the Beanstalk	Dark Beauty Castle
Mickey's Mechanical Man 1	Tomorrow City
Mickey's Mechanical Man 2	Tomorrow City
Mickey's Steamroller	OsTown/Mickeyjunk Mountain
Oh, What a Knight	Mickeyjunk Mountain
Plutopia 1	Mean Street/Tomorrow City
Plutopia 2	Tomorrow City
Shanghaied	Pirates of the Wasteland
Sleeping Beauty	Beating the Blot
Steamboat Willie 1	Gremlin Village
Steamboat Willie 2	Gremlin Village
Steamboat Willie 3	Gremlin Village
The Whalers	Pirates of the Wasteland
Thru the Mirror	Mean Street/OsTown
Trolley Trouble	Mickeyjunk Mountain
Ye Olden Days	Beating the Blot

Junction Points

Junction Points are quests or events that influences your game future, and they can be decisions such as defeating a boss with Paint or Thinner, choosing to help an NPC with a task or not, and other game-changing moments. These are the key Junction Points that appear in the game in chronological order:

JUNCTION POINTS	
Name	**Description**
Small Pete	The end-game movie will play one choice if you got Pete and the Gremlins to be friends by completing Small Pete's ship log quest in Gremlin Village or another choice if you chose not to complete the ship log quest.
Clock Tower	The end-game movie will play one choice if you used Paint to defeat the boss or another choice if you used Thinner. Your Paint or Thinner capacity will also increase based on this choice.
Big Bad Pete	The end-game movie will play one choice if you befriended all the other Petes (Small Pete, Petetronic, Pete Pan), plus finished all the optional quests for Big Bad Pete in Mean Street. The end-game movie plays a second choice if you did not complete all that.
Horace	The end-game movie will play one choice if you finished all the optional quests for Horace in Mean Street. The end-game movie plays a second choice if you did not complete all the optional quests.

JUNCTION POINTS	
Name	**Description**
Animatronic Goofy	The end-game movie will play one choice if you restored Animatronic Goofy by finding or buying all the parts, or a second choice if you did not restore Goofy.
Moody	If you destroy the safe with Moody standing underneath, Moody will no longer be available in OsTown and you shut off all future Moody quests, including raising Donald's tugboat.
Petetronic	The end-game movie will play one choice if you used Paint to defeat the boss or another choice if you used Thinner. Your Paint or Thinner capacity will also increase based on this choice.
Animatronic Daisy	The end-game movie will play one choice if you restored Animatronic Daisy by finding or buying all the parts, or a second choice if you did not restore Daisy.
Hostiles in the Jungle	If you choose to complete the quest, you find Starkey at the Skull Island projector screen, and you can collect sketches from any pirates you freed from the jail. If you choose not to complete the quest, Starkey never makes it back to Tortooga, and the harbor is overrun with enemies.
Hook's Machine	If you choose to fill the pumps with Paint, you can collect a special pin. If you use Thinner on the pumps, you alter the environment in Skull Mountain. However, if you ignore the pumps, the pirates in Ventureland can't return to Tortooga. When you return to Ventureland, your choice to stop or ignore Hook's Machine determines which quests are available.
The Jolly Roger	The end-game movie will play one choice if you freed the Sprite and got Pete Pan to fight Hook or another choice if you beat Hook by yourself by forcing Hook to walk the plank. If you chose the Sprite path, you increase your Paint capacity; the Hook path increases your Thinner capacity.
Bog Easy	Siding with the ghosts and scaring the local townsfolk opens up more ghost-related quests. Siding with the townsfolk and helping them against the ghosts opens up more townsfolk-related quests.
Lonesome Manor Ballroom Organ	Repairing the organ sends all the ghosts in Bog Easy back to Lonesome Manor. Leaving the organ alone means the ghosts will still inhabit Bog Easy when you exit Lonesome Manor.
The Mad Doctor	The end-game movie will play one choice if you used Paint to defeat the boss or another choice if you used Thinner. Your Paint or Thinner capacity will also increase based on this choice.
Animatronic Donald	The end-game movie will play one choice if you restored Animatronic Donald by finding or buying all the parts, or a second choice if you did not restore Donald.
The Shadow Blot	The end-game movie will play one choice if you used Paint to defeat the boss or another choice if you used Thinner. Your Paint or Thinner capacity will also increase based on this choice.
Throne Room	Exit the room using Thinner to access the Fantasia 1 level. Exit the room using Paint to access the Fantasia 2 level.

Pins

There are 20 Bronze Pins, 17 Silver Pins, 20 Gold Pins, and 48 special pins for a total of 105 pins in *Disney Epic Mickey*. To collect them all, plan to play the game at least three times and follow this handy guide to all the pin locations in chronological order, from the early pins in Dark Beauty Castle and Gremlin Village to the later pins in your battles against the Shadow Blot.

BRONZE PINS	
Level	**Location**
Dark Beauty Castle	
Lab	In the room opened by defeating the arm
Gremlin Village	
Ticket Booth	Repair the teacup ride
Jungle Boat Ride	Paint in the gears behind the scenes

BRONZE PINS	
Level	**Location**
Asia Boat Ride	Turn off the steam valves in the air duct
World of Gremlins	Inside Gus' house after you paint it in
Europe Boat Ride	Pete's Treasure Room (Must have Petes log from crashed boat in World of Gremlins)
Mean Street	
Mean Street V1	Secret alcove covered by Toon on the Roof of the Detective Agency; Turn in 4 Reels to the Usher
OsTown V1	Restore the power boxes for the Phone
Mickeyjunk Mountain	
None	
Mean Street	
None	
Tomorrow City	
Lagoon	Rescue the Gremlin under the Thinnerfall and win the UFO challenge
Space Voyage	Near the Beetleworx Spawner
Mean Street	
None	
Pirates of the Wasteland	
Tortooga V1	Light the Lamps to raise platform from the thinner bay; Hit the Gear at the bottom of the Well to raise platform from the thinner bay
Pirate Boat Ride	Hidden Alcove on the upper Right Side near start of burning city section
Jolly Roger Boss Fight	Behind the breakable wall on the Ship deck lower left side
Mean Street	
None	
Lonesome Manor	
Manor House	Behind and left of the Spladoosh on the other side of the thinner pool near the level start
Ballroom	Use the possessed tables to reach the second floor alcove
Mean Street	
Bog Easy V2	Paint the Bridges for Metairie (Play the Organ for quest giver to be present)
Mickeyjunk Mountain	
None	
Mean Street	
None	
Tomorrow City	
None	
Dark Beauty Castle	
Lab V2	Behind the Oswald Statue in a Hidden Room
Inside the Blot	After the player is stopped by Gus and you jump down the ledge on the left side, paint in the red chest. (This chest is located BEFORE you enter the main room with Mickey's heart)

SILVER PINS	
Level	**Location**
Dark Beauty Castle	
None	
Gremlin Village	
Jungle Boat Ride	Chest near the exit - use the retractable ledge by freeing all four Gremlins in the level
Europe Boat Ride	Ride the Clouds to the Upper Level/Take the Windmill Exit from World of Gremlins
Mean Street	
Mean Street V1	Behind the Train Station
Mickeyjunk Mountain	
Heaps	Dial 349 on the Phone to stop the Thinnerfall
Piles	Use the Thinner Path and ride the 3rd screw down.
Caverns	Pass through the Wasteland Model Room.
Mean Street	
Mean Street V2	Reward for turning in 12 reels to the Usher
Tomorrow City	
Space Voyage	Behind the Beetleworx Spawner
Mean Street	
None	
Pirates of the Wasteland	
Pirate Boat Ride	Free the Gremlin and rescue Rigger Greene, obtained in the treasure room with Rigger Greene (red chest)
Skull Island	On the roof of the starting cave with the projector
Mean Street	
Ventureland V2	Bosun Blake Moves In Quest (Do not stop the Machine in Skull Rock, give Henrietta Ice Cream); Damien and Henrietta Moves In Quest (Do not stop the machine in Skull Rock, give Henrietta Flowers); Buy Damien and Henrietta a Tiki Mask (Do not stop the Machine in Skull Rock, give Henrietta Flowers)
Lonesome Manor	
Foyer	Thin out the right lower section of the foyer wall, the red chest is behind a Spladoosh on the left
Library	Collect the six Books floating around the library (you can also pay the Gremlin 50 E-Tickets once you free him behind the wall on the right side of the level from the starting projector)
Mean Street	
None	
Mickeyjunk Mountain	
None	
Mean Street	
None	
Tomorrow City	
None	
Dark Beauty Castle	
Utilidor 4	Hidden Side Hallway
Utilidor 7	Free floating pin in the first hallway atop the first chandelier. Need to thin out the toon wall on the left and go onto the balcony. Follow the path to where the gears are and thin out the toon wall to gain access to the chandelier.

GOLD PINS	
Level	**Location**
Dark Beauty Castle	
Castle Entrance	From rescuing the Gremlin on the Catapult
Gremlin Village	
Asia Boat Ride	In the wall near the machine to raise the fire bridge, paint in all gears on the platform
Mean Street	
Mean Street V1	On the roof of the Museum
Mickeyjunk Mountain	
Piles	Alcove near the exit, use the disabled claws to reach (need to free the Gremlin from the ledge below the thinner path as you enter the room, or dial 512 on the phone pad)
Slopes	In the Hidden Basketball Room
Caverns	Paint in all the Wasteland Models, climb the Castle to the top.
Mean Street	
None	
Tomorrow City	
Great Big Tomorrow	Defeat the Slobber using Thinner
Tomorrow City Square	When exiting the level just past where the people movers come out turn left for the chest
Mean Street	
Ventureland 1	Give Flowers to Damien to access the Red Chest
Pirates of the Wasteland	
Jungle	Paint in a Chest at the bottom of the Thinner River near the Hangmans Tree (The two ways to gain access to the thinned chest that is submerged under the thinner creek, is to paint in the gear near the thinnerfall dam or to free the gremlin. In order to free the gremlin you must paint in the three lamps in the level)
Skull Island	Thin out a large Toon Rock on the left side of Skull Island just past the anchor cave with two spatters in it
Mean Street	
Ventureland V2	Solve all the Riddles for Jim and return to him after doing each one. The first riddle is solved by using a steady stream of paint on the Tiki mask above the Tiki shop in Ventureland for part one. Thin out the light green clock (or if its thinned paint in the round gear section then thin it out again) located on the left upper side of the Train Station building in Mean Streets to access the lower left brown double doors and get the candle for the second part. For the third part travel to Bog Easy and go into Louis's shack in the far back and right section from level start. Once inside his shack talk to the Radio to complete the third section of the quest. (All Paint/All Thinner in the four Machines in Skull Island to have access to the quest giver)
Mean Street V4	Turn in 18 Film Reels
Bog Easy V1	Gather the courage medal which is located in the sunken steamer near the start of the level and behind the ghosts during the initial meeting. Do not sell the medal to the ghost who offers 200 E-Tickets but instead take it to Louis's shack located in the far back and right section of the HUB from level start. Talk to Bertrand near the edge of the city who will ask you to paint in the lanterns located around the small main city section. After you have given the medal to Louis and painted in the lanterns for Bertrand speak to Metairie who will thank you, open the door to Lonesome Manor and give you a gold pin.
Lonesome Manor	
Stretching Room	Paint in both smaller gears and spin the main gear to access the third level sections of the paintings. The red chest is behind the mural of the lady sitting on top of the grave stone. Spin attack the mural until the correct section is in front of the player and thin it out to access.
Attic	Chest above the Exit located around the last Beetleworx spawner where the Mad Doctor was/is
Mean Street	
None	
Mickeyjunk Mountain	
None	

GOLD PINS	
Level	**Location**
Mean Street	
None	
Tomorrow City	
None	
Dark Beauty Castle	
Throne Room	Located above the starting projector in the air
Grief Tower	Paint in Chest near Entrance
Loss Tower	After second arena, below entrance to third arena.
Utilidor 7	Obtainable from a chest in the second hallway. Either use a watch sketch in the first hallway and run across the collapsing floor before it falls or make a timed jump from the swinging chandelier to the second floor.

SPECIAL PINS	
Level	**Name and Location**
Dark Beauty Castle	
Castle Entrance	Dark Beauty Castle Pin (Behind the Toon Door)
Gremlin Village	
World of Gremlins	Gremlin Pin (Turn in Pete's Log to Gremlin Shaky)
Clock Tower Boss	Stop the Music; Unwind the clock (Use Paint/Thinner to defeat the Clock)
Mean Street	
Mean Street V1	Welcome to Wasteland (Buy at shop); Gremlin Village (Buy at Shop); Small Pete Pin (Given by Mean Street Pete if you give the ships log to Small Pete in Euroboat Ride); Swashbuckler Pin (Get Hooks Sword from the Cinema); Cartoon Buff Pin (Turn in 36 film reels)
Mickeyjunk Mountain	
Caverns	Mickeyjunk Mountain (Given at the end of the Wasteland Model Room exit door)
Mean Street	
OsTown V2	Happy Birthday (Deliver the Ice Cream Cake and return to Clarabelle)
Mean Street V2	Mean Street Romance(Deliver the Ice Cream Cake to Horace in the Detective Agency); Pie Delivery (Deliver the Pie to Horace in the Detective Agency)
Tomorrow City	
Great Big Tomorrow	TV Pin (Obtained by obtaining a TV sketch for the first time)
Mean Street	
Mean Street V3	Mystery Solved (Turn in the Dog Tags from Space Voyage); Redeem Petetronic (Use Paint on Pete); Tomorrow City (Buy at shop); Defeat Petetronic Pin (Use Thinner on Pete); Symphony Sunflower (Solve Horace's Mystery)
OsTown V2	Animatronic Goofy (Restore Goofy by gathering parts in Tomorrow City or buying from Mean Street Shop for 1,000 E-Tickets a piece after finishing Tomorrow City); Mickey Mum Pin (Give Flower to Clarabelle); Sparkle Daisy Pin (Give Flower to Clarabelle); Swamp Iris Pin (Give Flower to Clarabelle)
Ventureland 1	Ventureland Romance Pin (Give Flowers to Damien)

SPECIAL PINS	
Level	**Name and Location**
Pirates of the Wasteland	
Tortooga V1	Watch Pin (Return Beluga Billy's Bag, given for obtaining a Watch Sketch for the first time)
Tortooga V2	Pirate Hero (Defeat all the enemies in Jungle and talk to Starkey)
Skull Island	Pirate Friend (Use paint to shut down the machines, go into the mouth of the large center island Skull and paint in the red chest next to the Pirate and fixed main machine);
Jolly Roger Boss Fight	Captain Hook Pin (defeat Captain Hook by solving the deck puzzle and making him walk the plank. You can also run him into objects or make him fall on deck five times to defeat him)
Mean Street	
Ventureland V2	1) Animatronic Daisy (Gather the four Pal parts located all through Pirates of the Wasteland levels in Blue chests or given to the player by Smee. The first is in the Jungle well which is accessed by gathering all orange gems in the level and placing them into the stone head statues near the Beetleworx Basher, while painting in the other toon eyes as needed. This will unlock the locks from the well and you can then platform up and go into the well for the Pal piece. The second Pal piece is in Tortooga V2 and is located to the left of where you enter from and across the bay in the spot you gave the bag and sword to the pirate. The third is on the very top of the center of the island. This is accessed by traveling to the far back and left section of the island from the starting projector and platforming up. (The piece is located near the very top by Pete Pan). The last piece is given by Smee after you leave the Jolly Roger Boss Battle (He gives you the last piece if you use all thinner or all paint in the four machines in Skull Island. If you ignore the four machines or use paint in some and thinner in others he will not give you the last piece in which case you must buy it for 1,000 E-Tickets in the Tiki Hut Shop) ; 2) Pirates of the Wasteland (Buy at the Shop); 3) Ice Cream Pin (Paint/Thin the four Machines in Skull Rock, Get Henrietta Ice Cream from the Mean Streets Ice Cream shop)
Mean Street V4	Hook vs Pete Pan (Paint in the stairs that Hook thins out during the start of the battle and platform up the Jolly Roger to free the Sprite who will then get Pete Pan to do battle with Hook)
Lonesome Manor	
Manor House	Anvil Pin (Given for obtaining an anvil sketch for the first time. You can get an anvil for the pin by going to the red chest on the upper balcony which can be accessed by thinning out the support columns and the upper railing, then platforming up. Once on the upper balcony you can also get a sketch by thinning out the far left wall and freeing the Gremlin located near the Spladoosh)
Ballroom	Play a tune (Help the Organ. This is done by following the notes helping him complete his tune)
Attic	Mad Doctor (Defeat the Mad Doc)
Mean Street	
Bog Easy V2	Animatronic Donald (Put Donald together); Lonesome Manor Pin (Buy at Shop if the Organ is repaired); Well Read (Turn in the Runaway Book to Madame Leona);
Mean Street V5	Case Closed (Find the Hatchet in Library); Mean Street
Mickeyjunk Mountain	
Shadow Blot Fight	Shadow Boxing Pin (Defeat Shadow Blot with Thinner), Me and my Shadow(Defeat Shadow Blot with Paint)
Mean Street	
Mean Street V6	No More Bloticles (obtained after defeating Bloticles in all the HUB levels, just before you enter Tomorrow City projector); Repair Mean Street (Free floating on the grass section where the one Bloticle was in Mean Street V6)
Tomorrow City	
	None
Dark Beauty Castle	
Control Room V1	Oswald Pin (Restore the Throne Room)
Loss Tower	Skydiver (This pin is in a red chest at the bottom of the tower section Mickey falls through)
Inside the Blot	Gremlin Guardian Pin (Rescue all the Gremlins in the entire game)

Quests

QUESTS	
Quest Name	**Description**
BOG EASY	
Battle in Bog Easy	The Blot is taking over! You've got to do something! The blisters on the Bloticles are weak points that can be thinned to defeat it.
Fix Donald's Boat	Donald wants you to fix his boat by taking his boat gear to Moody in OsTown. Donald's tugboat has sat at the bottom of the Thinner lake for a very long time. Moody can use the special gear to raise the old tug.
Fix the Bridges	Metairie wants you to paint in all of the bridges around Bog Easy. Metairie can't stroll through the swamp with the bridges out.
Free the Trapped Ghosts	Ghost Ian wants you to free all the ghosts from the candles around the bog. Some of Ian's friends have been trapped inside candlesticks, and are wandering the swamp unable to free themselves.
Gilbert Wants to Fish	Gilbert wants you to free the boat that is stuck under the dock. Dropping something solid and heavy on the dock will provide just the shock needed to shake the stuck boat loose.
Go Back to Mean Street	Return to Mean Street. Look for Oswald in Mean Street. You may explore Bog Easy along the way, if you wish.
Help Bertrand Open His Store	Bertrand wants to reopen his store but needs his store sign. The sign was last seen near Louis's shack. When replaced, it will remind customers that the store is open for business.
Help Gilbert Scare Someone	Find Gilbert in the town square. Gilbert has moved to the square and awaits your help in unleashing a new wave of boo scares on the locals.
Investigate Donald's Pains	Donald is having mysterious pains and wants you to find out what is causing it. Donald is not in control of his own limbs since being reassembled. The answer to this mystery lies in the swamp.
Light the Lamps	Bertrand is scared and wants you to light the eight lamps in the area. Bertrand would never admit to being afraid of the dark, but when all the lamps are lit, he is undeniably more comfortable.
Lonesome Manor Gate	Open the gate to Lonesome Manor. The means to open the gate to Lonesome Manor can be found somewhere in Bog Easy. Explore and investigate to figure it out.
Pipe Organ Madness	Visit the Pipe Organ. Smooth things over with the Pipe Organ in Lonesome Manor so the Lonesome Ghosts can go back home.
Recover Louis's Courage	Louis wants you to find his courage medal, lost near the partially submerged boat. Louis was bravely exploring the swamp when his courage fell off. He quickly retreated to his cabin and has been afraid to leave it.
Recover the Runaway Book	Find a lost book somewhere in Bog Easy. Ian the ghost wants you to find the book that ran away from Leona's Library, in Lonesome Manor, as a result of his horseplay.
Restore the Bell	Louis wants you to find the two pieces of the broken bell. Two segments of the bell were lost when mischievous ghosts broke it and sold the parts.
DARK BEAUTY CASTLE	
Defeat the Blot	Enable the three fireworks batteries and launch them into the Blot. Climb the Sorrow Tower and activate the first gem. This will enable the first batch of fireworks.
Escape Dark Beauty Castle	Find a way out of Dark Beauty Castle. Gus will guide you and share his knowledge along the way.
Meet Oswald in the Control Tower	Make your way to the Control Tower. Find a way to reach the Fireworks Control Tower at the heart of Dark Beauty Castle.
Rescue All Gremlins	Rescue all of the trapped gremlins in Wasteland. Forces loyal to the Mad Doctor have been caging troublesome gremlins wherever they find them.
Return Home	Find out how to escape Wasteland. Oswald the Lucky Rabbit was involved in your arrival here. Perhaps he knows how you can get home.

QUESTS	
Quest Name	**Description**
GREMLIN VILLAGE	
Ambush Down Below	Either defeat the Spatters with Thinner or turn them friendly with Paint.
Clock Tower	Defeat or befriend the Clock Tower. Use Thinner to defeat the Clock Tower or Paint to make it an ally.
Find Small Pete's Ship's Log	Recover the ship's log from Small Pete's crashed boat.
Get Inside the Colosseum	Topple the Parisian Tower or take the cloud path to the Colosseum.
Navigate the Asian Boat Ride	Find the path to the door leading out of the Asian Boat Ride. Talk to the trapped gremlins, repair the machines, and explore to find hidden clues to navigate through the Asian Boat Ride.
Open the Gate	The exit from World of Gremlins is controlled in the Village Tower. Reach the top of the Village Tower, and then operate the pump at the top.
Patch Steam Pipes	Paint in all of the leaking steam pipes you see in the tunnels. Leaking steam pipes can usually be patched by painting in the area around the leak. But do it from a safe distance.
Raise the Fire Bridge	Use the machinery to escape. The machinery in the back corner of the Asian Boat Ride controls something called fire bridge.
Reach the Clock Tower	Proceed through the European Boat Ride to reach the Clock Tower.
Save Gus' House	Stop the Thinner from continuously spraying on Gus's house. Repairing some of the damage in World of Gremlins will enable you to shut off the Thinner flow that douses Gus's house.
The Leaning Tower	Cause the Leaning Tower to fall over and form a bridge or fix the whirlpool problem.
Ticket Booth	Gremlin Tim needs help! Blotlings have trapped Gremlin Tim in the ticket booth. Remove the threat and stop new Blotlings from entering the area.
Tiestow's Door	Gremlin Tiestow wants to get the door open. Repair the door by painting the gears. Or take the direct approach and use your spin move to break it.
Tiestow's Treasure	Gremlin Tiestow asked you to paint in all of the pipes as you go through the tunnels. Leaking steam pipes can usually be patched by painting in the area around the leak. But be sure to do it from a safe distance.
LONESOME MANOR	
Battle the Beetleworx	Defeat the three Beetleworx generators in the Attic. Watch for the vulnerable points and use Thinner.
Catch the Flying Books	Madame Leona asks you to collect the six flying books that are loose in the Library... If you have the time.
Enter Lonesome Manor	Enter Lonesome Manor.
Help the Ghost in the Foyer	Free the Lonesome Ghost. The ghost in the bottle needs your help to get free! You must activate the two switches in front of his prison to reach him.
Match the Paintings	Match the paintings in the Stretching Room. Use the spin move on a section of painting to spin it into the correct position. You've got to match them all!
Oswald in Mean Street	Oswald awaits you in Mean Street. Travel to Mean Street and make contact with Oswald.
Play the Pipe Organ	Help the Pipe Organ play its song by performing along with it on the keyboard.
Restore Leona's Paintings	Madame Leona asks that you repair and straighten her four paintings around the Library... If you are inclined to do so.
Retrieve Rocket Part	Find the Mad Doctor's rocket part.
Return to Ian in Bog Easy	Go back to Ian. You have aided Leona in the Lonesome Manor. Return to Ian in Bog Easy for your reward.
Settle the Library Bookcases	Calm the Library spirits. Find the hidden skulls and restore them with paint. This will pacify the spirits that possess the bookcases.

QUESTS	
Quest Name	**Description**
MEAN STREET	
Battle of Mean Street	Clear out the Bloticles from Mean Street, quickly! The Bloticles here must be removed to weaken the Blot for a final assault.
Bog Easy Projector Screen	Talk to Gremlin Markus about the Bog Easy projector screen.
Bunny Children & Power Sparks	Get the power sparks back from the Bunny Children. Three Bunny Children have run away with a batch of power sparks. Use Paint or Thinner to recover them.
Bunny Roundup I	Round up the Bunny Children by luring them to the pipe sitting next to the City Hall.
Bunny Roundup II	Round up the Bunny Children by luring them to the pipe sitting next to the City Hall.
Bunny Roundup III	Round up the Bunny Children by luring them to the pipe sitting next to the City Hall.
Bunny Roundup IV	Round up the Bunny Children by luring them to the pipe sitting next to the City Hall.
Collect Film Reels	The Usher will reward you for collecting film reels from the cartoons around Wasteland.
Confront Petetronic	Big Bad Pete wants Petetronic to get with the program.
Detective Mickey I	Look for clues as to the whereabouts of Horace's lost book. Shifty characters always leave behind clues. Sometimes toon footprints can be revealed with Paint.
Detective Mickey II	Horace wants you to recover Clarabelle's flower. Follow the trail of footprints from Clarabelle's window to find out who took the flower.
Detective Mickey III	Help Horace solve the Missing Mask case. A thief took a Tiki Mask from Tiki Sam in Ventureland. Track down the culprit.
Detective Mickey IV	Find the missing candle for Horace. Travel to Bog Easy and search the vicinity of Louis's cabin for clues leading to the missing candle.
Find Casey's Key	Casey dropped his storeroom key somewhere near the Ice Cream Parlor. Recover it.
Find Dog Tags	Help Horace solve the case of the missing dog. Horace wants you to find dog tags in Tomorrow City, where the missing dog was seen last.
Find the Hatchet	Find Constance Hatchaway's hatchet in Lonesome Manor. For ages it has been suspected that Constance did away with her husbands, but no evidence has ever been found.
Find the Missing Pirate	Find Moody's cousin, Rigger Greene. Horace wants you to find out what happened to the missing pirate in Tortooga.
Gilda's Lost Axe	Find Gilda's Axe on Mickeyjunk Mountain. Gilda lost her climbing axe on Mickeyjunk Mountain. If you find it for her, she'll reward you.
History of Colonel Pete	Recover the lost cartoon of Colonel Pete. Enter Lonesome Manor, via Bog Easy, and locate the vintage cartoon that features Colonel Pete.
Museum Power Spark	Find something to trade for the power spark in the Museum. Ask the Usher at the Cinema about getting an item to trade for the power spark.
OsTown Projector Screen	Get the projector screen to OsTown working again. Gremlin Markus needs you to collect the gears from Pete and Horace to get the projector screen machine back in action.
Oswald Needs Help	Join Oswald atop Mickeyjunk Mountain. Forces loyal to the Blot are attacking Mickeyjunk Mountain. Get any equipment you need and go to the top.
Recover Horace's Book	Horace needs his book back. Horace will give you a machine gear if you recover his book from Casey, the Emporium owner.
Restore Pete Pan	Pete wants you to help Pete Pan regain his powers. Pete thinks that Pete Pan is a weakling and embarrassing since he became powerless.
Secret Door	Gremlin Markus needs 30 power sparks to power the mysterious machine. What does the extra compartment on the projector screen machine unlock? Turn in 30 power sparks to find out.
Seek out Oswald	Find Oswald at the top of Mickeyjunk Mountain.
Tomorrow City Projector Screen	Talk to Gremlin Markus about fixing the Tomorrow City projector screen.

QUESTS	
Quest Name	**Description**
Ventureland Projector Screen	Save Gremlin Markus from the Spatters. A group of Spatters chased Gremlin Markus into a cage. Remove the threat and free the Gremlin.
MICKEYJUNK MOUNTAIN	
Ascend the Mountain	Proceed to the top of Mickeyjunk Mountain. Oswald is somewhere atop this mountain that's crawling with Beetleworx, Blotlings, and other hazards.
Knock Knock	Subdue the Blotlings so Jack Trade can repair the door, or repair it yourself by restoring TVs in the area.
Power the Crane	Paint in the TVs to power the crane. Decker has informed you that the crane runs off TV power. The TVs are probably nearby and require Paint to be recharged.
The Shadow Blot	Face the Shadow Blot. Use Thinner or Paint on him when he's weak to defeat or befriend him.
Three Challenges	Complete three challenges, based on Oswald's adventures, to gain audience with Oswald.
OSTOWN	
Back to Mean Street	Go back to Mean Street to see what's happened while you were away.
Battle of OsTown	The Blot is taking over! You've got to do something! The blisters on the Bloticles are weak points that can be thinned to defeat it.
Bridge Repair	Find someone to fix the bridge to Mickeyjunk. To reach Mickeyjunk Mountain, the bridge must be repaired by someone in OsTown.
Bridge to Mickeyjunk Mountain	The bridge leading to Mickeyjunk Mountain is broken, so find a way to get it repaired. Gremlins are always a safe bet for fixing things, but the gremlin who lives in OsTown hasn't been seen in some time.
Deliver the Cake to Horace	Take the cake to Horace at the Detective Agency in Mean Street. With the ice cream you provided, Clarabelle was able to create a wonderful confection for Horace.
Deliver the Pie to Horace	Take the pie Clarabelle baked and deliver it to Horace Horsecollar in Mean Street.
Find Goofy's Parts	Help Goofy by finding his missing parts. Goofy was disassembled by unknown minions of the Mad Doctor and his parts strewn about Tomorrow City.
Found: One Gear	Find an owner for the gear from the Telephone. Find someone in Mean Street that might want the gear left behind when Gremlin Prescott disassembled the Telephone.
Gather the Flowers	Clarabelle will make a bouquet. Clarabelle wants you to gather at least three flowers from OsTown and Mean Street to make a bouquet.
Gremlin Prescott's Wrench	Recover Gremlin Prescott's wrench for him. Gremlin Prescott will restore the bridge to Mickeyjunk Mountain when he has his wrench back. It was last seen in your house.
Ice Cream Cake	Clarabelle needs ice cream before she can finish making her ice cream cake. Fetch ice cream from Paulie on Mean Street. Clarabelle will craft a special treat for Horace that he has craved for years.
Ice Cream for Henrietta	Bring Henrietta some ice cream from Mean Street. Go to Mean Street and buy some ice cream. Bring the ice cream back to Henrietta in Ventureland.
Mickeyjunk Mountain Phone Network	Restore the Mickeyjunk Mountain phone network. Dial 726 on a phone in Mickeyjunk Mountain to restore part of the Wasteland telephone network.
Noisy Safe	Investigate the racket emanating from the suspended safe in OsTown. Clarabelle wants someone to investigate the noises coming from the safe across the street from her house.
Ortensia's Locket	Who might want the locket from Ortensia's house? Keep an eye out for whomever might be interested in a locket with a cameo of Ortensia, the love of Oswald's life.
OsTown Phone Network	Restore the telephone network in OsTown. The Telephone wants you to paint in the phone boxes that are hidden around OsTown.
Paint Moody's House	Moody needs his house painted before he can remember the code to the safe. Moody is very forgetful when his mood is down. Restore his house to perk him up and get the combination that only he knows.
Thin the Gag Factory	Thin out all the color from the Gag Factory. Abner is sick of tourists bothering him when they show up to see the Gag Factory. It's closed, so you might as well thin it out.

Appendix

QUESTS	
Quest Name	**Description**
PIRATES OF THE WASTELAND	
Billy's Lost Bag	Find and return Billy's bag. Beluga Billy lost his bag while fleeing Tortooga. It is somewhere around the harbor.
Billy's Lost Belongings	Find the contents of Billy's bag. The pirates locked up in the jail must have looted the contents of Billy's bag. Maybe you can talk some sense into them.
Find Starkey	Find Starkey somewhere within the Jungle. Gentleman Starkey can help you reach Captain Hook. Locate him to find the answers you seek.
Find the Jungle Symbols	Find three symbols hidden in the Jungle. Three stones, engraved with ancient symbols, are hidden in the Jungle. Find them and return to Starkey.
Fix the Pumps	Use Paint or Thinner on the pumps.
Go back to Mean Street	Leave Pirates of the Wasteland and head back to Mean Street to see what happened while you were away.
Hook's Machine	Use either Paint or Thinner to disable or reverse the machine inside Skull Island. Look for the four Paint and Thinner Pumps.
Hostiles in the Jungle	Clear the jungle for Starkey. Eliminate all threats to Gentleman Starkey's well-being. This includes all Beetleworx and Spladooshes in the area.
Into the Well	A gear inside the well is linked to an old ride. Go down the well, find the gear there and use it. Be careful. The Thinner tide can flood the well.
Jungle Lanterns	Find the all the lanterns in the Jungle and paint them. Hidden in the Jungle are an unknown number of lanterns. It might be rewarding to find and restore them all.
Mysterious Mystery Gems	Find a use for the gems.
Open the Skull Gate	Activate the projector screen. Both Beluga Billy and Starkey can activate the projector screen out of Tortooga.
Paint the Lanterns	Paint in the lanterns to raise the ride from beneath the Thinner. The lanterns are part of an ancient ride system that could be activated by painting them all.
Save the Sprite	Find a way to save the Sprite! Either defeat Captain Hook or avoid him and save the Sprite from his grasp!
Smee's Boat	Find and raise Smee's boat to reach the Jolly Roger. Locate the anchors and cut them loose.
TOMORROW CITY	
Battle in Space Voyage	Defeat all three Bloticles attached to the rocket. The rocket cannot lift-off until all of the Bloticles have been removed.
Battle in Tomorrow City	Defeat all three Bloticles in Tomorrow City. The Bloticles in Tomorrow City are blocking access to Space Voyage.
Collect All Rocket Parts	Collect all of the rocket parts scattered all over Wasteland by the Mad Doctor.
Defeat the Slobber	Get through the Carousel of Progress and onward to Tomorrow Square! But a Slobber stands in the way!
Enter Space Voyage	Enter Space Voyage. Repairing the Rocket Ride is one step in clearing a path to Space Voyage.
Find the Elevator	Confront Petetronic. Find the elevator that leads to Petetronic's quarters.
Open the path to the Great Big Tomorrow	Disable the Thinnerfall to enter the Great Big Tomorrow. Fix the valve system to shut down the Thinnerfall. Once it's stopped, the door to Great Big Tomorrow can open.
Raise the Notilus	Figure out how to raise the Notilus. Get the two cranes operational again by using your Paint and Thinner abilities.
Redeem or Defeat Petetronic	Use your Spin Move to deflect Petetronic's discs. Deflect Petetronic's discs back at him. Then, when the moment is right, fill him with Paint or Thinner!
Repair the Rocket Ride	Find the mechanisms that prevent the Rocket Ride from functioning and repair them.
Restore the Pipes	Restore the pipe system. Restoring the pipes will repair the pistons, giving you access to the launchpad.

QUESTS	
Quest Name	**Description**
Shut Down the Valves	Turn the valves here to shut off the Thinnerfall. Find the valves that control the steam pressure and turn them off. Follow the pipes to locate them.
Talk to Mister Rover	Move on to Tomorrow Square! Mister Rover will open the way for you to move on to Tomorrow Square.
UFO Challenge	Investigate the UFO. Go check out that downed UFO in the sea of Thinner.
VENTURELAND	
A Keeper for Donald's Doll	Donald wants you to find someone responsible to take care of the doll so that it doesn't bother him anymore.
A Pirate's Love	Help Damien win the heart of Henrietta. The only way to really know what she would want is to ask her.
Battle in Ventureland	The Blot is taking over! You've got to do something! The blisters on the Bloticles are weak points that can be thinned to defeat it.
Bosun Blake Moves In	Bosun Blake needs a place to live. Clear any junk out of the treehouse, so that Bosun Blake can move in.
Damien Salt and Henrietta Move In	Damien Salt and Henrietta need a nice place. Clear any junk out of the treehouse, so that Damien Salt and Henrietta can move in.
Find Daisy's Album	Daisy has asked you to find her scrapbook. She lost it near the Train Station in Mean Street. Pete should have more information.
Find Daisy's Parts	Daisy wants you to recover all of her missing parts from Pirates of the Wasteland. The Mad Doctor disassembled Animatronic Daisy and her parts were scattered over Pirates of the Wasteland.
Find Donald's Parts	Daisy wants you to recover all of Donald's missing parts from Lonesome Manor. The Mad Doctor disassembled Donald and his parts are now in the Library, Ballroom, and Attic of Lonesome Manor.
Find Hook	Captain Hook holds a part of the rocket. Find Captain Hook and retrieve that missing part of the rocket! He is sailing about near Skull Island.
Housewarming	Damien Salt wants a Tiki Mask for his new home. Find a Tiki Mask for Damien Salt as a housewarming present for his new home.
Jim's Third Riddle	Solve Jim the Puzzled's third riddle. My voice carries, near and far. I work in homes, in planes, in cars. I'm rarely hearing, always talking. Turn my dials and I start squawking.
Plant Painting	Paint back in all of the plants and trees in Ventureland. Pirates left a trail of thinned plants behind them when they left. Repaint as many of them as you can.
Restore Bog Easy Plants	Restore plants in Bog Easy. Botanist Darvin in Ventureland wants you to restore all 20 plants in Bog Easy.
Return to Mean Street	The next step in your adventure lies in Mean Street. You may explore Ventureland all you like, but the true continuation of your adventure is in Mean Street.
Scurvy Pat's Compass	Find the treasure for Scurvy Pat or buy the Compass from him. Search Ventureland to find the treasure Scurvy Pat seeks or pay him in e-tickets. Either way he will give up his Compass.
Solve Another Riddle for Jim	Solve Jim the Puzzled's second riddle. My hands, they move about my face. I am the master of every race. Who I am, time will tell. Thin me out for a gift that's swell.
Solve Jim's Riddle	Solve a riddle for Jim the Puzzled. "I smile upon Ventureland, frozen in time. To seek your help, I ask this rhyme. Hunger is my only complaint. To sate my desire, please feed me some Paint."
Talk to Smee	Find Smee and learn how to reach Hook in Skull Island. Smee can tell you, in detail, what needs to be done to traverse Ventureland and enter Tortooga.
The Door in Ventureland	Collect the Figurehead, the Ship's Wheel, and the Compass to reopen the door. Tiki Sam has the Ship's Wheel. Scurvy Pat claimed the Compass. Damien Salt has some sort of fixation on the Figurehead.
Tiki Sam's Masks	Find three of Tiki Sam's masks hidden around Ventureland.

Disney Epic Mickey

PRIMA Official Game Guide

Written by:

Michael Searle and Nick von Esmarch

Prima Games
An Imprint of Random House, Inc.
3000 Lava Ridge Court, Suite 100
Roseville, CA 95661
www.primagames.com

Product Manager: Shaida Boroumand
Design & Layout: Jody Seltzer & Bryan Neff
Manufacturing: Stephanie Sanchez
Copy Editor: Asha Johnson

Important:
Prima Games has made every effort to determine that the information contained in this book is accurate. However, the publisher makes no warranty, either expressed or implied, as to the accuracy, effectiveness, or completeness of the material in this book; nor does the publisher assume liability for damages, either incidental or consequential, that may result from using the information in this book. The publisher cannot provide any additional information or support regarding gameplay, hints and strategies, or problems with hardware or software. Such questions should be directed to the support numbers provided by the game and/or device manufacturers as set forth in their documentation. Some game tricks require precise timing and may require repeated attempts before the desired result is achieved.

ISBN: 978-0-307-47085-0
Printed in the United States of America

10 11 12 13 LL 10 9 8 7 6 5 4 3 2 1

Credits

Junction Point Studios	Disney Interactive Studios
Warren Spector	Phil Hong
Paul Weaver	Steven Dodson
Adam Creighton	Tina Kwon
Scott Green	Tamara Johnston
Jason Habel	Patrick Sager
Chase Jones	Keyur Shah
Raul Ramirez	Stephanie Martinelli
Mark Stefanowicz	Matt Owczarek

About the Author

Mike Searle was born before regular, everyday people—not those scientist types—had computers in their houses. Some might say that makes him a dinosaur, but others think him a grizzled veteran of the gaming world. He's played 4,380 more video games than his lovely wife, Deb—she has no clue what the initials "FPS" stand for—but his kids Raina, Henry, Tristan, and Nate are quickly catching up to him.

We want to hear from you! E-mail comments and feedback to msearle@primagames.com.